PASSAGES TO
FREEDOM

THE UNDERGROUND RAILROAD
IN HISTORY AND MEMORY

FREEDOM

Edited by DAVID W. BLIGHT

Published in association with the National Underground Railroad Freedom Center

SMITHSONIAN BOOKS • Washington

COPY EDITOR: Nancy Eickel
PRODUCTION EDITOR: Robert A. Poarch
DESIGNER: Janice Wheeler

LIBRARY OF CONGRESS CATALOGING-IN-PUBLICATION DATA
Passages to freedom : the Underground
Railroad in history and memory / edited by
David W. Blight
         p.   cm.
    Includes bibliographical references and
    index.
    ISBN 1-58834-157-7 (cloth : alk. paper) —
    ISBN 1-58834-158-5 (pbk. : alk. paper)
    1. Underground railroad. 2. Antislavery
    movements—United States—History—19th
    century. 3. Abolitionists—United States—
    History—19th century. 4. Fugitive slaves—
    United States—History—19th century.
    5. Slavery—United States—History.
    6. Historic sites—United States. 7. United
    States—History, Local. I. Blight, David W.
    E450.P27 2004
    973.7'115—dc22   2003044289

British Library Cataloguing-in-Publication Data
available

Manufactured in China
10 09 08 07 06 05 04   5 4 3 2 1

The paper used in this publication meets the
minimum requirements of the American
National Standard for Information Sciences—
Permanence of Paper for Printed Library
Materials ANSI Z39.48-1984.
For permission to reproduce illustrations
appearing in this book, please correspond
directly with the owners of the works, as listed
in the individual credits. Smithsonian Books
does not retain reproduction rights for these
illustrations individually or maintain a file of
addresses for photo sources.

To all the slaves who never got out, and those who did

CONTENTS

PART 3: THE STORY ENDURES IN HISTORY AND LEGEND

FOREWORD

The story of the Underground Railroad is inextricably woven into the history of the nation as well as the state of Ohio. For both entities, the issue of slavery and its impact on everyone it touched shaped legislation, public discourse, and the actions of Americans both free and enslaved. One of the earliest pieces of legislation passed by Congress regarding slavery related to the Northwest Territory and land once claimed by Virginia and Pennsylvania. As part of the creation of this new region, Congress banned the institution of slavery within its borders. Therefore, from its very inception, Ohio, then part of the Northwest Territory, theoretically represented a safe haven for enslaved African Americans who were seeking their freedom. As a consequence, Ohio has a long history of attracting those who hoped to escape enslavement as well as those who actively opposed the institution of slavery.

Numerous stories exist about freedom seekers who made their way to the Ohio River—the river Jordan in the eyes of some—with the goal of crossing it to freedom. In the process they took their fate into their own hands, knowing full well that failure could result in terrible retribution. Margaret Garner, the inspiration for the book *Beloved* by Toni Morrison, provided one of the most dramatic examples of this burning desire for freedom. Enslaved in Kentucky, Garner ran away and relocated in Cincinnati to live with her mother. When slave catchers sought the return of Garner and her family to Kentucky, she chose to kill one of her children and was prevented from killing a second child rather than have them re-enslaved. Fortunately, not all fugitives were forced to make the choice that confronted Margaret Garner.

"Modern Medea," Margaret Garner with her slain child, from *Harper's Weekly,* May 18, 1867, from a photograph of a painting by Thomas Noble.

Levi Coffin, a Quaker and a native of North Carolina, moved to Indiana in 1826 and to Cincinnati in 1847. Known widely by the unofficial title of "President of the Underground Railroad," Coffin helped hundreds of fugitive slaves toward freedom from his Cincinnati home and store.

More of the fugitives were like Tice Davids, who reached the Ohio River with his pursuer hot on his trail. With no time to find a boat, he plunged into the water and swam to the opposite shore. His master saw Davids climb up the banks and then disappear from view. After rowing across the river, he inquired about the runaway in the city of Ripley. No one could recall seeing anyone fitting Davids's description. Eventually, the man left town empty-handed. Frustrated by his experience, he returned to Kentucky and wryly commented to his friends that Davids must have disappeared on an "underground railroad."

This comment came close to the actual truth of the situation. While Davids took the most important step in the process—deciding to seek his freedom—the help of others greatly enhanced his success. In this particular instance, sympathetic residents of Ripley, Ohio, came to his aid. Their network moved him through the city and con-

nected him with others who transported him to safety and freedom. The citizens of Ripley were hardly unique. All along the Ohio River, residents, both black and white, were ready to assist fugitives. They linked up with people of similar conviction in other parts of the state who participated in this Underground Railroad. This confederation existed in other areas of the nation as well, but Ohio was a particular hotbed of activism.

Many well-known individuals associated with the Underground Railroad and abolition lived in this state. Levi Coffin, often referred to as "the president of the Underground Railroad," made his home in Cincinnati. The Reverend John Rankin, noted for his antislavery writings and his active involvement in the Underground Railroad, resided in Ripley.

Harriet Beecher Stowe was inspired to create *Uncle Tom's Cabin* from the time she lived in the Cincin-nati region. Just as importantly, well-established African American communities in Cincinnati and Antioch, as well as the Gist settlement near Ripley, were home to John Hattfield, John Hudson, Polly Caldwell, John Parker, and other less well-known activists. Extremely important to runaways, these often overlooked individuals played a critical role in the success of the Under-ground Railroad. Fugitives frequently sought out African American communities and depended upon their residents for food, shelter, empathy, and support.

At the height of this activism, Ohio was a leading state in the antislavery effort. By 1837 at least one hundred fifty antislavery societies operated within the state. Ohio also had a reputation as a leading destination for runaways. Cincinnati in particular had a negative reputation among slaveholders as a place where many fugitives traveled and disappeared. They were especially wary of the boats traveling up and down the Ohio River. Workers on these vessels often dashed for freedom when they docked in Cincinnati. Once fugitives entered the city's African American community, recapturing them became an extremely difficult undertaking.

Thus, Ohio's long and intimate association with the Underground Railroad is a topic with great resonance for many of its citizens. The landscape of the state is dotted with structures that were once integral to its success. This rich tradition serves as the foundation for the efforts of the National Underground Railroad Freedom Center in Cincinnati, Ohio. The mission of the Freedom Center is to highlight the courage, cooperation, and perseverance that characterized the efforts of the individuals involved in the Underground Railroad. They risked their lives and their futures to oppose laws that favored the rights of slaveholders. Their personal sacrifice for a larger good still sends a powerful and inspirational message. Their actions illustrate the impact dedicated people can exert upon a society and how they can influence that society to live up to its principles. Instances of interracial cooperation and collaboration represented a countervailing force to the institution of slavery and eventually helped bring about the destruction of the peculiar institution.

One of our tasks at the Freedom Center is to separate myth from reality. Due to the secretive nature of the Underground Railroad, few written records detail its operations. Oblique references and code words more often characterized communication among participants. This approach not only adds to the mystique of the system, but it also makes it more difficult to depict accurately. Who the participants were, how they operated the system on a day-to-day basis, and which structures were actually used in the network are subject to great conjecture. It is certain that some of the homes and buildings that now claim to have been a part of the Underground Railroad definitely were not, despite the lore that surrounds them. Only more extensive research into the history and participants of the Underground Railroad will help clear up the mysteries attached to this endeavor of separating truth from fiction. Whenever it can, the National Underground Railroad Freedom Center will work with researchers in the field to add clarity and more data to the fragmented picture that exists. This volume, we believe, is an important addition to the literature on slavery and the Underground Railroad. The distinguished scholars represented here have increased our understanding of a very complex set of issues, and in the process they have shed more light on this system that undermined slavery. Most importantly, this book provides a bedrock of sound and engaging history on which we can address the fascinating question of the Underground Railroad's hold on American memory and legend.

The National Underground Railroad Freedom Center hopes to play a major role in telling the story of this important activity and of the men and women who were critical to its success. As the Freedom Center opens, its exhibitions and programs focus on the Underground Railroad. It will also direct attention to the importance of freedom in the nineteenth century and the continued significance of that concept today. Those involved in the Underground Railroad fervently believed freedom was worth the effort they made on its behalf. At the Freedom Center, we believe these individuals offer powerful examples of the impact people can have when they refuse to be bystanders and instead decide to make a difference. Their lessons still have great resonance today. By highlighting their bravery, we hope to inspire similar efforts on behalf of freedom in the modern-day world. Choices made today can result in a

Louise Minks, *Crossing the River*, 2003.

difference, just as they did during the era of the Underground Railroad. The Freedom Center seeks to make this clear and persuasive to everyone we touch through telling and retelling the story of the Underground Railroad.

ACKNOWLEDGMENTS

Numerous people and institutions have helped me conceive, write, edit and produce this book. First, I want to thank all the authors who agreed to write essays that reach out beyond our own scholarly disciplines. All are distinguished scholars or public historians, and each writer did his and her part to make this an original work of essays intended for a broad reading audience. I am grateful to all the authors for their professional dedication, attention to deadlines, and their assistance in locating illustrations. John Vlach and Milton Sernett were especially valuable in providing photographs for their essays. My friends, Jim and Lois Horton, advised me repeatedly on how to imagine this book. Richard Blackett was, as usual, a clear and astute counselor.

From its inception, The National Underground Railroad Freedom Center in Cincinnati has been the sponsor and the parent of this book. John Fleming originally recruited me to edit and conceive the book, and his leadership was valuable and insightful. Orloff Miller was my confidant and the skilled officer of the Freedom Center who managed the overall production of the book from start to finish. Orloff's background as a cultural anthropologist was essential to me at various stages of the book's evolution. Ed Rigaud provided important executive leadership as well in the early days of thinking about a book to accompany the opening of the Freedom Center. At the Freedom Center I am also grateful to staff members, Rita Organ and Tamara Williams. In the early years of the Freedom Center's planning, Richard Rabinowitz and Fath Davis Ruffins were inspirations as a curators, historians, and friends. And, Spencer Crew, the director and chief executive officer of the Freedom Center, has been an unfailing supporter of this project since his arrival in Cincinnati. I am most grateful to Spencer for his leadership.

At Amherst College I received the expert assistance of Nancy Board in converting all the essays into a uniform format and in helping me at various stages of editing and revision, from Frank Ward in reproducing dozens of illustrations and photographs, and from

archivists Daria D'Arienzo and John
Lancaster of Archives and Manuscripts, at
the Robert Frost Library. Without the
Amherst College Archives and its marvelous staff, I would not have been able to
research and secure at least two-thirds of
the nearly two hundred and fifty illustrations in this volume. Pembroke Herbert, of
Picture Research Associates, is an angel of
the illustration world. Pembroke was indispensable to me in finding and reproducing
the pictures that now make this book
unique in histories of slavery and the
Underground Railroad. At Yale University,
where I moved in the midst of this project,
I want to thank David Brion Davis, Robert
Forbes, and Jon Butler for their support,
and Owen Williams for many valuable conversations. Among my former colleagues at
Amherst, Jeffrey Ferguson and Martha
Sandweiss deserve special thanks for their
patience and their expertise as I was com-
pleting this book. Shawn Alexander and
Katherine Mooney were crucial as research
assistants and for their Web savvy.

Many people made special contributions to this work along its extended road
to publication. I thank Louise Minks for
her wonderful and original paintings which
were done exclusively for this volume. I am
grateful to my cousin, Kenneth Blight, who
took me on a special tour of Battle Creek,
Michigan where I first saw the magnificent
Harriet Tubman and Underground Railroad

monument in that city's center. Peter Hinks
was most gracious in sending me a copy of
his report on the validity of the many
alleged sites on the Underground Railroad
in Connecticut, as was Carol Lasser in providing me a copy of her fine essay about
the rich history of the Underground
Railroad in Oberlin, Ohio. The staff of the
National Park Service's "Network to
Freedom" have been helpful in many ways,
with both information and advice.

At Smithsonian Books I have been very
fortunate to work with a superb editor,
Caroline Newman, who helped me from
the beginning to conceive this as a book
that would reach out to a large reading
public. Robert Poarch and Emily Sollie
have been faithful and patient in all the
stages of production. And Nancy Eickel has
been a diligent and talented copyeditor.

Finally, to all those thousands of
Underground Railroad historians, devotees,
tour directors, curators, site managers,
researchers, and enthusiasts of all kinds, I
thank you for your work and your dedication. I thank Larry Gara for a book that still
stands up to scrutiny. I thank Frederick
Douglass for leaving so many of his words
to hear in my head over the years. In the
end I hope we have not committed too
many blasphemies for the devout, nor too
many scholarly blunders for the non-
believers. This subject merits a devotion
from all of us, each in our own way.

DAVID W. BLIGHT

INTRODUCTION

The Underground Railroad in History and Memory

By the winter and spring of 1836, the eighteen-year-old-slave Frederick Bailey, along with five male companions, had conceived a plan to escape from their bondage under William Freeland, their owner on the Eastern Shore of Maryland. Although he was the youngest of the group, the future Frederick Douglass served as their leader, and as far as we know, he was the only one who eventually achieved his freedom by flight and lived to write about it. (He changed his name after his escape.) This band of brothers met at night and on Sundays to plot their liberation across the Chesapeake Bay. Douglass remembered them repeatedly singing,

> O Canaan, sweet Canaan,
> I am bound for the land of Canaan.

Douglass assured his reader that their goal was not merely to reach "heaven." "We meant to reach the *north*—and the north was our canaan," he recalled. Another favorite spiritual among the young men was,

> I thought I heard them say,
> There were lions in the way,
> I don't expect to stay
> Much longer here.
> Run to Jesus—shun the danger—
> I don't expect to stay
> Much longer here.

These expressions of stealing away, said Douglass, had a "double meaning." They helped the young men imagine not only a freedom in the "world

1

of spirits" but also "a speedy pilgrimage toward a free state, and deliverance from all the evils and dangers of slavery."[1]

Although the group on Freeland's farm was betrayed, discovered, and jailed, and Douglass had to wait two more years for his own liberation, in such double meanings as in the songs these young men sang we find the deepest meanings of the Underground Railroad in American history. The escape of the slave required both faith and practical cunning, courage of the spirit and earthly knowledge. Fugitive slaves had to conquer fear, face down enormous odds against their success, and test their fate against a police and legal structure that was designed to rivet them in slavery.

"Why should I be a slave?" Douglass remembered asking while contemplating his escape. "There was *no* reason why I should be the thrall of any man." At the same time, he acknowledged that fear controlled the spirit of the would-be runaway slave. He and his brothers tried to be "bold and determined," but just as often they were "doubting, timid and wavering; whistling like a boy in the graveyard, to keep away the spirits." For all runaway slaves, fear and hope marched and huddled together. Indeed, Douglass left a warning to all modern enthusiasts of the drama of the Underground Railroad story. "No man can tell the intense agony which is felt by the slave," confided Douglass, "when wavering on the point of making his escape." The fugitive risked all, according to this most eloquent veteran of the story. "All that he has is at stake," Douglass maintained, "and even that which he has not. . . . The life which he has, may be lost, and the liberty which he seeks, may not be gained."[2] In this impossible choice between life and liberty, with neither a certainty, thousands of American slaves ventured all to be free. Those who succeeded and those who failed together forged a story we rightly celebrate as the "Underground Railroad," but we should do so with a cautious understanding of the relationship between legitimate history and the enduring collective memory and abiding mythology that surrounds this process by which some American slaves achieved liberation and many more never made it to any geographic or spiritual Canaan of the North.

The Underground Railroad is one of the most enduring and popular threads in the fabric of America's national historical

E. W. Bouve, illustration for "The Fugitive's Song" by Jesse Hutchinson Jr., 1845.

memory. It is widely heralded as a part of local heritage across the United States. Historically, what we today call the Underground Railroad was the process—sometimes organized in a network but more often not—by which slaves escaped northward to the free states, to Canada, or to points south, west, and out to sea. Broadly, it consisted of the individual and collective actions of thousands of enslaved people who were trying to achieve liberty and a new beginning to their lives. This traffic in escaped slaves exerted pressure on slavery itself, caused significant political tensions between North and South, and prompted a small but important group of abolitionists to resist the law by aiding fugitives to freedom. Most often, fugitive slaves fled on their own volition, with their destiny at the mercy of fate and the limits of their own courage.

The origin of the term "Underground Railroad" has several versions. One story says that in 1831 a fugitive slave named Tice Davids escaped from Kentucky to safer ground in Sandusky, in northern Ohio. When Davids's master looked in vain for him in Ripley, just across the Ohio River, he is said to have commented, "The nigger must have gone off on an underground rail-road." Another version explains that the term came into use among slave hunters in Pennsylvania who experienced similar frustrations. Yet a third story places the origin in Washington, DC, in 1839, when allegedly a fugitive slave, after being tortured, claimed that he was to have been sent north, where "the railroad ran underground all the way to Boston."[3] Whatever the actual first use of the term, it was common by the mid-1840s to speak and write of the Underground Railroad as a clandestine system for runaway slaves. It was already in part a legend, a construction of historical *memory*, as much as it was *historical*, by the time of the Fugitive Slave Act of 1850.

What are the differences as well as the mutual values between *memory* and *history*? What do we mean by these terms, so widely in use today and in the title of this book? Memory resides at the heart of our humanity. As individuals, and perhaps as societies as well, we cannot function in practical or moral terms without memory. Memory provides a physical, and sometimes an ethical, compass in our daily lives. In one of the most compelling meditations on memory every written, Saint Augustine, in his *Confessions,* refers to memory as the "vast court," the "treasury" in the mind. He stands in awe of its force—a great "cham-

Leigh Richmond Miner, "The Memory," from Higgins and Coombs, *Some Time Ago,* 1980.

ber," he calls it, and no one had yet "sounded the bottom thereof." Augustine approaches this quintessentially human trait with suspicion and respect. "Great is the power of memory," he writes, "a fearful thing. O my God, a deep and boundless manifoldness; and this thing is the mind, and this am I myself."[4] Augustine seems convinced that we *are* our memories; they dictate to us, we respond to them, and we endlessly revise them to fit our needs.

Memory can, therefore, control us, overwhelm us, or poison us. It can also save us from confusion and despair. As individuals, we cannot live without it, but it is part of the human condition to live with its burdens as well. Moreover, memory can sometimes become a safe haven in the past; it can cast romantic and sentimental spells over our imagination. Those spells can serve not only as survival mechanisms but also as obstacles to genuine understanding of what actually happened in the past. None other than Abraham Lincoln, capable of both highly legalistic

and imaginative thought, left a warning in verse about this dilemma. After visiting his boyhood farmstead in Indiana, a place where he had experienced true hardship, he penned this poem.

> O memory! Thou midway world,
> 'Twixt earth and paradise,
> Where things decayed and loved ones lost
> In dreamy shadows rise,
>
> And, freed from all that's earthly, vile,
> Seem hallowed, pure and bright,
> Like scenes in some enchanted isle
> All bathed in liquid light.

In our need to find an ennobling past through which to establish our identities, we have sometimes used the story of the Underground Railroad as a comforting "midway world" between the "earth" we currently inhabit and the "dreamy shadows" of local or family lore. When appealed to unquestioningly, memory can provide, as the philosopher George Santyana put it in his definition of religion, "another world to live in."[5]

Ed Dwight, *The Underground Railroad*, 1993. The Kellogg Foundation funded the monument, now located in Battle Creek, Michigan.

Is all of this equally true when memory takes on the collective, social form? Do whole societies or nations derive their very sustenance from memory as individuals do? Historians rightly have come to study the past through the lens of "memory" because they have returned to the realization that peoples of all cultures define themselves through the "myths" they live by. With time, the deeply encoded stories or metaphors from history acquire a symbolic power in any society. The great story of the Underground Railroad's role in America's struggle over slavery offers many lessons in how a public, collective memory has formed in the United States. It says much about who we are as well as who we say we want to be.

But what of discretion in the practice of history, as opposed to the formation of memory? How are history and memory distinct? They can represent two antagonistic attitudes toward the past, two streams of historical consciousness that at some point must flow into one another, often with turbulence, and form a collaboration. Historians are custodians of the past, the preservers and discoverers of the facts and stories out of which people imagine their civic lives. Professional historians also need a sense of humility and engagement in the face of public memory and the deep myths upon which it draws. "The remembered past," warned John Lukacs, "is a much larger category than the recorded past."[6]

History is what trained historians do, a reasoned reconstruction of the past rooted in research. It tends to be critical and skeptical of human motive and action, and therefore it is more secular than what we commonly call memory. History can be read by or belong to everyone; it is more relative, and contingent on place, chronology, scale, and multiple causation.

If history is shared and secular, memory tends to be a sacred set of absolute meanings and stories, possessed as the "heritage" or identity of a community. Memory is often *owned;* history is *interpreted.* Passed down through generations, memory frequently demands filial piety; history is revised generation after generation. Memory often coalesces in objects, monuments, or sites (houses, caves, tunnels, crossroads, place names, a slave jail, a preserved letter, a precious reminiscence); history seeks to understand contexts in all their complexity. History investigates a world with many actors; memory sometimes requires a duty to focus exclusively on our own ancestors. History asserts the authority of academic training and canons of evidence; memory carries the often more immediate authority of community membership and experience.[7]

Both history and memory, with all their divergences, provide indispensable means by which to inspire a sense of the past. Without grass roots research, bolstered by the zeal and imagination that it entails from hundreds of local historians and curators, we could not begin to distinguish the wheat from the chaff in the story of the Underground Railroad. Without an imagination for drama and past heroism, the resources to build the National Underground Railroad Freedom Center could never have been marshaled. Without exceptional teachers and local historians, the ability to see the past occurring in real places would not be disseminated to young people. The National Park Service's broad effort to establish a "National Network to Freedom" based on verifiable sites relies heavily on local knowledge and research. The past should make us *feel* as well as *think* about its challenges.[8]

Likewise, without professional historians to ask new, critical questions, to probe for original archival evidence, and to look carefully into and beyond local memory to larger terrain, we might never grasp the overall significance of the past. We might miss the historical world beyond our own horizons, which are often ringed with myths that serve our needs rather than stretch our understanding. Without the skeptical academic who, by training, must resist a spiritual or emotional approach to the past, the depth of the drama and the uses of the spirit in the past might never be comprehended. If history were never "revised," a word that makes some enthusiastic lovers of history uncomfortable, how would we ever understand our changing world? Should the past always be made to serve the present, or should it be guarded from Douglass's notion of the "world of spirits" or Lincoln's idea of the "dreamy shadows" in order to protect scholarship from the influence of wish fulfillment? Indeed, who should guard the past and determine how it informs the present? None of these questions has a pat answer. Quite simply, all of us who are concerned about history are its guardians and its advocates.

The pastness of the past is everyone's business, as is the present relevance of any great historical problem. To a large extent, all memory, like all politics, is local. The obligation of the professional historian is ultimately to cultivate the local story in order to offer the best possible interpretation of the global story. We need to *interpret* both history and memory in order to write good histories *of* memory. Anyone researching the Underground Railroad should listen attentively to their great-grandparents, and then get thee to an archive! Look with informed eyes at the architecture of alleged sites, remember how much *slavery* existed behind this *freedom* story, and search for the differences between belief and knowledge.[9]

Above all, none of us, whatever our perspective, training, or yearnings, can avoid the knotty problem of myth and legend and their relationship to history itself. Something in our human spirit, in our hard wiring, if you will, probably draws us to *story*, to narratives with beginnings, middles, turning points, and endings. Sometimes we love a story because it makes us feel good or takes us to desirable, imagined places. At other times we are attracted by the ancient patterns of melodrama: heroes and villains with perils and resolutions. Ideas or events that become mythic in any culture can serve the ends of social stability and unity, but they can also be counter-myths that are innovative and liberating. Like it or not, all modern cultures, tyrannies and democratic societies alike, use the past this way. Historian Richard Slotkin defines myth effectively as "usable values from history" that are "beyond the reach of critical demystification," while the critic Roland Barthes describes myths as clusters of ideas or stories that have lost "the memory that they were ever made." We are mistaken if we think we can deny great myths once they take hold. Deep myths have their "resilience," writes historian Michael Kammen, and are "not completely controllable."[10]

The Underground Railroad in American history has been just such a dilemma and an inspiration. We need to think clearly about its real and its legendary dimensions, its history and its memory. If we are unafraid, both ways of seeing the past will tell us much about ourselves.

In this volume of essays and more than two hundred fifty illustrations, we have endeavored to deliver both sides of this historical equation. The chapters are original pieces by many of the country's most distinguished scholars of slavery, abolitionism, and emancipation and its aftermath. In Part I, Ira Berlin and Deborah Gray White provide a short history with arguments about American slavery from the early colonial period to the beginning of the Civil War. They describe what changed and did not change about slavery over the generations and examine the relationship between the absolute power of slavery and the human will to survive. James Brewer Stewart accomplishes in a single essay an overall understanding of the antislavery movement, both black and white, as an organized resistance to tyranny and oppression.

Part II contains seven chapters, most of which tell documented, real stories of liberation and rescue. The opening essay by John Michael Vlach offers an engaging history of the origins and physical remains of the Underground Railroad, especially as it survives in architectural "places" and in current local enthusiasms. Jane Landers introduces the complex story of slave flight to Florida and black assimila-

tion among the Seminoles from the Spanish colonial period to the early nineteenth century. Bondsmen escaped southward as well as northward. Florida was no Canada, but it served as a frontier of possibility for former slaves. R. J. M. Blackett and Lois E. Horton illuminate the crisis of the Fugitive Slave Act of 1850, the increasingly violent resistance to the hated law, and the problem of the kidnapping of former slaves in the North in the turbulent decade of the 1850s. James Oliver Horton and Catherine Clinton look at the lives and heroic work of two of the Underground Railroad's most important

HARPER'S WEEKLY.
JOURNAL OF CIVILIZATION

Vol. XIX.—No. 978.] NEW YORK, SATURDAY, SEPTEMBER 25, 1875. [WITH A SUPPLEMENT. PRICE TEN CENTS.

THE SONG OF THE KETTLE—AN EVENING REVERIE.—[SEE PAGE 786.]

"The Song of the Kettle," from *Harper's Weekly,* September 25, 1875. The text accompanying this image reads in part: "Auntie sits in her own little room at evening time dreamily puffing the smoke from her pipe, and thinking of bygone days. . . . Poor old Tom is dead. . . . Who shall say what memories the Song of the Kettle recalls? Massa and Missus and the children, the old plantation scenes, the evening dance, the Sunday hymns, the dreaded auction block, the driver's whip all come up before her as she thinks of olden times. It is like a dream to her now, and often she wonders if it can indeed be true that she is free."

"Uncle Tom Brown,"
former slave photo-
graphed in old age,
from Essie Collins
Matthews, *Aunt Phebe,
Uncle Tom and Others,*
1915.

operatives, William Still and Harriet Tubman. Both have become the stuff of legend, while in historical time they were as important as anyone in supplying the body and blood of the real story of the Underground Railroad. Ending the second section is Bruce Levine's rich short history of emancipation and the destruction of slavery in the midst of all-out war and conquest. Only the first chapters of the fugitive slave story had been written before the Union and Confederate armies clashed in 1861 or Abraham Lincoln signed the Emancipation Proclamation. If war is an agent of liberation and social change, it was never more so than in the Civil War.

Finally, Part III addresses the problem of legacies and current uses of the Underground Railroad in modern thought, tourism, and public history. David W. Blight probes the issue of why so much attention, locally and nationally, has been given to the story of the Underground Railroad in our own time. In doing so, he examines the question of Underground Railroad "lore" over more than a century and ultimately suggests that almost nothing is new in our current enthusiasm, save possibly the scale. Jane Williamson contributes a poignant account of one Underground Railroad site—the Rokeby Museum in Vermont—with thorough documentation and a multigenerational story to tell about fugitives slaves who were aided to freedom by devout Quakers. Her essay is also a splendid discussion of how mythic memory creeps into the history of such sites, and what local historians and curators can do to control it. Milton C. Sernett writes as both a historian and a resident-observer of the remarkable degree of current Under-

"Aunt Lucy," former slave photographed in old age, from Essie Collins Matthews, *Aunt Phebe, Uncle Tom and Others*, 1915.

ground Railroad commemoration in New York State. As in many other Northern states, grass roots researchers, preservationists, and enthusiasts in New York are refashioning the Underground Railroad story to fit a new era. Diane Miller surveys the criteria and operation of the National Network to Freedom, a major initiative of the National Park Service to verify and establish official sites associated with the history of the Underground Railroad. Religious scholar Eddie Glaude Jr. concludes with a forceful meditation on the significance of the biblical story of "Exodus" in African American thought and life before emancipation. One of the oldest stories in western literature is indeed the template for how many blacks comprehended their own attempts to flee their "Egyptian" bondage for freedom in New Canaan.

Together, these essays and illustrations pick up where traditional historians and hundreds of grass roots workers along the many paths of "the Road" leave off. This book is the story of slavery's deep significance in American history. It is intended as a quilt of many colors, with the dark hue of the broad background representing the multiple dimensions of slavery and with the Underground Railroad woven throughout as threads of primary colors. By presenting the history and the memory of the Underground Railroad, we aim to stimulate wider discussions of the true nature of this great American story as well as determine why we have so dearly needed it to fashion our multifaceted national identity.

PART ONE
SLAVERY AND ABOLITION

IRA BERLIN

BEFORE COTTON

African and African American Slavery in Mainland North America during the Seventeenth and Eighteenth Centuries

The destruction of slavery amid a bloody civil war has fixed the way in which most Americans view chattel bondage and has led them to identify it with the states of the Southern Confederacy and the cultivation of cotton. Yet that characterization belies slavery's long history in the portions of mainland North America that initially formed the United States. Indeed, for most of slavery's history, it was a colony-wide or national institution that reached every corner of the continent. Until the nineteenth century—some two hundred years after the first African slaves arrived in mainland North America—few slaves grew cotton and hardly any lived in the "blackbelt," that rich band of alluvial lands that extends westward from upcountry South Carolina to the Mississippi River and became the heartland of the Confederacy. In short, most American slaves experienced slavery not as cotton cultivators or residents of the blackbelt. Even after King Cotton had been crowned, the years "before cotton" continued to shape the lives of American slaves.

The story of slavery during those first two centuries was not of one piece. Slavery was constantly changing, as slaves confronted their owners in a panoply of diverse circumstances. Depending upon their origins, their time of arrival in the Americas, their numbers, the terrain upon which they lived, and the crops they grew, the lives of enslaved Africans and African Americans were different—sometimes radically so. The continual transformation of slavery remade the lives of those held in bondage and suggests how and why slavery would be transformed in its final half century, when it became identified with the blackbelt and cotton. In the two centuries prior to the growth of cotton culture, the history of slavery can be divided into three

parts or generations: a Charter Generation, composed of the first arrivals; a Plantation Generation, which experienced the imposition of staple production; and a Revolutionary Generation, which was transformed by the egalitarian movements of the late eighteenth century. The experiences of each generation differed, and with them so did the lives of enslaved peoples, although most were of African descent and black in color.

The Charter Generation refers to people of African descent who arrived as slaves in mainland North America prior to the advent of the plantation in the seventeenth and eighteenth centuries. Disproportionately they were drawn from the Atlantic littoral. Their world focused outward onto the larger Atlantic region. They spoke, among other languages, the creole dialect that had developed among the peoples of the Atlantic world in the fifteenth and sixteenth centuries, a language with a Portuguese grammar and syntax but with a vocabulary borrowed from every shore of the Atlantic. They understood something

about the trading etiquettes, religions, and laws of the Atlantic world. Many were employed as interpreters, supercargoes, sailors, and compodores (all-purpose seaboard handymen) for the great sixteenth- and seventeenth-century trading corporations—the Dutch West India Company, the French Company of the West, and the Royal African Company—as well as a host of private traders and privateers. They entered societies in which many people of European descent, although not slaves, were held in various sorts of servitude. Almost immediately they began incorporating themselves into those societies by taking familiar names, trading independently, establishing families, acquiring property, and employing their knowledge of the law to advance themselves and secure their freedom in remarkably high numbers. About one-fifth to one-quarter of those in the Charter Generation gained their liberty.[1]

Little is known about these men and women, whose telling names—Anthony Johnson of Virginia, Paulo d'Angola of New

Amsterdam, and Francisco Menéndez of Saint Augustine—speak of the larger Atlantic world. Their history can be glimpsed through the life of another of their number: Samba Bambara of New Orleans.

Samba Bambara's name first appears in the historical record while he was working for the French Company of the West on the Senegal River in west Africa at the beginning of the eighteenth century. He is known because he disputed his pay and complained that his wife "dishonored" him. Working along the river, moving cargo—perhaps human cargo—from Saint Louis on the coast of Senegal to the African interior, Samba Bambara rubbed shoulders with saltwater sailors of various European and African nationalities, traders from the continent's interior, the corporate bureaucrats who directed the French Company of the West, and the soldiers who protected them. He doubtless spoke the creole language of the Atlantic along with his own

language and a bit of French. Like others who followed his path, Bambara became a cultural broker negotiating among the various peoples who had come together in the Atlantic.

Sometime in the 1720s, Samba Bambara became implicated in a slave insurrection in Saint Louis on the west coast of Africa, or perhaps he was merely accused of being involved. Nonetheless, he was enslaved and transported to Louisiana, a desultory society-with-slaves that stood at the outer edge of the French empire. That in itself was an interesting development, for almost all the slaves leaving Senegal for the New World were going to Martinique or Saint Domingue, colonies that were fast becoming the great sugar factories of the Atlantic world. Perhaps someone realized it was dangerous to send one like Samba Bambara, a man who knew how the system worked, to the revolutionary tinderboxes of Martinque and Saint Domingue.

J. H. M., "African Slave Trade," from *The History of Slavery and the Slave Trade*, 1860.

Doubtless, Samba Bambara was not happy about his enslavement, exile, and forcible separation from everything and everyone he held dear, but once in New Orleans, he resumed his life almost without losing a beat. Within a decade, Samba Bambara—still a slave—was successively the overseer of the largest company-owned plantation in Louisiana and then the chief interpreter in the Louisiana Superior Court.[2]

Samba Bambara's success suggests something about the unity of the Atlantic world. It reveals how New Orleans on the Mississippi River was not much different from Saint Louis on the Senegal River. Both ports were filled with saltwater sailors from the Atlantic, native traders from the interior, European corporate bureaucrats, and settlers from all nations. New Orleans was, in short, a place in which a cultural broker like Samba Bambara could not only survive but could also enjoy a modicum of success.

Similar stories of modest success can be found among other members of the Charter Generation throughout mainland North America. The story of Anthony Johnson, sold to the English at Jamestown in 1621 as "Antonio a Negro," reveals one of the parallel paths the Charter Generation followed. During the dozen years after his arrival in North America, Antonio labored on the Bennett family's plantation on Virginia's middle peninsula, where he was among the few who survived the 1622 Indian raid that all but destroyed the colony, and where he later earned an official commendation for his "hard labor and known service." His loyalty and his industry also won the favor of the Bennetts, who became Antonio's patron as well as his owner, perhaps because worthies like Antonio were hard to find among the rough, hard-bitten, and often sickly men who comprised the mass of servants and slaves in the region. Whatever the source of the Bennetts' favor, they allowed Antonio, a slave, to farm independently, marry, and baptize his children. Eventually he and his family escaped bondage. Once free, Antonio Anglicized his name, transforming Antonio a Negro into Anthony Johnson, a name so familiar to English speakers that no one could doubt his identification with the nationality of the colony's rulers.

Johnson, his wife Mary, and their children—who numbered four by 1640—followed their benefactor to the Eastern Shore of Virginia, where the Bennett clan had established itself as a leading family and where the Johnson family began to farm on its own. In 1651 Anthony Johnson earned a 250-acre headright, a substantial estate for any Virginian, let alone a former slave. Johnson's son John did even better than his father, receiving a patent for 550 acres, and another son, Richard, owned a 100-acre estate. When Anthony Johnson's Eastern Shore plantation burned to the ground in 1653, he petitioned the county

J. W. Orr, "Gathering Cane," from *The History of Slavery and the Slave Trade,* 1860.

Unidentified artist, "Slaves Dancing the Juba," ca. 1800.

court for relief. Reminding authorities that he and his wife were longtime residents and that "their hard labors and knowne services for obtayneing their livelihood were well known," he requested and was granted a special abatement of his taxes. Like other men of substance, Johnson and his sons farmed independently, held slaves, and left their heirs sizeable estates. As established members of their community, they enjoyed rights in common with other free men and frequently employed the law to protect themselves and to advance their interests. Still, when Anthony Johnson's slave—a black man named John Casar (sometimes Casor, Cassaugh, or Cazara)—claimed his freedom and gained sanctuary with Robert and George Parker, two neighboring white planters, Johnson did not immediately attempt to retrieve his property. The Parkers had already exhibited considerable animus toward the Johnson fami-

ly, accusing John Johnson of "fornication and other enormities." Antagonizing rancorous white men of the planter class was a hazardous business, even if Johnson could prove they had conspired to lure John Casar from his household. At length, however, Anthony Johnson decided to act. He took the Parkers to court and won Casar's return along with damages against the Parkers.[3]

Johnson and the Parkers wrestled over Casar because labor—whether European, Native American, or African in origin—was the key to success on the mainland, as ambitious men competed for status, land, and yet more labor. In their rush to seize the main chance, planters might trample their workers, but they made little distinction among their subordinates by age, sex, nationality, or race. While the advantages of this peculiar brand of equality may have been lost on its beneficiaries, it was precisely the shared labor regimen of Africans, Europeans, and Native Americans that allowed some black men, such as Anthony Johnson, to escape bondage and join the scramble that characterized life in the Chesapeake during the seventeenth century.[4]

The Johnsons were no more unique in the Chesapeake region than Samba Bambara was in the lower Mississippi Valley. John Francisco, Bashaw Ferdinando (or Farnando), Emanuel Driggus (sometimes Drighouse, probably Rodriggus), Anthony Longo (perhaps Loango), and "Francisco a Negroe" (soon to become Francis, then Frank, Payne and finally Paine) and similar men could be found throughout the Chesapeake and most especially on the Eastern Shore of Virginia and Maryland. Their number remained tiny. In 1665 the free black population of Virginia's Eastern Shore (Northampton and Accomack Counties) amounted to less than twenty adults and perhaps an equal number of children. The black population of the region was itself small, totalling no more than 300 on the Eastern Shore and perhaps 1,700 in all of Maryland and Virginia, yet the proportion of the black people enjoying freedom was substantial— and perhaps more importantly, it was growing. In Northampton County, free people of African descent made up about one-fifth of the black population at mid-century and rose to nearly 30 percent in 1668, which was not radically different than other mainland settlements.[5]

As elsewhere, members of the Charter Generation in the Chesapeake ascended the social order and exhibited a sure-handed understanding of the area's social hierarchy and the complex dynamics of patron-client relations. Although still in bondage, they began to acquire the property, skills, and social connections that became their mark throughout the Atlantic world. They worked provision grounds, kept livestock, traded independently, and married white women as often as they married black.[6] More important, they found advocates among the propertied classes, often their owners, and identified themselves with the colony's most important institutions by registering their marriages, baptisms, and children's godparents in the Anglican church and their property in the county courthouse. They sued and were sued in local courts and petitioned the colonial legislatures and governors.

The Charter Generation's experiences in the French colony of Louisiana and the English colony of Virginia were repeated across mainland North America prior to the advent of the plantation. Variations of the stories of Samba Bambara and Anthony Johnson can be found in French Canada, Dutch New Netherlands, and Spanish Florida. Although their tales differed from place to place, success in gaining entry into the new societies of the mainland became a hallmark of the Charter Generation.[7]

Its successor—the generation of men and women who came to North America with the advent of the plantation—were not nearly as fortunate. Members of the Plantation Generation worked harder and died earlier. Their family life was truncated, and few could claim ties of blood or marriage. They knew—and probably wanted to know—little about Christianity and European jurisprudence. They had but small opportunities to participate in independent exchange economies, and they rarely accumulated property. Most lived on large estates deep in the countryside, cut off from the larger Atlantic world. Few escaped slavery.

Their names often reflected the contempt with which their owners held them. Most answered to some European diminutive: Jack and Sukey in the English colonies, Pedro and Francisca in places under Spanish rule, and Jean and Marie in the French dominions. As if to emphasize their inferiority, some were tagged with names more akin to barnyard animals. As a kind of comic jest, others were assigned the name of some ancient deity or great personage, such as Hercules or Cato. The most insignificant received the greatest of names. Whatever they were called, they rarely bore surnames, as their owners sought to obliterate marks of lineage and deny them adulthood. The anonymity of the Plantation Generation is reflected in the biographies of individual men and women. To the extent that they can be reconstructed, their life stories are thin to the point of invisibility. Less is known about these men and women than any other generation of American slaves.[8]

The degradation of black life had many sources, but the most significant was the growth of the plantation. Offering staple commodities for an international market, these production centers required a radically different form of social organization and commercial enterprise controlled by a class of men whose appetite for labor was nearly insatiable. Drawing power from the metropolitan state (England, France, and Spain), planters transformed slavery, and in the process they redefined the meaning of race, investing color—white and black—with far greater weight in defining status. Blackness and whiteness took on new meaning.[9]

The Plantation Revolution came to mainland North America in fits and starts. Beginning in the late seventeenth century in the Chesapeake region, planters moved unevenly across the continent over the next 150 years, first to lowland South Carolina in the early eighteenth century and then, after failing to establish a plantation regime in the colonies north of the Chesapeake, to the lower Mississippi Valley. By the beginning of the nineteenth century, slave soci-

Thomas Coram, "View of Mulberry Plantation," 1792.

eties dedicated to cultivating tobacco in the Chesapeake, rice in low-country South Carolina and Georgia, and sugar in the lower Mississippi Valley had swept away the Charter Generation.[10]

Although variations in the nature of settlement, the character of the slave trade, and the demands of particular staple crops produced striking differences in the Plantation Generation, the trajectory of the Plantation Revolution was always the same. With the advent of staple production, be it

Nanſemond, June 20, 1768.

RUN away from the ſub-ſcriber ſome time in *April* 1767, a new Negro man named TOM, belonging to the proprietors of the *Diſmal Swamp*. He is about 5 feet 6 inches high, has his country marks (that is, four on each of his cheeks.) Any perſon that apprehends the ſaid fellow, ſo that I may get him, ſhall have three pounds reward, paid by
JOHN WASHINGTON.

tobacco, rice, or sugar, the number of slaves lurched upward. No longer did slaves dribble into the mainland from various parts of the Atlantic littoral. Instead, planters turned to the African interior as their primary source of labor and imported slaves by the boatful. The proportion of the population that was African in origin grew steadily, and in some places reached a majority.

For many European settlers, it seemed like the mainland would "some time or other be confirmed by the name of New Guinea." African men and women, often marked by ritual scarification that slave owners called "country markings" or "negro markings," filed teeth, and plaited hair, were seen everywhere. Their music, particularly their drums, filled the air with sounds that frightened European and European American settlers, and their pots,

pipes, and other material objects became distinctive features of everyday life. The language of black slaves in America turned from the creole lingua franca of the Atlantic world to the tongues of the African interior. An Anglican missionary found "difficulty of conversing with the Majority of Negroes themselves," because they have "a language peculiar to themselves, a wild confused medley of Negro and corrupt English, which makes them very unintelligible except to those who have conversed with them for many years." Whereas Atlantic creoles had beaten on the doors of the established churches to gain a modicum of recognition, the new arrivals showed neither interest in nor knowledge of Christianity. Jesus disappeared from African American life not to return for most people of African descent until well into the nineteenth century. The religious practices of the new arrivals, dismissed as idolatry and devil worship by the established clergy, placed them outside the pale of civilization as most European and European Americans understood it.

The Africanization of American slavery accompanied a sharp deterioration in the conditions of slave life. With an eye for a quick profit, planters imported a disproportionate number of males. Generally men outnumbered women more than two to one on slaver ships entering the region, and this imbalance soon manifested itself in the sexual balance of the plantation population. The number of men and women, which had previously been roughly equal, swung heavily toward men. The sharply skewed sex ratio made it difficult for the newly arrived to establish families, let alone maintain the deep ancestral lineages that framed so much of life in Africa. The familial linkages that bound members of

the Charter Generation attenuated, undermining the ability of the slave population to reproduce itself. Just as direct importation drove birth rates down, it pushed mortality rates up, for the transatlantic journey left transplanted Africans weak and vulnerable to New World diseases. Fertility remained low and mortality high, and the number of slaves grew slowly, if at all, by natural means. Whereas Anthony and Mary Johnson, like other members of the Charter Generation, had lived to see their grandchildren, few of the newly arrived Africans would even reproduce themselves.

Confined to the plantation, African slaves faced a harsh work regimen as planters escalated the demands they placed on those who worked the tobacco, rice, indigo, or sugar fields. The number of hours spent in the field expanded, and slaves worked well into the evening, often seven days a week. To squeeze more labor

from their workers, planters also reorganized their work force into squads or gangs, often placing agile young workers at the head of each one. They hired overseers to supervise their slaves and sometimes employed stewards to supervise their overseers, dividing their work force by age, sex, and ability. Slaves found their toil subject to minute inspection, as planters or their minions monitored the numerous tasks that the cultivation of tobacco, rice, indigo, and rice necessitated. Slaves suffered as planters prospered.

Living on isolated plantations, the slaves' world narrowed. Physical separation not only denied the new arrivals the opportunity to integrate themselves into the larger society, but it also prevented them from finding a well-placed patron and enjoying the company of men and women of equal rank. The planters' goal of stripping away all ties upon which the enslaved persona

Slave quarters at Hermitage Plantation in Savannah, Georgia, ca. 1900–10.

rested—village, clan, household, and family—and leaving slaves totally dependent upon their owners was nearly realized.

The new regime left little room for free blacks. Planter-controlled legislatures systematically carved away at their liberty. Statute books soon filled with legislation that distinguished between the rights accorded black and white persons, barring free persons of African descent from the most elemental liberties and denying slaves access to freedom. In various places, free black people lost the right to employ white indentured servants, hold office, bear arms, muster in the militia, and vote. They were required to pay special taxes, punished more severely for certain crimes, and subjected to fines or imprisonment for striking a white person, no matter what the cause. Having destroyed such rights, lawmakers closed the door to freedom, constricting and in some places prohibiting manumission. The number of free people of African descent declined, if not in absolute num-

bers, certainly as a proportion of the black population. It became increasingly difficulty to equate freedom with blackness.

Such a social order required raw power to sustain it. Planters mobilized the apparatus of coercion in the service of their new regime. The level of violence escalated. Slaves faced the pillory, whipping post, and gallows with far greater regularity and in far larger numbers than ever before. Even as slave masters routinely employed the rod, the lash, the branding iron, and the fist, they invented new punishments to humiliate and demoralize as well as correct. What else can one make of planter William Byrd's forcing a bed-wetting slave to drink "a pint of piss" or Joseph Ball's placement of a metal "bit" in the mouth of persistent runaways. Beyond the dehumanizing affronts were the grotesque mutilations, as slaveholders terrorized those they deemed to be their human property.

The state ratified the planters' actions, affirming even the masters' right to take a

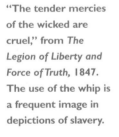

"The tender mercies of the wicked are cruel," from *The Legion of Liberty and Force of Truth*, 1847. The use of the whip is a frequent image in depictions of slavery.

slave's life without fear of retribution. After 1669 the demise of a slave "who chance to die" while being corrected by his or her owner or upon orders of their owner no longer constituted a felony in Virginia. Such legislation, which soon became a general attitude throughout the mainland, stretched the masters' authority far beyond anything previously enjoyed. In the years that followed, lawmakers expanded the power of the slaveholder and diminished the slaves' rights until the masters' dominion over the slave was nearly complete.

Evidence of the degradation of slave life was everywhere. Violence, isolation, exhaustion, and alienation often led African slaves to profound depression and occasionally to self-destruction. Most slaves, however, refused to surrender to the dehumanization that accompanied the Plantation Revolution. Instead, they contested the new regime at every turn, protesting the organization, pace, and intensity of labor and challenging the planters' definition of property rights.

Slaves answered the planters' ruthless imposition with an equally desperate resistance, as the creation of the plantation regime sparked bloody reprisals. The mainland grew rife with conspiracies and insurrectionary plots, but resistance required guile as well as daring. If the planters' grab for power began with the usurpation of African names, slaves soon took back this signature of their identity. Of necessity, slaves answered to the names their owners imposed on them, but many clandestinely maintained their African names. If secrecy provided one shield against the planters' power, seeming ignorant offered another. In the stereotype of the dumb, brutish African that planters voiced so loudly, newly arrived slaves found protection by

Omar Sayyid was a Muslim slave born in Senegal.

using their apparent ignorance of the language, landscape, and work routines to their own benefit.

In resisting the planters' rule, slaves began to create their own distinctive culture. Whereas the Charter Generation had searched for ways to incorporate themselves into the larger society, members of the Plantation Generation wanted no part of the world of their owners, whose economy, religion, and laws only conspired to oppress them. Drawing upon the memory of Africa—itself renewed and refreshed with the continual arrival of new African imports—slaves joined the many cultures of Africa with their own diverse experience in mainland North America. The result was

Samuel Jennings,
"Liberty Displaying,"
undated.

a plethora of new cultural forms, manifested in a variety of new languages, patterns of leadership, family structures, religious forms, songs, dances, and cuisines. These African American cultures became the basis of black life in slavery.

At the end of the eighteenth century, as a new generation of black men and women, many of them American born, reconstructed African life in mainland North America, a series of revolutionary changes again remade slavery. The great democratic revolutions—the American (1776), the French (1789), and the Haitian (1793)—marked a third transformation in the lives of black people, propelling some slaves to freedom and dooming others to nearly another century of captivity.

The War for American Independence and the revolutionary conflicts it spawned throughout the Atlantic region gave slaves new leverage in their struggle with their owners. By shattering the unity of the planter class and compromising its ability to mobilize the metropolitan state to slavery's defense, the war offered slaves new opportunities to challenge both the institution of chattel bondage and the allied structures of white supremacy. In many instances, the state—whether understood as the planters' former British, French, or Spanish overlords or their own representatives—turned against the master class. As the slaveholders stumbled, so did the support nonslaveholders once rendered them.

Some abandoned longstanding ties with planters to fashion new connections among themselves. A few formed alliances with slaves. The emergence of such combinations compelled slave masters, now divided into Loyalist and Patriot factions, to make previously unimagined concessions, occasionally extending to freedom. Such concessions, no matter how skillfully parried, eroded the planters' position atop slave society and opened the way for some slaves to secure their freedom and for others to improve their lot. Yet, slaveholders did not surrender their power easily. In most places they recovered their balance, sometimes overwhelming their opponents and at other times acquiescing just enough to revitalize their shaken institution. Even then, however, slave owners could not recreate the status quo antebellum. The shock of revolution profoundly altered slavery.[11]

24   PASSAGES TO FREEDOM

To a large degree, the warfare itself—the intensity of the fighting and the internal divisions it created—shaped the slaves' ability to challenge the old order. Where the fighting remained distant and invading armies were little more than rumor, masters generally parried the slaves' threat, but where rival armies clashed and occupied large portions of the countryside, creating civil disorder and social strife, the advantage fell to the slaves. Often slaves found opportunities for freedom amid the chaos of war, camouflaging themselves among the tramping soldiers and occasionally taking up arms and becoming soldiers themselves.

The turmoil of war marked only the beginning of the slaveholders' problems. The invocation of universal equality, most prominently in the American Declaration of Independence and the French Declaration of the Rights of Man, further strengthened the slaves' cry for freedom. The Patriots' loud complaints of enslavement to a distant imperial tyrant and their insistence on the universality of liberty overflowed the narrow boundaries of the struggle for political independence. How can Americans "complain so loudly of attempts to enslave them," mused Thomas Paine in 1775, "while they hold so many hundreds of thousands in slavery?" Paine's query unsettled many, including numerous slaveholders.[12]

Revolutionary ideology was only one source of the new spirit of liberty and equality. In English North America, an evangelical upsurge that presumed all were equal in God's eyes complemented and sometimes reinforced revolutionary idealism and placed new pressure on slaveholders. The evangelicals, with Baptists and Methodists in the fore, despised the planters' haughty manners and high ways,

and welcomed slaves into the fold as brothers and sisters in Jesus Christ. Black men and women who joined—and led, as did Richard Allen and Harry Hoosier—the evangelical churches considered temporal freedom an obvious extension of their spiritual liberation, and many white congregants enthusiastically agreed.[13]

The war and the libertarian ideology that accompanied it extended beyond the boundaries of the newly established United States, deeply affecting the rest of mainland North America. As the fighting spread to the lower Mississippi Valley and from there to the Gulf Coast, planters in those regions found themselves on the defensive, their position threatened by international rivalries among imperial powers and eroded by internal divisions. Events in France, Spain, mainland South America, and the islands of the Caribbean initiated new assaults on slavery and compounded these breaches. No place was touched more deeply than the French colony of Saint Domingue on the island of Hispaniola, where *gens de couleur* seized notions of liberty, equality, and fraternity and pressed their case for full citizenship. Planters denounced the free people of color as presumptuous upstarts and imprisoned their leaders, even executing

RUN away from the subscriber in *Albemarle*, a Mulatto slave called *Sandy*, about 35 years of age, his stature is rather low, inclining to corpulence, and his complexion light; he is a shoemaker by trade, in which he uses his left hand principally, can do coarse carpenters work, and is something of a horse jockey; he is greatly addicted to drink, and when drunk is insolent and disorderly, in his conversation he swears much, and in his behaviour is artful and knavish. He took with him a white horse, much scarred with traces, of which it is expected he will endeavour to dispose; he also carried his shoemakers tools, and will probably endeavour to get employment that way. Whoever conveys the said slave to me, in *Albemarle*, shall have 40 s. reward, if taken up within the county, 4 l. if elsewhere within the colony, and 10 l. if in any other colony, from
THOMAS JEFFERSON.

Thomas Jefferson, future author of the Declaration of Independence, published this advertisement for his runaway slave Sandy in the *Virginia Gazette* on September 14, 1769.

many after torturing and mutilating them. Driven to the brink, the free people resisted and, when defeat loomed, armed their slaves, who needed no primer on revolution. The dispute between free people—white and brown—quickly escalated into a full-fledged slave insurrection, pitting white against black, free against slave. Interventions by the British and Spanish advanced the cause of the slave as one belligerent after another bid for the slaves' support. By the time France tried to retake the colony and reimpose slavery, an independent Haiti had emerged under Toussaint L'Ouverture. The reality and the rumors of events in Saint Domingue cast a long shadow that reached the deepest recesses of mainland North America society.[14]

Unidentified artist, "Toussaint L'Over-ture," undated.

As the realities of worldwide revolution manifested themselves, slaveholders retreated and slavery faltered in the new North American republic. In the North—first in areas where slaves were numerically few and economically marginal and then throughout the region—slavery collapsed, as one state and after another abolished slavery by legislative actions, judicial fiat, or constitutional amendment. In the states of the Upper South (Delaware, Maryland, Virginia, and North Carolina), slave owners successfully resisted the emancipationist onslaught, but they were nevertheless forced to give ground. Upper South lawmakers loosened the strictures on manumission. The free black population, which had declined for nearly a century, expanded rapidly. Some masters freed their slaves; some slaves purchased their freedom, and many fled and found safety in the greatly enlarged free black population. As a result, the number of black people enjoying freedom increased, so that some 10 percent of the black population in the Upper South had gained its freedom by the beginning of the nineteenth century. For the first time since the demise of the Charter Generation, freedom came into the possession of large numbers of black men and women.

Once freed, former slaves began reconstructing their lives. Newly freed men and women commonly celebrated emancipation by taking new names as both a symbol of personal liberation and an act of political defiance. A new name reversed the enslavement process and confirmed the free black's newly won liberty, just as the loss of an African name had earlier symbolized enslavement. In assuming new names, former slaves also fused emancipation and the changes that accompanied a century or more of American captivity. With a single stroke they claimed their freedom and obliterated lingering reminders of the past. African names were gone, and so too were the derisive names slave owners had forced upon slaves, as black people shrugged off connections with slavery and Africa in the same motion. In place of Caesar and Pompey, Charity and Fortune, and Cuffee and Phibbee stood Jim and Bett and Joe and Sarah, common Anglo-American names often with biblical connections. And, as if to emphasize the new self-esteem that accompanied their libery, freedpeople usually elevated their names from the diminutive to the full form: Jim became James and Bett became Elizabeth.

The dual process of social and cultural change can also be seen in the choice of surnames. In bondage, most black people had but a single name; freedom allowed them the opportunity to select another. The Freemans, Newmans, Somersets, and Armsteads scattered throughout the new republic suggest how a new name provided an occasion to celebrate slavery's demise. Most frequently, black people took familiar Anglo-American surnames, such as Jackson, Johnson, Moore, and Morgan, to accompany forenames of like derivation. These names, underscored by the singular absence of the names of the great slaveholding families, again suggest how black people identified with free society as they shucked off their old status.

For many former slaves, establishing a new address was also a part of the process of securing freedom. Freedpeople tried to escape the stigma of slavery by deserting their owner's abode for a new residence. Fleeing the memory of slavery and the subtle subordination that the continued presence of a former master entailed were reasons enough to abandon old haunts. For others, however, freedom required a return

Manumission paper for "Jack," who was freed by his owner, Samuel White, on February 1, 1808, in Harrison County, Virginia.

to the site of their enslavement. Whether they fled from their old residence or returned to it, the process of emancipation set thousands of black people in motion and gradually transformed the geography of black America. For former owners, this massive migration was just additional evidence of the chaotic character of black life in freedom. In fact, most newly freed blacks knew where they were going. Looking for a fresh start and new opportunities, many headed toward places that promised economic advancement and a richer social life. The great ports of Baltimore, Boston, New Orleans, New York, and Philadelphia promised both, and the free black population became increasingly urban during the post–Revolutionary War period, as black people identified cities with freedom.

For most, the hoped-for opportunities never appeared. In many places, former slaves plummeted into occupational hierarchy. Skilled craftsmen had difficulty finding work at their old trades once they were free, as white employers refused to hire free blacks for any but the most menial tasks. At best, such work was hard, dirty, irregular, and unremunerative. Often it could be demeaning and shameful, such as sweeping streets and disposing of night soil. Black women rarely worked outside the service trades—work that had been identified with slavery—and thus reinforced their identification with domestic labor. Nonetheless, some newly freed black men and women found prosperity in the middle ranks of American society by entering the professions and mechanical trades and securing small proprietorships. Many of the most successful black businessmen

and women took up these trades, opening barbershops, bath houses, catering establishments, coal yards, oyster houses, and stables. A handful, including James Forten and Paul Cuffe, became manufacturers and merchants of the first rank.

Economic independence provided the basis of family security, and no goal stood higher among the newly freed than establishing a household under their own control. Given the opportunity, former slaves legitimated relations that previously had no standing in law, joining together to celebrate weddings and to register their marriages in official records, often of their own making. The legitimatization of longstanding relationships allowed black people a freer hand in performing familial duties and assuming the roles of husbands and wives, parents, and sons and daughters, but giving family life a basis in fact as well as in law was generally the last step in a long process. Before a family could be united under one roof, spouses, parents, and children had to be located, an arduous task amid wartime and postwar disorder.

As families joined together new communities formed and soon sprouted a host of institutions—churches, schools, fraternal organizations, and friendly societies. Many of these institutions rested upon the informal, clandestine associations black people had created in slavery. Others drew on the experiences former slaves had gained in interacting with the white abolitionists who had assisted in their passage from slavery. Yet others were a product of the novel circumstances of freedom. The need for a whole range of services, from maternal care to burial, arose from the freedpeople's desire to articulate their own moral and social commitments.

"View of the Capitol of the United States after the Conflagration in 1814," from *A Portraiture of Domestic Slavery in the United States*, 1817. Slave labor was crucial in the reconstruction of the Capitol and other buildings in Washington, DC, after the British burned the city during the War of 1812.

The universal adoption of the term "African" in the designation of African American institutions marked the final creation of an *African* nationality. Just as black people in the North no longer called themselves or named their children in the traditional African manner, they celebrated their origins on the placards that adorned the largest buildings and the biggest organizations in the black community. The Free African Society of Philadelphia introduced its articles of incorporation with the words, "We, the free *Africans* and their descendants." Some spoke earnestly about returning to Africa, although few actually made the journey. The acceptance of *African* as an institutional designation also denoted the passing of distinctive national identities: the descendants of Africa were no longer Igbos,

This original slave medallion of ca. 1790 was based on one designed by the English potter Josiah Wedgwood in 1787 and was framed in the United States. Images of kneeling, supplicant slaves became a central symbol of the antislavery movement in colonial America.

Coromantees, or Gambians. Henceforth, all people of African descent would be one people. African nationality, which had no significance on the continent of Africa itself, took on new, weighty meaning among the descendants of the first African diaspora.

The establishment of independent African organizations, whether churches, schools, or mutual aid associations, marked the culmination of two centuries of struggle. Yet, even while former slaves joined together in their churches and schools to press for greater liberty, slavery itself expanded. The American Revolution greatly enhanced the power of the planter class, particularly in the Lower South. Having lost a large proportion of their slave labor force in the war, Lower South planters talked not of abolition—not even in the most distant future—but of more slaves. They reopened the African trade and, in the years before 1808, when Congress permanently ended American participation in the international slave trade, South Carolina and Georgia imported some 100,000 slaves, the greatest infusion of African people in the mainland's history. Even this massive importation failed to satisfy the needs of planters in the Lower South. They initiated an internal slave trade, taking slaves from the North and the Upper South and transferring them to the expanding plantation frontier. The so-called Georgia trade, which boomed in the years immediately following the American Revolution, laid the basis for the great forced migration of the nineteenth century.

The growth of slavery in the Lower South was no simple expansion of the old regime. Slaves, whether newly arrived Africans or forced immigrants from the mainland, faced a harsh regime on the frontiers of the Lower South. As they carved plantations out of the forests and prairies, westward-moving planters pushed their slaves to the limits. Slaves found the old compromises with their owners, hewed out with enormous difficulty, abrogated and the level of exploitation increased. If emancipation and the growth of the free black population at the end of the eighteenth century presaged the assault on slavery in the nineteenth century, this postwar expansion was a harbinger of the massive economic growth in cotton that sent slavery across the blackbelt and remade it into a more arduous and exploitative bondage.

The years before cotton were not simply a prologue to this expansion. Rather, the first two hundred years of African American life on mainland North America embraced a distinctive experience that gave the concepts of master and slave, black and white, unique definitions. When the struggle for freedom took place on different terrain, it was no less intense.

William L. Sheppard, "The First Cotton Gin," from *Harper's Weekly*, December 18, 1869.

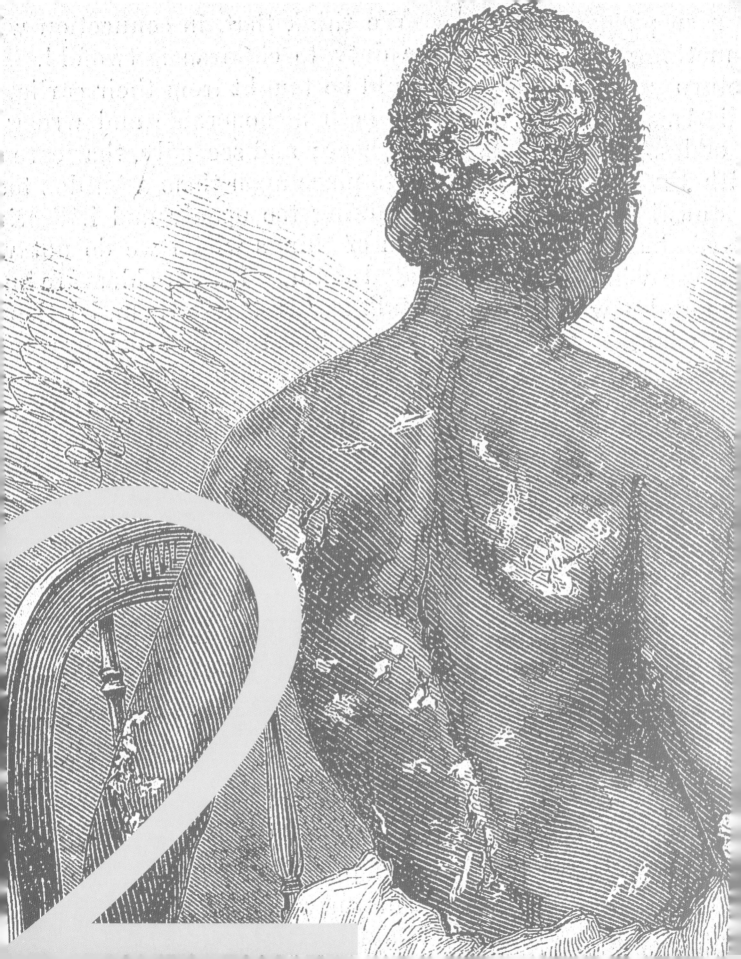

DEBORAH GRAY WHITE

SIMPLE TRUTHS

Antebellum Slavery in Black and White

Emerging from all of the sophisticated and complicated studies of enslavement are two simple truths: white folks had all the power, and black folks survived. These two truths anchor the history of antebellum slavery. Whether the subject under study is the community, religion, childhood, and female network of the enslaved, or slave work in the cotton, tobacco, sugar, and rice crops, or the lumber, turpentine, iron, or maritime industries, these two facts remain constant. They reside at the heart of our analysis of the slave trade, antebellum Southern life, and the free and enslaved black family. They form the core of our ideas about slave resistance and its centerpiece, the Underground Railroad. They are the simple truths of slavery: white power and black survival.

WHITE POWER

They jus' whipped me 'cause they could—'cause they had the privilege.[1]

Above all else, slavery was an awesome system of forced labor. From the very beginning of the plantation system Africans were forced to do work that white labor would not do and could not be made to do. The ability and willingness to treat Africans as outsiders who could be exploited differently than white people are what made slavery so vicious and profitable, and white power so daunting.[2]

At the heart of the labor system was gang labor, the highly systematized organization of labor that was unrivaled in the Western world for its specificity and efficiency. Wherever one went in the South between 1820 and 1860 one could expect to see these enslaved gangs of laborers toiling at some kind

33

"On the side of the Oppressors there was power," from *Legion of Liberty*, 1847.

of work. They worked as lumberjacks and turpentine producers in the forests of the Carolinas and Georgia. In Virginia and Kentucky slaves labored in the gold, coal, and salt mines. On the steamboats that plied the Mississippi River they performed as deckhands and boiler stokers. In Georgia and Louisiana they worked as textile laborers. Slave labor was so profitable that in 1847 the owners of the Tredegar Iron Works in Richmond, Virginia, shifted from using white laborers to slaves. In addition to being factory workers, slaves also made up a significant portion of the South's skilled artisans—carpenters, coopers, blacksmiths, silversmiths, and the like.[3]

Mostly, though, the four million enslaved African Americans worked on the plantations and in the fields of the South.

First came, led by an old driver carrying a whip, forty of the largest and strongest women I ever saw together; they were all in a simple uniform dress of a bluish check stuff, the skirts reaching little below the knee; their legs and feet were bare; they carried themselves loftily, each having a hoe over the shoulder, and walking with a free, powerful swing, like chasseurs on the march. Then came the plow-hands with their mules, the cavalry, thirty strong, mostly men but a few women. . . . A lean and vigilant white overseer, on a brisk pony, brought up the rear.

They worked on an average day fourteen hours in the summer and ten hours in the winter. During harvest time they worked backbreaking eighteen-hour days in the piercing sun and the sweltering heat. The average slave worked in cotton production, and during harvest season was expected to pick about 130 to 150 pounds of cotton per day. Work in sugar and rice was equally arduous, if not more so. Both crops demanded constant cultivation and the digging of drainage ditches in snake-infested

fields. At harvest time for the sugar crop, slaves had to cut, strip, and carry cane to the sugarhouse for boiling. This was extremely strenuous work. Rice cultivation was even more miserable. Since rice is grown under water, the enslaved spent long hours standing in water up to their knees.

> I have often worked without half enough to eat, both late and early, by day and by night. I have often laid my wearied limbs down at night to rest upon a dirt floor, or a bench, without any covering at all, because I had no where else to rest my wearied body, after having worked hard all day.[4]

Slaves who worked in the master's house had a totally different regimen, one that was physically easier but mentally taxing. Women predominated in the house, and like male slave artisans, they performed tasks that allowed for more creativity and self-direction than the work done by field hands. Working indoors, they cooked, cleaned, and labored as seamstresses, nursemaids, and laundresses. Although they could count on better food and clothing than their counterparts in the field, they were under closer supervision, were on call both day and night, and were more

In this undated stereograph, a woman guides a man pulling a plow in a rice field near Savannah, Georgia.

small holdings of one to nine, slave work and life was constantly monitored and supervised so that enslavers could reap maximum profits.[6]

Pregnant women and those with small children were not exempted from day and evening work. Women who were far along in their pregnancy were assigned to work gangs that did "light hoeing," and if they toiled on cotton plantations they were expected to do some picking until well into their pregnancy. When pregnant women were very far advanced, they were not allowed just to rest. On the contrary, they spun thread, wove cloth, and made plantation clothing. Women with infants or small children had an especially tiring day. As outlined by ex-slave Clayborn Gantling, women on the plantation of Judge Williams in Terrell County, Georgia, had it hard. "Women with little babies would have to go to work in de mornings with the rest, come back, nurse their children and go back to the field, stay two or three hours, then go back and eat dinner; after dinner dey would have to go to de field and stay two or three more hours and go and nurse the chillun again, go back to the field and stay till night." Frances Kemble, the English wife of a Georgia planter, sympathetically observed some of the slave women she saw every day.

> Fanny has had six children; all dead but one. She came to beg to have her work in the field lightened. . . . Charlotte has had two miscarriages, and was with child again. She was almost crippled with rheumatism, and showed me a pair of poor swollen

often involved in personality conflicts with the white family. As put by one house servant, "We were constantly exposed to the whims and passions of every member of the family."[5] This meant everything from assignment to petty jobs, to insults, spontaneous angry whippings, and sexual assaults.

Although house servants were under the closest surveillance, compared to slaves in other parts of the Americas, all slaves in the United States were under relatively close supervision. Unlike in Caribbean slave societies or in Latin America, slaves, slaveholders, and overseers in the United States lived in very close proximity to each other. In Jamaica, for instance, one-third of all slaves lived on estates with two hundred slaves or more, and three-quarters of all slaves lived on holdings of at least fifty. Such large numbers of bondmen made close supervision of slave life and work impossible. In contrast, such large plantations were rare in the United States. Only one-quarter of all slaves lived on plantations with more than fifty slaves. Since most lived on holdings of ten to forty-nine slaves, and about one-quarter lived on very

knees that made my heart ache. Sarah had had four miscarriages, had brought seven children into the world, five of whom were dead, and was again with child. She complained of dreadful pains in the back, and an internal tumor which swells with the exertion of working in the fields; probably, I think, she is ruptured. . . .[7]

The enslaved did all of this work because they had to: the national, state, and local governments gave enslavers the absolute power to compel them to do it. Of course, slave owners liked to think that slaves were happiest when they were at work. Some even made this claim as part of the proslavery argument. Most slaveholders, however, well understood that it was the threat of physical punishment and their power of life and death over the slave that kept enslaved African Americans hard at their jobs. "It is a pity," wrote a North Carolina planter, "that Slavery and Tyranny must go together and that there is no such thing as having an obedient and useful Slave, without the painful exercise of undue and tyrannical authority." This authority was what made white power so ominous

and what put it at the center of the master-slave relationship. A Southern judge summed it up best when he said, "The power of the master must be absolute, to render the submission of the slave perfect."[8]

In the antebellum South the omnipresent symbol of white power was the whip. Whipping and work went hand in hand. For instance, on one Alabama estate, women who had just given birth and were still confined to the slave cabins had to spin thread. According to an ex-slave named Cato, "If they did not spin seven or eight cuts a day they got a whipping." Ben Simpson, a Georgia slave, remembered how his master would use a "great, long whip platted out of rawhide" to hit a slave in the gang who would "fall behind or give out."[9]

> He tied my wrist together and stripped me. He hanged me by the wrist from a limb on a tree and spraddled my legs round the trunk and tied my feet together. Then he beat me. He beat me worser then I ever been beat before, and I faint dead away. When I came to I'm in bed. I didn't care so much iffen I died.[10]

"Mothers with young children at work in the field," from *Illustrations of the American Anti-Slavery Almanac for 1840*, 1839.

Overseers and drivers told the same gruesome story. These black and white men who worked for slaveholders were immediately responsible for the production of the crop. Charged with managing slaves to ensure that the plantation turned a profit, and faced with the loss of their position if it did not, they used any means necessary to make slaves work as hard as possible. This was especially true on plantations where owners were absent. Without the supervision of slaveholders, who might be more interested than their managers in protecting their investment, overseers and drivers could and often did use as much force as they wanted. This disturbed even those who were vigorous supporters of slavery. Slaveholder Daniel R. Hundley admired and defended the South's institutions but admitted that "the overseers on many southern plantations, are cruel and unmercifully severe."[11]

Even those overseers and drivers who were not considered especially brutal revealed the inherent violence of the system. For example, in one of his weekly reports Robert Allston's overseer casually noted that he had "flogged for hoeing corn bad Fanny 12 lashes, Sylvia 12, Monday 12, Phoebee 12, Susanna 12, Salina 12, Celia 12, Iris 12." George Skipwith, a black driver for John Hartwell Cocke, a Virginia planter, was equally liberal with the whip. In 1847 he reported to his master that several slaves who worked under him "at a reasonable days work" should have plowed seven acres apiece but had only done one and a half. Skipwith's response was to give them "ten lick a peace [sic] upon their skins. . . ." With no seeming sympathy for one of his own race he "gave Julyann eight or ten licks" for the unforgivable sin of "misplacing her hoe."[12]

BOTH PAGES: A. R. Waud, "Scenes from a Cotton Plantation," from *Harper's Weekly*, February 2, 1867.

RATION DAY.

If punishment was used to ensure maximum work, it was also employed to ensure "perfect submission." Indeed, slaveholders could command a slave's labor only if they could minimize the slave's resistance to their authority. Resistance, no matter how slight, was rightfully perceived as a reflection of independence. Since independence was clearly incompatible with slavery, all behavior on the part of the slave that suggested even a hint of self-determination had to be squelched. Dependence had to be instilled. Slaves who showed too much self-direction were deemed rebellious and judged dangerous. Punishment, therefore, served the purpose of making the enslaved work, but it also functioned to awe them

with a sense of the master's power—and power was what the master used to make the slave stand in fear.[13]

The slaveholder and his family demonstrated their power in a variety of ways. To begin with, they always made the slave show deference, not just to them but to all white people. Slaves had to bow in the presence of whites, they had to give way to whites walking in their path, and they were subject to whippings given even by white children. When they approached the overseer or the master, they had to show humility. On Charles Ball's plantation the slaves "were always obliged to approach the door of the mansion, in the most humble and supplicating manner, with our hats in our

hands, and the most subdued and beseeching language in our mouths."[14]

Hand in hand with humility went cheerfulness. Slaveholders feared the rebelliousness of slaves who expressed dissatisfaction; therefore, they did not tolerate sullen or sorrowful moods. Henry Watson attested to this when he noted that "the slaveholder watches every move of the slave, and if he is downcast or sad—in fact, if they are in any mood but laughing and singing, and manifesting symptoms of perfect content at heart—they are said to have the devil in them. . . ."[15]

The power to make slaves work as well as to show deference and false happiness was granted to slaveholders by state and city legislatures through statutes called slave codes. Slavery differed from one region of the South to another, from one crop to another, even from one master to another. What gave the system its uniformity, however, was the consistency of social thought on the matter of slaveholder power. Manifested throughout the South in the slave codes, the white South's thinking about slavery left the enslaved no legal

redress for actions committed against them in violation of the law.

The Louisiana slave code was typical of other state and city codes. The very first provision pronounced that the slave "owes to his master, and to his family, a respect without bounds, and an absolute obedience. . . ." The code defined slaves as property that was "subject to be mortgaged" and that could be "seized and sold as real estate." Most of the provisions stated what the enslaved were prohibited from doing. For instance, they could neither travel without a pass nor assemble in groups. They were prohibited from buying and selling any kind of goods, and they could not carry arms nor ride horses without the permission of their master. Besides proscribing the behavior of blacks, the codes also restricted the actions of whites. They could not sell to, or buy anything from, slaves. Whites could not teach the enslaved to read or write, and slaveholders could not free a slave without posting a $1,000 bond guaranteeing that the freed slave would leave the state. The code also declared that if a slave willfully harmed the master, mis-

tress, their children, or the overseer, the penalty was death. If a slave set fire to the crop or any part of the owner's property, or if a slave raped any white female or assaulted any white person in an attempt to escape from slavery, the code made death their punishment.[16]

In Louisiana, as in the rest of the South, the slave codes were enforced by masters, mistresses, overseers, and that ubiquitous institution, the slave patrol, a police system designed specifically to watch and control black people.

> If a master had slaves he just could not rule . . . he would ask him if he wanted to go to another plantation and if he said he did, then he would give him a pass that would read: "Give this nigger hell." Of course, when the patrollers or other plantation boss would read the pass, he would beat him nearly to death and send him back.[17]

In the countryside and in the city the patrol's job was to watch, catch, and beat slaves. Armed with guns, whips, and binding ropes, patrollers punished blacks who congregated without whites, stole food or other goods, harbored runaways or weapons, or traveled without a pass. In cities they enforced the slave curfew and whipped any slave found outside after the curfew bell had sounded. In Richmond, Virginia, for exam-

"Abhorrence of the African color and smell," from *Legion of Liberty*, 1847.

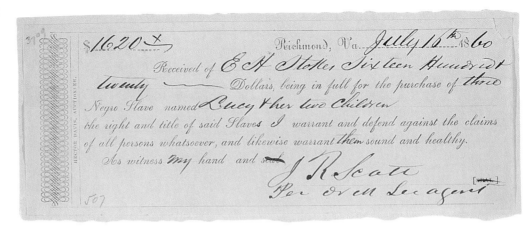

Receipt for the sale of "Lucy and her two children" for $1,620 on July 16, 1860, in Richmond, Virginia.

ple, any slave taken up by the town patrol after 9 p.m. was carried to "the cage," the name of the slave jail. Members of the patrols were drawn mostly from the lower classes (with the possible exception of patrols in North Carolina). The patrol was among the many Southern institutions that gave every white man and woman power over every black man and woman. Like slave owners, slave traders, overseers, and slave catchers, the patrollers formed another group of whites that was invested with the power of the state to discipline, contain, and control black people. As one former slave remarked, "It was always some low-down white men, that never owned a nigger in their life, doing the patrolling and a stripping the clothes off men like Pappy right before the wives and children and beating the blood out of him."[18]

Whether or not the slave codes were enforced, the stories told by ex-slaves reveal this system of exploitation and forced labor to be just as cruel and inhumane as the statutes suggest. Even the "kindest" owners kept their slaves illiterate, broke up families through sale, burdened them with too much work, and fed the enslaved a diet that lacked fresh meat, dairy products, and vegetables. Throughout the South, black chil-

dren were denied proper physical care and emotional support, while adult slaves were stripped naked and whipped in front of family and friends for the slightest infractions. Sadly, too, the presence of thousands of mulatto children gave undeniable testimony to the frequency of the sexual abuse of black women.

In the antebellum period, a time that saw few lynchings, rape was the quintessential expression of white male sexual power against black people. It was wielded like a weapon of terror. It demonstrated white male supremacy over not only white women, who had no means to challenge their father's, husband's, brother's, and son's right to the black female body, but also black men and women, who had to risk life and limb to repel white male sexual aggression. Since no state in the South made it a crime for *any* male to take a black woman against her will, black women went totally unprotected against molestation, and they bore the brunt of white sexual violence. "Slavery is terrible for men," wrote former slave Harriet Jacobs, "but it is far more terrible for women. Superadded to the burden common to all, they have wrongs, and sufferings, and mortifications peculiarly their own."[19]

Eyre Crowe, *Richmond Slave Market Auction*, ca. 1850s. Artists frequently depicted the auction block in images of slavery.

Sexual abuse took many forms. There was, of course, unabashed rape.

> Us niggers knowed the doctor took a black woman quick as he did a white and took any on his place he wanted, and he took them often.

In one cruel example, Celia, a slave in Missouri, was bought by sixty-year-old Robert Newsom, not to be a field slave and not to relieve his two daughters of domestic drudgery, but to serve as his sexual slave. She was but fourteen years old when she was purchased and was first attacked by him, and for five years she endured his relentless assaults. When she could take it no more, Celia struck and killed Newsom with a log one fateful night. With that, the full machinery and wrath of the state came into play. In Missouri, the sexual assault of a slave woman by white males was consid-

ered merely trespass, not rape. Obviously, an owner could not be charged with trespassing upon his own property. At her trial Celia was accused of killing a white man, and the prosecution instructed the jury that neither her motives nor her intentions could be taken into account. In other words, even if Celia killed her owner in self-defense, the jury was to render a verdict of guilty, which it did. Celia was tried and hanged.[20]

Sexual violence also permeated the whippings women received. The man who whipped Henry Bibb's wife was often heard by Bibb, a slave, to exclaim that "he had rather paddle a female than eat when he was hungry." Based on one account, the whipping of a slave girl in Georgia had sexual overtones as well. The girl was put on all fours, "sometimes her head down, and sometimes up," and beaten until froth ran

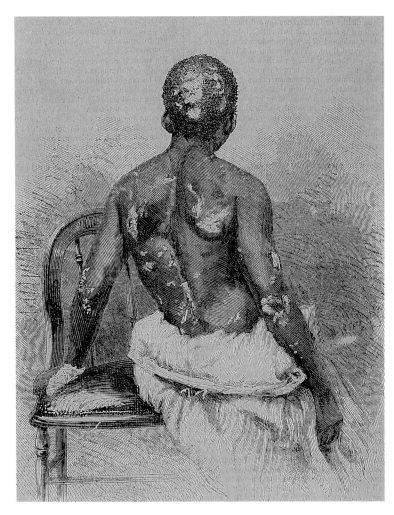

"Marks of punishment inflicted upon a colored servant in Richmond, Virginia," from *Harper's Weekly*, July 28, 1866.

exploitation. Few calculations made by masters and overseers failed to take a slave woman's childbearing capacity into account. So important, and exploitive, was this aspect of slave management that major periodicals carried articles detailing the optimal conditions under which bonded women were known to reproduce, and the merits of a particular "breeder" were often the topic of conversations in the parlor or around the dinner table. Once reproduction became a topic of public conversation, so did the black female body. Where layers of clothing adorned the "respectable" white woman, who never presented her legs or arms to public view, the black woman's tattered clothing revealed her nakedness. Deliberately exposed and touched during sale and whippings, the black female body was treated contemptibly at best and brutally at worst.

Women wasn't nothing but cattle.[22]

Among the more insidious aspects of sexual exploitation, though certainly not the most sadistic, was the manipulation of the enslaved woman's environment to increase the number of children she could have. This did not always translate into easier working conditions, but enslavers usually assigned pregnant slaves less work and more food than nonpregnant women. A typical instruction was like the one Richard Corbin of Virginia gave to his manager: "Breeding wenches more particularly you must instruct the Overseer to be Kind and Indulgent to, and not force them when with child upon any service or hardship that will be injurious to them." Although designed to increase slave numbers, this practice doubled as an incentive for overworked slave women to have children.

from her mouth. Solomon Northup's owner used to beat a slave named Patsey in the same manner. According to Northup, his master's "brute passion" was best satisfied by having a few drinks and whipping Patsey.[21]

In addition to rape and whippings, black women's childbearing was manipulated. After 1808, when enslavers could no longer legally import Africans into America, the slave system became dependent on the reproductive abilities of black women. Since it was up to them to produce the laborers on which the system depended, the manipulation of their procreation emerged as an integral part of their sexual

Writing about the women on her husband's rice plantations in Georgia and South Carolina, Frances Kemble claimed that the extra clothing and weekly rations bestowed on the family, "as small as they may seem, act as powerful inducements" for women to have children. Other enticements might include an extra dress, Saturday afternoons off, or money. "If de massa had a good sow that wuz a givin' birth to a lot of pigs eve'y year, you don't think he goin' to take a stick an' beat her do you? Dat's de way he wuz wid his niggars."[23]

When these inducements proved unsuccessful to get women of childbearing age to have children, enslavers resorted to force. Ex-slave Rose Williams of Texas was forced by her master, a brute named Hawkins, to sleep with a slave called Rufus. When she refused, Hawkins told her point blank that her duty was to "bring forth portly children," that he had paid "big money" for her "cause I wants you to raise me childrens." As fearful of the whip as she was of the auction block, Williams gave in.

"I thinks 'bout Massa buying me offen the block and saving me from being separated from my folks and 'bout being whipped at the stake. There it am. What am I's to do? . . . I yields."[24]

Williams was among the millions of enslaved women who faced the prospect of being sold if they did not have children. It was such a common practice for enslavers to sell women who could not or did not have children that Southern judges and juries established a policy for dealing with cases of fraud in the buying and selling of women of childbearing age. If a buyer took possession of a woman who the seller had certified as fit to bear children, and it could be demonstrated that the seller knew the woman was incapable of having children, the sale was voided and the money returned. Thus, when an Alabama master unwittingly bought three infertile women, he had his money returned. Similarly, when a Georgia farmer paid for a young woman only to find, a week later, that she was suffering from a uterine infection that made

Henry Byam Martin, "The Land of the Free & Home of the Brave," 1833. The work shows the slave market in Charleston, South Carolina, on March 4, 1833.

her infertile, he too had his money returned. An ex-slave summed it up: if a woman was a good breeder, "they was proud of her"; if not, "they got rid of her."[25]

White power was real. It was menacing and omnipresent. The only limits to the enslaver's power were those imposed by conscience, which more often than not was overshadowed by economic needs, social wishes, puerile desires, and sexual appetites. Still, black submission was far from perfect. Although designed to exact fear and humility, dependence and awe, twenty-four hours a day, seven days a week, the system failed to nullify black humanity. While we must never forget or underestimate the reality, effects, and legacy of white violence on black Americans, neither should we trivialize the indomitable spirit that made it possible for African Americans to survive.

BLACK SURVIVAL

Us ain't hogs or horses. Us is human flesh.[26]

Try as they might to induce black people to believe in their own inferiority, whites only convinced blacks that whites had superior power, not superior souls. Black people possessed an unshakable belief in their own humanity and an indelible conviction in the equality of master and slave before God.[27] Never convinced that they were like animals, the enslaved defied the slave codes that reduced their status to that of chattel, and every day they bore witness to white people's dependence on their humanity. African Americans lived under repressive white power, but they survived by building a life around it and in spite of it.

At the heart of black survival was a belief system that profoundly differed from that of whites.

White folks 'jes naturally different from darkies. We's different in color, in talk and in 'ligion and beliefs. We's different in every way and can never be spected to think or live alike.

Christianity is a primary example. Whites saw religion as a means of social control, as a way to inculcate black inferiority. "You will find," wrote Thomas Affleck in his instructions to overseers, "that an hour devoted every Sabbath morning to [slave's] moral and religious instruction would prove a great aid to you in bringing about a better state of things amongst the Negroes." From the slaveholder's point of view, a better state of things meant more obedience, less stealing, and more hard work. Most white preachers' standard text was, "Servants, be obedient to them who are your masters according to the flesh, with fear and trembling, in singleness of your heart, as unto Christ."[28]

Although presented one way, Christianity was digested another. African Americans took at face value the idea that all men were equal in the sight of God. They did not consider seriously the white preacher's text, "Slaves, obey your masters." "Before God, we are white as he is," said Mary Chesnut's slave Maria in complaint of a white preacher, "and in the pulpit he no need to make us feel we are servants."[29] Almost all African Americans shared Maria's perspective. If God was the all-powerful master with no one, not even the slave master or mistress, above him, and if all men and women were God's children, without regard to rank and station in life, then all God's children must be equal, white and black alike. All, including enslavers, ultimately had to answer to a higher authority.

The enslaved believed that the slaveholder, not the slave, was the sinner, and the Bible provided them with the evidence that they were right. Had not God sent Moses to deliver the Israelites out of bondage? Had he not punished the Egyptians for enslaving his chosen people? Had he not sent his son, Jesus, to redeem the world, and was not Jesus, like the slave, a humble sufferer, a servant? By identifying with the Israelites and with Jesus, the enslaved turned the master into the sinner and gave themselves the inner strength that flowed from the belief in their own salvation in the next world. "It's going to be an awful thing up yonder," said one former slave, "when they hold judgement over the way that things was done down here."[30] In the everyday world, this inner strength gave the enslaved enough psychic freedom to resist becoming completely subservient to white people.

Nowhere was this strength more evident than in the courage slaves revealed in conducting their own religious services, even when they had been forbidden to do so. Sometimes they would meet after the mandatory white service. At other times they would steal away in the middle of the week to hold services in a brush arbor or other secret place, far from white eyes fearful of the independence such services spawned. Recalled former slave Beck Ilsey, "When we'd have meetin' at night, wuz mos' always 'way in de woods or de bushes some whar so de white folks couldn't hear, an' when dey'd sing a spiritual an' de spirit 'gin to shout some de elders would go 'mongst de folks an' put dey han' over dey mouf an' some times put a clof in dey mouf an' say: Spirit don talk so loud or de patterol break us up."[31]

Mean-spirited whites were not thought to be superior to blacks; indeed, it was the other way around. The enslaved revealed this attitude in their songs. Slaves, not the master, were "de people dat is born of God . . . de people of de Lord." When African Americans sang, "I'm a child ob God, wid

A. R. Waud, "Prayer Meeting," from the series "Scenes from a Cotton Plantation," from *Harper's Weekly*, February 2, 1867.

PRAYER MEETING

my soul sot free," they sang of salvation in the afterlife and deliverance in this world. Together, away from the master's eyes and ears, black men and women worshiped a God they felt would deliver them the same way he delivered Joshua, Jonah, Moses, and Noah. "O my Lord delivered Daniel, O why not deliver me too?"[32]

The deliverance for which African Americans prayed was not just for the next world. They wanted to be free in this world, and many of their sacred songs contained elements of protest and messages of liberation.

> You got a right, I got a right. We all got a right to the tree of life.

For example, when Frederick Douglass and many of his fellow slaves sang, "O Canaan, sweet Canaan, I am bound for the land of Canaan," they were singing not only about someday going to heaven but also about reaching the North. "The North was our Canaan," said Douglass. The North was also the implied destination in the song, "Run to Jesus, shun the danger, I don't expect to stay much longer here." In the same vein, when slaves sang "Steal Away to Jesus," they were just as likely to be announcing a secret worship service as they were to be talking about salvation.[33] The service, conducted under the direction of preachers that African Americans chose themselves, gave the enslaved a sense of autonomy. This kind of freedom, it is true, did not liberate them from their enslavers, but it did give them the courage to assert themselves more than they otherwise would have done. It provided some parents with the will to stand up

Lewis Miller, "Lynchburg Negro Dance," 1853. Slaves make music with fiddle, banjo, and the bones, and perform their own distinctive dances.

O carry me back, O carry me back, to old Virginia — Shore, home Spun, and human block, & Corn. this very valuable grain in Virginia and much is raised.

Lynchburg — negro dance, August 18th 1853,

for their children, some husbands the strength to defend their wives, and many the permission they needed to steal from the master. Slave religion presented an alternative view of the world, one different from that of the master, and as such it put enough distance between the master and the slave to allow the latter to survive and sometimes even defy white power.

So, too, did folk beliefs, another crucial part of what one historian has called the enslaved's "sacred world." Though most whites, and some slaves, generally found beliefs in fortunetellers, witches, magic signs, and conjurers to be at odds with Christianity, for most blacks no chasm existed between the two. The same slave who believed fervently in Christ could also insist that the dead returned to the living in spiritual visitations, that children born with teeth or as twins came under an ominous sign, and that conjuring caused insanity and other illness.[34]

In slave folk religion signs were important. A screech owl's cry signaled death, but it could be countered by turning shoes upside down at a door or by turning one's pockets inside out. A black cat crossing one's path was bad luck unless one spit on the spot where the paths met. Many slaves believed that a cross-eyed person could cast a spell unless one crossed one's fingers and spit on them.[35]

Dreams were also taken seriously. A former South Carolina slave reported that he dreamt he saw his three uncles skinning a cow and cutting it open while women and children sat around crying. When he told his mother about the dream, she told him that fresh meat in a dream was a sign of death. "Sure enough that very evening Uncle Peter Price died." According to the former slave, his dreams came true so often that the older

people on his plantation used his dreams as a way of predicting the future.[36]

In a way, folk beliefs were all about prediction. The enslaved lived in a world over which they had little control. For them, life held many uncertainties, and little was predictable. Folk beliefs provided a way of imposing order on a capricious environment. Like Christianity, slave folk beliefs

"Meeting in the African Church, Cincinnati, Ohio," undated.

could not be controlled by whites, and therefore they became another source of strength.[37] Looked at another way, folk beliefs provided the slave with a source of power that lay totally outside the world of the master. It was different from and yet still competed with the power held by whites.

Although all slaves could utilize this power, conjurers were thought to possess a special gift for reading signs and dreams, and for affecting change through the use of spells, herb mixtures, and charms. Most slaves feared conjurers as much as they feared the master because they believed these men and women could bring about all manner of bad or good luck. They could make mean masters kind and kind masters mean. They could prevent or cause whippings, separations, illness, or death, or they could ensure love and happiness or friction and hate. They were especially known for the evil they could do. Ex-slave Rosana Frazier, for instance, blamed a conjurer for her blindness, while Nicey Kinney of Georgia thought "some old witch man conjured me into marrying Jordan Jackson."[38]

Enslavers were also concerned about conjurers because they had to share power and influence with them. Slaves were known to believe themselves invulnerable when carrying a conjurer's charm. In 1842 the Reverend Charles C. Jones, a slaveholder, wrote that slaves "have . . . been made to believe that they were under a protection that rendered them invincible. That they might go any where and do anything they pleased, and it would be impossible for them to be discovered or known." Jones's observation was significant, not so much because conjurers *could* work magic but because so many black folk believed they did. In doing so, they acknowledged that one of their own had power, different than white power, for sure, but power nonetheless. "Dey couldn't whip her. Dey used to say she was a conjer' and dey was all scared of her."[39]

That sense of power was shared by the cadre of herb doctors, midwives, and nurses who tended the needs of the sick and the pregnant. If masters and mistresses could have had their way, the enslaved would have looked to them to meet their every blessed need and want. Since whites thrived on black dependence, this would have made white power more invincible than it already was. African Americans, however, usually preferred to treat their own illness and make their own medicines, mostly because they did not trust whites.

De people never did put much faith in de doctors in dem days, mostly, dey would use de herbs in de fields for dey medicine.[40]

This was especially the case with sick or pregnant women, who, with absolutely no reason to trust white men, looked to black midwives and "doctor women" for care and sustenance. Any number of broths, made from the leaves and barks of trees, from the branches and twigs of bushes, from turpentine, catnip, or tobacco, were used to treat whooping cough, diarrhea, toothaches, colds, fevers, headaches, and backaches. Although they cared for both men and women, these particular "healers" specialized in the treatment of women and children. Menstrual cramps, for example, were sometimes eased with a tea made from the bark of the gum tree, and at least one woman treated colic by giving the fretting infant a syrup made from a boiled rat's vein. If the efficacy of this last treatment seems questionable, so too did the folk practice of putting an axe under the delivery mattress to "cut the pain" of childbirth.[41] The point, however, is not how effective these treatments actually were. The nineteenth-century medical practice of bleeding a patient proved just as ineffective a cure as did slave practices. The important consideration is that slaves looked to their own when they were sick or in need of spiritual guidance. This strengthened their own community and gave men and women in their own group a chance to gain status and be important— and it mediated the impact of white power and helped make black survival possible.

The strong ties of the black family also made survival possible, though this was not the aim of masters and mistresses. For enslavers, slave families provided a way to organize the plantation, a means of social control, and a vehicle through which to increase their property ownership. Rather than the barrack-style accommodations found in the Caribbean and Latin America, slaves in the American South lived in quarters with their families. From the master's perspective, such living arrangements cut down on rebelliousness. As early as the 1770s the Earl of Egmont, then governor of a colony the British were trying to establish in eastern Florida, wrote requesting women be sent to serve as companions for the slave men there. Fearing the men would run away, he wrote that women "would greatly tend to keep them at home and to make them Regular." Many years later a slave in Raleigh, North Carolina, confirmed the earl's observation. When asked by a curious Northern traveler why he did not run away, the man replied, "I might be sold away from them [his family], which I won't be if I don't try to run away. . . ."[42]

Husbands and children had the same effect on slave women. In 1838 a slave named Clarissa was sent to Philadelphia even though there was some concern about her running away once she reached free territory. What kept Mrs. Trigg, her mistress, from worrying about her escape was the fact that Clarissa's husband and children remained in Kentucky. As put by Clarissa, "I was certain my children were to be put in their power, in order to give them a stronger hold upon me."[43]

Although enslavers saw the slave family as a way of cutting down on rebelliousness and escapes, their most obvious use for the family was to reproduce the slave population. Rather than simply breed slaves, enslavers encouraged birth within families. It was the cheapest, easiest, and the most natural way to reproduce their

Five generations of a South Carolina slave family in 1862.

labor force, and fertility statistics prove the wisdom of this approach. In each year between 1800 and the Civil War, more than one-fifth of the black women between the ages of fifteen and forty-four years of age bore a child. On average, female slaves had their first child at age nineteen, two years before the average Southern white woman had hers. She continued having children at two-and-a-half-year intervals until she reached the age of thirty-nine or forty. This high fertility rate made the sex ratio among blacks relatively even and family life possible. It bears repeating that this did not happen in most other slave societies in the Americas, where enslavers purchased new slaves from Africa rather than depend on natural reproduction. In North America the slave population reproduced itself, and in so doing it made family, community, and

James F. Gibson,
"Contrabands at Mr.
Foller's House,
Cumberland Landing,
Virginia, May 14,
1862."

survival possible.[44]

Indeed, the African American family softened the impact of white power because it allowed the enslaved a point of reference that did not begin and end with the master. It put bonded men and women in the role of parents. Their children assumed the roles of siblings, which evolved into the roles of aunts and uncles. With the family, slaves became the providers and protectors of their spouses and their own children. Few parents were lucky enough to reach old age without being separated. Usually a mother survived with a daughter, and the mother could count on her daughter to take care of her. Clearly, family life happened within the constraints of slavery and was victimized by white power, but it nevertheless served as a buffer between master and slave, and the family was made sacred because of it.

My child him is mine.[45]

Another way the slave community and the family absorbed so much of the pain and desperation of enslavement lies in courtship patterns. For instance, during the week field workers wore tattered and dirty clothes, but on Sundays blacks put on their best clothing. This made a real difference in their otherwise dreary lives, especially those of enslaved women. On Sundays they donned dresses that had been packed all week in sweet-smelling flowers and herbs to attract the opposite sex. Ex-slave Gus Feaster had pleasant memories of the women who "took their hair down outen the strings," who charmed the men "wid honeysuckle and rose petals hid in dere bosoms," and who "dried chennyberries and painted dem and wo'em on a string around dere necks."[46]

If courtship allowed for feminine expression, it also gave men the opportunity to demonstrate their masculinity in a domain not controlled by the master. Men went to great lengths to attract the attention of young women. One Louisiana man

Former slaves in front of their quarters in Beaufort, South Carolina, ca. 1864. During the Civil War photographers took hundreds of images of the South and the lives of slaves.

named Sam danced away an entire Christmas party, trying to impress his sweetheart by proving himself to be the best dancer on the plantation. Abraham, a slave in Georgia, used a different tactic to get female attention. He "borrowed" his master's boots and horse and went off to a nearby frolic where, as predicted, he "got all the gals attentions." John White, an Oklahoma ex-slave, was also adept at "borrowing." He remembered how he used to take food from the master's kitchen and give it to his girlfriends. According to him, "I favor them with something extra from the kitchen. Then they favors me—at night."[47]

When these courtship rituals resulted in marriage, the slave could count on an even greater variety of roles, not to mention a new kind of companionship. From each other, slave husbands and wives could depend on compassion. Remembering his father, one ex-slave recalled, "My mother just rejoiced in him. Whenever he sat down to talk she just sat and looked and listened."[48]

In what was, by necessity, an equalitarian marital relationship, both parents provided what extras they could for each other, for their children, and for other family members. Men made furniture and chopped firewood. If the master had given them a garden plot, they helped grow food. In addition, they hunted and fished to supplement the food provided by the master.

My old daddy partly raised his children on game. He caught rabbits, coons an' possums. He would work all day and hunt at night.[49]

Women also worked for their families. They made and mended clothing, cooked meals, and helped supplement the family diet. Like men, they hunted, fished, and grew garden vegetables. Female house servants often stole food for their families and sometimes for other slaves as well. Sarah Fukkes, a cook on a Virginia plantation, remembered that whenever the whites left, the cook "had a habit of making cookies and handing them out to the slaves before the folks returned."[50]

As parents, slaves were responsible for the socialization of their children. Part of that process included teaching the children how to provide for their family and be a parent when they grew older. Fathers took pride in teaching their sons how to trap wild turkeys and rabbits, how to run down and catch raccoons, and how to build canoes out of great oak logs. Mothers taught their daughters how to quilt and sew, and hunt and fish, too. And usually, at their own peril, both parents did what they could to show their children how to protect their own. A case in point involved the mother of Fannie Moore. With pride, Moore recalled that in the face of hatred from "de old overseer," her mother stood up for her children and would not let them be beaten. For that, "she get more whippin' . . . dan anythin' else."[51]

The stories that parents told their children say as much about the way enslaved parents socialized their children as how black people survived white power. Take, for example, the story of Brer Rabbit, the Wolf, and Tar Baby. It begins when the strong and powerful Wolf creates a sticky doll, or Tar Baby, to trap the inquisitive and sly Rabbit. While walking through the woods one day, Rabbit comes upon Tar Baby sitting by the side of the road where Wolf has placed it. Being a friendly sort, Rabbit greets it with a "Hello, howdy do." When Tar Baby does not reply, the angry Rabbit hits the baby doll. First, one hand gets stuck, then the other. Losing his temper even further, Rabbit kicks Tar Baby and butts it with his head, only to get his entire body stuck to the doll. When Wolf arrives to collect Rabbit, he decides to kill him by burning him in the brush. Instead of cringing in fear, Rabbit's clever response is to pretend that he wants to feel the warmth of the fire on his coat. Wolf falls for Rabbit's deception and decides that the thorny briar patch might be a more suitable punishment. Rabbit, however, knows that if he gets thrown in the briar patch, he can work his way loose from Tar Baby and escape. He pretends to cringe at Wolf's threat: "Mercy,

mercy, whatever you do, please don't throw me in the briar patch." Believing Rabbit's feigned terror, Wolf throws him in the briar patch, whereupon Rabbit makes a quick escape.[52]

Another story told to the young involved a very talkative slave. In the tale the slave comes across a frog that can speak. Amazed at such a wonder, the slave runs and tells his master of this miracle. The master does not believe the slave and threatens to punish him if he is lying. When the frog refuses to talk for the master, the slave is severely beaten. Only when the master leaves does the frog speak, saying, "A tol' yuh he othah day, yuh talk too much."[53]

Although these are only two of the hundreds of tales told in the slave quarters, they say a lot about life under slavery. They tell us that powerful whites did not always have their way. Wolf had Rabbit in his control, but he was still unable to conquer him. From this, the enslaved learned that a quick wit was essential to survival. Deception could give the weak some control over the strong and allow the powerless to endure with a minimal amount of physical or emotional assault. The story of Brer Rabbit also illustrates that might does not always make for right, and rash behavior, like that indulged in by Rabbit, seldom yields rewards. These were important lessons for the slave child. They were not distant or abstract ideas, but practical points that the slave needed to survive.[54]

The same held true of the second story. Although simple in its storyline, it showed young blacks that the enslaved's world was an unpredictable one. Where else but in a world filled with uncertainty could a frog speak—and speak to the powerless at that? In the real world, masters and mistresses, angry at God knows what, might lash out

"Sold to Go South," from *Suppressed Book of Slavery*, 1864.

at a slave at any moment. A mistress might suddenly find fault with her housemaid and strike out with a fist or a foot. A year or two of bad harvests might lead to a slaveholder's financial ruin and force him to sell some of the slaves. This could separate parent from child, husband from wife, brother from sister.

The slave learned from this story that the best defense against unpredictability was silence, the key to secrecy. Silence kept masters ignorant of things going on behind their backs: the food slaves stole, the religious services held in secret, the escapes made by the boldest of slaves, the anger and hatred that blacks felt towards whites. Silence protected the slave quarters. It kept the slave's family and religious life removed from white invasion. In other words, the story taught the slave child how to protect African American plantation communities, its families, its religious life, and its sacred world. It taught the basic lesson of antebellum black life: how to survive under white power.

Yet, for all the good the family and community could do for the enslaved, it could also be a source of heartbreak and weakened resistance. Few men who had romantic relationships with women escaped without wounded pride, enduring anger, and a diminished sense of manhood. Louis Hughes stood stark still, blood boiling, as his master choked his wife for talking back to the mistress. His wife was then tied to a joist in a barn and beaten while he stood powerless to do anything for her. The family was also the scene of domestic violence. Ellen Botts's mother showed up in the kitchen of a sugar plantation with a lump on her head, put there by her hot-tempered husband. For all that parents could do for their offspring, and the community could do for its members, they could not shield them from the painful realities of perpetual servitude. Masters and mistresses held the ultimate authority.[55]

Despite all that could go wrong with it, the slave's family was the most important unit on the plantation. When family members were separated by sale or death, members of the slave community stepped in and acted as fictive kin. If a child lacked a mother or a father, an aunt or uncle or a close friend served as a fictive parent. Older community members became grand-parents to children who had none. Men more often than women were sold sepa-rately from their families, and on their new plantations they made fictive brothers and sisters of other slaves. Always present was this familial bonding, this search for an identity that made them unlike chattel. To the extent that the family and the commu-nity protected, sheltered, or even hurt its members, both provided a world apart from the one controlled by the master.

This separate world gave the enslaved a reason to resist white power. Sometimes it provided them with the impetus to run away and be free from slaveholder control altogether. Records of antebellum American slavery show that, given the mil-lions of African Americans who were enslaved, relatively few fled to freedom. Fewer still participated in large-scale rebel-lions aimed at overthrowing the institution of slavery. Many, many blacks, however, took a stand against their servitude and somehow managed to be slaves in form but not in fact. These men and women resisted the worst aspects of slavery. Some refused

to be whipped; others ran away for short periods of time. Some feigned ignorance of how to do a particular chore, and others pretended to be ill rather than work to the limits that the master and mistress wanted. Still others used individual acts of violence to counter enslaver authority. Unlike run-ning away, this kind of resistance only sep-arated the slave from the worst aspects of white power. Along with the slave family and slave Christianity and folk religion, acts of violence form an important chapter in black survival.

Whatever other circumstances came together in the life of a slave to cause an act of individual resistance, one thing is sure: the slaves who resisted did not stand in abject fear of their masters, nor did they completely lose those qualities that made them whole human beings. The slave who stole extra food, for example, cared enough about his or her own well-being to defy the slaveholder's rationing system. Slaves who risked their lives in their struggle not to be whipped were, in fact, making a personal statement about their sense of self-esteem and individual honor. Women who kicked and clawed their sexual abusers fought for their personal dignity. Those who burned

William H. Brown, "Hauling the Whole Weeks Picking," 1842.

HAULING THE WHOLEWEEKS PICKING

gin houses, barns, corncribs, or smoke-houses, even as acts of anger, served notice that they could be pushed only so far. Some slaves used poison or outright physical force to kill their masters. Capture always meant certain death, but they did it nevertheless. Whatever the individual act of resistance, it signified an attempt to retain or take back some control over a life that was by law assigned to someone else.

The story of Frederick Douglass is instructive. Some time in the early 1830s his master hired him for a year to Edward Covey, a man widely known for his ability to break the spirit of unruly slaves. Covey had almost succeeded in working and beating Douglass into the most abject obedience when, by chance, Douglass visited a conjurer who gave him a root reputed to prevent whippings. With the root in his pocket Douglass resisted Covey's attempt to beat him. In fact, Douglass seized Covey around the throat, flung him to the ground, declared that he would no longer be treated as a brute, and fought off the other slaves Covey ordered to assist him. In the end, Douglass won out over Covey, and he was never again whipped by him or any other white man.[56]

The victory Douglass achieved over Covey was small compared to the one he won over his own fear. As he put it, "I felt as I never felt before. . . . My long crushed spirit rose, cowardice departed, bold defiance took its place; and I now resolved that, however long I might remain a slave in form, the day had passed forever when I could be a slave in fact." Four years later Douglass escaped from slavery and made his way to New York.[57]

The thousand or so slaves who escaped each year, and the many more who mustered the courage to try, displayed a special kind of bravery. Runaway slaves knew that with capture they faced the worst abuse the system could offer, and even the most successful flight was laden with incredible danger. They had to outrun dogs that would rip their flesh at a patroller's command. Poisonous snakes, mosquitoes, black flies, and alligators all proved as formidable as hunger, thirst, and winter's frost. Always looming in the mind of the runaway was the fear of betrayal.

Still they fled. Georgia slave John Brown ran away several times before he finally succeeded in reaching freedom. One time he got as far as Tennessee. Another time, thinking he was traveling north, he walked almost all the way to New Orleans. Each time he was captured he was whipped, chained, and had bells attached to him. Over and over again he escaped until he finally reached Indiana. Charles Ball also escaped from Georgia. Beset by dogs, hunger, cold, and exposure, he made his way to Baltimore. After finding work and settling in as a free man, he was seized by slaveholders and taken back to Georgia. Determined to be free, he escaped again, this time by stowing away on a ship bound for Philadelphia.

> They didn't do something and run. . . . They run before they did it. . . . In them days they run to keep from doing something.[58]

Aunt Cheyney of the Kilpatrick cotton plantation in Mississippi was not so fortunate. One of her master's concubines, she had recently given birth to the fourth of her master's children when she ran away. Kilpatrick set his dogs on her trail. When they caught up with her, he ordered them to attack. According to her friend Mary Reynolds, "The dogs tore her naked and et the breasts plumb off her body." This not

"Letting the oppressed go free," from *Legion of Liberty,* 1847.

only served as a punishment for Cheyney, but it was also Kilpatrick's way of warning all slaves, especially women, of the punishment for running away.[59]

However much African Americans were haunted by these kinds of horrors, there were still those who would not be deterred. Their stories of escape reveal as much relentless perseverance as they do ingenuity. Adams Express mail service, for example, carried Henry "Box" Brown for twenty-seven hours from Richmond to Philadelphia in a box three feet long and two feet deep. Brown literally mailed himself to freedom. The light-skinned Ellen Craft escaped by pretending to be a sickly white man traveling in the company of his slave, who was in fact her darker skinned husband William. Together the two traveled by coach, boat, and train from Georgia to Philadelphia. They stopped at some of the best hotels along the way, and disguised as a white man, Ellen even conversed with slaveholders about the trouble of runaway slaves.

> I was sick and tired of being a slave, and felt ready to do almost anything to get where I could act and feel like a free man.[60]

The person who seemed to give the South the most runaway trouble was Harriet Tubman. Born a slave sometime around 1821 on Maryland's Eastern Shore, Tubman lived in slavery for twenty-eight years. Like most slaves in this upper region of the South, Tubman lived in dread of being sold and forced to move to the Deep South. In 1849, when she learned that she was indeed going to be sold, she joined the thousands of others who took to the woods and stole themselves.

What made her unique is that she returned, not once but over and over again, to rescue others, including her sister, her sister's two children, and her parents. Given African Americans' self-identification with the Israelites, it should come as no surprise that Tubman was called "Moses." It is also not surprising that when Tubman said, "Tell my brothers to be always watching unto prayer, and when the good ship Zion comes along, to be ready to step on board," this was her signal to leave, not for heaven but for freedom. She supposedly returned nineteen times and rescued more than three hundred slaves. She was so good at this that Maryland planters offered a bounty of $40,000 for her capture.[61]

Indeed, Tubman was unique among all slaves, especially women. William Still of the Philadelphia Vigilance Committee well knew this. Writing about female runaways, he observed that "females undertook three times the risk of failure that males are liable to." William Penn, another worker for the Underground Railroad, made a similar observation. Speaking of two female runaways, each of whom had two children, he noted, "None of these can walk so far or so fast as scores of men that are constantly leaving."[62]

"The Domestic Slave Trade," from *Legion of Liberty*, 1847.

The observations of Still and Penn are reflected in statistics on runaways. Men, much more than women, swelled their ranks, in part because women were more reluctant to leave without their children. Often the fear of losing them provided the incentive to flee. Escaping alone was difficult enough; escaping successfully with children was close to impossible.

Some women accomplished it. A Kentucky woman took to the woods when she learned that her two daughters were to be sold. Surviving only on fruits and green corn, she managed to make her way across the ice floes of the Ohio River. A Maryland slave named Vina fled to New Jersey with her two daughters. Vina's journey was tortuous in many ways. Not only was she haunted by the memory of the two sons she left behind, but also at one point the journey grew so difficult that she had to leave one of her daughters alone on a road to await a time when Vina's husband could retrieve her.[63]

Undoubtedly, male runaways regretted leaving their wives and children behind, but women, it seems, suffered a special agony when faced with such a decision. Harriet Jacobs, for instance, was sure that her mistress's vengeance would put her son and daughter in danger of severe punishment, or even sale. She sought advice, but it only served to confuse her and increase her anxiety. Her friend and accomplice Betty, who was childless, encouraged Harriet to escape. "Lors, chile! What's you crying 'bout? Dem young uns vil kill you dead. Don't be so chick'n hearted! If you does, you vil nebber git thro' dis world." In contrast, Harriet's grandmother, who had helped raise three generations of black children, admonished, "Stand by your children, and suffer with them till death. Nobody respects a mother who forsakes her children; and if you leave them, you will never have a happy moment." Harriet was one of the lucky few. She escaped, and years later so did her son and daughter.[64]

Truancy seems to have been the way many enslaved women reconciled their desire to flee and their need to stay. Men also practiced truancy, but women made the most likely truants because they nursed and were directly responsible for their children. Benjamin Johnson remembered that sometimes when women would not take a whipping, they "would run away an' hide in de woods. Sometimes dey would come back after a short stay an' den dey would have to put de hounds on dere trail to bring dem back home." As one antebellum Virginia planter put it, "The negro women are all harder to manage than the men."[65]

Women's short-term flight was by no means a reflection of their lesser courage or greater accommodation to slavery. Truants faced punishment when they returned, yet many braved it over and over again. Moreover, truancy involved as much danger as running away. As Johnson's comment indicates, dogs hunted them down, and the woods and swamps they hid in held all kinds of dangers.

Instead, truancy mirrored the different slave experiences of men and women as well as their different ways of resisting. The division of labor on most farms and plantations conferred greater mobility on male than on female slaves. Few of the chores performed by bondwomen took them off the plantation. Usually masters chose male slaves to assist in transporting crops to market and in bringing supplies and other materials to the plantation. Males commonly worked as artisans and craftsmen, and they were more often hired out than were females. Fewer women therefore had a chance to vary their work experience. As a consequence, more men than women were able to test their survival skills under different circumstances.

Another factor affecting slave mobility was the "abroad marriage," a marriage between slaves who resided at different locations. When "abroad" spouses visited each other, usually once a week, the husband frequently traveled to the wife. All in all, female bondage, more than male

bondage, meant being tied to the immediate environment of the plantation or farm.

This was a liability when it came to running away, and it accounts for the tendency of women to become truants rather than runaways. The would-be female fugitive had to consider her unfamiliarity with the surrounding countryside as well as how conspicuous a lone black woman, or a group of black women, would appear. Like Tubman, some female fugitives overcame this last problem by disguising themselves as males. However, the small number of female runaways indicates that more bondwomen than bondmen just "stayed put."[66]

By and large, women resisted in more subtle ways. For instance, they "played the fool" more often than men. To avoid doing some onerous chore, they would smile humbly and pretend to misunderstand instructions. The use of poison also suited women in their capacity as cooks and nurses on the plantation. As early as 1755 a Charleston slave was burned at the stake for poisoning her master, and in 1769 a special issue of the *South Carolina Gazette* carried the story of a woman who had poisoned her master's infant child. Since slaves who resorted to poison did not intend to get caught, we will never know just how many whites they ushered to an early grave.[67]

We also can never know how many instances of illness were actually ruses to escape backbreaking labor.

> They don't come to the field and you go to the quarters and ask the old nurse what's the matter and she says, "Oh, she's not . . . fit to work sir"; and . . . you have to take her word for it that something or other is the matter with her, and you dare not set her to work; and so she will lay up till she feels like taking the air again, and plays the lady at your expense.[68]

Women had an advantage over men in this realm because slave owners expected women to bear children. In an age when women's diseases, menstruation, and childbirth were still shrouded in mystery, white slave owners were forced to play a guessing game of how to get the maximum amount of work from women of childbearing age without damaging the female reproductive organs. Few men wanted to play this game of feigning illness, and few could afford to lose it.

Whether they also got away with birth control and abortion is another thing we will never know. Some women were brave enough to risk sale by choosing to be childless, but these matters were exclusive to the female world of the slave quarters. When such problems arose they were handled in secret and were intended to remain that way. Slaveholders were convinced that slave women knew how to avoid pregnancy and also how to bring on a miscarriage. While Tennessee physician Dr. John H. Morgan wrote that slave women used the herbs of tansy and rue, the roots and seeds of the cotton plant, cedar berries, and camphor to bring about miscarriage, Dr. E. M. Pendleton responded that planters regularly complained of whole families of women who failed to have any children.[69]

More serious were cases of infanticide. Women who chose this form of resistance were clearly desperate. They struck the system where they knew it would hurt—in the increase of the slave population—but they hurt themselves more than they harmed the master. In these rare cases of infanticide, the women were either prosecuted and hanged, or they suffered emotional grief forever.[70]

And yet, grief and a feeling of being trapped led them to perform this desperate

act. One Alabama woman killed her child to save it from the mistress's abuse. She claimed the master was the baby's father. Her mistress knew this and treated the child so cruelly that she had to kill her own offspring to save him from further suffering. Another woman killed her newborn because she knew the master had plans to sell her baby, the same way he had sold her three other children. Years later former slave Lou Smith recalled the incident. "When her fourth baby was born and was about two months old, she just studied all the time about how she would have to give it up, and one day she said, 'I just decided I'm not going to let Old Master sell this baby: he just ain't going to do it.' She got up and give it something out of a bottle, and pretty soon it was dead."[71]

African Americans would have overthrown this system that forced such tragic decisions upon them if they could have, but unlike other slave nations in the Americas, black people here were overwhelmingly outnumbered by whites, and they were grouped in small numbers on plantations located miles apart. Whites controlled the guns, the ammunition, the horses, the dogs, and the law. They had the resources to crush any revolt by slaves, and slaves knew it. Resistance had to be largely individual and local because whites put down the few large-scale rebellions and planned revolts with a viciousness that made one obvious point: revolt was futile.

The revolts that did occur proved this regrettable fact. Among the first was the largest one—an uprising of close to four hundred slaves in the parishes of Saint Charles and Saint John the Baptist in Louisiana. Led by the slave Charles Deslondes in 1811, the slaves sent whites fleeing their plantations for safety in New

Orleans. Farther east in 1817 and 1818, blacks joined the Seminole Indians in their fight to retain their Florida homelands. In what was actually a battle for the rights of the Seminoles and the runaway slaves who had settled among them, units of blacks and Indians raided plantations in Georgia, killing whites and carrying off slaves. Again in 1835, blacks joined the Seminoles in their unsuccessful fight against the militias of Florida, Georgia, and Tennessee. Seminole lands continued to be safe havens for runaway slaves, and by the 1830s President Andrew Jackson was determined to eliminate these autonomous communities and seize all Indian lands for white slaveholders. By that time, however, it was difficult to refer to Seminole land as Indian territory because blacks and Indians had intermarried to the extent that they were often indistinguishable. Indeed, so many hundreds of blacks fought with the Seminoles that General Thomas Jesup declared, "This, you may be assured, is a negro, not an Indian war. . . ."[72]

General Jesup understood what all slaveholders knew—that resistance had always accompanied slavery. The century had begun with Gabriel Prosser's attempt to seize Richmond, Virginia, and the year he died, 1800, was the year that Denmark Vesey bought his freedom from his master and began his life as a free man. It was also the year Nat Turner was born. Both men proved to be the slaveholder's worst nightmare.

Although historians debate the extent, even the existence, of Denmark Vesey's 1822 conspiracy against the city of Charleston, South Carolina, Vesey turned the tables on white people and made them, if only for a while, tremble in fear.[73] A free African American carpenter, Vesey worked hard enough to become more than just self-supporting. By the standards of the day, he was relatively wealthy. Vesey was a proud, literate, free black man who hated slavery and despised seeing his people bowing and scraping to whites. At age fifty-three, he reputedly gathered around him trusted black men, both free and slave, with the idea of capturing the city of Charleston. One of them, Gullah Jack, was a conjurer. It was said that for months they planned their attack on the arsenal at Charleston as well as their assault on plantations surrounding the city. They recruited slaves and free men who were brave enough to carry out the plan. When the alleged plot was betrayed and became public, whites shivered with fright at the very thought of a slave rebellion. In a violent frenzy they seized and murdered blacks even remotely associated with Vesey. As they put many to death and whipped and exiled many more, the whites revealed the depth of their fears. Their confidence in their power had been shaken, if only temporarily. Vesey and his conspirators had unveiled one truth about slavery: while the punishment of slaves was designed to make blacks stand in fear, whites *never* rested easy as long as African Americans tenaciously survived.[74]

Nat Turner laid bare the same truth.

"Instrument of Torture Used by Slaveholders," from *Harper's Weekly*, February 15, 1862.

"Carrying Cotton to
the Gin," from
*Harper's New Monthly
Magazine*, February
1854. Labor remained
the central reality of
the slaves' lives even
as they struggled to
resist their condition.

Proud and self-confident, literate and articulate, he saw visions of God delivering black people from bondage. He believed himself to be the Moses who would lead his people to freedom. Acting on that feeling, Turner led about seventy slaves in an assault on the whites of Southampton, Virginia. In one of the most clear-cut cases of slave rebellion that occurred in this country, Turner went from one plantation to the next, killing whites along the way. His instructions to his fellow insurrectionists were followed to the letter. They spared no one. Age and sex made little difference.[75]

In the end Nat Turner was caught. By the time his murder count reached around sixty, bands of white men caught up with his men and put down the revolt. Turner took to the woods and managed to evade capture until most of his followers had been put to death. As had happened in the Prosser and Vesey conspiracies, the fear of large-scale insurrection spread across the South with alarming speed. In response, whites lashed out mercilessly at blacks, especially those in the vicinity of the rebellion. Anyone suspected of aiding Turner was put to death. All acts of disrespect were taken as a direct challenge to white authority, and slaves who did not behave in the most humble manner were punished severely, even killed. Blacks were not allowed to hold religious services or gather in groups of any kind. All African Americans, slave and free, were watched by patrols with their firearms ready. On a pole along the roadside the decapitated head of a slave was hoisted for all to see. It sent a message loud and clear. White power would not tolerate black resistance. Revolts for freedom were for white men only.

African Americans nevertheless did resist white power. Yes, individual resistance did not overthrow slavery, but it might have encouraged masters to make perpetual servitude more tolerable and lasting. Still, for many African Americans, individual rebellions against the authority of slaveholders fulfilled much the same function as did the slave family, Christianity, and folk religion: it created the psychic space that enabled black people to survive.

And it did much more. Resistance was always present, always growing, and always haunting. It gnawed at the American conscience as it proved a daily reminder that African Americans craved freedom as much as any other group. Out of place in a nation whose founding document proclaimed "all men are created equal," slavery ate away at the country's self-assuredness, especially the conventional wisdom that black people were happier as dependents of whites rather than as their equals. Black resistance demonstrated black equality, and while it helped ensure black survival, it also seeded the tradition of black protest that for generations would force the United States to expand its definition of liberty. Whatever else can be said about the nearly two hundred fifty years of African and African American enslavement, this much is true: white power was irrepressible, but no more so than black survival.

JAMES BREWER STEWART

FROM MORAL SUASION TO POLITICAL CONFRONTATION

American Abolitionists and the Problem of Resistance, 1831–1861

I n January 1863, as warfare raged between North and South, the great abolitionist orator Wendell Phillips addressed an enormous audience of more than ten thousand in Brooklyn, New York. Just days earlier, President Abraham Lincoln, in his Emancipation Proclamation, had defined the destruction of slavery as the North's new and overriding war aim. This decision, Phillips assured his listeners, marked the grand culmination "of a great fight, going on the world over, and which began ages ago . . . between free institutions and caste institutions, Freedom and Democracy against institutions of privilege and class."[1]

A serious student of the past, Phillips's remarks acknowledged the fact that behind the Emancipation Proclamation lay a long history of opposition to slavery not only by African Americans, free and enslaved, but also by ever-increasing numbers of whites. In Haiti, Cuba, Jamaica, Brazil, and Suriname, slave insurrection helped to catalyze emancipation. Abolition in the United States, by contrast, had its prelude in civil war among whites, not in black insurrection. This would have been impossible to imagine had not growing numbers of Anglo-Americans before 1861 chosen to resist the institution of slavery directly and to oppose what they feared was its growing dominion over the nation's government and civic life. No clearer example of this crucial development can be found than Wendell Phillips himself. His career provides a useful starting point for considering the development of militant resistance within the abolitionist movement and its influence in pushing Northerners closer first, to civil war, and then, to abolishing slavery.

This compelling Boston orator burst onto the national stage in 1837 when he vociferously denounced a mob of proslavery rioters in Alton,

Illinois, that had murdered abolitionist editor Elijah Lovejoy. Thereafter, Phillips
developed a rich abolitionist career in
which he all but covered the spectrum of
resistance, legal and extralegal. On a day-
to-day basis, he claimed the role of agitator
by making speeches, publishing articles,
and petitioning legislatures, all forms of
resistance protected by the Constitution's
Bill of Rights. At various junctures he relied
on these protections to urge defiance of
proslavery law and government, to engage
in peaceful civil disobedience, and even to
give rhetorical encouragement of the use of
violence. More specifically, he customarily
defied legally sanctioned white supremacy
by seating himself in railway cars reserved
for "colored only," agitating in favor of
desegregating Massachusetts's public facilities (schools in particular), and demanding
that citizens organize vigilante actions in
the free states to protect against the recapture of fugitive slaves.[2]

These actions were the logical consequences of his most fundamental conviction of all: slavery itself was so heinous a
crime in the eyes of God and so fundamental a violation of all principles of American
freedom that it ought, by every measure of
justice, to be destroyed in the twinkling of
an eye. Like all fully committed abolitionists, black and white, Phillips demanded
"immediate abolition." By the 1840s and
1850s, he had followed this logic to justify
still more militant forms of resistance. He
announced that moral Americans must
deny the legitimacy of the nation's proslavery Constitution, welcome slave revolts in
the South, openly defy federal law enforcement officers in order to prevent the recapture of fugitives, and celebrate the insurrectionist John Brown for his raid on Harpers
Ferry, Virginia, in 1859.[3]

Most important of all, when Phillips
voiced his insurgency, the American public
paid close attention, and as the decades
passed, increasing numbers of Northerners
felt compelled to agree with him. From the

mid-1840s onward, Phillips achieved wide renown as an extraordinary orator who presented the most radical abolitionist opinions in a way that audiences always found compelling, even enchanting. "You heard him . . . an hour, two hours, three hours," listeners typically recalled, "and had no consciousness of the passage of time. . . . He steals upon the audience and surprises them into enthusiasm." The fullest testimony to Phillips's preeminence as "abolition's golden trumpet," however, came from slavery's defenders, who feared him as "an infernal machine set to music," an exponent of racial upheaval and political chaos so eloquent in his espousals of resistance that he simply overpowered his listeners' better judgment. "For the present generation, he is a most dangerous agitator," one such critic observed, because he possessed an unerring ability "to take premises we all grant to be true and to weave them into an enchantment of logic from which there is no escape."[4]

Explaining Phillips's remarkable impact involves more than appreciating his oratory. His unusual public appeal reflects a broadening agreement among white Northerners about the necessity of resisting slavery. As Phillips's reputation grew, so did both his espousals of resistance and his audiences' receptivity to his ever more militant message. Between 1831, when white immediate abolitionists first began mobilizing, and 1860, after that most violent resister of all, John Brown, had been hanged, powerful insurgent impulses increasingly permeated the abolitionist movement. Much to the advantage of Wendell Phillips as a public speaker, they also radiated ever more powerfully into the broader political culture of the North, a fact that angry slaveholders fully appreciat-

ed when voting to secede from the Federal Union. To comprehend the significance of this growing antislavery impulse, we need to examine the roots of white abolitionists' postures of resistance, the evolving forms that this resistance took, and the reasons why increasing numbers of white Northerners joined with Phillips and other abolitionists to register defiance to the slave South.[5]

When launching their movement against slavery in the early 1830s, the first white exponents of immediate abolitionism presented themselves as apostles of Christian reconciliation, not as agents of insurgent resistance. Most of these early crusaders drew their inspiration from a wave of Protestant religious revivalism, the Second Great Awakening, that swept the nation in the 1820s. Led by powerful evangelical ministers such as Charles Grandison Finney and Lyman Beecher, this religious outpouring emphasized the individual's free will choice to renounce sin and to strive for personal holiness. Once "saved," the individual should bring God's truth to the "unredeemed" and combat the evils that sin inevitably perpetuated: drunkenness, impiety, sexual license, and exploitation of the defenseless. To the ears of young white abolitionists-to-be—Congregational revivalists Arthur and Lewis Tappan, Theodore Dwight Weld, and Elizur Wright Jr., Baptists such as William Lloyd Garrison, and the radical Quakers Lucretia

Portrait of Wendell Phillips, ca. 1853–60.

William Lloyd Garrison, ca. 1835, four years after beginning the publication of his newspaper, *The Liberator.*

Mott and John Greenleaf Whittier—these doctrines confirmed that slavery was the most God-defying of all sins and the most corrosive behavior of all to bringing harmony among his people.[6]

In what other system did exploitation of the defenseless occur more brazenly? Where was sexual wantonness more rampant than in the debauchery masters forced upon their female slaves? Where was impiety more deliberately fostered than in masters' refusals to permit their slaves to read the Scriptures? Where was brutality more evident than in the master's heavy use of whips, or his willingness to dismember the family ties of slaves? The solution to all these terrible questions was the truth of "immediate emancipation," pressed urgently upon the slumbering consciences of American citizens, slaveholders and non-slaveholders alike, by means of peaceful exhortations of Christian morality.[7]

Calling this strategy "moral suasion," these neophyte abolitionists believed that theirs was a message of healing and reconciliation best delivered by Christian peacemakers, not by divisive insurgents. Their goal was not simply to resist slavery but actually to obliterate it, rapidly and forever. They appealed directly to the (presumably) guilty and therefore receptive consciences of slaveholders with cries for immediate emancipation. This would inspire masters to release their slaves voluntarily and thereby lead the nation into a redemptive new era of Christian reconciliation and moral harmony. Guided by such visions, they quite naturally insisted that immediate emancipation would do away with racial conflict by ending the bitter enmity between masters and slaves, and it would relieve dangerous political tensions already inflaming North against South. "Our object is to save life, not destroy it," William Lloyd Garrison stressed in 1831. "Make the slave free and every inducement to revolt is taken away, every possibility ended for servile as well as civil war."

Moreover, these abolitionists felt certain that the practice of "immediatism" would enrich daily living for everyone by expanding adherence to time-honored values to which morally upright citizens already held fast. As Garrison sharply questioned, "Are we then fanatics because we cry 'Do not rob! Do not murder!'?" And finally, immediate abolitionists saw themselves as harmonizers, not insurgents, because the vast majority of them forswore violent resistance. The American Anti-Slavery Society's founding declaration, published in 1833, made this requirement clear when its signers pledged to reject "the use of all carnal weapons" and to adhere to Christian principles that forbade "the doing of evil that good may come." "Im-mediatists," in short, saw themselves not as resisting slavery by responding to it reactively, but instead as uprooting it by spiritually revolutionizing the corrupted values of its practitioners and supporters.[8]

By adopting Christian pacifism and regarding themselves as revolutionary peacemakers, these earliest white immediatists woefully underestimated the power of the forces opposing them. Well before they launched their crusade, slavery had secured formidable dominance in the nation's economy and political culture. To challenge so deeply entrenched and powerful an institution eventually meant adopting postures of intransigence for which these abolitionists were, initially, wholly unprepared. A review of slavery's actual position within the nation's political economy and culture suggests why this was so.

From the 1830s until the onset of the Civil War, enslaved humans constituted the nation's second largest form of capital investment, exceeded only by investment in land itself. After 1810, when Eli Whit-ney's gin had opened vast new opportunities for planters to adapt slave labor to an important new commodity, cotton quickly replaced rice and tobacco as the South's most lucrative product. Slavery's geographical center shifted rapidly southwestward from Virginia and Maryland into the newly admitted states of Mississippi, Alabama, Louisiana, Missouri, and Arkansas. Multiplying slave populations mirrored this expanding geography. In 1790 the nation's enslaved had numbered six hundred thousand. By 1830 they counted for close to two million and were concentrated increasingly in these newly developing western lands. To hasten this process, masters developed a far-flung interstate slave trade by uprooting enslaved families in the Upper South and selling their scattered members to eager buyers on the "cotton frontier." Meanwhile in New England, wealthy industrial entrepreneurs with names such as Lowell, Appleton, and Lawrence linked southwestern cotton and slavery to their own region's emerging leadership in the industrial revolution. Throughout the 1830s they established

"The Coffle Gang," from *Suppressed Book of Slavery*, 1864. In this antislavery drawing, the slaves are barefoot, smiling fiddlers play, and the US flag is prominently displayed.

water-powered textile mills across New England. These mills transformed raw cotton into fabric that clothed ever-increasing millions of Americans, thereby uniting North with South in ever-tightening bonds of commerce, investment, and credit.[9]

In politics as in the economy, slaveholding interests predominated as the nation expanded its boundaries and consolidated its systems of government. Back in 1787, the framers of the United States Constitution had provided slavery with a legal legitimacy and a significant political advantage that became increasingly obvious during the antebellum years. Article Four confirmed masters' rights to recover runaways, and the Tenth Amendment forbade the federal government to interfere with slavery on the state level. The former provision ensured the legal sanctity of slaves as property, and the latter gave slaveholders ample constitutional support for adding new slave states to the Federal Union. Most crucially, the Constitution guaranteed slaveholders political power that far exceeded their actual numbers when it provided, in Article One, that in addition to the free population, three-fifths of the slave population also be counted for purposes of taxation and representation in the House of Representatives. This imposing advantage for Southern planters took on still greater importance in the 1830s when politicians assembled a national two-party system based on universal white manhood suffrage.[10]

The men who perfected this expansive new approach to politics competed as Whigs and Democrats. Influential among them were representatives of the same elite groups that underwrote slavery's southwestern expansion and fostered the economic transformation so closely related to slavery—Northern industrialization. Rousing unprecedented numbers of voters by organizing speakers, parades and rallies, barbecues and partisan newspapers, their two parties offered contrasting approaches to fiscal policy, banking, tariffs, the opening of western lands, and support for roads and canals. Concerning slavery, however, their differences were superficial. Led by the slaveholding war hero Andrew Jackson and organized by talented party operatives in North and South, Democrats across the nation stood foursquare behind the institution of slavery. Whigs in both sections sometimes phrased their support in more measured accents when embracing the leadership of Kentucky planter-politician Henry Clay along with that of Daniel Webster, New England's powerful spokesman for industrialization. In either case, strategies for victory required parties to mobilize a white majority of voters that encompassed both regions. This, in turn, led politicians to suppress sectionally divisive disagreements over slavery and to appeal forcefully to powerful new ideologies of white supremacy that circulated freely in both North and South. As the 1830s opened and abolitionists launched their crusade, it was deepening racial prejudice even more than slavery's entrenched positions in politics and the economy that secured it as the nation's most formidable institution.[11]

In the South, of course, it had long been established that heavily enforced white supremacy constituted the cornerstone of a free, "white" society. By contrast, the racial tensions that developed in the 1820s in the North were of a much newer sort. As urban life in the North rapidly grew more complicated during this decade, feelings of white supremacy and conflict

between people of differing colors became increasingly chronic as well. In Northern cities, industrialization fostered a rapid transition from artisan work to wage labor, which, in turn, attracted waves of immigrants from all over the British Isles, particularly from Ireland. When encountering the traumas of adjustment to unfamiliar circumstances, these newly arrived workers saw in the "blackness" of their African American neighbors unwelcome competition in a tightening labor market and, even more important, a mirror of their diminishing ability to shape their own futures as "independent" men. Irish Catholics in particular feared personal "enslavement" to the Protestant "bosses" who paid their wages. Acting on these anxieties, they claimed to be "white," just like all other presumably "free" citizens, and then asserted this "whiteness" through acts of aggression against free blacks. On the opposite

end of the social spectrum, elite white ministers, lawyers, and businessmen noted these growing frictions and increasingly convinced themselves that free African Americans constituted an ever more turbulent, dangerous people. Such blacks should be encouraged to "return" to Africa under the auspices of the American Colonization Society, a "benevolent" movement favored by prominent Northerners.

Free blacks, for their part, refused to abandon their hard-fought struggles, dating from the American Revolution, to claim full citizenship and build "respectable" communities around their churches, schools, and voluntary associations. In their view, invitations to resettle in Africa were gross insults and ominous signs that whites were planning their forced deportation. Threats by these white elitists as well as by the white rabble required the sternest of responses.[12]

Edward W. Clay, "Practical Amalgamation," 1839. From their portraits on the wall, abolitionists gaze down on the antics of these interracial couples.

These volatile racial tensions turned the 1820s into a decade of white racial tyranny. Lower-class whites felt a mounting impunity to harass, abuse, vandalize, and even murder blacks. Typical were the Philadelphia rioters in 1824 who hurled garbage and paving stones when driving away their dark-complexioned fellow citizens from the Fourth of July ceremonies in which everyone had, until then, participated amicably. Particularly horrifying was the Cincinnati "race riot" of 1829. Armed mobs returned for three successive nights to terrorize black neighborhoods, leaving homes and churches in rubble, several dead, and more than six hundred in stupefied exile, with some moving permanently to lower Canada. While less-disastrous incidents disrupted other major cities such as New York, Boston, and Hartford, racial bigotry

overtook state legislatures in the North as politicians methodically stripped free African Americans of their citizenship. Legislators in Ohio, Indiana, and Illinois opened the franchise to all white males while they simultaneously enacted "black codes" that all but eliminated the political rights of free African Americans. Pennsylvania, New York State, and Connecticut likewise approved universal white manhood suffrage while requiring blacks to "qualify" as voters by satisfying all-but-impossible property requirements. Newspapers, barrooms, and theaters suddenly teemed with viciously racist cartoons and satires. White Americans in the North no less than in the South had now made color the primary criterion for living unchallenged or in oppression on "free" American soil.[13]

With the nation's most powerful institutions so tightly aligned in support of slavery and white supremacy, it is clear that young white abolitionists were profoundly self-deceived when they characterized their work as "the destruction of error by the potency of truth—the overthrow of prejudice by the power of love—the abolition of slavery by the spirit of repentance." When so contending, they were deeply sincere and grievously wrong. To crusade for slavery's rapid obliteration was, in truth, to stimulate not "the power of love" and "repentance," but instead to promote the opposition of not only an overwhelming number of powerful enemies—the entire political system—but also the nation's most potent economic interests—society's most influential elites—and a popular political culture in the North that was more deeply suffused with racial bigotry than at any previous time in the nation's history. Three headline events that opened the 1830s ominously suggested what the future actually held for these young idealists.[14]

The first, the Nullification Crisis in South Carolina (1828–32), revealed just how enraged by immediate abolitionism slaveholders were likely to become. Well before the start of the abolitionists' crusade, extremist planters in this state were already mobilizing armies and threatening secession in order to protect slavery from "meddling outsiders" and the power of the federal government. The second, involving militant pamphleteer David Walker, underscored just how desperate race relations across the nation had actually become. Walker published his *Appeal to the Colored Citizens of the World* in Boston in 1829 and 1830, and immediately it became a landmark expression of African American political ideology. With angry accents and

uncompromising ideas, Walker excoriated whites for their bigotry and free African Americans for their apathy and called, in extreme circumstances, for slaves to rise in violence. As Walker made all too clear, white oppression was driving black leaders in the free states to desperation even as angry planters closed ranks around their "peculiar institution." Then in late 1831 in Southampton County, Virginia, insurrectionist Nat Turner led a bloody uprising that took the lives of fifty-five whites and a far greater number of blacks. Yet when responding to all this turmoil, newly committed immediatist Samuel E. Sewall saw only portents of redemption, offering the prediction that "the whole system of slavery will fall to pieces with a rapidity that will astonish." Garrison even went so far as to prognosticate that "the day is not far off when black skin will be not simply endurable, but even popular!"[15] To these "Bible believing" abolitionists, sectional crisis and racial upheaval did not portend disaster, but instead it gave reassurance that a God who hated slavery was making his anger manifest.

For all its obviousness, this enormous naiveté was actually one of the abolitionists' greatest initial strengths. Their fervent belief that God would make all things right as slavery was rapidly swept aside motivated them to shoulder otherwise unthinkable tasks and endure otherwise unimaginable risks. Thus, for a full six years, from 1831 through 1837, abolitionists transformed themselves into whirlwinds of agitation. Fully intent on not simply resisting but actually uprooting the institution of slavery, they energetically canvassed the free states, creating hundreds of antislavery societies, dozens of newspapers, blizzards of pamphlets and broadsides, and innumerable local controversies over the

Photographed in 1846, the Jacksons were an extended family of abolitionists who participated in the Underground Railroad. William Jackson (seated at table, fourth from left) was said to have helped many fugitives from the Boston area to freedom westward and on to Canada.

"sin of slavery." Working closely with long-established groups of free African American activists in the Northern cities, they also struck directly at what they termed "color phobia" by founding schools, churches, and voluntary associations in which people of all ancestries and both genders associated freely. In the same spirit, abolitionists met as "promiscuous assemblies" (as detractors called them), with men mixing publicly with women and light-skinned people with dark. By 1835 abolitionists had exploited the United States Postal Service to flood slave-holders' mailboxes with warnings of impending damnation and pleas to repent and emancipate. The next year they launched a "Great Petition Campaign," sending to the US House of Representatives a tidal wave of citizen requests that Con-gress legislate against the interests of slavery.[16]

Judged by the urgency of the issues they raised and the controversies they pro-voked, the abolitionists' initial impact vast-ly exceeded their modest numbers. (Fully engaged immediatists were never more than a minuscule portion of the North's population.) Judged by their self-professed goals and expectations, however, these first campaigns led them straight to a disaster that changed their movement forever. Elected officials from President Andrew Jackson on down, civic leaders of every variety, ministers from nearly all denomi-nations, and masses of ordinary people in both North and South responded to imme-diatism with a harrowing barrage of repres-sion. In response, white abolitionists had no choice but to redirect their movement from a crusade for rapid emancipation into a long-term resistance struggle against the intractable tyranny of slavery and white supremacy.

In the slave states, mobs urged on by elected officials invaded post offices and burned abolitionist mailings, while state legislatures voted cash bounties for the capture of leading abolitionists. White Southerners suspected of "abolitionist sympathies" faced harassment, indictment, and sometimes the whip or the tar bucket as public criticism of slavery all but ended throughout the Lower South. Meanwhile, in Washington, DC, Whigs and Democrats joined in 1836 to pass a gag rule that prohibited all discussion of abolitionists' petitions to the House of Representatives, a truly unprecedented restriction of citizens' freedom of political expression. In elections across the nation, these same two parties competed for votes by stressing antiabolitionism and white supremacy as

central to their beliefs. This sudden emergence of intensely competitive two-party politics based on mass participation and universal white manhood suffrage was thus inextricably tied to campaigns to suppress the abolitionist movement and visit still further woe on people of dark complexion.[17]

While politicians legislated against immediatism and campaigned for white men's votes, mayhem erupted in cities and towns throughout the free states. Utica, Boston, Philadelphia, Rochester, Pittsburgh, and Syracuse witnessed unruly gangs that disrupted abolitionists' meetings and threatened black citizens with rocks, garbage, fists, and firebrands. Similar conflicts broke out in dozens of small towns and crossroads villages as well. When immediatist Prudence Crandall attempted to establish an academy for young women of color in the hamlet of Canterbury, Connecticut, in 1831 and 1832, her neighbors tried to burn her schoolhouse and ultimately succeeded

"New Method of Assorting the Mail, As Practised by Southern Slave-holders, or Attack on the Post Office, Charleston, SC," 1830s.

THE RESULTS OF ABOLITIONISM!

Bring up the mortar you white rascals.

You bog-trotters, come along with them bricks.

White man Hurry up them bricks.

Sambo hurry up the white laborers.

"The Results of Abolitionism!" ca. 1835.

in driving her from the state. Soon thereafter, the state legislature made schools such as Crandall's illegal and passed laws restricting abolitionists' rights to move freely within the state. In Dover, New Hampshire, the local residents used a brace of oxen to destroy a building that abolitionists had purchased to house a school open to both black and white students, while in 1831 in New Haven, Connecticut, simply the proposal by abolitionists to develop a manual labor school for young black men provoked stern condemnation from Yale University's administrators. Arthur Tappan's home was attacked, and two days of racial warfare erupted in the city's black neighborhoods. On and on the mayhem went. For abolitionists, whatever their color, disillusionment compounded as the damage mounted.[18]

In Hartford in 1836, for example, the Reverend Hosea Easton surveyed the smoking rubble of what had been the First Congregational Church, his African American congregation's treasured symbol of spirituality and community achievement. In this instance, white marauders had not even bothered to use abolitionism as their pretext when deploying arson against free people of color. In New York City in 1834 and (again) in Cincinnati in 1836, unconcerned sheriffs and constables looked on as buildings in black neighborhoods burned, pillagers looted, and people of color either hid or fled. Unlike the riots of the 1820s, however, these marauders sought out white abolitionists as well as blacks. The targets in New York City were Arthur and Lewis Tappan, millionaire merchants and militant white immediatists who underwrote a variety of abolitionist projects and associations. The victim in Cincinnati was James G. Birney, editor of the immediatist newspaper *The Philanthropist*. Mobs there repeatedly sacked his office and hurled his printing press into the Ohio River. A practitioner of "nonresistance," Birney himself escaped unharmed, although his offices did not, and neither, predictably, did the dwellings and businesses of Cincinnati's African Americans.[19]

Another embattled abolitionist, editor Elijah Lovejoy, scorned "nonresistance" as mobs in Alton, Illinois, repeatedly destroyed his presses and threatened his life in 1837. Fronting on the Mississippi River and located in the southernmost part of the state, Alton (like Cincinnati) teemed with men who supported slavery fervently, who deeply despised abolitionists, and who were eager to harm Lovejoy. Seizing his rifle, Lovejoy descended from his second-story office toward his tormentors as they attempted to flush him out with arson. As he came down the stairs, they cut him down with a fusillade of gunfire. Thus did white abolitionism enroll its first "martyr." Thus, too, did this unprecedented movement for racial equality begin a momentous transition from a hopeful religious crusade to eradicate slavery to a dogged struggle to resist this formidable institution, protected as it so heavily was by religious denominations, the state, the courts, the two political parties, the bigoted opinions of most white Americans, and now by vigilante violence. In the wake of Lovejoy's murder, Garrison captured perfectly the shocked realization sweeping through the movement that abolitionists must now rethink and revise their fundamental premises.

> When we first unfurled the banner of the *Liberator* . . . we did not anticipate that, in order to protect southern slavery, the free states would voluntarily trample under foot all law and order, and government, or

brand the advocates of universal liberty as incendiaries and outlaws. . . . It did not occur to us that almost every religious sect, and every political party would side with the oppressor.[20]

Historians have provided clear accounts of the deep divisions that finally shattered the white abolitionist movement once its leaders began acting on this realization. By 1840 three quarreling factions had emerged. One, led by Garrison, argued that the nation's values had now been revealed to be so utterly corrupted that abolitionists must flee from proslavery churches, spurn the proslavery political process, and oppose the proslavery Federal Union with demands for Northern secession. Religious perfectionism and espousals of female equality also seasoned this iconoclastic ideology (referred to as "Garrisonianism" by supporters and detractors alike) and sustained the American Anti-Slavery Society throughout the antebellum decades. A second group,

"The destruction of Birney's Philanthropist press in Cincinnati," from *Nye, Fettered Freedom,* 1949.

headed by James G. Birney and others, insisted that abolitionists must shift their fight to the political arena, where voters should be exhorted to "vote as they prayed and pray as they voted" for immediate emancipation. This was possible, they argued, because the United States Constitution derived its organic authority from the Declaration of Independence's assertion that "all men" were "created equal." Thus the Constitution actually supported a legislative end to slavery. Their Liberty Party first campaigned for the presidency in 1840, garnering no more than seventy-five hundred votes, but it continued, undaunted, to field immediatist candidates up to and including the 1860 election of Abraham Lincoln. And finally, a third group, led by Lewis Tappan, founded the American and Foreign Anti-Slavery Society in the hope of sustaining the original version of moral suasion. To them, Garrisonians were heretical iconoclasts who had deflected the crusade

for slave emancipation into a morass of perfectionist, anticlerical heresy, while the Liberty Party's initiatives pandered dangerously to proslavery voters.[21]

Yet for all their conflicting approaches, these three factions still felt they relied, just as abolitionists always had, on moral appeals to "the nation's conscience." All, in other words, saw themselves as remaining wedded to moral suasion. Certainly none felt suddenly compelled to advocate broadly conceived programs of overt resistance, let alone resort to violence. Nevertheless, by the later 1830s everything had changed, as was symbolized by the murder of Elijah Lovejoy. A seven-year reign of terror now forced these white immediatists to begin exploring, not new approaches for rapidly abolishing slavery, but instead how to grapple successfully with this intransigent institution and its equally uncompromising alter ego, white supremacy. In short, they started to fashion the tools of resistance. When

Wendell Phillips responded to Lovejoy's death by dramatically embracing the abolitionist cause in 1837, his reasons for so doing illustrate how this process began.[22]

What disturbed Phillips most about Lovejoy's murder was not the sin of slavery (heinous though he thought it was) but rather the institution's seemingly unstoppable capacity to corrupt every aspect of American life, even to the point of destroying not only those it kept in chains but also those who opposed it in the North. The mob that murdered Lovejoy, Phillips insisted, was driven by a soulless, unchecked power in human relations, one founded in tyranny, that spread increasing destruction all over America—the institution of slavery. Here, he believed, was "an abnormal element" in American political culture that "no one had counted on. No check and no balance had been provided" in the nation's laws or government to stem its corrupting influences. Phillips, as he explained, suddenly became "conscious that I was in the presence of a power whose motto was victory or death." All that stood between slavery's unchallenged predominance and the last glimmerings of American liberty were, according to Phillips, the abolitionists themselves, few, despised, and powerless though they were.

When Phillips decided to devote his life to presenting compelling speeches in order to turn public opinion against slavery, his participation injected a sharp new tone of resistance into abolitionism. He forswore pacifism, celebrated the nation's revolutionary traditions of patriotic blood sacrifice, and sought effective political tactics for resisting the "unchecked" onslaught of slavery in the free states. A staunch Garrisonian when it came to Northern disunion and women's rights, Phillips's militancy spoke to a rapidly growing fear among abolitionists and Northerners. Slavery's pernicious influences (race riots, gag rules, and legislated repression) would surely overwhelm the free states as it had the South unless a new generation of abolitionist patriots rallied to resist it. The contrast between this desperate viewpoint and Garrison's ebullient prediction, made six years earlier, that "black skin will be not simply endurable, but even popular" measures well how far abolitionists had journeyed from their original hopes of glorious victory.[23]

Yet even as this momentous transition proceeded, African American activists

Portrait of James G. Birney, a Southern-born slaveholder who freed his slaves and became an abolitionist. He ran as the Liberty Party candidate for president of the United States in 1840.

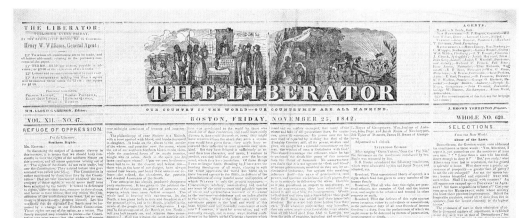

Masthead of the *Liberator,* William Lloyd Garrison's abolitionist newspaper, published in Boston from 1831 to 1865

involved in the abolitionist movement also reordered their assumptions and changed direction in a manner that pushed their white associates still further along the pathways of resistance. A review of the evolving roles of Northern black abolitionists in the early white-dominated immediatist movement will clarify how this process unfolded.

From the beginning, black activists such as James Forten, Hosea Easton, and William Watkins had gravely doubted the white immediatists' assumptions that Southern planters would embrace moral suasion, or that Northern whites would soon cast off their color phobia. Their long and bitter trials with racial tyranny hardly fostered such optimism. Nevertheless, several reasons compelled them to respond with great enthusiasm to the initial white crusade for moral suasion. One such incentive involved the white abolitionists' implacable hostility toward the American Colonization Society.[24]

No proposition more openly scorned free African Americans' claims to citizenship than did the idea that they be "returned" to their "homeland" across the ocean, which is exactly what the American Colonization Society proposed. Like so many of the North's black activists, these leaders regarded their ongoing struggles as being rooted in the irrevocable achievement of citizenship that had been attained for all people of color by "colored patriots" who had rallied to the cause during the

The capture of a female fugitive slave in the North, from *Legion of Liberty*, 1847.

American Revolution. Wedded to this conviction, they hailed the white immediatists' full-throated condemnations of the American Colonization Society and joined them to amplify it as fully as they could. Overburdened by racial bigotry, these Northern black activists also felt understandably heartened by the sudden appearance of whites who took their views seriously by inviting them to abolitionist meetings and publishing their thoughts in the abolitionist press. Black and white abolitionists discovered, furthermore, that they shared many of the same moral values, primarily those stressing piety, thrift, sobriety, self-control, and self-improvement. Black leaders had long been accustomed to advocating these qualities when exhorting their communities to sustain programs of self-help in order to uplift themselves to ever higher levels of "respectability." That meant building and strengthening churches and schools as well as sponsoring adult education groups, fraternal organizations, and temperance societies. "Uplift" constituted an ideology well suited not only for fortifying communities of color in Northern cities but also for inviting close collaboration between black community leaders and white immediatists to foster African American "respectability" as a demonstration of racial equality.[25]

Never before in the nation's history had people of color and Euro-Americans worked together so closely for racially egalitarian goals of uplift and respectability. Together they moved decisively during the early 1830s in cities throughout the free states to establish academies, colleges, and libraries, to foster temperance societies, and to underwrite cultural enrichments, such as debating societies, literary clubs, and "juvenile associations." One monument to this brief crescendo of interracial creativity endures to this day: Oberlin College in Ohio. It was founded in 1835 as the nation's first institution of higher learning open to students of both genders and of all complexions. Oberlin, unfortunately, is all that endures. On every other front, these unprecedented efforts to face down color phobia with racial uplift backfired completely. Instead, they gave the mightiest impetus of all to fears of racial "amalgamation" and the most compelling of motives for applying mob rule and legislated repression.[26]

While white immediatists were responding to racial tyranny by moving beyond moral suasion, their African American colleagues felt driven to recognize the costly limitations of uplift and to design new militant approaches of their own. Both groups, in other words, drastically revised their initial strategies and tactics. Most white immediatists turned from converting the planter class to focusing efforts to resist and unmask slavery's Northern sources of power, as Wendell Phillips did. Northern black activists, for their part, continued to seek the uplifting of their communities but only as part of militant new campaigns to face down bigots, demand the full rights of citizenship, and assist individual slaves in escaping their masters. On every front, and among those of every complexion, abolitionists displayed an ever more militant spirit of resistance from the 1840s onward.

The next generation of talented African American activists that rose to leadership in the 1840s did much to move abolitionism in these new directions. As often as not, these forceful black abolitionists now set agendas for their white associates and refused to tolerate their paternalistic

James W. C. Pennington, former fugitive slave from the Eastern Shore of Maryland, worked as an abolitionist and minister in New York City. From *A Text Book of the Origin and History of the Colored People*, 1841.

David Ruggles, for example, was a black who first refused to sit in the "colored only" sections of steamboats and railway cars operating in Massachusetts. After being physically ejected from several of these conveyances in 1841, he filed a series of antidiscrimination lawsuits and invited Garrison, Phillips, and other leading white abolitionists to join him in campaigns of civil disobedience. On a warm August day that same year, Phillips thus found himself on the open-air "Negro deck" of a steamer bound to New Bedford, Massachusetts, defying segregation by mingling with forty black and white abolitionists, William Lloyd Garrison and Frederick Douglass prominent among them. Soon thereafter, individual acts of civil disobedience and concerted efforts by integrated groups against segregated transportation systems spread throughout New England and quickly expanded to address the issue of segregation in public schools.[28]

In the early 1840s, when black abolitionists began rallying their communities to boycott segregated schools, they again found useful allies in white abolitionists. In Massachusetts towns such as Salem, Lynn, New Bedford, and Nantucket, these boycotts proved successful, as did another led by Douglass in Rochester, New York. The most significant struggle, however, took place in Boston and was led by previously obscure local blacks and supported by some of the North's most prominent whites. Black abolitionists William C. Nell and John T. Hilton began an antisegregation petition campaign in 1846 directed against the Boston School Committee. When their petitions were rejected, they launched boycotts and rallied parents in mass demonstrations to prevent students from registering for segregated classes.

impulses. This was a dramatic reversal from the early years of moral suasion and African American uplift, when whites made most of the basic decisions and expressed, unchallenged, their sense of cultural superiority. Some, such as James McCune Smith, Martin Delany, and James W. C. Pennington had Northern roots and abolitionist educations while others, notably Frederick Douglass, Samuel Ringgold Ward, Sojourner Truth, and Henry Highland Garnet, were survivors of slavery. Whatever their backgrounds, they seldom flinched when confronted by Northern bigotry, and they quickly began involving Wendell Phillips and other whites in their protracted struggles to resist segregation.[27]

Horace Mann, secretary of the Massachusetts School Board, tried to broker a compromise, but Wendell Phillips intervened with bitterly sarcastic speeches and editorials. Meanwhile, black and white activists merged their assets and expertise to force desegregation by instigating expensive lawsuits. In 1849 African American attorney Robert Morris and white, Harvard-educated Charles Sumner brought a suit against the Boston School Committee on behalf of Benjamin Roberts, whose five-year-old daughter walked each day past five "all-white" elementary schools before arriving at the grossly inferior "colored school" to which she had been assigned. Although their lawsuits failed, continuing agitation led by Phillips and Garrison and bolstered by energized black communities headed by Roberts and Nell finally resulted in victory. In 1855 the Massachusetts legislature voted to outlaw segregation in public schools across the state.[29]

When abolitionists turned their efforts to Northern politics, however, the results were much less satisfying. During the early and mid-1840s, for example, black abolitionist Henry Highland Garnet led a sustained campaign to force the repeal of New York State's qualification that required all black males who wished to vote had to own at least two hundred dollars' worth of property. In this case, the white abolitionists who came forward to assist Garnet were not Garrisonians but leaders of the emancipationist Liberty Party, among them Henry Brewster Stanton, Joshua Leavitt, and Alvin Stewart. This marked just one of many instances when white Liberty Party members supported black activists' attempts to resist and repeal discriminatory

laws. Their efforts resulted in a statewide referendum to repeal the restriction, which whites then rejected in 1846 by a nearly two-to-one margin. This proved to be a fair measure of the power racial tyranny wielded in one significant free state. In Pennsylvania, white opinion stymied a similar effort before it ever reached the voters.[30]

As abolitionists of all backgrounds well knew, none of these struggles did much to force emancipation in the South. Yet on a deeper level, such challenges to their region's boundaries of inequality magnified as nothing else could the growing conflict of fundamental values between the "free" North and the "slave" South. Below the Mason-Dixon line, granted, slavery continued to flourish and expand in the absence of organized opposition of any sort. Above it, however, especially in New England, in Upstate New York, and in northern Ohio, militant blacks, struggling to liberate themselves from humiliating denials of their citizenship, were joining whites pledged to

"Colored Scholars Excluded from Schools," from *Anti-Slavery Almanac for 1840,* 1839.

immediate abolition in sustained campaigns to make the law serve racial justice. And most significantly, as in Massachusetts, they sometimes succeeded. To be sure, as the abolitionists' defeat in New York State made clear, the free states remained mired

"The branding of Captain Jonathan Walker, for aiding runaway slaves," from *Nye, Fettered Freedom,* 1949.

in white supremacy at practically every level. This was particularly true in cities, in deeply conservative Connecticut, in "downstate" New York, and in the central and southern regions of Pennsylvania, Ohio, Indiana, and Illinois. Yet even in these locales, attorneys such as Salmon Chase in Ohio occasionally put their legal expertise at the disposal of African Americans ensnared in a highly prejudicial legal system. Southern congressmen and senators, in turn, noted these multiplying signs of racial insurgency within the free states and found them increasingly disturbing. In this manner, the abolitionists' turn from reform to resistance more and more distressed the white South and its supporters during the 1840s and 1850s.[31]

Short of black insurrection, nothing undermined political harmony between North and South more deeply than did abolitionists who aided escaping slaves. In the larger history of slave escapes, to be sure, African Americans involved in the "underground railroad" usually relied on one another and largely distrusted the participation of whites. Starting in the 1840s,

however, white abolitionists in ever-increasing numbers grew eager to encourage slaves to escape and then to protect them once they resided in the North. By the mid-1840s, "slave stealing" ranked high on slaveholders' lists of complaints, and the impact of abolitionist resistance on Southern concerns was becoming increasingly easy to measure.

A few venturesome souls actually moved to the South, assisted escapees, and were heavily punished for their trouble. Charles T. Torrey from Massachusetts ranked high in the abolitionist Liberty Party before he moved to Baltimore in 1844 to engineer slave escapes. Caught, convicted, and sentenced the next year, he died an abolitionist "martyr" in the Maryland penitentiary in 1846. A decade earlier Garrisonian sea captain Jonathan Walker shipped out of New Bedford, Massachusetts, for Pensacola, Florida, where he assisted fugitives until he was arrested in 1844, branded with the letters *SS* (for slave stealer), and imprisoned for a year. The punishment for the Reverend Calvin Fairbank was far harsher in 1844: fifteen years of hard labor for abetting numerous slaves to escape in and around Lexington, Kentucky. William Chaplin, another prominent immediatist, proved the most ambitious slave stealer of all. When he visited Washington, DC, in 1848, he hired two seafaring adventurers, Drayton and Sayres, and their transport ship and made plans to ferry seventy-seven fugitives to the free states. The plot was betrayed just as the ship left port, and a pursuing steamer captured it. The angry masters—some were influential members of

Congress—sold most of the escapees and made sure that the accomplices received harsh sentences. Drayton and Sayres both languished in prison for several years; Chaplin, who evaded prosecution, was later convicted for abetting fugitive slaves in Maryland.[32]

Slave stealers operating in the free states feared no such punishments (although escapees certainly did). On the contrary, during the 1840s abolitionists discovered to their surprise that Northerners who were in no sense immediatists nonetheless began voicing their support for protecting fugitives as a way to express their own growing worries over the political impact of slavery in the nation's affairs. Prompting these feelings were the same general concerns that had so troubled Wendell Phillips over the murder of Elijah Lovejoy, that is, the slaveholders' seemingly unstoppable determination to undermine the freedom of Americans everywhere, not simply rule over those they enslaved. Increasing numbers now joined with the abolitionists, not to endorse immediate emancipation but instead to express their worry over gag rules, assaults on the freedoms of speech and assembly, the mobs that disrupted orderly communities, the ransacking of federal post offices, and the terrorizing of innocent African Americans. Compounding these concerns after 1845 was the prospect of adding still more slave states to the Union, the result of annexing the Republic of Texas and opening a war of conquest against Mexico. When immediatist James G. Birney warned that "whilst our aristocracy would preserve the domestic peace of the South, they seem totally to disregard the domestic peace of the North" and that "the liberties of those yet free are in imminent peril," he also addressed

directly the growing fears of what Northerners had started to term the "slave power." Responding to this growing political concern, Northern state legislatures began enacting "personal liberty laws" that relieved judges and law enforcement officials from the obligation to enforce the 1793 Fugitive Slave Law within their particular state's borders. Constitutional arguments over "states' rights" now were beginning to furnish a means not only for politicians to oppose the influence of slavery in the free states but also for slaveholders to protect the institution in the South.[33]

When Boston authorities seized fugitive George Latimer in 1842, Wendell Phillips's angry response perfectly conveyed why state legislatures felt compelled to enact such laws. His remarks also suggest why the abolitionists' spirit of resistance was now beginning to stimulate such strong sectional feelings in Northern political culture and why his own appeal to Yankee audiences was growing so rapidly. The answer, in both cases, involved revulsion against the "slave power's" invasive

Albert Sands Southworth and Josiah Johnson Hawes, "The Branded Hand of Capt. Jonathan Walker," August 1845.

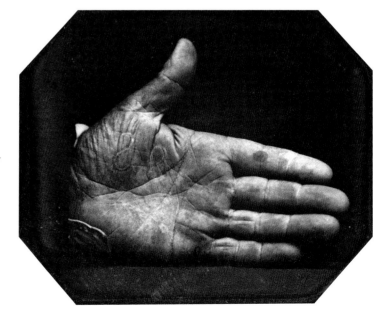

attempts to make Northern freemen serve the commands of Southern planters.

Who was really responsible for Latimer's plight? Phillips queried his audience. Not his jailers, the sheriff, or even the slave catcher. "No!" Phillips exclaimed, "they are but your tools. You are the guilty ones. . . . It is you that bolt and bar the door to that poor man's dungeon." Demanding the passage of a personal liberty law, Phillips insisted that the state of Massa-chusetts "cannot allow her soil to be polluted with the footprints of slavery without trampling on her Bill of Rights and subjecting herself to infamy. . . . She is solemnly bound to give protection to all who may escape the prison of bondage, and flee to her for safety." Clearly, Phillips expressed the feelings of most Massachusetts voters. The following year the legislature did as he demanded by prohibiting Massachusetts justices from acting under the 1793 Fugitive Slave Law and barring state officials from arresting presumed escapees. By the mid-1840s several other state legislatures had done likewise. In major cities black activists who

had long before established vigilance committees of their own to protect runaways now found their work shielded from interference on the state level. For their part, worried planters felt quite certain the law of the land in the free states legitimized slave stealing. Meeting this threat, they decided, required stringent new measures on the part of the federal government. They managed to secure these measures as part of the legislative compromise of 1850. Congress designed the compromise to resolve all outstanding sectional disagreements, including those derived from slavery's expansion into territories conquered during the Mexican War as well as those raised by fugitive slaves and abolitionists.[34]

Proslavery politicians obtained what they wanted when Congress enacted an extraordinarily harsh new Fugitive Slave Law as part of the compromise measures. It authorized federal commissioners, not state judges, to process escapees, and it obliged every citizen to assist in capturing runaways. Those who protected fugitives risked severe penalties, while the escapees themselves were stripped of the right to trial by jury and the opportunity to testify. Free blacks found themselves in jeopardy of summarily being claimed as escapees, seized, and shipped south without so much as a hearing. Though conflict over slavery's future in western territories, not over fugitive slaves, ultimately propelled the sectional collisions that led to civil war, this repressive new law inspired abolitionists to acts of militant resistance that undermined inter-sectional good will. As conflict over reserving the West for "free soil" or opening it to slavery split Whigs and Democrats irrevocably along North-South lines following the Kansas-Nebraska Act (1854), the Kansas Border Wars (1855–57), and the Dred Scott decision (1857), abolitionists hungered for confrontation with "slave catchers and for ways to defy the federal government openly. To the heightened dismay of the planters who had demanded this fugitive law, slave stealing, for abolitionists, now constituted their high moral injunction. To a growing majority of "free soil"–minded Northerners who were certainly not abolitionists but who nevertheless supported the new Republican Party, resistance also seemed imperative if hope were to remain for arresting the spread of the "slave power." After almost three decades of constant agitation, abolitionists were finally being heard and, in a restricted sense, believed by powerful blocs of Republican Party voters. While these Republicans certainly opposed the desires of the slave South, they also promised to leave Southern slavery alone and held no necessary brief for racial equality.[35]

As blacks and whites united in defying the fugitive law, resistance sometimes turned violent. An abolitionist shot a slaveholder in Christiana, Pennsylvania, in 1851,

and three years later an attempt to free a fugitive in Boston by storming the courthouse and overpowering his guards led to a fatality. And even when physical violence did not result, Wendell Phillips (now the best paid and most highly sought after public speaker in the North) and other oratorical militants increasingly urged their audiences to resort to physical destruction if more peaceable methods failed to stop federal slave catchers. On several occasions well-organized groups of abolitionists overwhelmed the marshals and spirited fugitives to safety. At other times they stored weapons, planned harassing maneuvers, and massed as intimidating mobs. In any case, most agreed with Phillips when he declared that any black American "should feel justified in using the law of God and man in shooting [any] officer" attempting to enforce the fugitive law.[36]

For African American activists, these appeals to arms and open defiance of slave catchers represented nothing new, but instead they built on militant traditions that could be traced back at least to David Walker's radical pamphlet *Appeal*, published in 1829. Leaders such as Douglass, Ward, and Garnet were hardly innovators when they declared in the 1850s that the killing of tyrants was obedience to God. Neither were the black insurgents in Detroit acting in isolation when they drove away federal marshals with volleys of paving stones. For white abolitionists, by contrast, the journey away from moral suasion was marked by ambivalence. From one perspective, moral suasion had yielded so little that more extreme measures seemed perfectly justifi-

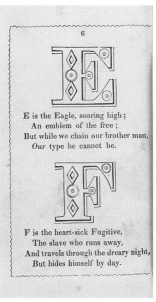

Antislavery Alphabet pamphlet, Philadelphia, 1847.

Hale Woodruff, "The Revolt," a depiction of the rebellion aboard the *Amistad* in 1839.

able. More than two decades of peacefully preaching against the sin of slavery had yielded not emancipation but several new slave states and an increase of over half a million held in bondage, trends that seemingly secured a death grip by the "slave power" on American life. As for the new Republican Party, its opposition to slavery appeared to many abolitionists, as Garrison put it, "mean, partial, dwarfed and twisted," blighted by white supremacy and an easy acceptance of slavery's continuance in the South.[37] Surely, none of this was progress.

Yet from a second perspective, the white abolitionists' commitment to pacifism upheld their movement's highly religious vision at a time when free soilers and proslavery settlers slaughtered each other in Kansas, and Senator Charles Sumner recuperated from a vicious beating he received from an enraged South Carolina congressman. Then, too, nonresistance had always

registered the white immediatists' sincere abhorrence of black insurrection. To jettison that conviction now was, perhaps, to embrace the prospect of servile revolt. That, however, is precisely what many white abolitionists began to do. A few quite consciously abandoned it, but most went through a hesitant process of rationalization that left them without defenses when they found themselves in the overpowering presence of the formidable John Brown.

"Old Brown" was truly a complex and dangerous man, endowed with a personality of immense authority. His magnetism, his skill at manipulating others, and his prophetic vision of God's retribution helped him to convince frustrated immediatists to support his cause of capturing the federal arsenal in Harpers Ferry, Virginia, arming the slaves, and inciting insurrection. During the 1850s he made a familiar figure of himself at abolitionist meetings, where he came to know many leading immediatists. All were well aware that Brown possessed a killer's instinct. It had been widely documented that he had butchered six unarmed settlers during the Kansas wars in 1857 and that leading abolitionists, Phillips among them, had given him money to purchase rifles and pikes. Now, as Brown laid plans for fomenting slave insurrection, immediatists again gave him cash and asked few questions. Some black activists, such as Harriet Tubman and Jermain Loguen, generally were aware of Brown's plotted insurrection, but they did not know where, when, or how. (Wendell Phillips suspected Brown's intentions but claimed no direct knowledge of them.) Among the most violence-prone abolitionists of all were those who knew all that Brown would tell them in exchange for directly financing his attack. These included Liberty Party leaders Gerrit Smith and Frederick Douglass, and in Boston four of Phillips's strong allies in the struggle against the Fugitive Slave Law of 1850: Thomas Wentworth Higginson, George Luther Stearns, Franklin L. Sanborn, and Samuel Gridley Howe. Brown satisfied these men's romantic desires to engage in conspiracy as well as their yearnings for creating a dramatic example of direct action that would shatter slavery.

After many weeks of preparation, Brown and his band of eighteen descended on Harpers Ferry, seized the arsenal, and were quickly routed by troops commanded by Colonel Robert E. Lee. As abolitionists everywhere rushed to embrace his insurrectionary deeds, Brown was arraigned, tried, sentenced, and hanged by Virginia authorities in December 1859. His raid can perhaps be best understood less as Brown's supreme act of will and more as the predictable result of the abolitionists' frustrat-

ing struggles in the unremitting cause of resistance, their ambivalent feelings about the Republican Party, and their mounting desires for a morally definitive confrontation with slavery.[38]

In the aftermath of Brown's raid, many abolitionists rallied around Brown's insurrection, while others, such as Garrison, attempted to separate their belief in the slaves' inherent right to rebel from Brown's act of terrorism. As usual, Phillips captured feelings of the insurrectionist's admirers unusually well. He proclaimed to an enormous audience in Boston's Faneuil Hall that Brown had "twice as much right to hang Governor Wise [of Virginia] as Governor Wise has to hang him." Brown's deeds, Phillips emphasized, did not aim at creating social chaos. Instead, Brown had sought to destroy a turbulent, anarchic society that had tormented the nation for nearly a century. The South itself was in "chronic insurrection," not John Brown, peopled by a "barbarous horde who gag each other, imprison women for teaching children to read, abolish marriage, condemn half their women to prostitution and devote themselves to the breeding of people for sale." By contrast, Brown at Harpers Ferry stood "as a representative of law, of

Augustus Washington, portrait of John Brown, ca. 1846.

"GET OFF THE TRACK!"

A song for Emancipation, sung by
THE HUTCHINSONS,
Respectfully dedicated to
NATH⁺ P. ROGERS,
As a mark of esteem for his intrepidity in the cause of Human Rights.—By the Author.
JESSE HUTCHINSON JUNⁱ.

Price 25 cts net
BOSTON

"Get Off the Track!" cover for sheet music by Jesse Hutchinson Jr., Boston. The Hutchinsons were a famous abolitionist family of singers. Note the use of antislavery newspaper titles and "railroad" language in the illustration.

government, of right, of justice, of religion." Brown, in short, embodied moral order, not insurrection, a rationalization that permitted Phillips and many other abolitionists to celebrate the bloody deeds of the most dangerous resister of all.[39]

With Abraham Lincoln's election as president in 1860, the full political significance of the abolitionists' long pilgrimage from moral suasion to resistance and (finally) to insurrection at last became clear. Long observation of the abolitionists' behavior over almost three decades had utterly convinced the slaveholders that exactly the opposite of what Phillips believed was the truth. The North, not the

South, had collapsed into anarchy. Race mixers, lawbreakers, and armed insurrectionists had overrun the (supposedly) free states. What once had been a civil society now wallowed in moral chaos. Despite all their reassurances about never meddling with slavery where it presently existed, Lincoln and the party he led were actually "black Republicans," no different in the final analysis than Frederick Douglass or Wendell Phillips. Fully alienated, the planters elected secession and commenced with civil war. In this respect the abolitionists influenced the course of the nation's history to an extent greatly disproportionate to their meager numbers. In the process, their work had also done much to prepare a white majority in the free states for its ultimate wartime reckoning with Southern slavery.[40]

Subsequent events would drive white Americans to recreate new forms of racial tyranny that continue into our time. Nevertheless, the history of resistance on the part of the abolitionists makes clear that at least some Americans before the Civil War entertained far more democratic visions of the nation's future. While the abolitionists continued their work throughout the Civil War and well into Reconstruction, their antebellum struggles had already secured their ultimate legacy. From 1831 to 1860 they had engaged the nation and one another honestly, exploring their movement's internal tensions and identifying its most fundamental obligations while making searching critiques of society's deep injustices. This compelling example of civic engagement gives the history of the abolitionists' struggles significance for their own age, and for ours.

PART TWO
STORIES OF THE
REAL UNDERGROUND
RAILROAD

JOHN MICHAEL VLACH

ABOVE GROUND ON THE UNDERGROUND RAILROAD

Places of Flight and Refuge

In 1855 Frederick Douglass complained that a flood of jubilant reports about successful escapes from slavery via the Underground Railroad was transforming that clandestine network into an *"Upper-*ground railroad." The net effect of these accounts, he thundered, was to provide slaveholders with useful advice on how they might prevent their bondsmen from running away. He counseled that it was best the ways and means of successful flight be kept a secret until the system of slavery was completely abolished.[1] While Douglass's caustic substitution of the word "upper" for "under" was meant chiefly to quell premature celebration of African American courage, the term also serves as a reminder that this famous resistance movement was carried out above ground.

Successful runaways necessarily had to pay careful attention to the varieties of terrain they encountered. They were always looking for opportune spaces and places where they could carry out their escapes. To appreciate fully their quests for freedom, we too must pay close attention to the places through which they traveled. The array of locales that offered opportunities for successful escape covered almost half of the United States. In order to make good on their plans to get away, slaves first had to choose a point of exit and then find their way through a sequence of protective sanctuaries. Given that slave catchers most closely patrolled the borders of the free states, runaway slaves had to look carefully for the most promising places of entry into the Northern states and then cautiously determine the safest routes for further travel. Eventually they had to focus on a final destination, a location they might claim as their new home. This place could have been in Canada, some Northern city, or a secluded rural haven created by free blacks.

An antislavery "moral map" of the United States, from *Legion of Liberty*, 1847.

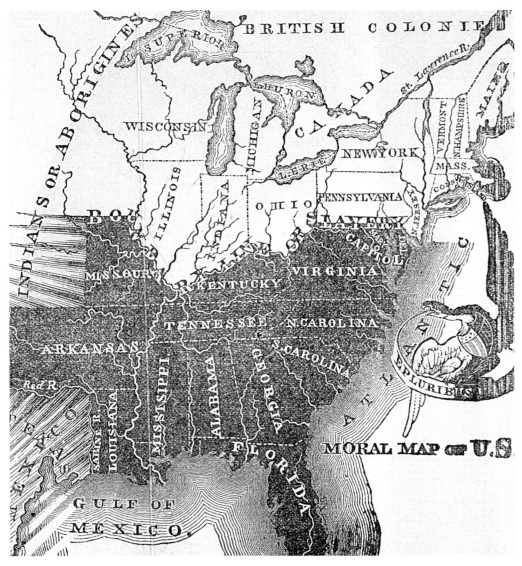

The range of places and pathways used by fugitive slaves might suggest a random, haphazard effort, but all of these locations and routes did coalesce, over time, into a coherent network. This "upper-ground railroad" emerged incrementally through the collective experience of numerous runaways. Slaves, being ever watchful for anything they might use to improve their lives, routinely noted the places where they could hide themselves should they ever decide to escape. With the lure of freedom as a powerful motivation, they paid careful attention to reports of preferred trails they might follow and of possible places where they could find shelter. They gradually learned that within the empire of slavery were means enough for a resourceful person to launch a successful quest for liberation. In fact, slaveholders unwittingly fostered their bondmen's hopes of escaping by telling them they would be poorly treated in the Northern states and Canada was a dismal, cold place. While visiting communities of successful escapees who had settled in Ontario, black abolitionist Samuel

Ringgold Ward learned of the unintended effects of slaveholders' campaigns of misinformation. Ward was told on several occasions, "We knew Canada was a good country for us because master was so anxious that we should *not* go there."[2]

Runaway slaves did not just wander aimlessly, hoping to meet up with a charitable person who would help them. Rather, they knew a good deal about how to get away and how to survive on their own. Often they chose to run off during the Christmas season, a period of time when slaves were routinely given passes permitting them to travel to other plantations in order to connect with family members who had been sold to nearby estates. During this time of year black people were regularly seen out on the road alone and thus were less likely to be stopped and questioned. The late fall season was another good time

to escape because farmers would have gathered and stored their harvest by then. A runaway could readily feed himself with rations pilfered during his journey, as William Wells Brown confirmed in his account of his escape across Ohio. "On the first night after my food was gone, I went to a barn on the road-side, and there found some ears of corn. I took ten or twelve of them, and kept on my journey. During the next day, while in the woods, I roasted my corn and feasted upon it." John P. Parker, a free black who also served as an Underground Railroad conductor, noted the resourcefulness of fugitive slaves and praised their ability to live off the land. Having assisted hundreds of them across the Ohio River, Parker identified them as superior people who were "usually strong physically, as well as people of character, and were resourceful when confronted with trouble, other wise they never would have escaped." He could have added that they were also skilled at reading and using the landscapes through which they traveled.[3]

Charles Gilpin, "W. Wells Brown," London, 1849.

WHO DROVE THE TRAIN?: GETTING BEYOND THE RAILROAD IMAGE

The Underground Railroad was neither underground nor a railroad but a multi-pronged attack on the system of chattel slavery carried out over a period of more than half a century. All those who took part in this lengthy and widespread expression of civil disobedience, both the runaways and their helpers, risked beatings, imprisonment, and other penalties. The Underground Railroad was, first of all, a community of conscience. While considerable

courage was required of all those involved,
the runaway slaves were most vulnerable,
and their actions should be judged as the
most valiant. Yet, the heroism of African
Americans is diminished by the use of railroad metaphors that divert most of the
attention to "conductors" and their "stations." Historian Larry Gara has convincingly documented the rise of a widespread
mythology about the Underground
Railroad during the last quarter of the
nineteenth century, a set of tales that
described a carefully organized conspiracy
managed by virtuous white people for the
benefit of pitiable blacks.[4] The Underground Railroad of popular legend casts
blacks mainly as the passive "customers"
who were fortunate enough to receive a
"ticket" allowing them to ride on the
"Liberty Line."

That a link would be forged between
escaping slaves and railroad imagery during the 1830s was understandable enough,
given that "railroad fever" was sweeping
across the United States during this period.
Steam-powered locomotives with such
inspirational names as Rocket, Racer,
Hercules, or Giant suggested the unparal-
leled power of the train as some thirty
thousand miles of track were under construction. The railroad quickly rose to
prominence as a compelling national sym-

bol suggestive of American efficiency, competence, and heroism. In such a context,
the editors of the Western Citizen, a Chicago
newspaper with abolitionist sympathies,
enthusiastically published a celebratory
notice about local Underground Railroad
activities and illustrated it with a train. In
the drawing a locomotive and its four cars
enter a tunnel that leads right to "Liberty-
ville, Upper Canada," and potential passengers are encouraged to apply for seats "at
any of the trap doors." Also in the 1830s a
Boston publishing firm issued sheet music
for the popular abolitionist song "Get Off
the Track!" The cover sheet included an
image of a locomotive named Liberator
pulling a car labeled "Immediate
Emancipation."

Railroading analogies were eventually
applied to all facets of the black quest for
freedom. Safe houses became "stations";
helpers might be referred to variously as
"conductors," "stationmasters," "superin-
tendents," or "stock holders"; pathways
between destinations were called "lines" or
"tracks"; and escaping slaves were identified
as "passengers" or "packages." Using this
form of coded speech, abolitionists framed
the struggle for African American emancipation as a problem that would be solved, at
least metaphorically, by employing the most
efficient and modern of machines. Their

solution to the problem of slavery was thus aligned with the ongoing national dilemma of how to best create a virtuous republic with the means provided by modern industrial technology.[5]

This view was quite alien and irrelevant to many African Americans. Their pursuit of personal freedom had nothing to do with the national goals of the United States. When former slave Arnold Gragston was asked if he was a participant in the Underground Railroad, he replied, "I don't know as we called it anything." Gragston, who had been a slave on a plantation in northern Kentucky, rowed many runaway blacks across the Ohio River toward their first steps on free soil. He acted not out of any sense of organized conspiracy against slavery but from a sense of moral mission. He understood from personal experience that, if given a choice, no one would want to be a slave. "We just knew there was a lot slaves always a-wantin' to get free, and I had to help 'em." Henry Bibb, a slave who had made his way safely to Canada, wrote in 1853 that "self-emancipation is now the order of the day." He had escaped from Missouri in 1837 after gathering the modest sum of $2.50 and a new suit of clothes. Agonized over the prospect of leaving his wife and child behind, he nevertheless sought his freedom alone. Bibb's behavior was typical of most runaways: they were mainly younger males who took off on their own. Historians John Hope Franklin and Loren Schweninger calculate that by the 1850s, 95 percent of all escaping slaves were running away alone or with only one or two companions. Illinois abolitionist W. H. Lyford confirmed this self-reliance in 1896. "I do not know of any fugitives ever being transported by anyone, they always had to pilot their own canoe, with the little help that they received." While some white conductors were very active, Lyford's testimony challenges common assumptions about the Underground Railroad. He suggests that the greatest number of fugitives were self-emancipating individuals who, upon reaching a point in their lives when they could no longer tolerate their captive status, finally just took off for what had to be a better place.[6]

RUNNING AWAY WITHIN THE SOUTH: SHORT- AND LONG-TERM ESCAPES

Southern plantations actually served as the training grounds for those most inclined to seek their freedom. It was a common practice among slaves to obtain at least a measure of temporary relief from their regimen of dawn-to-dusk labor by running away for short periods of time. Planters referred to this behavior as "absconding" or "lying out." While they did not approve of this absenteeism, slaveholders nevertheless tolerated such acts because, in most cases, the truants returned after a few days.[7] In fact, the whereabouts of their campsites were often known, and a slave emissary might even be dispatched to request that the fugitive return to the plantation. Periods of lying out can be viewed as trial runs for a future escape.

Often these plantation truants snuck back to the plantation to obtain provisions, sometimes stealing a few chickens or even a pig, before returning to their forested hideouts. M. E. Abrams, an ex-slave from

Images of lone fugitives became ubiquitous symbols of runaways in newspaper advertisements as well as in abolitionist literature. This one first appeared as the cover of the *Anti-Slavery Record* in July 1837.

South Carolina, testified, "We used to steal our hog ever sa'day night and take off to de gully whar us'd git him dressed and barbecued." Frederick Douglass recalled with considerable delight the frequent theft of pigs in order to supply the main course for a surreptitious feast held out in the woods. He referred to these regular occurrences as "crimes, high-handed and atrocious" that "could be committed there with strange and shocking impunity."[8] Paired with the risk of disobedience was the joy of winning a small victory over a master's claims of absolute control. Even if the theft of property seemed to be little more than an occasional nuisance to a slaveholder, such acts confirmed in the minds of slaves that a more substantial prize—personal liberty—was possible if planned carefully.

Short-term escapes were often used as bargaining tools in much the same way that factory workers employed strategic work stoppages to negotiate for better pay. Delicia Patterson, who served as a kitchen maid on a Missouri plantation, reported

that she ran away to the woods when she was reassigned to work in the fields. Her owner, Thomas Steele, sent word that if she would come back she could continue to work in the house. Upon her return she reported, "No one ever bothered me anymore either."[9] Brief escapes not only served to build the self-esteem of the absconding slave, but they also signaled to others that through bold action they too would be able to improve their lot. The next logical step for those who repeatedly fled for short periods was ultimately to run away for good.

In 1825 an entire slave family from Christ Church Parish in South Carolina ran into the woods, connected with a company of other fugitives, and managed to avoid being recaptured for three years. Prolonged escapes of this sort were a stage in the development of full-scale maroon societies, which were permanent outlaw communities of former slaves. According to Herbert Aptheker, fifty-nine maroon colonies were formed all across the South between 1672 and 1864, usually in places isolated by thick forests or formidable swamps. The fugitives living in these colonies did more than merely camp in the wilderness and launch raids on nearby farms. As far as they were able, maroons tried to establish a stable social life. A black outlaw community in Mobile County, Alabama, erected a formidable stockade fort to repel attacks by the state militia. Similarly, another group of runaways that settled in the marshes near Lumberton, North Carolina, set up a "very secure retreat," where they "had cleared a place for a garden, had cows, & c in the swamp." Maroons were sometimes able to create independent towns, communities that were noted not only for their black occupants but also for the chance they offered to elude a white master's grip.[10]

David Hunter Strother, "Horse Camp," from *Harper's New Monthly Magazine,* **September 1858. Maroons and teams of African American shingle cutters built these flimsy shelters in the more inaccessible portions of the Dismal Swamp.**

The best-known maroon settlement was located within the Great Dismal Swamp. Here, as many as two thousand former slaves were encamped throughout a thousand square-mile area of forested peat bog that straddled the Virginia–North Carolina border. Sustaining themselves by hunting, fishing, and gardening, they lived in the deepest, least-accessible areas of the swamp and were regarded as dangerous people by whites and other blacks alike. When landscape architect Frederick Law Olmstead visited the Great Dismal in 1856, he was told of maroons who had been born in the swamp and subsequently lived their entire lives in "huts in 'back places' hidden by bushes, and difficult of access." Ishreal Massie, a former slave from nearby Greenville County, Virginia, described how slaves who ran away to the swamps—or dismals, as they were called—built subterranean houses that allowed them to avoid detection and capture.

David Hunter Strother, "Osman," from *Harper's New Monthly Magazine*, September 1858. This drawing was based on Strother's chance meeting with a black man whom he took to be a Dismal Swamp maroon.

We had one slave dat runned away an' he had a vault in th' woods fixed jes like dis room an' he had a wife an' two boys dat he raised under dar. . . . Dar wuz a hole cut in de groun'. I don' cut many a one an' stole lumber at night to kiver hit over wid. Den dirt was piled on top of dis plank so dat hit won't rain in dr. Den he had him some piping—trough-like—made of wood dat runned so many feet in de groun'. Dis carried smoke away from dis cave. Fer fire [he] used oak bark 'cause hit didn't give much smoke. He had him a hole to come up on lan'. Dar wuz sticks, pine beard, and trash to kiver de hole. . . . Ya could stan' right over dis hole an' wouldn' now it.

That Massie visited this cleverly camouflaged den on several occasions indicates that the survival techniques practiced by maroons were also known to the slaves who remained on plantations. Enslaved blacks viewed these communities as the sites of full-fledged liberty and considered them a reasonable response to the problem of their captivity. Massie reported with an appreciative laugh that his half-brother who built the "cave" house was able to live there "until Lee surrendered."[11]

Those slaves who ran away from Georgia and South Carolina to find refuge among the Seminole Indians in Florida are generally not thought of as travelers on the Underground Railroad, yet their quest for liberty is undeniable, even if Canada was not their goal. Indeed, the practice of escaping southward had a long history. So many took advantage of the possibility of freedom in Florida that in 1739 the Spanish governor was able to garrison a fort on the outskirts of Saint Augustine exclusively with fugitive slaves. Called Fort Mose, it was the first known free black community in North America. (See chapter 5 for more on Fort Mose.)

Late in the eighteenth century the Seminoles began to absorb black fugitives into their communities. During the series of battles with the United States Army that have come to be known as the Seminole Wars (1817–18, 1835–42, 1855–58), black men proved to be very effective fighters. Understanding that defeat meant they would be returned to bondage, they were so ferocious in battle that General Thomas S. Jesup was moved to write in one of his field reports, "This, you may be assured, is a negro, not an Indian war. . . ."[12]

African Americans first joined with the Seminoles when the Indians were living on the banks of the Apalachicola River in the panhandle area of Florida. Over the course of the Seminole Wars the various Indian villages were forced to move, first to the Alachua Prairie near Saint Augustine and finally to the Everglades in southern Florida. Regardless of the duress caused by forty years of skirmishes, the Seminole always organized their villages into parallel camps, one for Indians and the other for blacks. This pattern shows up clearly on General Andrew Jackson's battle map for his 1818 attack on Chief Bowlegs's village along the shores of the Suwannee River. The evident segregation was intended not to marginalize the black Seminoles but to provide them with the greatest possible domestic autonomy.[13]

African Americans, it seems, brought with them a typical Southern settlement pattern in which buildings were most often set out in casual semicircles. While no surviving documents indicate exactly what kinds of houses the black Seminoles built for themselves, considerable extant evidence suggests that they intended to create enduring communities on the lands provided by their Indian partners. Their town of Peliklakaha in central Florida had, according to a merchant-diplomat who traveled through the region in 1823, one hundred acres cultivated in corn, rice, and peanuts as well as a herd of cattle. They may have lived in buildings made of round logs notched at the ends. This typical mode of pioneer housing on the Southern frontier was used by freeholder and slave alike. Moreover, a group of black Seminoles that was able to escape to the Bahamas in 1828 built there what were recalled as "pole houses," while another group that returned to Texas in 1870 after two decades of exile in Mexico also built cabins with poles. By constructing log houses near Concho, Texas, these black Seminoles signaled their intent to claim a territory in their own way.[14]

Renty Grayson, a black Seminole scout, was a descendent of fugitive slaves who escaped into Florida.

RUNNING AWAY ON THE WATER: MARITIME MEANS OF ESCAPE

When he was just eighteen years old, Frederick Douglass realized it was possible to sail to one's freedom rather than face the daunting challenges of running to the woods. One day while gazing out on what he termed "the noble waters of the Chesapeake," he recognized that this vast estuary might serve as "a broad road of destruction to slavery." Douglass was not alone in realizing that waterways offered an effective route of escape from the South. Indeed, records from eighteenth-century Virginia indicate that 14 percent of all runaways were watermen who fled in stolen vessels. The most ambitious attempt at a maritime escape occurred in 1848 in Washington, DC, when abolitionist William L. Chaplin arranged passage to Philadelphia for seventy-seven blacks aboard the sailing schooner *Pearl*. The whole group was recaptured when this ill-fated ship was found becalmed on Chesapeake Bay. While the plot proved a failure, it demonstrated that slavery was clearly vulnerable to the possibility of a maritime escape.[15]

In his account of Underground Railroad activity, William Still, corresponding secretary for the Pennsylvania Anti-Slavery Society, carefully recorded the stories of many fugitives who arrived safely in Philadelphia via boats and ships. In 1859 William Peel of Baltimore had himself wrapped in straw, secured in a wood crate, and then shipped to his abolitionist colleagues by the regularly scheduled coastal steamer. A few years earlier five slaves from Portsmouth, Virginia, several of whom had worked as oystermen and thus were quite familiar with small vessels, commandeered a skiff and sailed out into the Atlantic and up through Delaware Bay. Similarly, four men from Lewes, Delaware, stole a small boat and rowed themselves for a day and a night through a fierce gale over to the south Jersey shore. Thoroughly exhausted by the rigors of their crossing, they had the good fortune to be discovered by a sympathetic captain of an oyster schooner, who piloted them up to Philadelphia. Others, such as Susan Brooks of Norfolk, Virginia, found a way to get aboard a northbound ship. Boldly explaining to the officer on deck that she was just a laundress delivering some freshly pressed

Louise Minks, *Ocean Passage*, 2002.

shirts, Brooks took the opportunity to hide below decks until the vessel had reached its final destination. The escape of Savannah slave Edward Davis in 1854 proved considerably more challenging. He came to be known as the "saltwater fugitive" because he chose to hide himself in a tiny space in the bow of the steamship *Keystone State*. There, the waves swept over him repeatedly from the moment the ship left Georgia until it reached the mouth of the Delaware River three days later. Calling for help in a hesitant whisper, he was found near death from exposure to the icy water and the constant buffeting he had endured.[16] Year after year, Still recorded successful, albeit always challenging, passages to freedom made by African Americans willing to travel over the water.

Maritime escapes proved to be so effective mainly because so many free men of color served as sailors. Their considerable numbers effectively converted rivers, coastal trading lanes, and even the vast Atlantic Ocean into places where potential escapes could be successfully carried out. Records of all the seamen known to have shipped out of Providence, New York, Philadelphia, Baltimore, and Savannah between the years 1803 and 1866 reveal that, on average, 14 percent of them were African American. In some years the number of black sailors operating out of a particular port might be considerably higher. In 1836, for example, 31 percent of the men who signed up for berths on Providence ships were black. Interestingly, this was also the year when 41 percent of Providence's African American seamen served as members of all-black crews. The sight of vessels operated by men of color from bow to stern was not uncommon; 40 percent of Baltimore's African American sailors went to sea as members of all-black crews in 1857. Consequently, any slave looking to escape from the South via an ocean route could find willing accomplices in one of the region's port cities. Tom Wilson, who escaped from New Orleans in 1858, reported that "some of the coloured crew of the American cotton ship *Metropolis* took me on board, and hid me away among the bales." Wilson testified further that these men protected and fed him throughout a three-week voyage until he reached safety in Liverpool, England. An almost identical escape was arranged for William Grimes, who fled from Savannah in 1818 aboard the brig *Casket*. He was hidden on deck in a prearranged space within the ship's cargo of cotton bales. When the vessel sailed beyond the sight of land, the crew gave

three cheers to signal Grimes that he was now a free man.[17]

Because the economy of the antebellum South focused chiefly on the production of agricultural commodities, the growth of its cities lagged far behind the urban centers of the North. The most prominent Southern cities were almost all port towns located around the region's coastal and riverine boundaries. From their wharves great harvests of cotton, rice, or sugar were shipped to various destinations. That Southern cities served mainly as exit points for agricultural produce also offered fugitive slaves one of their best chances to escape. One frustrated planter described Wilmington, North Carolina, as "an asylum for Runaways," not only because it was an active port but also because its population was largely black. Indeed, 52 percent of all Wilmington residents were slaves in 1840.[18]

The mere presence of slaves in a city proved problematic to slaveholders because in order to perform their assigned tasks, these captive men and women had to be out and about on their own. According to Frederick Douglass, a city slave, being so frequently beyond an owner's immediate scrutiny, was "almost a free citizen." Given that Southern port cities were populated by large numbers of slaves as well as by sizeable populations of free blacks, a fugitive slave escaping from the countryside might readily find an ally to provide shelter and assistance. This was particularly true upon reaching the waterfront. In any harbor a runaway encountered black fishermen, stevedores, carpenters, caulkers, sailmakers, blacksmiths, chandlers, hucksters, roustabouts, and ferrymen, in addition to sailors, pilots, and even a few ship's captains, such as George Henry and Moses Grandy. The feeling of quasi-liberty that characterized urban slavery was heightened even more at the water's edge, where black people managed many of the essential tasks required to get the great masted ships under way. Well placed to facilitate escapes, black workers regularly helped fugitives hide amidst the piles of goods standing on the docks until a vessel could carry them away. For runaway slaves, the harbor districts of New Orleans, Mobile, Savannah, Charleston, Norfolk, and other port cities opened a potential doorway to liberty.[19]

FLEEING TO NORTHERN HAVENS: THE PROTECTION OF RURAL ENCLAVES

The Fugitive Slave Act of 1850 armed Southern slaveholders with the means to reclaim bondmen who had fled to the states above the Mason-Dixon line. The passage of this controversial law meant that blacks would now have to run all the way to Canada if they wanted to live with certainty as free people. Some of them, however, discovered another solution: they sought out rural enclaves established by free blacks all across the Northern states. There they could either receive trustworthy guidance for the next move on their journey or simply stay put and essentially become Northern maroons. This "halfway" escape offered personal freedom and the supportive fellowship of a black community, while it eliminated the need for a lengthy and more dangerous passage.

Snow Hill, established in the wooded outskirts of Haddonfield, New Jersey, was one such place where a runaway slave might find shelter. Mary Thomas, a black woman born in this community in 1874,

explained that "so many people came from Maryland that they changed the name of the little village to Snow Hill, which was the name of the town nearest the farms from Maryland all or most of the people had run away from." When Ralph Smith, secretary of the Philadelphia Vigilance Committee, first purchased this tract of land in 1840, he called it, appropriately enough, "Free Haven." Feeling the strong urge to take charge of their lives and their new home, the Maryland fugitives selected a name that would always signal the first step of their journey toward freedom. The town was called Snow Hill until 1907, when the US Post Office changed the community's name to Lawnside, allegedly to accommodate the request of the Reading–Atlantic City Railroad.[20]

One surviving house from the antebellum period suggests something of the way of life for African Americans living in Snow Hill-Free Haven during its first decades. Built by Peter Mott around 1845, this modest wood frame house conveys both his skills as a carpenter and his desire to stay put. Mott, who also served as preacher at the Snow Hill Church (now the Mount Pisgah African Methodist Episcopal

The Peter Mott House, Lawnside, New Jersey.

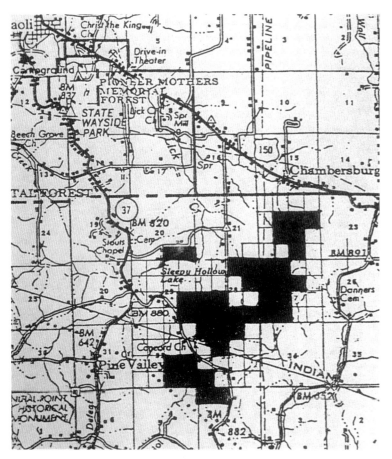

Total acreage owned by the African American community in the Lick Creek Settlement, Orange County, Indiana, in 1855. From Robbins, *Forgotten Hoosiers*, 1994.

support of a Quaker community in the nearby town of Mount Holly. Here, a small group of free and fugitive blacks cleared lands for their farms and built themselves a school and a church. The citizens of Mount Holly occasionally visited the settlement when they held camp meetings on the shores of Rancocas Creek, which ran past the village. While the approximately 125 black residents of Timbuctoo went largely unnoticed, they were not immune to threats. In 1860 slave catchers from Delaware came to Timbuctoo searching for Perry Simmons. A black man who had lived there for twelve years, Simmons vowed not to be taken alive, and he held off his attackers with two rifles and an axe while an alarm was raised throughout the village. In what was described in a local newspaper as the "Battle of Pine Swamp," the citizens of Timbuctoo protected Simmons and drove off his attackers. To make such a show of force against white people was always a risky proposition for blacks, even when they had just cause to do so. That the citizens of Timbuctoo rose so quickly to the defense of one of their own reveals both the intensity of their bonds of community and their shared sense of vulnerability.[22]

The rugged, hilly terrain across the southern portions of the Midwestern states, some parts of which are still covered by stands of first-growth forest, provided excellent protective cover for runaway slaves. Among the first black settlers to enter the region were former slaves who had attained their freedom either via official manumission or by self-purchase. One group of black migrants reached Lawrence County, Ohio, where they established a cluster of farmsteads they called Pokepatch. Located only twenty miles from

Church), probably felt that it was his duty to set a positive example for other blacks. He accomplished this, in part, by constructing a home that was four times the size of the average sixteen-feet-by-sixteen-feet slave cabin.[21] His was definitely the home of a free man who had run to freedom but now would run no more. Something akin to Mott's sense of purpose and striving is manifested as well by the longevity of the Snow Hill community itself. Some of its original settler families still live near Lawnside after more than 150 years.

Not far from Snow Hill was the black community of Timbuctoo, known to some as Buckto or Bucktown. This exotically named settlement of small farms was established sometime around 1825 with the

the Ohio River, this community regularly sheltered fugitive slaves, some of whom decided to stay on as residents. The origins of the Lick Creek Settlement just south of Chambersburg, Indiana, parallel the formation of Pokepatch. In this case, groups of blacks from Virginia and North Carolina, traveling in the company of Quaker settlers, began to arrive in Indiana in 1832. Carrying certificates of freedom, they quickly acquired forty-acre parcels, the smallest units the federal land office could sell them. Over the next three decades their farms prospered and they increased their holdings. Many doubled the size of their farms, and one man was able to acquire an additional 140 acres. One hundred seventeen African Americans resided along the banks of Lick Creek in 1850 and stood ready to assist fugitives headed north out of Owensboro, Kentucky.[23]

During the 1840s groups of free blacks were forced out of Tennessee because whites feared their presence would induce slaves to riot. Some of these black families found their way into the Shawnee Hills region of southern Illinois. In a rugged area of upland forest riven by steep sandstone canyons they organized a community called Miller Grove, in honor of one of their pioneer families. These black Tennesseans developed small farms and built a church and a school, all protected by the seclusion of the wilderness.[24] A stable community, Miller Grove endured until the 1920s. All of these black settlements, while located deep within a thick virgin forest, were no more than a journey of one or two days from the Ohio River. Fugitive slaves who found their way to one of these black "islands" were offered not only a place to rest but also evidence of the better life that awaited them outside the South. Hidden places like these

were probably their first evidence of the promise of freedom. Here, they could judge for themselves what black people might accomplish if given the opportunity to master their own lives.

In contrast, nothing secret or clandestine surrounded the town of New Philadelphia. Laid out in 1836 on the rolling prairies of Pike County, Illinois, under the direction of former slave Frank McWhorter, the town's boundaries enclosed an area of forty acres. Designed with a grid pattern of prominent avenues, the town was sectioned into twenty blocks that were subdivided further into 144 individual lots.[25] Even though New Philadelphia never attracted many residents, it was nevertheless a promising prairie village as well as an active way station for fugitive slaves on their way to Canada. Crossed by two major roads—one of them ran due east from the Mississippi River—the town was easy for runaways to find. Moreover, McWhorter, who was also known as Free Frank, had a reputation for generosity. A former slave, he was always a sympathetic host to runaway blacks. Since one of his sons had previously lived in Canada for several years,

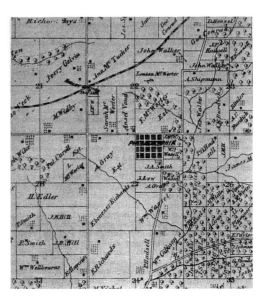

Portion of Hadley Township, Pike County, Illinois, showing the town of New Philadelphia, founded by Free Frank McWhorter, as well as McWhorter's farm and the holdings of some of his family members. From *Atlas Map of Pike County, Illinois*, 1872.

he also had useful information about what they might expect to find there. Admittedly, Free Frank had developed his town primarily in the hope of becoming a wealthy land speculator, but he did not forget his obligation to his people. Under his direction, New Philadelphia became an ideal refuge for the harried fugitive.

As runaway slaves slipped farther away from the South, their chances of being recaptured diminished considerably. Some groups of blacks that had been guided northward into Michigan via a network of Quaker safe houses decided that they had traveled far enough when they reached Cass County. About fifty of them decided to settle in Penn and Calvin Townships. They may have been attracted by the presence of a community of forty-seven former slaves from Cabell County, Virginia. Their former owner, Sampson Saunders, had granted their freedom as a condition of his will, and he provided them with $15,000, which they used to acquire 485 acres of land as well as the necessary equipment to start their own farms. The efforts of local farmer Stephen Bonine further confirmed Cass County's status as a freedom destination. He offered fugitive slaves small tracts on his thousand-acre farm if they would promise to clear and develop their assigned parcels. Their plots of five to ten acres scattered randomly across his property came to be known as Ramptown.[26]

THE ARCHITECTURE OF ESCAPE: VARIETIES OF SAFE HOUSES

It is often claimed that Underground Railroad stations included special features that could be used to hide slaves from their pursuers: a place under the floor accessible only by a trap door, a secret space behind a particular wooden panel in the hallway, or an area behind a knee wall up in the attic. The most impressive stations are those said to be equipped with tunnels extending from the cellar to a safe location as much as a hundred yards beyond the house, if not more. Recent attempts to verify the presence and use of such architectural features, however, generally show them to be elements of fanciful legend. Explicit searches for tunnels in reputed stations confirm that either there never was a tunnel or the remnants of old cisterns had been mistaken for the entrances to tunnels. Further, the cellars, trap doors, crawl spaces, and storage spaces tucked behind knee walls that all seem so exotic to us today usually prove to be nothing more than the normal details of the average nineteenth-century house. That they are presented as tangible proof of Underground Railroad activity is evidence mainly of the persuasive power of the mythology surrounding its legend and of attempts to project a current belief onto past events. The legend of the Underground Railroad, writes historian Larry Gara, portrayed abolitionists as unfailingly kind people who led groups of apprehensive slaves toward the happy ending of a better life on free soil. He cautions, "The actual men and women of the abolition movement, like the slaves themselves, are far too complex to fit into a melodrama."[27] Similarly, the thousands of safe houses, when viewed collectively, also constitute a complex and varied array of structures that cannot be made to fit a single standardized profile.

A survey of those buildings with unassailable credentials as Underground Railroad stations would include homes,

churches, schools, mills, warehouses, stables, barns, and various smaller outbuild-
ings. The houses might be simple structures, such as the Todd House in Tabor,
Iowa, a small wood frame dwelling consist-
ing principally of two rooms with a loft;
substantial townhouses constructed with
thick stone walls, similar to the William
Johnson House in Germantown, Pennsylvania; or mansions much like William
Seward's residence in Auburn, New York, a
rambling brick edifice constructed in several stages over a period of thirteen years.
Stations might stand at the edge of forested
wilderness, on open farmland, in small
towns, or in the middle of thriving cities.
Most of them were modest houses, garbed
with just enough decoration to signal the
cautious expression of respectable middle-
class taste. That they did not usually stand
out from neighboring houses helped to
deflect suspicion from the subversive acts
transpiring inside.

Contrary to popular legends, very few
Underground Railroad stations were outfitted with secret hiding places. Most fugitive
slaves were sheltered in existing rooms and
spaces, such as cellars, attics, extra bedrooms, or barn lofts, to name a few. Levi
Coffin operated an active station in
Newport (now Fountain City), Indiana,
where, over a period of twenty years, he
claimed to have given refuge to approximately two thousand fugitives. Even though
it was a bit inconvenient at times, he simply
had them sleep on bedrolls that he and his
wife laid out on the floor of the kitchen.
Frederick Douglass did much the same at
his home in Rochester, New York, recounting how on one occasion eleven black
escapees were "provided a strip of carpet on
the floor for a bed." Similarly, when Harriet
Beecher Stowe visited Lewis Hayden's com-

Levi Coffin House, Fountain City, Indiana.

RIGHT: Lewis Hayden House, Boston, built in 1833. Hayden first rented the house in 1844 and finally purchased it in 1853. Many fugitive slaves passing through Boston took refuge in this house and its surrounding neighborhood, located in today's Beacon Hill district.

hunters were so close on his trail that a Mr. Brown of Bloomfield thought it best for Green not to stay at his farm. Instead, Brown erected a small hut out in the middle of a nearby marsh, a place where his pursuers definitely would not look. Green, after "laying out" for a few days, continued on to Canada without incident. A certain measure of caution and the prudent use of available spaces were generally all that was required to hide a slave from pursuers.[29]

Some safe houses were indeed outfitted with specially constructed rooms, but those buildings prove to be rare exceptions. Given the considerable number of fugitives moving through the busiest stations, tiny closets and cramped crawl spaces would simply not have provided enough space. The resourcefulness demonstrated by so many stationmasters indicates that any house—even a rather small one—could effectively hide runaway slaves. What was needed most was

pact row house on Boston's Beacon Hill, she reported that she encountered thirteen runaways on the premises. Sometimes an upstairs space might be used to hide fugitives if greater privacy or protection were required. Coffin recalled that after he moved into a townhouse in Cincinnati runaway slaves were kept in the third-floor bedrooms. "Our house was large and well adapted for secreting fugitives," Coffin reported. "Very often slaves would lie concealed in upper chambers for weeks without the boarders or frequent visitors at the house knowing anything about it."[28]

Since many slaves traversed extensive tracts of Midwestern farmland, barns were frequently offered as places for a night's shelter. The farms owned by Aaron Benedict in Morrow County, Ohio, and by Seth Marshall in Lake County, Ohio, are two sites where fugitive slaves were quartered. In fact, during one month in 1855, sixty of them stayed in Benedict's barn. Temporary shelters were also improvised by arranging piles of firewood or stacks of hay and straw with open spaces hidden in their centers. When George Green was making his way across Ohio, the slave

a person willing to undertake the challenges of running a station, someone who was ready to endure social censure, threats from slave catchers, personal assaults, and even imprisonment. A station's appearance gave no hint that anything unusual or illegal might be occurring within its walls. Its secret was not that it contained special hiding places but that the station's operator was convinced of the evils of slavery. Stations on the Under-ground Railroad were created mainly by acts of courage and conscience rather than by clever carpentry.

While the actions of station operators were generally cloaked by a veil of secrecy, the Reverend John Rankin was one operator who made a bold public display of his Underground Railroad activities. A Southerner by birth, he had long been dismayed by the practice of chattel slavery. Opposed to the slave-owning practices he encountered in Tennessee and Kentucky, he moved his family to Ripley, Ohio, a small town of four hundred people on the shores of the Ohio River. Here, in 1822, he immediately began to help slaves who were running away from plantation captivity by offering them assistance in the usual private manner. Six years later he moved to a new house built on the highest point of the hill overlooking the town. There he put his role as a conductor for the Underground Railroad on full public display. Standing as it did in the middle of a twenty-acre parcel of open land, the house was plainly visible from the Kentucky side of the Ohio River. The building stood out like a fortress on a battle line: it was an intentional declaration of Rankin's willingness to oppose slavery. Runaways arrived at his door every week. At times he had as many as a dozen people waiting in his barn while he arranged for a wagon that would carry them northward to the next station. To ensure further that fugitive blacks would know which was his house, every night he raised a lantern to the top of a flagpole in his front yard. According to former slave Arnold

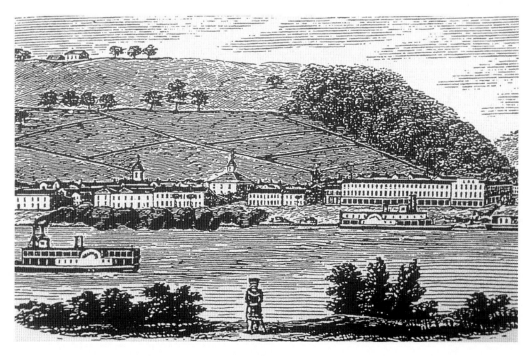

Ripley, Ohio, seen from the Kentucky side of the Ohio River, 1846. The Rankin House stood at the top of the hill.

Gragston, "Mr. Rankins had a regular station for the slaves. He had a big lighthouse in his yard, about thirty feet high, and he kept it burning all night. It always meant freedom for the slave if he could get to this light." By transforming his house into a highly visible gateway to freedom, day and night alike, Rankin aggressively dared slave owners to stop him. While bounties in excess of $2,500 were offered for his death, Rankin managed to evade his assailants while helping to liberate almost three thousand African Americans.[30]

Crucial to the success of many white stationmasters were the partnerships they formed with their African American neighbors. When Rankin first began to help slaves escape from Kentucky, he usually forwarded them to his abolitionist allies in Sardinia, a village some twenty miles away. Over the years he realized that he could get his refugee charges to safety more quickly by sending them to one of the nearby "Negro settlements." Levi Coffin recalled that the local black community in Newport was the first to take in arriving runaways. His chief role was then to provide them with adequate clothing, food, and transportation to their next destination. He later developed alliances with free blacks in Cincinnati and regularly employed black men as wagon drivers. Thomas Garrett, the much lionized stationmaster in Wilmington, Delaware, relied on black men to serve as guides for groups of slaves attempting to escape from Maryland. Foremost among them was Samuel D. Burris, who was once captured while leading runaways across Delaware. Garrett's compatriots had to rescue Burris from the auction block.[31]

Elmira, New York, was home to many abolitionists, including such noteworthy men as Jervis Langdon and Thomas Beecher. They provided shelter in their homes for runaway slaves but counted on their black neighbor, John W. Jones, himself a former slave from Virginia, to guide the escapees up to Lake Ontario, where they might find a vessel to transport them to Canada. From 1851 to 1860 Jones reportedly led some eight hundred African Americans to freedom. Dr. Julius Lemoyne, who joined the American Anti-Slavery Society in 1837, not only became an active promoter of abolitionist events but also offered his home in Washington, Pennsylvania, as a place of shelter for runaway slaves. Free blacks living in the surrounding county had already established a network of escape routes leading from Virginia northward to Pittsburgh. Three of these pathways ran through Washington very close to Lemoyne's house.[32]

The partnership between blacks and whites in the cause of freedom was readily apparent in Boston, where the Massachusetts Anti-Slavery Society was fully integrated. Over the years, however, a clear division of labor evolved among the organization's members. Runaway slaves were usually sequestered somewhere within the black enclave on the north side of Beacon Hill, while whites made arrangements for their passage by boat or train to Canada.[33] Not too surprisingly, the Underground Railroad seems to have functioned most efficiently in places where strong connections extended across the usual dividing lines of race.

CANADIAN SANCTUARY: FINAL FREEDOM IN THE QUEEN'S DOMINIONS

Slaves fleeing to Canada most often settled in the province of Ontario, which was then known as Canada West. Of the approximately 17,000 black people residing in Ontario in 1861, roughly 9,800 of them were born in the United States, and of this group not more than 3,400 identified themselves as having been born in one of the slave states.[34] These fugitives, understandably wary about living in what they saw as an unfamiliar country, tended to remain close to their point of entry. Those who arrived via Detroit settled near Amherstburg, Dresden, and Windsor, while those who entered through Buffalo generally went no farther than the nearby towns of Saint Catherine's and Hamilton. The first black fugitives to reach western Ontario assumed the role of pioneers as they acquired and cleared tracts of forested land. Of these people, Samuel Gridley Howe, a member of the Freedmen's Inquiry Commission, wrote:

> Those who have come from the United States, within a year or two, live in a log cabin, in a small cleared lot; round which is the forest or wild land. Older settlers have built houses, cleared larger fields; and they keep a cow, a pig, and some poultry. A few have well-cleared farms and good outbuildings, with plenty of farm tools, horses, oxen, cows, and the like.[35]

What Howe found most remarkable was that homes constructed by blacks were, in his estimation, identical to those built by whites. To him, it seemed the fugitives had quickly learned to live like Canadians.

The first African American settlers in Canada West did more than clear the land: they put their own distinctive marks on it. Many of them had come from Kentucky, and almost immediately they began to raise burley tobacco, a crop they had previously cultivated on plantations. Pungent tobacco fields, together with their crops of hemp

and droves of hogs, made the area around Amherstburg seem like a piece of the American South that had been transferred to Canada. Most important to these black settlers was not the crops they raised but rather their discovery that they might at last be recognized as persons. They concentrated on proving their competence as productive citizens by building schools and homes. Education and the ownership of property were, according to black leader Josiah Henson, the "two great means by which our oppressed and degraded race could be elevated to enjoy a participation

in the blessings of civilisation, whereas they had hitherto been permitted to share only its miseries and vices."[36]

New black settlements established across Ontario were brimming with optimism, especially in the larger black towns. Dawn, founded in 1842 as a labor school for former slaves, suggested hopefulness just by its name alone. By the 1850s it was home to five hundred black settlers who had cleared two thousand acres and built a sawmill, gristmill, rope factory, and a brickyard. These settlers went so far as to send a load of their best timber to England, where it was put on display at the Crystal Palace. The Refugee Home Society was another sizeable colony founded to shelter former slaves. Established near Amherstburg in 1851, its one hundred fifty families were each given twenty-five-acre plots to farm in any manner desired. Of all the attempts to create black villages, Buxton proved to be the most enduring and successful. It was overtly marked with signs of liberation. The town's name honored British abolitionist Thomas Fowell Buxton, and one of its principal streets was called Wilberforce to recall the efforts of the famous antislavery advocate William Wilberforce. By 1860 the community boasted of several thriving businesses, including a sawmill, brickyard, potash factory, blacksmith shop, and two hotels. Its three hundred families brought almost five thousand acres under cultivation.[37]

Buxton was a carefully planned model city laid out in a long gridiron pattern to underscore order and a clear sense of place. Visitors admired its solidly constructed dwelling houses, which were carefully aligned exactly thirty-three feet back from the road. Further, each house had a large garden where family members could raise whatever vegetables they desired. When Buxton resident Mary Jane Robinson wrote to a friend who had remained in Brooklyn, she was almost giddy with delight. She bragged that in Buxton, "We had turnips as big as the crown of your husband's hat, and cabbages as large as a water-pail. O, don't laugh for it's a fact—for the ground is so rich it raises up everything in no time." Her portrayal of this new black town as a place of almost edenic abundance stemmed, no doubt, from her excitement of being, for the first time, able to manage her own life. No doubt, she also marveled at the efforts of her neighbors, all of whom had homes and gardens just like hers. More pointed was the comment made by Joseph Tabor. From his new home in Saint Catherine's, Tabor wrote to his former owner back in Virginia, "I have enjoyed more pleasure with one month here than in all my life in the land of bondage."[38]

THE UNDERGROUND RAILROAD AS A LANDSCAPE OF FREEDOM

During the antebellum era Southern newspapers were filled with advertisements offering rewards for the return of escaped slaves. These notices were always accompanied by an image of a black person walking in full stride while carrying a small bundle of possessions, as if to suggest that an overland route was the assumed path of escape. In reality, runaway slaves used whatever mode of travel might prove most promising. Ships were to Frederick Douglass "freedom's swift-winged angels, that fly round the world." Others escaped by appropriating horses and carriages. One group, assisted by Levi Coffin, received tickets for the night train to Cleveland. James Lindsey Smith made his way from Heathsville, Virginia, to Norwich, Connecticut, in 1838 traveling by canoe, on foot, aboard a series of ships and boats, and finally on foot again.[39]

Just as runaway slaves might sometimes have to decide among various modes of travel, so too might they choose from a range of potential places of refuge. Their first priority was to rid themselves of slavery's indignities: the daily drudgery, the constant surveillance, the seemingly endless list of capricious cruelties. They could achieve this goal by escaping to a number of sites, from the nearby woods or a maroon camp, to the nearest city, a town in a Northern state, or even another country. While some of these places certainly offered more advantages than others, all options were worth considering. It is important to remember that those slaves who ran just beyond a plantation's fence lines for only a brief time were as much involved in an Underground Railroad action as were those who might have fled all the way to Canada.

African Americans struck out against slavery using all available means, environmental as well as tactical. While helped on occasion by white people, escaping slaves most often trusted only themselves and other blacks. Noted Ohio abolitionist James Birney confirmed this pattern of black self-reliance in a letter written in 1837, in which he told how a slave couple had arrived in Cincinnati by steamboat and had been passed on safely via stagecoach toward Canada. "Such matters are almost uniformly managed by the colored people. I know nothing of them generally till they are passed."[40]

Thinking about the Underground Railroad as a user-determined system allows us to focus on the choices a slave might make on his or her own behalf. Landscapes of flight and refuge, places that provided the means of both escape and shelter, were carefully assessed during these perilous journeys toward freedom. The ways in which African Americans navigated through this loosely linked array of spaces reveals both their intelligence and their bravery. It was regularly remarked, by slaveholder and abolitionist alike, that runaway slaves were "uncommonly bright," shrewd "men of mark," and "persons of superior talents."[41] They were thoroughly capable of reading the places and spaces through which they traveled. This ability was crucial to finding those passages and destinations of freedom they so ardently desired.

JANE LANDERS

SOUTHERN PASSAGE

The Forgotten Route to Freedom in Florida

The Underground Railroad's central place in American history and memory is constructed within a fairly consistent temporal and geographic framework. The dramatic escapes organized by such well-known figures as Harriet Tubman, William and Ellen Craft, Henry "Box" Brown, and others have been immortalized not only in scholarly works and school textbooks but also in movies, historic markers, land and house registries, monuments, and other forms of public memorialization. A quick look at the numerous Web sites now devoted to the Underground Railroad confirms that the popular perception of the "railroad" is that it operated in the decades leading to the Civil War and that its route took Southern slaves northward to freedom—and eventually across the international border to Canada. In fact, the very use of the terms "railroad" and "conductor" reinforces this Northern and late antebellum conception. However, if the historical objective of such memorialization is to acknowledge the steadfast determination of slaves to become free through flight, one must look to a much earlier time and track a Southern passage that has been largely forgotten.[1] More than a century before escaped slaves established the famed Underground Railroad of the antebellum period, hundreds of Africans risked their lives to flee southward—to Spanish Florida. Taking astute advantage of the international border and the political and religious enmity existing between Spain and its neighbors to the north, runaways sought and gained freedom and religious sanctuary among the enemy of their enslavers.[2]

African resistance to slavery in what became the United States began as early as 1526, when slaves joined an Indian revolt that destroyed the Spanish settlement of San Miguel del Gualdape on the modern-day Georgia coast.

Spaniards finally managed to establish a permanent settlement at Saint Augustine in 1565, but African slaves also escaped from that outpost and found refuge among the Ays Indians.[3] For the next three centuries, the vast Indian nations of the Southeast would be one destination for escaping slaves.

Meanwhile, Spanish settlers in Saint Augustine established a two-tier system of African slavery similar to that found in other Spanish colonies. As recently enslaved and unacculturated Africans, called *bozales*, did hard labor on cattle ranches and built government fortifications and other public works, Spanish-speaking Catholic slaves, known as *ladinos*, filled a wide range of urban domestic, artisanal, and lower-status economic roles. Urban slaves (who were usually ladinos) generally received better treatment than their rural counterparts, due to older metropolitan slave relations, their access to legal and religious protections, and their integration into a cash economy. In Saint Augustine, as in Havana and other circum-Caribbean cities, slaves were allowed to work for

slaves could accumulate sufficient income to buy their freedom or that of their kin through a legal mechanism called *coartación*. Owners and the state also freed slaves, resulting in the coexistence of African freedom and enslavement in all Spanish colonies.

Freed slaves became Spanish subjects with the same rights as any other resident. Men and women of African descent held property, lived scattered throughout Spanish communities, petitioned government officials and even the king for redress of grievances, testified in courts, and were active participants in the many public rituals of the Catholic Church. Women entered into the cash economy by creating hand-crafted items and by raising and selling pigs, chickens, and garden produce. They also took in laundry and ran taverns. A few even became plantation mistresses and managed more significant business transactions. Freedmen generally enjoyed broader occupational options than did women and became shoemakers, tailors, carpenters, masons, fishermen, sailors, and lumber-jacks, to name only a few. They ran small businesses and farmed on lands granted them by the governor. Men also became members of the free black militias that helped Spain maintain its precarious hold on an empire too vast for soldiers on the Florida peninsula to control.

For the first century of its existence, Saint Augustine was a small military outpost of the Caribbean, existing to defend the treasure fleets and supported by annual Spanish payrolls. In the seventeenth century ranching, agriculture, and timbering somewhat diversified the economy, but Florida was slow to develop labor-

Stereograph of Slave Market House, Saint Augustine, Florida, 1870s.

themselves on Sundays and feast days and also to hire themselves out for an agreed-upon return to their owners. With effort,

intensive plantations. It was "a society with slaves" rather than "a slave society," to use historian Ira Berlin's categorization.[4]

The Lower South took on a different profile in 1670, however, when, after more than a century of Spanish settlement in the region, Barbadian planters already hostile to Spain established an English colony at Charles Town (in what became South Carolina) "but ten days journey" from Saint Augustine. The English settlers were intent on establishing profitable plantations such as they had known in Barbados. This would require the hard work of African slaves—and many of them. The slave codes English planters developed in the Caribbean and transplanted to Carolina deemed slaves as chattel or "moveable property," not unlike cattle or furniture. These codes featured harsh regulation and minimal protections and strongly discouraged manumissions. Spanish slavery, on the other hand, was based on Roman law, which considered slavery "against the laws of nature" and a mutable legal condition. Slaves were always still human and, as such, entitled to legal protections, church membership, and freedom via testament, self-purchase, and state or private manumission. Slaves were quick to learn the critical differences in these slave regimes.

Following the founding of Charles Town, Spanish governors mounted raids against the "usurpers" to the north. Their forces always included free black militiamen whose very presence continually advertised the difference between the Spanish and English slave systems and may actually have inspired later escapes. Only a year after Governor Diego de Quiroga led a force of Spaniards, Indians, and free black militiamen on a raid against Edisto Island, eight men, two women, and a nursing child

A runaway slave being chased through tall grasses.

escaped from Carolina to Saint Augustine in a canoe and requested baptism into the "True Faith." As required by law, Governor Quiroga saw to the runaways' Catholic instruction, baptism, and marriage, but he also took advantage of their skills. The men became ironsmiths and laborers on the Castillo de San Marcos, and the women served as domestics in the governor's own household. He reported paying wages to all of them: the men earned a peso a day—the wage paid to male Indian laborers—and the women earned half as much. When an agent from Carolina traveled to Saint Augustine to reclaim the runaways the following year, the Spanish governor refused to return them. Instead, he offered to pay the Carolina slave owners their asking price

A fugitive slave fighting off dogs in pursuit.

for the group—sixteen hundred pesos—as soon as Saint Augustine's annual subsidy arrived. Satisfied with that promise, the agent returned to Charles Town empty-handed.[5]

The slaves' "telegraph" must have quickly reported the outcome of the negotiations, for soon other fugitives began arriving in Saint Augustine. The Spaniards recorded new groups of runaways reaching Saint Augustine in 1688, 1689, and 1690, and Carolina's governor, James Colleton, complained to his Spanish counterpart that slaves ran "dayly to your towns." Unsure

about how to handle the incoming refugees, Saint Augustine's officials repeatedly solicited Spain for guidance. Finally, on November 7, 1693, Charles II issued a royal proclamation "giving liberty to all . . . the men as well as the women . . . so that by their example and by my liberality others will do the same."[6] Hundreds of slaves did—risking all the dangers of the swamps and the patrollers and Indians hired to recapture them. The eight men and two women who left Carolina for freedom in 1687 instigated a major policy revision at the Spanish court that would shape the geopolitics of the Southeast and the Caribbean for years to come.

Although the Spanish Crown emphasized religious and humane considerations for freeing the slaves, political and military motives were equally, if not more, important. In harboring the runaways and eventually settling them in their own town, Florida's governors were following a traditional Spanish policy of populating and holding territory threatened by foreign encroachment. If the interests of Spain and Florida were served by this policy, so too were those of the ex-slaves. It offered them a refuge within which they could live free and maintain their families. In the highly politicized context of Spanish Florida, fugitives made creative use of Spanish institutions to improve the conditions of their freedom.[7]

The provocation inherent in the Spanish sanctuary policy increasingly threatened the Carolinians. Despite the institution of regulatory slave codes, ticket systems (passes to travel on public roads), and land and water patrols, Carolina slaves continued to flee—southward to Florida. Not only did each runaway represent an economic loss, but planters also feared that the success of the few might inspire the many. By the beginning of the eighteenth century, blacks outnumbered whites in Carolina, and in that colony as in all other slave systems, uprisings of slaves were a chronic source of fear. Carolina slaves did revolt in 1711 and again in 1714, and the following year many slaves joined the Yamasee Indian War against the English. That war almost succeeded in eradicating white settlement in South Carolina, but after reinforcements from Virginia and North Carolina helped turn the tide, the defeated Yamasees and their black allies

who managed to escape from Carolina sought refuge among the Spaniards.[8]

Historian Peter Wood asserts that of all the Carolinians' conspiratorial concerns, none seemed to worry them more after 1720 than did the existence of Saint Augustine. That year the townspeople of Charles Town uncovered a major slave conspiracy in which at least some of the participants "thought to gett to Augustine." Fourteen escaped slaves reached Savannah before being captured and executed. Still, slaves continued to take the risk. In 1724 ten more runaways reached Saint Augustine, assisted by English-speaking Yamasee Indians. According to their statement, the slaves knew that the Spanish king had offered freedom for those seeking conversion and baptism.[9]

Initially at least, Governor Antonio de Benavides honored the 1693 edict that freed slaves of the English upon their conversion. In 1725 he sent a delegation to Charles Town to negotiate boundary disputes and an agreement on the runaways. Following the precedent set by his predecessor in 1687, the governor offered to purchase the newly arrived fugitives for two hundred pesos apiece. Angry Carolina slave owners rejected the offer as insufficient, claiming their property was worth much more and asking to be compensated as well for the loss of the slaves' labor since they ran away. Governor Benavides wrote to authorities in Spain to inquire whether the fugitives, who had entered Florida during a period of truce between England and Spain, were entitled to receive sanctuary, but no reply was immediately forthcoming. When the English threatened to reclaim their lost slaves by force, Benavides sold the unlucky fugitives at public auction to the leading creditors of Saint Augustine's treasury.

Although the governor gave the auction proceeds to the planters' envoy, the Carolinians charged that Benavides "Makes Merchandize of all our slaves, and ships them off to Havanah for his own Profit." They were at least partially correct in that assessment.[10]

Undeterred, more Carolina slaves continued to flee to Florida. Thomas Elliott and other planters near Stono "had fourteen Slaves Runaway to Saint Augustine" in 1726. The acting governor of Carolina, Arthur Middleton, complained to officials in London that the Spaniards not only harbored their runaways but also "They have found a New way of sending our own slaves against us, to Rob and Plunder us." Some of the runaways were seasoned soldiers who had fought with the Yamasee against the English, and some may have been warriors in their homelands. They became effective additions to Saint Augustine's black militia and, like their predecessors, joined in Spanish raids against their former masters. Governor Middleton claimed that "Six of our Runaway slaves and the rest Indians" in two canoes attacked near Pon Pon in the fall of 1727 and carried away white captives. Another account of the same raid said that "Ten Negroes and fourteen Indians Commanded by those of their own Colour, without any Spaniards in company with them" had taken the action and that they had also brought back to Saint Augustine one black man and a mulatto boy. That same year Spanish raiders and former Carolina runaways struck again at a plantation on the Edisto River and carried away another seven slaves. Governor Benavides admired the military abilities of the runaways and recognized their diplomatic potential as well. He sent another party of four dozen Yamasees northward and offered thirty pieces of eight for every English scalp and one hundred pieces "for every live Negro they should bring."[11]

The following year the Carolinians struck back, and the black militia fought vigorously to defend Saint Augustine. The Spanish Crown commended the black militia for its bravery in that action and in 1733 reiterated its offer of freedom, but due to the local uncertainty about how to interpret the original decree, some of those who had entered Saint Augustine remained enslaved.[12] Francisco Menéndez, captain of Saint Augustine's slave militia, led a determined campaign to make Florida's officials live up to the promises of the Spanish king. He presented petitions to the governors and to the auxiliary bishop of Cuba, who toured the province in 1735, but to no avail. When Manuel de Montiano became the new governor of Florida in 1737, however, the group's fortunes changed. Captain Menéndez once more petitioned for freedom, listing thirty-one individuals unjustly enslaved, including some who had been shipped to Havana, and the names of the persons who claimed ownership over them. This time his petition joined another from his Yamasee ally, Chief Jorge, who stated that he and the other Yamasee chiefs "commonly" made treaties with the slaves and that Captain Menéndez and three other escaped slaves had fought bravely for him for several years until they were ultimately defeated. Jorge related that when the Yamasees fled southward, their black allies joined them, hoping to receive in Saint Augustine the Christian sanctuary promised by Spain.[13]

War with England was expected at any moment, and the combined petitions of the African and Indian leaders must have made an impression on a governor in need of experienced fighters. After reviewing all relevant documentation, and against the vehement protests of powerful owners, Governor Montiano granted unconditional freedom to all the fugitives from Carolina. When the Spanish Crown reviewed Montiano's actions, it approved and ordered that not only all the blacks who had already come from Carolina "but all those who in the future come as fugitives from the English colonies" should be given prompt and full liberty in the name of the king. Further, to prevent any additional pretext for selling the former slaves, the royal edict should be publicly posted.[14]

In 1738 the runaways from Carolina began new lives as freed men and women on the Spanish frontier, establishing the new town of Gracia Real de Santa Teresa de Mose about two miles north of Saint Augustine. This became the first free black town legitimately constituted in what is today the United States, and the site has now been designated a National Historic Landmark. Captain Menéndez, who earlier had initiated the successful suit for freedom and who still led the black militia, also governed this settlement, and Governor Montiano referred to the inhabitants of Mose as Menéndez's "subjects." Governor Montiano clearly considered the benefits of a northern outpost against anticipated British attacks. Who better to serve as an advance warning system than grateful ex-slaves carrying Spanish arms? The freedmen apparently understood their expected role for, upon receiving the land, they vowed to be "the most cruel enemies of the English" and to risk their lives and spill their "last drop of blood in defense of the Great crown of Spain and the Holy Faith."[15] The new homesteaders were pragmatists: their own interests were clearly served by fighting those who would return them to chattel slavery.

News regarding Spain's sanctuary policy in Florida and the existence of Fort Mose spread rapidly northward through the fledgling English colony of Georgia (where slavery was still prohibited) to the expanding plantations of South Carolina, where roughly thirty thousand blacks were enslaved to the arduous rice economy by the mid-1730s. Carolina planters complained that Spain's 1733 edict had been proclaimed publicly (as, in fact, it was) "by Beat of Drum round the Town of St. Augustine (where many Negroes belonging to English vessels that carried thither Supplies of provisions had the Opportunity of hearing it)."[16] They also alluded to secret measures taken by the Spaniards to disseminate their offer among English slaves and frequently reported suspicious visitors from Spanish Florida. As word spread, more slaves were emboldened to flee for liberty.

On November 21, 1738, twenty-three men, women, and children escaped from Port Royal, Carolina, and made it safely to Saint Augustine in a stolen launch. Governor Montiano promptly honored their request for sanctuary, and they joined their predecessors at Fort Mose. Nineteen of the newcomers had belonged to Captain Caleb Davis, an English merchant who had been trading merchandise (and intelligence) in Saint Augustine for years. Despite his useful relationship with the Spaniards, Governor Montiano refused Davis when he attempted to reclaim his slaves the following month, and the frustrated Davis reported that his slaves laughed at his fruitless efforts to recover them. Twelve years later Davis submitted a claim to the Spanish government for twenty-seven of his slaves "detained" by Montiano, whom he valued

at seventy-six hundred pesos, as well as for the launch in which they had escaped and supplies they had taken with them.[17]

Each successful escape generated more attempts. In February 1739, Carolina authorities captured, but later released, several runaways headed for Saint Augustine. The following month four slaves and an Irish Catholic servant from Carolina made their escape to Florida on stolen horses. The English angrily reported that, although the runaways had killed one man and wounded another, "They were received there [in Saint Augustine] with great honours, one of them had a Commission given to him, and a Coat faced with Velvet."[18] The same month another group of envoys from Carolina traveled to Saint Augustine to press for the return of the runaways. Governor Montiano was cordial but refused to comply, citing the royal edict of 1733 that promised religious sanctuary. Carolina's governor, William Bull, wrote that the planters were very dissatisfied "to find their property now become so very precarious and uncertain." He added that Carolina's planters feared "Negroes which were their chief support may in little time become their Enemies, if not their Masters, and that this Government is unable to withstand or prevent it." In April frustrated members of the South Carolina Commons voted to offer bounties, even for adult scalps "with the two ears," to dissuade other slaves from trying to escape. For added emphasis they staged the public whipping and execution of two newly captured runaways.[19]

Despite the increasingly harsh measures taken against them, the enslaved still sought their freedom, and the level of their own desperate violence escalated proportionally. In August, Don Diego Pablo, an

Indian ally from Apalachee sent word to Governor Montiano that the British had attempted to build a fort nearby, but the hundred black laborers had revolted, killed all the whites, and hamstrung their horses before escaping. Several days later some of the escaped blacks encountered the same Indians in the woods and asked directions to reach the Spaniards, presumably to request sanctuary.[20]

The following month, on September 9, 1739, a group of "Angolan" slaves revolted near Stono, South Carolina, where they killed more than twenty whites and sacked and burned homes before heading for Saint Augustine. Governor Bull quickly gathered a retaliatory force, which struck the rebels later that day when they stopped along the road for what the white pursuers viewed as a drunken dance, but which historian John Thornton identifies as a traditional feature of war in Central Africa. Kongo had long been a Catholic kingdom with many Portuguese speakers. Thornton contends, as did contemporary Carolinians, that the rebels could well have understood both Spanish (a sister language to Portuguese) and the offer of Catholic protection, and that they based their flight plans on this knowledge. Those rebels who survived the first day's battle fought on for another week, moving southward toward Saint Augustine. Thornton attributes their success to their possible training and service as soldiers in the eighteenth-century wars that wracked the Kongo.[21] Historian Eugene Sirmans has argued that the Stono Rebellion was "less an insurrection than an attempt by slaves to fight their way to St. Augustine." Even if this is true, the political nature of the action, as well as the risk taken by its participants, remains significant. After a week's worth of fighting, a larger white militia force finally

Fort Mose, undated.

caught and killed most of the surviving rebels, yet all reports say that some escaped the final battle as well. If any did make it to their destination, they would have been sheltered at Fort Mose.[22]

Historian Peter Wood argues that Stono led to a "heightened degree of white repression and a reduced amount of black autonomy" in South Carolina. Either factor would have made escape to Saint Augustine worth the greater risk. An estimated one hundred fifty slaves rebelled near the Ashley River outside Charles Town in June 1740. Like the Stono rebels, they also may have hoped to reach safety in Saint Augustine. They chose a dangerous time for

Louis Manigault's runaway reward poster for his slave "Dolly," Augusta, Georgia, 1863.

BELOW: Stereograph of "Remains of Slave Quarters, Fort George Island, Florida," undated.

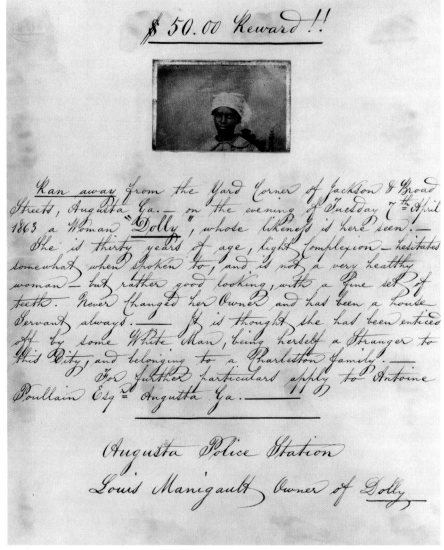

$50.00 Reward!!

Ran away from the Yard Corner of Jackson & Broad Streets, Augusta Ga. — on the evening of Tuesday 7th April 1863 a Woman "Dolly", whose likeness is here seen. — She is thirty years of age, light Complexion — hesitates somewhat when spoken to, and is not a very healthy woman — but rather good looking, with a fine set of teeth. Never changed her Owner, and has been a house Servant always. — It is thought she has been enticed off by some White Man, being herself a Stranger to this City, and belonging to a Charleston Family. — For further particulars apply to Antoine Poullain Esq Augusta Ga. —

Augusta Police Station

Louis Manigault Owner of Dolly

Remains of Slave Quarters, Fort George Island, Florida

their escape since Carolina and Georgia were at that very moment joined in attacking Spanish Florida. That fact, however, may have triggered the revolt. Carolinians captured fifty of the rebels and hung them at the rate of ten a day, but nothing is known of the fate of the other hundred. Some may have reached Florida and joined their compatriots at Fort Mose.[23]

Fort Mose was created as a polyglot community, and this may have facilitated the incorporation of new and diverse runaways. The leader of Mose, Francisco Menéndez, was an African-born man of the Mandinga nation (possibly a Muslim), who upon conversion to Catholicism adopted his Spanish name. Others of the freed Africans came from Senegambia, Calabar, the Kongo, and Angola. Some brought Indian wives with them from Carolina. Whatever their origins, because the residents had sworn "to shed their last drop of blood in defense of Spain and the True Faith" and had converted, they were considered loyal vassals and free subjects. The men formed themselves into a free militia, commanded by Captain Menéndez, and they and their families became valued homesteaders on Spain's northern frontier. Over the next decades the people of Mose adapted to Spanish religious and cultural expectations and battled English invaders and Indian raiders to defend their hard-won gains.

The militia at Fort Mose fought bravely when General James Oglethorpe of Georgia invaded Florida in 1740. When Menéndez wrote to the king asking for appropriate rewards for his service, Florida's governor supported that petition. The following year Menéndez and others took to the seas as corsairs for Spain. After several successful expeditions Menéndez was taken prisoner, tortured, re-enslaved, and sold as a prize of

war in the Bahamas. Other free sailors from Cuba faced similar fates in New York because the British presumed that, because they were not white, they must be slaves. Remarking that Spain could not man its navies without people of color, Florida's governor went to great lengths to provide the British admiralty courts with legal proofs of their freedom, and some were eventually freed. This may be what happened to Francisco Menéndez, who reappeared as the leader of Mose by 1752.

Truly an Atlantic creole, Menéndez had been enslaved and transported from West Africa to Carolina years earlier. After fighting for three years in the Yamasee War, he spoke Yamasee and English in addition to the African languages he already knew. In Florida he learned Spanish and wrote it beautifully. He may well have been literate in Arabic at an earlier time. He sailed the Atlantic from Havana to Ocracoke and planned to travel to Spain, where he would present his credentials to the king. After a tumultuous life, Menéndez ended his days in Cuba at some seventy years of age. His seems an amazing story, and yet it is only one of many recorded in Spanish documents that relate this forgotten chapter in the history of African resistance in North America.

Throughout the 1740s and 1750s enslaved people from South Carolina and Georgia made their way to freedom in Spanish Florida, where they became part of the Mose community. Male runaways outnumbered females, but despite the grave dangers involved, women continued to try for freedom. Runaway slave notices in newspapers from colonial South Carolina describe some of them. Delia, who spoke very little English, took her "sucking child" and ran with Clarinda, whose English was good. They escaped in their owner's cypress canoe. Amoretta and Sarah joined three African men in their own successful escape. The door to freedom in Spanish Florida slammed shut in 1763, however, when the Treaty of Paris ceded Florida to Great Britain. Rather than be re-enslaved, the Mose community of about a hundred persons left Florida on a new southward passage: they joined the Spanish exodus to Cuba, where they became homesteaders again on the Matanzas frontier.[24]

As the Spanish community sailed away, British investors rushed in to create a whole new plantation society in Florida, and soon chattel slavery stretched along the Atlantic coast. Ambitious planters, such as Richard Oswald and Governor James Grant, imported hundreds of Africans from slave factories on the Sierra Leone River to do the backbreaking work of carving new plantations out of the Florida wilderness. One contemporary estimated that as many as a thousand African slaves were imported into Florida in 1771 alone, a peak year of the Africa-Florida trade. As a result, the labor force in British East Florida came to be predominantly black and African-born. When British Loyalists were forced by the course of the American Revolution to evacuate Savannah and Charleston, British East Florida provided a haven, and the refugees brought more than eight thousand slaves with them. The new influx meant that blacks outnumbered whites in Florida three to one.[25] In the brief twenty years the British ruled Florida, the province became "Africanized" and began to look much like the Carolina society after which it was modeled. With no other hope of freedom, unknown numbers of British slaves escaped from plantations along the Saint Johns and Saint Mary's Rivers to became vassals and

allies of the Seminoles, with whom they soon formed family ties as well.

At the conclusion of the American Revolution, Spain regained Florida from the British, and in the chaos of the change of governments a new generation of runaways claimed freedom. Some were slaves of the departing British.[26] Others came from South Carolina and Georgia, as before. Florida's new governor doubted the religious motivation of the incoming slaves, but he was bound by the religious sanctuary edict to receive and shelter them. He ordered any whites "having in their control Negroes or mulattoes, either free or slave" to register them and "every vagrant Negro without a known owner or else a document that attests to his freedom" to report to the authorities within twenty days to clarify his or her status and obtain a work contract. Those failing to report would forfeit their freedom and be enslaved by the king.[27] In the next months more than two hundred individuals reported to Spanish officials and became free. Almost twice as many men as women presented themselves, but more than half of the ex-slaves belonged to a family unit. The numerous groupings, the tender ages of many of the children, and some of their harrowing accounts of flight indicate that the fugitives sought to maintain family and friendship ties, even in extremely difficult circumstances.

One family achieving freedom was that of Prince Witten. In the summer of 1785, after several failed attempts, Prince, his wife, Judy, and their children, Polly and Glasgow, escaped from the Loyalist colonel who had abducted them from their South Carolina plantations, only to be seized anew in Georgia. Undaunted, one Sunday morning a year and a half later, they managed to flee again and cross the newly established international border into Spanish Florida, where they finally found refuge. Prince was born in "Guinea," and Judy and their children were born in South Carolina. A runaway notice described Prince as "negro, six feet, strong built and brawny . . . talkative, with a large mouth." Judy was said to be "country-born . . . 5'7 . . . a smart, active wench." Glasgow, who was about eight at the time, was "a well looked boy of an open countenance and obliging disposition," while Polly, age six, possessed "lively eyes" and was "gently pitted with the small pox." The runaway notice stated: "It is supposed that Prince has carried them with him to Florida to avoid a separation from his family . . . to which he is much attached."[28]

Prince and Judy made a successful transition to the freedom they had risked so much to achieve. A skilled carpenter, Prince readily found ready work in Saint Augustine. The Wittens acquired a home and a slave, and Prince enjoyed a heroic career in the black militia. Prince and Judy were married, and they and their children were baptized in the Catholic Church. Each took a new Spanish name. Glasgow, now called Francisco, was educated in Saint Augustine's Catholic school alongside other sons of slaves and Spanish planters. He became a shoemaker and, like his father, joined the black militia. Polly, now María, married a former slave rebel from Saint Domingue. Members of this family became popular choices as godparents and marriage sponsors for both free and enslaved Africans, and they were leading citizens of the free black community in Saint Augustine as long as it was Spanish.[29]

The new government of the United States, however, responding to pressures from its Southern constituents, found the idea of a slave haven on its border intolerable. Secretary of State Thomas Jefferson warned the weakened Spanish Crown that the community's continued presence could mean a rupture in the friendly relations between their two nations. By 1790 Spain was forced to abrogate the sanctuary policy that had existed since 1693, but all run-

Stereograph of cooks, chambermaids, and a hostler in Saint Augustine, Florida, undated.

aways already in Florida retained their freedom.[30]

As long as the Seminoles controlled the interior of middle Florida, runaway slaves still had possibilities for obtaining freedom across the Saint Mary's River, the international border separating Spanish East Florida from the new United States of America. With the departure of the British, Chief Payne and his successors, Micanopy and Bowlegs, reshaped Seminole foreign policy and became allies of the Spanish government. The Spaniards recognized and feared the land hunger of the ambitious new government to the north and depended heavily on their Seminole allies to act as a buffer against Anglo encroachment. They assured Seminole loyalty through treaties and annual gifts, and in times of crisis they posted free black militiamen in their villages. The Spaniards stood to lose their colony, the Seminoles their rich lands and cattle herds, and the former slaves their freedom. This convergence of interests bound them together during Spain's sec-

ond tenure in Florida (1784–1821). Initially, blacks allied to the Seminoles lived in pre-existing villages, such as Payne's Town and Bowlegs Town, but many eventually resided in autonomous villages— Pilaklikaha, Mulatto Girl's Town, King Heijah's Town, Bucker Woman's Town, Boggy Island, and Big Swamp—that were ruled by black leaders. The black Seminoles provided the chiefs with whom they were associated an annual tribute of agricultural surplus and military service, and visitors later described their flourishing villages.[31]

Soon after the conclusion of the American Revolution, however, the adolescent government of the United States began testing its strength against its Spanish and Seminole neighbors. The significant, and armed, free blacks who were living in Florida and were reputed for both their militancy and their alliance with the Seminoles set an unacceptable example for plantation slaves of the Anglo South. Thus, the United States government not very covertly supported a number of hostile

LEFT: Chief Coacoochee, called Wild Cat, led Seminole and black Indians during the Florida War and was later exiled in Mexico.

RIGHT: John Horse, a black Seminole leader in the nineteenth century, joined Wild Cat in helping his people escape slavery.

actions against Spanish Florida, including the Patriot War of 1812, the naval attack on the black fort and settlement at Prospect Bluff on the Apalachicola River in 1815, and Andrew Jackson's devastating raids against black and Seminole villages along the Suwannee River in 1818. After that calamity, black and Indian refugees dispersed to the west and south of Florida, where they joined others who had anticipated the attacks at Prospect Bluff and at the Suwannee and had already resettled in traditional hunting villages near Tampa Bay. From Tampa the desperate Seminoles and their black allies sent repeated diplomatic missions to the British in the Bahamas and the Spaniards in Cuba.[32]

In 1821 Florida became a territory of the United States and part of the plantation South, but Spain did not abandon its black subjects. As in Louisiana, cession treaties required the incoming government to respect the legal status and property rights of free blacks. Some free blacks, who had acquired property and invested years of hard work in improving it, decided to stay in Florida and risk trusting the newcomers to honor their treaty promises. Most of the free black community, like their predecessors in 1763, instead joined in a mass exodus to Cuba. Once again Africans and African Americans cast their lot with the government that offered them freedom. Others continued to fight with the Seminoles and shared their fate.

The new governor of the territory was none other than General Andrew Jackson, who promptly recommended removing the fugitive Creeks, Seminoles, and free blacks from the Florida peninsula. The Seminoles and their black allies fought one more war before being forced westward to the Indian Territory, where their free status was often ignored by slave catchers. Some remembered the freedom offered by the Spanish system and headed southward again, across the border to Mexico.[33]

For more than three centuries, persons of African descent helped shape the geopolitics of the American Southeast through their determination to escape bondage. They judged Anglo slavery by "voting with their feet" and by risking their lives repeatedly to forestall its advance. In Florida some expanded the emancipatory potential of Spanish law and reshaped their lives by becoming loyal subjects of that empire. Others chose instead to become black Seminoles, but they too found freedom by crossing the international border into Florida. As we celebrate the courage and determination of the better-known generations and figures who followed their star and the Underground Railroad northward, it is also appropriate to remember that the quest for freedom began much earlier and was constant—and that many determined and courageous though lesser-known people, such as Francisco Menéndez and Prince and Judy Witten, remain a crucial part of the forgotten history of the southern passage to Florida.

6

R. J. M. BLACKETT

"FREEMEN TO THE RESCUE!"

Resistance to the Fugitive Slave Law of 1850

At the heart of the American dilemma lies the tension between slavery and freedom. The founding generation sought one solution in the Fugitive Slave Law of 1793. With an eye for legal niceties and the euphemistic phrase, the law ordered fugitives from labor, rather than slaves, be returned to their owners. Slaves had other ideas: the number of those who escaped continued to rise throughout the nineteenth century, with many of them fleeing either to the anonymity and security of free black communities in the North or to the safety of Canada. All the evidence suggests that by the middle decade of the nineteenth century fugitive slaves were a vital and substantial segment of these free black communities. At one time or another, for example, three hundred to seven hundred fugitives were in New Bedford, Massachusetts, between 1845 and 1863, and as many as four hundred may have been in Boston in 1850. There they found jobs, were married, and became active in all aspects of community life. One observer in 1850 expressed some surprise at the number of runaway slaves who had found refuge in Pittsburgh and the levels of integration they had achieved. "Many who have stood high in the estimation of the public, and who were considered freemen by birth," he concluded, "turn out to be fugitives."[1]

Although slaveholders had recorded some successes in recapturing runaway slaves in the years since 1793, the ease with which fugitive slaves were integrated into these and other Northern black communities exposed the ineffectiveness of the law. It was clear to many in the South that none of this would have been possible without the collusion of the North. As sectional tensions rose over the issue of how lands captured from Mexico at the end of the 1840s were to be divided, some feared the country could be torn apart.

"Effects of the
Fugitive Slave Law,"
ca. 1851.

They sought a solution to the problem in
what became the Compromise of 1850,
which dealt with, among other issues, the
admission of California, the boundaries of
Texas, the organization of Utah, and a
more stringent Fugitive Slave Law.

The new law attempted to plug the
holes in the old law created by the slaves'
search for freedom. Among other things, it
imposed heavy fines and imprisonment on
those found guilty of aiding fugitives to
avoid recapture; it created special federal
commissioners who were not constrained
by judicial traditions and so could act independently of state and local laws; it denied
trial by jury and the right to habeas corpus
for arrested fugitives; and it granted special
incentives to commissioners who ruled in
favor of slaveholders. The broad sweep of
its remit did nothing to differentiate
between those who were born free and
those who were slaves. How were black
people who were born free to prove their
status once they were accused of being

escaped slaves? Abolitionist Wendell
Phillips recalled the case of a seventy-year-
old free black woman who sought his
advice about leaving the country "fearful
. . . of being caught up by mistake." There
seemed to be no limit to the reach of the
law. Respected and productive members of
society, like those in Pittsburgh, were as
likely to be caught in the web of the law as
were recently escaped slaves. James
Phillips, for example, was arrested in
Harrisburg, Pennsylvania, in May 1852,
where he had lived and worked for fourteen years. The law, historian Benjamin
Quarles insists, was "ex post facto, reaching back to fugitives who had almost forgotten that they had always been free."[2]

To understand the instant and widespread condemnation and defiance of the
law is to appreciate the sense of outrage
and indignation felt by blacks throughout
the North. The law was a slight to their
dignity, an assault on their rights, and an
open assertion that they were not to be

accorded the rights of citizens. In the months leading up to the enactment of the law, blacks in Allegheny County, Pennsylvania, spoke for many when they pleaded with Congress not to adopt legislation that, they pointed out, would infringe upon their liberties as American citizens—their petition was ignored. Within days of President Millard Fillmore signing the bill into law, blacks organized massive protest meetings throughout the North. The anger and rage against those who adopted what abolitionist Lewis Hayden of Boston called this "ungodly and anti-republican law" was palpable. Frederick Douglass spoke of an "approaching calamity" that left black people with a feeling they were in an "enemy's land," where there was nothing but "danger, trials, bitter mockery, scorn and oppression. . . . There is no valley so deep, no mountain so high, no plain so extensive, no spot so sacred to God and liberty in all this extended country," he told a Rochester audience, "where the black man may not fall prey to the remorseless cupidity of his white brethren." Those attending a meeting in Philadelphia dismissed the law as wicked, atrocious, and "utterly at variance with the principles of the Constitution . . . subversive of the objects of the law, the protection of the lives, liberty, and property of the governed . . . repugnant to the highest attributes of God, justice and mercy . . . and horribly cruel in its expressed mode of operation." Abolitionists in Syracuse declared the law unconstitutional for its denial of due process, the right to habeas corpus, and access to legal council.[3]

Black communities throughout the North pledged open defiance of the law. "[W]e owe ourselves, our wives, our children, and to our common nature, as well as to the panting fugitive from oppression," a Philadelphia meeting resolved, "to resist this law at any cost and at all hazards." Blacks in Boston declared themselves ready to resist the law and to "rescue and protect the slave at every hazard." Those at a meeting at the African Congregational Church in Syracuse warned of the community's willingness to take "the scalp of any government hound that dares follow on our tracks as we are resolved to be free, if it is not until after death." William P. Newman, a Baptist minister on a visit to Cleveland, reported that blacks there were of a "fixed and changeless purpose to kill any so-called man" who attempted to take one of them. Abolitionists in New Bedford declared the law a "Dead Letter" and pledged to trample its provisions "under our feet, and our blood should flow freely from every vein, and mingle with the blood of our revolutionary fathers, who fell on the field of battle defending the liberties of our country, before we should consent to be taken from the pure soil of Massachusetts as fugitive slaves." Douglass reached for the ultimate calculus of resistance: "Two or three dead slaveholders," he suggested, "will make this law a dead letter."[4]

Not surprisingly, defiance came quickest from those who stood to suffer most from the law. To borrow an apt phrase from Benjamin Quarles, defiance became a "new commandment" of black communities and their white supporters throughout the North.[5] Meetings were called within days of the passage of the law. Those in attendance condemned the law's promoters, reviled the legislation for being antirepublican and unconstitutional, and made a commitment to do all within their power to ensure that its provisions were not implemented.

Communities were mobilized and organized to resist the law. In a broader sense, the speed with which meetings were summoned reflected the extent to which black communities had succeeded in creating an array of organizations to meet their needs. In the mid-1850s in Harrisburg, Pennsylvania, for instance, could be found three Masonic lodges, one Odd Fellows lodge, one Women's Good Samaritan Council, one Douglass Union, one Dorcas Society to aid the needy, one Fugitive Aid Society, one black militia, two Baptist churches, and one black Presbyterian

church. Large audiences attended public events held at community venues and joined organizations to resist the law. These groups, which relied on the leadership and participation of ordinary men and women in the community, either were created where they had not existed before or were reactivated where they had been dormant. At the first such event in Boston, Lewis Hayden was elected president of the

meeting; John Hilton, William Craft, and Henry Watson vice presidents; and William Nell and Isaac Snowden secretaries. This proved to be a mix of fugitive slaves (Hayden and Craft) and free blacks (Nell and Hilton). The group also called for the formation of a League of Freedom, with a mandate to include all "those who are ready to protect the slave at every hazard."[6] While leaders such as Hayden were important to the struggle against the law, the aim and success of such organizations rested on the involvement of as many members of the community as possible in making decisions about what exactly the group should do. Those most affected by the problem spoke their piece and became involved in acts of resistance. The speed with which meetings were called, and the large numbers of those who participated, suggest networks of resistance already existed within black communities and were able to mobilize at relatively short notice. These networks are not always easy to identify. Some with a long, continuous public history were still active in 1850 while others had been dismantled. Still others acted clandestinely, away from the gaze of public scrutiny. Created or inspired by the activities of an older generation, these networks were sustained and refashioned to meet the exigencies of this new challenge to the rights and dignity of black Americans.[7]

The Committee of Vigilance and Safety formed at a Boston meeting in October 1850 was modeled after the Vigilance Committee established in 1846. The Philadelphia Vigilance Committee took its cue from the activities of an earlier organization, as did the New York Vigilance Committee, which had its first incarnation in the work of David Ruggles and others in 1835 and had undergone two reorganizations in the 1840s.[8] In almost every instance, African Americans took the initiative in opposing the law. Committees in cities such as Syracuse, New York, and Harrisburg initially were all black. Once whites joined the efforts, as many subsequently did, these committees were reorganized to exploit the legal talents of many of its white members.[9]

Vigilance committees had always taken on a multiplicity of tasks, from protecting fugitive slaves against recapture to providing for such basic needs as food and clothes. In other words, they combined both direct action and social welfare. Some, such as the Detroit Colored Vigilance Committee, went even further by promoting manhood suffrage and temperance, establishing schools and literary societies, and organizing state Negro Convention meetings.[10] It is not always easy to trace the full range of the work of these committees, as much of what they did was necessarily clandestine. Beginning sometime in the 1830s, the Philanthropic Society of Pittsburgh, led by Martin R. Delany, the Reverend Lewis Woodson, and others, seemed to have used genuine benevolent activity to mask the more dangerous business of protecting the black community from the sort of attacks and riots that periodically plagued other cities. They also defended fugitives from recapture and spirited away suspected slaves traveling with their masters through Pittsburgh. One local newspaper reported in 1855 on the existence of "a regularly organized association of blacks in the city bound together by the most solemn oaths . . . whose object is the

abduction of Negro servants traveling with their masters." The society may very well have been the most vital arm of the local Underground Railroad. Similarly, a small group of blacks in Harrisburg came together in the early 1840s to "resist and punish slave hunters." In Detroit a secret order called the African American Mysteries: Order of the Men of Oppression, led by William Lambert, a tailor, and George DeBaptiste, a barber, was involved in aiding and protecting fugitive slaves.[11]

In the shadow of the law, self-defense and the protection of members of the black community came to dominate the activities of these organizations. The first order of business may have been the most difficult: persuading blacks that it was safe to remain where they were and protecting them from the reach of the law. The high number of people who chose to flee the United States in the days and weeks after the passage of the law reflected the depth of fear and the degree of uncertainty that plagued black communities throughout the North. One hundred Pittsburghers left the city within days. Forty others from across the river in Allegheny City joined the exodus. It was reported that by the end of September more than three hundred blacks had left the area. The Baptist Colored Church of Buffalo lost one hundred thirty of its members; its sister church in Rochester lost one hundred twelve. Thirty to forty members of the AME Church in Boston chose to leave, joined by ten from the AME Zion Church, forty from the First Independent Baptist Church, and sixty from the Twelfth Baptist Church. William Whipper, a local black leader, estimated that over half of the black population of Columbia, Pennsylvania, fled the town in the five years after 1850. This exodus, as

Daguerrotype of
Frederick Douglass,
ca. 1848. Douglass
presented this image
to Susan B. Anthony
as a gift.

ture sold off in preparation for leaving. The same occurred in Pittsburgh, where it was reported that the majority of those fleeing were male and married, implying that the wives and children left behind were free.[13]

It is safe to assume that those who left for the security of Canada represented only a fraction of the population that felt threatened by the provisions of the new law but, for one reason or another, decided to remain where they were. In protecting those who stayed behind, black communities mobilized to defend their homes, families, and institutions—the free spaces they had worked so hard to create over the years. Some declared their immediate communities and surrounding cities free zones that slave catchers entered at risk to their own lives. If no black person was to be safe, if free men were liable to be taken away at any time, then, as abolitionist Martin Delany told those attending a meeting in Pittsburgh, he was left with no other option: "If a slave pursuor [sic] enter my dwelling, one of us must perish. I have treasures there: there are a wife and children to protect; I will give the tyrant timely warning; but if the sanctuary of my home is violated, if I do not defend it, may the grave be to my body no resting place, and the vaunted heavens refuse my spirit." In Syracuse, the Reverend Jermain Loguen, a former slave, echoed Delany's sentiments. He did not respect the law, neither did he fear it, and he had no intention of obeying it. "It outlaws me, and I outlaw it, and the men who attempt to enforce it on me." All black communities and freedom-loving people, he declared, had "to meet this tyranny and crush it by force, or be crushed by it."[14]

Protecting the home and those in it became a metaphor for defending the community. While mobilization took on added urgency under threat of the new law, blacks

Frederick Douglass so aptly observed, was like "a dark train going out of the land, as if fleeing from death."[12]

These numbers do not begin to reflect the depth of despair, uncertainty, and disruption the law created. Abolitionists in the little Ohio town of Salem had warned the promoters of the legislation and "all their tyrant accomplices, that henceforth the citizens of this region will dispense their hospitality as readily by daylight as in darkness." Such commitments to protect fugitives in their midst may have worked their magic in Salem, which had strong abolitionist traditions, but in larger cities the law played havoc with black communities. Several families in New Bedford, "where either the father or mother were fugitives," were broken up and their furni-

and their white supporters were able to call upon a system of resistance they had fashioned in the struggle against efforts to enforce the earlier Fugitive Slave Law. The system rested on networks of associations, some permanent and others that flourished for a time and then disappeared only to be revived when the situation warranted it. The Philanthropic Society of Pittsburgh, created in the 1830s, was at the heart of almost every effort to protect fugitives down through the 1850s. In contrast, the Chicago Liberty Association, which was made up of forty-two men "working in teams" that patrolled the city looking for slave catchers, emerged in the wake of the new law and may have disappeared soon after its passage. Many of the vigilance committees formed in 1850 followed the lead of earlier committees. The success of the system rested in part on small groups of workers that could be assembled on very short notice. Many were employed as porters, waiters, chambermaids, and other workers at hotels and boarding houses, where they kept an eye out for slavehold-

ers traveling with slaves. In 1850, one hundred eighteen blacks worked as porters, waiters, or cooks in Pittsburgh's hotels. Thomas A. Brown, a night porter at the Monongahela Hotel in Pittsburgh, remembered a cold March night when a slaveholder and his slave arrived at the hotel. It took less than twenty minutes to get word out that a slave was at the hotel. While the planter dined, Brown and six others snatched the slave from her quarters, dressed her in men's clothes, and spirited her away in a carriage provided by a wealthy supporter. "Kind friends," Brown recalled, "dressed her in a dark traveling suit; gave her a well filled purse and by 10 p.m. she was on the North bound train speeding to Canada and freedom."[15]

Such abductions required an effective and extensive system of communications. The speed with which Brown got word to supporters to have a carriage ready outside the hotel attests to the effectiveness and sophistication of the communication system that Pittsburghers had developed. In towns,

"Desperate Conflict in a Barn" depicts the attempted capture or rescue of a fugitive slave. From Still, *Underground Railroad,* 1872.

church bells were usually tolled to announce the arrival of suspected slave catchers. Placards and posters also informed fugitives of potential danger. In one Philadelphia case, posters "3 feet square" were plastered throughout the city, warning of the activities of a notorious local slave catcher. Almost as soon as catchers arrived in Boston in search of the escaped slave Shadrach Minkins in

Lewis Hayden House, Boston.

February 1851, posters and hand-bills describing them were circulated. More than one slave catcher expressed genuine surprise at the speed with which crowds gathered to protest their arrival and to protect the suspected fugitive. On several occasions abolitionists in Philadelphia warned their counterparts in Pittsburgh of the arrival by train of a master traveling with suspected slaves.[16] Over the years, black and white abolitionists developed and refined a sophisticated system of protection to increase the likelihood of fugitives eluding their pursuers. This, indeed, was a real and verifiable element of the Underground Railroad.

Success also relied on the creation of a network of safe houses that Lewis Hayden, the leader of the Underground Railroad in Boston, called "temples of refuge." Barbershops, churches, and homes provided needed sanctuary. When, in 1850, two slave catchers from Georgia arrived in Boston in

search of William and Ellen Craft, Ellen was moved frequently from one safe house to another, first to the Bowditch's in Brookline, then to the Dodge's near Salem, and finally to the home of Theodore Parker in Boston. William initially armed himself and vowed to make his stand at his shop, but later he took the advice of supporters and moved to the home of Lewis Hayden. George Thompson, a British abolitionist, reported that the windows were barricaded and the doors double locked and barred. Around a table "covered with loaded weapons [sat] Lewis Hayden, his young son and a band of brave colored men armed to the teeth and ready for the impending death struggle with the US Marshal and his armed posse." No one, it was reported, could approach either Craft's shop or Hayden's home "without being seen by a hundred eyes." When Caroline Cooper, the suspected slave of a Mr. Slaymaker, was taken from the City Hotel in Pittsburgh in March 1855, she was hurried through a private alley leading on to Third Street to the barbershop owned by a Mr. Davis and subsequently moved to a safe house near Cherry Alley and Strawberry Alley. The authorities sometimes knew the whereabouts of these houses. Stephen Pembroke, a minister and the brother of former fugitive slave James W. C. Pennington, and his two sons, Robert and Jacob Pembroke, who had only recently escaped from slavery in Maryland, were captured at a safe house in New York City and returned to a Baltimore cell in spite of the efforts of the Pennsylvania and New York vigilance committees to protect them. Stephen later had his freedom purchased for close to $1,500, but his sons were sold farther south.[17]

As with the Crafts, black communities made it abundantly clear that they were more than willing to take up arms to pro-tect fugitives. Slave catchers and the offi-cers of the law who supported efforts to reclaim suspected fugitives were consid-ered invaders of the safe spaces that had been carved out of Northern cities and towns. One reporter observed that, in the midst of the threat to the Crafts, blacks on Belknap and Cambridge Streets fortified their homes and armed themselves with guns, swords, and knives. "The colored population," he wrote, "are really roused in this matter and are making their houses like barracks." Leaders of a meeting held a few days earlier called on blacks to arm themselves. They were to be "men of over-alls—men of the wharf—who could do heavy work in the hour of difficulty."[18] Given this willingness to defend their com-munities, and the federal government's determination to enforce the law, it is sur-prising that more instances of open vio-lence and even death were not reported.

In the case of William and Ellen Craft, the community did all within its power to frustrate the work of the catchers with a deft combination of legal and physical intimidation. In foiling the catchers, howev-er, and sending them back to Georgia with-out their quarry, the black community forced the hand of the federal government. No government, and especially one so deeply committed to a policy of compro-mise, could stand idly by and watch the law be openly flaunted. It had to act. President Fillmore's threat to send in the military made it obvious to those in Boston that they could no longer guarantee the Crafts' safety. They decided William and Ellen should leave for England. Had the Crafts remained in Boston, the government most likely would have sent in the military to ensure their return to slavery, just as it subsequent-ly did in the cases of Shadrach Minkins and Anthony Burns. In such celebrated cases as those of the Crafts, Minkins, and Burns in Boston, as well as Jerry McHenry in Syracuse, it appears that only exile in Canada or England would guarantee escape and security. The law was successfully defied in many more instances, but such accounting does not bring us any closer to understanding why people chose to defy the law and how they accomplished it.

William and Ellen Craft, from Still, *Underground Railroad,* 1872.

The heavy work, to use the apt phrase of one speaker at the Boston meeting, was to be borne by an organized black community that could turn out in large numbers at short notice. The armed crowd had always played a pivotal role in efforts to protect fugitives. The group of one hundred fifty blacks "armed with bludgeons" that attempted to rescue a fugitive on his way to a Philadelphia jail in 1824 was not atypical. One local editor expressed dismay when in 1836 a Boston crowd rescued two fugitive women from jail. "The prisoners have been forcibly rescued, at noonday, from the highest court, sitting in the heart of a populous city. The outrage was committed by a mob of several hundred, and after three days search, neither the prisoners nor the rioters have been arrested."[19]

Wherever rescues were attempted, whether in Harrisburg, Pennsylvania, or Sandusky, Ohio, commentators expressed genuine surprise at the size of the crowds, the speed with which they assembled, and how well armed they were. They all insisted, or at least left the impression, that these were the spontaneous acts of a disorganized rabble. When a large crowd of blacks seized Caroline Cooper from Mr. Slaymaker in Pittsburgh, eyewitnesses reported that the "whole affair was so sudden and precipitate, that it was difficult to tell how many colored persons were present or who positively laid hands on the woman." At least in this case, such high levels of coordination and an organized plan of action may have been intended to minimize the chances that the authorities later would be able to identify those who actually abducted Cooper. Such anonymity facilitated effective direct action. Evidence suggests that in some instances leaders of organizations formed in response to the

law gave the crowds their marching orders. More importantly, however, even if formal organizations sometimes played only minor roles in these activities, ample evidence indicates high levels of coordination were at work, along with the existence of what anthropologist James Scott has called "an enabling popular tradition." There is no other way to explain the appearance of two thousand people at the first arraignment of the fugitive suspect Jerry McHenry in Syracuse in October 1851 or the fact that within thirty minutes of Shadrach Minkins's arrest, a hundred blacks and fifty whites turned up at the courtroom. A high degree of coordination among opponents of the law must have been in place. Communities took this tradition of resistance so seriously that when errors occurred, every effort was made to rectify them. For example, it was soon discovered after a crowd took Caroline Cooper from Mr. Slaymaker that she was in fact a free woman. Martin Delany made immediate plans to have her brought from hiding and taken to the mayor's office. To ensure that the error was not repeated on their travels, Delany issued Slaymaker and Cooper letters of safe passage addressed to the "Friends of Liberty."[20]

Crowd actions are one way of measuring the extent to which communities were committed to the struggle against enforcing the Fugitive Slave Law. These activities also effectively applied pressure on local authorities and were part and parcel of an established system of resistance that included mass meetings, petitions, and legal challenges. In defending a suspected fugitive called Latimer in 1842, for example, Boston abolitionists held mass meetings, circulated petitions, published a newspaper, and challenged federal law in state courts.[21] In almost every instance, legal challenges followed the formation of a vigilance committee that could draw on the skills of a small group of talented lawyers. Whites became most actively involved in the work of resistance at this point. The legal subcommittee of the Boston Vigilance Committee, for instance, was made up of Samuel Sewall, Charles Sumner, R. H. Dana Jr., John C. Park, and George Minot. These lawyers raised questions concerning the constitutionality of the law in a variety of ways, such as filing writs of habeas corpus, a right denied to suspected fugitives. One aim of these challenges was to shift cases from federal to state courts, where, it was calculated, state law provided more protections for fugitives and local judges would be more sympathetic or more amenable to local pressure. The courts were also used to intimidate slave catchers and to prevent them from carrying out their assignments. When the slave catchers Knight and Hughes attempted to retake the Crafts, they were confronted by a number of suits brought by the Vigilance Committee, each of which required the posting of substantial bail. The slave catchers were accused of slander and of attempts to kidnap the Crafts. They were also charged with carrying concealed weapons, of smoking in the streets, and of cursing and swearing. In the end such legal intimidation, combined with the threat of possible violence from the crowds that followed them wherever they went, persuaded Knight and Hughes to abandon their quest and leave town. One observer, possibly a participant, captured the essence of the strategy employed to frustrate these and other slave catchers: "The combination of the tragical and the comical, the serious and the ludicrous, with the harassment of handbills, arrests, and

crowds at their heels wherever they went, and the certainty that their progress could not be served without bloodshed, overcame their obstinacy and they took the express train for the South, waited upon by a large and respectable committee."[22]

At a time when most blacks could not vote and when the economic, political, social, and legal systems were arrayed against them, these actions expressed the political will of the people and their determination to defend their communities. Their efforts were not always successful, but the organizations they created in the face of so many powerful forces reflects a high level of resolve, sophistication, skill, and above all else, collective action. The opposition was nothing if not daunting. It had at its disposal the might of the federal and, in many instances, state and local govern-

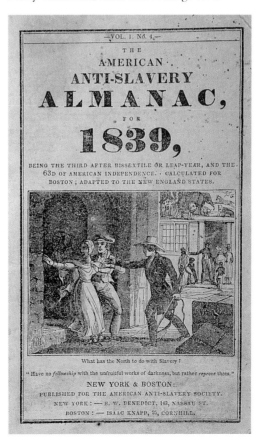

The title page of the *American Anti-Slavery Almanac for 1839* shows a fugitive slave being captured and asks, "What has the North to do with Slavery?"

Poster illustrating the
life of **Anthony Burns**,
ca. 1854.

THE ESCAPE ON SHIPBOARD.

ARREST IN BOSTON.

DEPARTURE FROM BOSTON.

THE SALE.

THE ADDRESS.

Anthony Burns

AUCTION

THE PRISON.

ments. It could rely on the support of commercial interests worried that their business connections with the South would suffer from the activities of those who assisted fugitives to escape and then protected them once they were settled in Northern communities. One Georgia newspaper reached to the core of the dilemma for those in the North who were concerned about protecting their commercial interests and preserving faithful adherence to the terms of the compromise: "Massachusetts owes to the South the fugitive slaves within her limits; efforts have been made to get several of them back. We lost the two Crafts and Shadrach, and recovered Sims. A faithful execution of the law, indeed! When costs have been subtracted, we should like to know how much has been gained."[23]

Even committed abolitionists feared that open and continued defiance of the law—of any law for that matter—marked the first step on the road to anarchy. Many white abolitionists who considered the law anathema nonetheless stopped short of counseling open resistance. The fear of not straying too far into illegality tempered their opposition. As historian Albert Von Frank has shown in his analysis of the speeches white abolitionists made at Boston meetings during the Anthony Burns case, nothing in "the whole record of the Burns affair is more striking to a modern audience or at first more off-putting than the apparent incapacity of even the most committed of the radicals to express a direct, authentic outrage on Burns' personal behalf." Ways had to found to persuade the national government to reverse course without openly defying the law. Some saw a solution around the dilemma in allowing fugitives to be retaken and then raising funds to buy their freedom. No one in the black community openly endorsed such acquiescence. In this they were supported by a handful of radical white abolitionists, such as Samuel J. May and Thomas Wentworth Higginson. May paraded five fugitives before an abolitionist meeting in Syracuse and dared the authorities to take them. For his part Higginson continually berated his associates for their lack of nerve and their unwillingness to oppose the law by rescuing the imprisoned Burns.[24]

While not surprising, these differences over how best to confront the law were relatively minor and not unexpected. More daunting was the array of forces lined up in support of the government's stance in favor of the rights of slaveholders. What were the black community and their white supporters in Boston to make of the hundred-gun salute that greeted the passage of the law, or the large meeting at Faneuil Hall in November at which people swore their allegiance to the government? In New York City supporters of the Fugitive Slave Law formed the Union Safety Committee "to resist every attempt to alienate any portion of our country from the rest, or to enfeeble the sacred ties which now link together the various parts." The committee easily raised $25,000 for its activities, persuaded clergymen to set aside one day in December for sermons about its cause, and called on friends of the Union to hold public meetings throughout the city. These committee members and their followers may have been the "pimps of power" that so angered Jermain Loguen or, in the words of Samuel Ringgold Ward, the "Northern dough-faces" who were willing to "lick up the spittle of the slavocrats, and swear it is delicious," but their power and influence could not be ignored. Wendell Phillips thought the country had entered a new phase remi-

niscent of those "foreign scenes" after the abortive European revolutions of 1848, "which have hitherto been known to us, transatlantic republicans, only in books." For the first time they had to think seriously about the personal cost of opposing the government. Some of them, according to Phillips in a letter he wrote to Elizabeth Pease, an English friend, were considering "putting property out of their hands, planning to incur penalties, and planning also that, in case of conviction, the Government may get nothing from them."[25]

The forces organized against black communities and their white allies were daunting and imposing. Experience told African Americans that conditions would only get worse. Not surprisingly, they and their supporters adopted multiple approaches to the crisis created by the law. Some

The Reverend Jermain W. Loguen, former fugitive slave and a prominent defender of escaped bondmen in New York State.

looked to personal withdrawal, others to disobeying the law. Many contemplated changing the government by forming new political parties, and yet others advocated attacking the government verbally and by violent means, if necessary. Those who fled to Canada in the weeks and months after the Fugitive Slave Act's passage were motivated by fear of being returned to slavery. For others, especially those born free, the law confirmed the nation's total disregard for the rights of black Americans. They saw no other option but to leave the country. In October 1850, William Powell, a free black who had long been involved in promoting the welfare of black seamen, chaired a meeting in New York City that repudiated the law and voted to petition both Congress and the state assembly to repeal

it. Not long after this, Powell decided to take his family to England, convinced there was no future for them in the United States. Powell did not return until the early years of the Civil War.[26]

In Harrisburg, African Americans held a series of debates in February 1853 on the question, "Which offers the greatest inducement for a permanent home for the colored man, Africa or America?" Among those promoting Liberia was the eighteen-year-old Thomas Morris Chester, whose parents had long been active in radical abolitionist circles that opposed all schemes to send blacks out of the country. The young Chester had first been exposed to "emigrationism," as it was called, while attending school in Pittsburgh. There he heard lectures by Delany, the leading proponent of

Runaway advertisements that appeared in the (Columbus, Georgia) Times and Sentinel on March 1, 1853.

BROUGHT TO JAIL,

ON the 8th inst., as a runaway negro man by the name of TONEY, who says he belongs to Zachariah Daniel of Sumpter county, Ga., said boy is dark complected, nineteen or twenty years old, weighs two hundred lbs., the right forefinger nail half white, the other full black. The owner is requested to come forward, prove property, pay charges and take him away, or he will be dealt with according to law.   JOSEPH REMBERT,
Columbus, Dec 14—50wtf   Jailor of Muscogee county.

$300 Reward.

ON the night of the 29th of December last, my negro man JACK made his disappearance, taking with him a large BAY HORSE belonging to my father.
Jack is about thirty years of age, rather dark complexion, stout built, weighs about one hundred and sixty lbs., has lost his upper front teeth.
If the said boy has been stolen, I will give a reward of Five Hundred Dollars for the apprehension of thief and negro, and their delivery to me, or Three Hundred dollars for the negro and horse.   W. T. LOFTIN,
Jan 19—3w 6t   Rocky Mount, Merriwether co. G

African emigration, and may even have read Delany's emigration manifesto, *The Condition, Education, Emigration, and Destiny of the Colored People of the United States*, published in 1852. Elsewhere in Pennsylvania, blacks were exploring the possibilities of settling and doing business in Liberia.[27]

Like Powell and Chester, those who chose to leave the country went in search of a new beginning free from American slavery and discrimination. For those who held out hope of reforming America, the message of the law was unequivocal: blacks had no rights that whites were bound to respect. In this way, the law anticipated the more famous legal ruling in the Dred Scott case seven years later. Such indignities fueled a rage among blacks that surprised even some of their white friends. When Loguen refused offers to have friends purchase his freedom and in essence dared authorities to arrest him as a fugitive, he became a symbol of the willingness and determination of blacks to stay where they were and defy the law. In so doing, they appealed to a vision of America that ran counter to that which asserted America's freedom could be assured only by the security of slavery. Years after the Civil War had resolved the question of slavery and apparently had addressed the issue of black political equality, Samuel May suggested that, ironically, the seeds of such profound changes may have been planted in resistance to the Fugitive Slave Law. "The historian of our country, if he be one worthy of the task, will linger with delight over the pages on which he shall narrate the uprising of the people generally, in 1850 and 1851, throughout the Northern States, in opposition to the Fugitive Slave Law."[28] May represented the pride of a victor in a struggle well fought, but in 1850 few would have anticipated that the issues would be resolved in the space of thirteen years at the end of a bloody civil war. Of one thing, however, they were certain: the law had to be resisted at all cost and by every means at their disposal.

LOIS E. HORTON

KIDNAPPING AND RESISTANCE

Antislavery Direct Action in the 1850s

From the nation's beginning, the founders of the United States compromised on the troubling issue of slavery. In determining the population for the purposes of representation in the House of Representatives, for example, the choice came to counting only free people or counting every person, including slaves. As a compromise, three-fifths of the slaves were counted, giving Southern states less power than they wanted but a larger voice than Northern representatives thought appropriate. Disagreement over the continuation of the slave trade resulted in a compromise that protected the trade from congressional action for twenty years, until 1808. The greatest compromise on this issue was the decision to leave the future of slavery for each state to decide. Compromise, according to James Madison, is the foundation of democracy, the way to reconcile the divergent views of the various factions that arise from the multiplicity of an open society.

Disagreements over slavery arose again and again in the nineteenth century, requiring compromises that became increasingly difficult to achieve. The question of whether or not slavery should exist in the territories and in new states as they entered the Union proved especially vexing. This issue was settled, Congress believed at the time, by the Missouri Compromise of 1820, which excluded slavery from the territory of the Louisiana Purchase north of the 36°30' parallel, the southern border of Missouri. Thomas Jefferson considered this compromise only a reprieve, believing that the resurgence of the question was, as he said, "like a fire bell in the night" that filled him with "terror" for the endurance of the Union. The source of Jefferson's pessimism was his perception that slavery was wrong and Southerners would not find a way to end it. "But as it is," he observed, "we have a wolf by the ears, and we can neither hold him, nor safely let him go. Justice is in one scale, and self-preservation in the other."[1]

African Americans never accepted such compromises with slavery. They argued during the Revolution that the patriots' rhetoric of freedom was incompatible with the existence of slavery, and they fought against slavery on many fronts during the nineteenth century. Free blacks organized and petitioned. They bought family members' freedom and helped relatives, friends, and strangers escape. Slaves resisted regulation and work regimens, rebelled, and ran away. When white abolitionist William Lloyd Garrison joined black abolitionists to create an integrated militant antislavery movement in the 1830s, he declared that freedom could not be compromised. There should be "no union with slaveholders," Garrison famously maintained. More and more abolitionists came to believe that allowing freedom and slavery to coexist,

compromising America's fundamental principles, was immoral and doomed to failure. The refusal of black Americans and their white allies to accept an accommodation with slavery contributed greatly to the failure of the Compromise of 1850 and to the disunion that led to the Civil War.

Desperate and brave fugitives had sought freedom from the beginning of African enslavement in America. Even Africans with little knowledge of the language or the terrain attempted to escape, though their chances of success were relatively slim. Most people who ran away left plantations for nearby havens in the woods, for neighboring farms, the mountains, the Dismal Swamp of Virginia and North Carolina, or growing urban settlements with free black populations. Some found their way to Spanish Florida, where often they were protected by the Seminole Indians. During and immediately after the American Revolution, Vermont and Massachusetts ended slavery outright, and by the early nineteenth century, the other

An abolitionist records the story of an escaped slave. From *A Portraiture of Domestic Slavery in the United States*, 1817.

Northern states had passed measures gradually abolishing slavery from their jurisdictions. New York State replaced gradual emancipation with immediate abolition in 1827. It was impossible for most slaves to reach freedom in the North, but some, especially those in states bordering the free states, did manage the dangerous journey. In 1791 Thomas Rotch, a white man from a wealthy Nantucket merchant and trading family, provided aid and shelter in New Bedford, Massachusetts, to a fugitive named John, who was accompanied by his wife and five children. Upon learning that John's owner intended to come to New Bedford to reclaim them, Rotch sent part of the family to Providence and the protection of Moses Brown, another prominent foe of slavery. In 1792 Thomas's brother, William Rotch Jr., reported that so many fugitives sought refuge in Massachusetts that he was busy "almost daily" in their aid.[2]

Massachusetts continued to attract fugitives throughout the first half of the nineteenth century. When Ohio, just across the river from Kentucky, was admitted to the Union as a free state in 1803, it too became a magnet for enslaved people seeking freedom. Fugitives could find greater safety, however, outside of the United States, where laws protecting Americans' property rights in slaves did not apply. The abolition of slavery in the British empire in 1833 made Canada a haven for fugitives. The antislavery sympathies of the Canadian government reinforced this attraction, and Canada became home to a number of black immigrant settlements, such as Wilberforce, Chatham, and Buxton, where the majority of the residents were runaway slaves. Many fugitives traveling the legendary Underground Railroad made their way from slavery in the Upper South

through Pennsylvania and New York or up the Mississippi River through Ohio and Michigan to freedom in Canada. Some escape routes went south into Mexico, where slavery had been abolished in 1821. Mexico's northern territory, however, was also home to white immigrants from the American Lower South, many of whom were determined to maintain slavery. Thus, in 1836 Texans declared their independence from Mexico, and in 1845 the United States annexed Texas as a slave state. Some fugitives from slavery in the western South did escape farther south to freedom in Mexico, where at least one settlement of African Americans existed.[3]

From the early days of the republic, all blacks, slave and free, were in danger of being kidnapped into bondage. Prince Hall and other Boston blacks petitioned the Massachusetts legislature in 1788 for the freedom of three free men who had been taken aboard a ship that sailed to Martinique. Governor John Hancock responded and arranged for the men to be returned home. The Massachusetts legislature then enacted a new law prohibiting the slave trade and stipulating that kidnap victims be compensated.

Kidnapping free blacks became a common practice in the border states in the late eighteenth and early nineteenth centuries. Early abolition societies in Pennsylvania, Delaware, and Maryland were all committed to freeing blacks who were illegally held in bondage. In 1775, for example, the Pennsylvania organization called itself the Society for the Relief of Free Negroes Unlawfully Held in Bondage. Several years later, in 1787, it added the abolition of slavery and improving the condition of Africans to its name. Kidnapping continued throughout the period before the Civil War

and escalated after 1820 as slavery expanded into the lower western South. One newspaper reported in January 1837 that the opening of the Texas slave market and the high price of cotton had occasioned an increase in kidnapping in New York, New Jersey, and Pennsylvania. As if to prove the case, two months later the newspaper reported that a free black woman named Morgan and her six children had been seized by a constable and slave catchers in New York City, transported to Maryland, and sold to a slave driver for shipment south.[4]

Certain African Americans were particularly vulnerable to being kidnapped. Children were at risk, since they were physically easier to subdue. People in the border states, where a large free black population developed, were targets of kidnappers who operated close to slave territory. Notorious gangs roamed the Pennsylvania-Maryland border with relative impunity from prosecution. Bringing kidnappers to justice was difficult, since it required financial resources, the cooperation of authorities in slave states, and jury decisions in favor of blacks and against whites. Settlements frequently required kidnappers to pay court costs and the jail fees of the victim. This was important for poverty-stricken African Americans, but it hardly deterred the profitable enterprise of kidnapping.[5]

Black sailors who traveled to ports in slaveholding states were another vulnerable group. Some states in the Deep South passed laws, such as South Carolina's Negro Seamen Act of 1822, that required free black sailors either to be confined to their ships or to be incarcerated in the local jail while their ships were in port. Southerners believed that free blacks from the North were likely to spread ideas about freedom and to foment slave insurrection if they mingled with the local black population. Under such laws, sailors sometimes risked being sold into slavery should the ship's captain refuse to cover the costs of their jailing or if papers proving their free status were confiscated or lost.

Sailors and border fugitives were the most vulnerable to being snatched from freedom into slavery, but virtually all

African Americans were at risk. The widespread practice of kidnapping, along with taking legal actions against free blacks thought to be fugitives and the inclination of authorities to believe that accused African Americans were slaves, made everyone's freedom precarious. Even the prominent Philadelphia black leader and minister Richard Allen was wrongly charged with being a fugitive slave by a Maryland slave owner and taken before a judge twenty years after he had purchased his own freedom. One of the best-known cases of kidnapping was that of Solomon Northup, a free black musician who played during the summers at resort hotels in Saratoga Springs, New York. In the winter of 1841 two white men offered him a job with their act. He traveled with them to Albany and New York City, and then continued on to Washington, DC, where they said they intended to get work with the circus.[6]

In Washington, Northup's employers drugged him, robbed him, and sold him to a slave dealer. His protestations that he was a free man earned him only beatings, and through a series of sales he ended up on a Louisiana plantation. Northup endured the horrors of slavery for twelve years and estimated that hundreds of other kidnapped blacks were living in slavery in Louisiana and Texas at that time. Eventually he was able to enlist the aid of Samuel Bass, a white Canadian carpenter, and cautiously entrusted him with his story. Authorities in New York and Louisiana finally confronted the plantation owner, and Northup was freed. *Twelve Years a Slave,* the narrative of Northup's life in slavery and his restoration to freedom, created a sensation when it was published in 1853. It sold eight thousand copies in the first month, and its harrowing tale of kidnapping and poignant

portrayal of life in slavery disseminated a powerful antislavery message.[7]

Early white and integrated abolitionist organizations pursued strategies shaped by the differences between legal and illegal enslavement. They sought legal remedies for kidnapped free blacks, pursuing their cases in the courts and seeking damages and freedom. In their attempts to protect captive fugitives, however, early abolitionists were more likely to raise money to purchase their freedom. This distinction was difficult to maintain. Kidnapping was so common that legal costs were soon well

"A Northern Freeman Enslaved by Northern Hands," from *Anti-Slavery Almanac,* 1839.

beyond the financial means of antislavery organizations. Most importantly, to the increasingly numerous militant abolitionists, maintaining a distinction between the kidnapping of free blacks and the capture of fugitives seemed to acknowledge the legitimacy of the slave system. Black abolitionists and their most radical white allies did not recognize a slaveholder's right to enslave human beings. Therefore, they considered both captured fugitives and captured free blacks to be kidnapped. To them, slavery was immoral, as were fugitive arrests and the whole arsenal of obligations

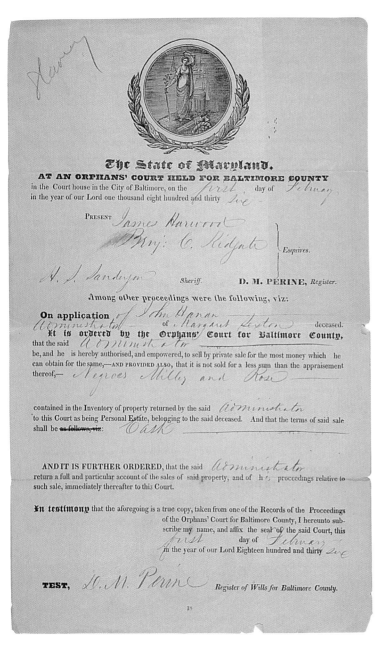

The State of Maryland.

AT AN ORPHANS' COURT HELD FOR BALTIMORE COUNTY

in the Court house in the City of Baltimore, on the _first_ day of _February_ in the year of our Lord one thousand eight hundred and thirty _six_

PRESENT _James Harwood_
Benj: C. Ridgate } _Esquires._

A. S. Sandwyn Sheriff. D. M. PERINE, Register.

Among other proceedings were the following, viz:

On application of _John Apnan_ _Administrator_ of _Margaret Liston_ deceased. **It is ordered by the Orphans' Court for Baltimore County,** that the said _Administrator_ be, and he is hereby authorised, and empowered, to sell by private sale for the most money which he can obtain for the same,—AND PROVIDED ALSO, that it is not sold for a less sum than the appraisement thereof,— _Negroes Milly and Rose_

contained in the Inventory of property returned by the said _Administrator_ to this Court as being Personal Estate, belonging to the said deceased. And that the terms of said sale shall be as follows, viz: _Cash_

AND IT IS FURTHER ORDERED, that the said _Administrator_ return a full and particular account of the sales of said property, and of h __ proceedings relative to such sale, immediately thereafter to this Court.

In testimony that the aforegoing is a true copy, taken from one of the Records of the Proceedings of the Orphans' Court for Baltimore County, I hereunto subscribe my name, and affix the seal of the said Court, this _first_ day of _February_ in the year of our Lord Eighteen hundred and thirty _six_

TEST, _D. M. Perine_ Register of Wills for Baltimore County.

18

Orphans' court sale in Maryland of "Milly" and "Rose" after their master's death, 1836.

and punishments associated with the Fugitive Slave Law. They believed that abiding by a higher law sanctioned illegal tactics and all manner of subterfuge to avoid anyone's return to slavery. African Americans' most important white allies, Quakers and Boston newspaper editor William Lloyd Garrison, made such arguments for the violation of fugitive slave laws. Garrison, like the Quakers, was a pacifist, however, and he strongly objected to any resort to violence in antislavery action. Black supporters of Garrison, even those who could agree with his doctrines of immediate abolition, reliance on moral suasion, and nonparticipation in politics, often struggled with his steadfast advocacy of nonviolence, even in self-defense.[8]

Although early abolitionists generally tended to use legal strategies and to purchase fugitives' freedom, they sometimes resorted to direct action. In the summer of 1836 Eliza Small and Polly Ann Bates, fugitives from Baltimore, were detained aboard the brig *Chickasaw* as it entered Boston harbor. Captain Eldridge held them at the request of a slave catcher named Turner, an agent for John B. Morris of Baltimore who claimed the women were his slaves. Reportedly, Morris had offered Small and Bates their freedom if they would emigrate to Liberia. They had refused his offer, saying they would be willing to go to Haiti, but Morris would not agree to this alternative. Both women held free papers for their voyage to Boston, but Turner managed to trick one into giving her papers to him. At their hearing, Justice Shaw declared that Captain Eldridge, not being the slave owner's agent, had no right to detain Small and Bates, and he decided the women should be discharged. Before he could pronounce them free to go, however, Turner stood up and declared his intention to make a new arrest, asking the judge if he needed a warrant. At the same moment, a constable went to lock the door leading downstairs, which greatly alarmed the African Americans seated in the courtroom. They all rose from their seats and rushed toward the fugitives. A group of black women burst into the courtroom, and when the deputy sheriff tried to intervene, a cleaning woman "of great size" seized him and threw him aside. The crowd hurried the captives down the stairs, out of the courthouse, and into a waiting carriage for their escape from the city. The successful rescue of the two women was accomplished in just a matter of minutes, and none of the rescuers was apprehended or identified.[9]

It is unclear whether Small and Bates were actually free or were fugitive slaves. Much of the reporting on the case presumed them to be fugitives, but they were never brought to trial to assess the validity of their freedom papers. There is, in fact, some reason to be suspicious of their claim to freedom. According to the recollections of Robert Purvis in Philadelphia, two market women in Baltimore—one black and one white—commonly helped fugitive slaves by providing them with freedom papers. They possessed a number of papers with physical descriptions that were general enough for several people to use, according to Purvis's memory of the Underground Railroad, because of whites' perception that "all negroes look alike." Successful fugitives returned the papers to the market women to be used by other runaways.[10]

Garrison's commentary in the *Liberator* on the rescue of Small and Bates is telling. He condemned any violence that might have been committed but condoned the crowd's actions, contending that they believed the women had been discharged and simply wanted to protect them from "the kidnapper." "Resistance to the legal authorities we never hesitate to disapprove," Garrison wrote, "but we see no evidence in the conduct of the accused that they intended any disrespect to the court, or any transgression of the law." To rein-

force this condemnation of violence, the Massachusetts Anti-Slavery Society formally expressed "deep regret and decided disapprobation" of the rescuers' actions.[11]

Important disagreements circulated among African Americans on using violence or the threat of it to defend fugitives. In April 1837 a crowd estimated at one thousand gathered at the courthouse and a nearby park in New York City to protest the trial of Dickson, a fugitive slave. Samuel Cornish, black editor of the *Colored American*, penned an article addressed "To the Thoughtless part of our Colored Citizens," in which he admonished readers to act with more dignity and self-restraint when fugitive slaves were captured. Cornish urged African Americans to leave the defense of fugitives to the lawyers who had been hired by the vigilance committee. Reportedly, the crowd had precipitated what the paper called "a disgraceful riot"

A poster announcing the raffle of "Star," a dark bay horse, and "Sarah," a stout mulatto girl, suggests slaves were held in the same regard as work animals. Such comparisons might have led some to conclude that slavery had to be resisted by means outside the law.

when an attempt was made to rescue a fugitive and two or three black people had been arrested. Public protest, even public assembly, Cornish warned, would risk the loss of support from respectable allies. He was especially shocked by the involvement of black women in this protest, singling them out for "everlasting shame" and charging that they "degraded" themselves by their participation. "We beg their husbands," he continued, "to keep them at home for the time to come, and find some better occupation for them."[12]

The *Colored American* placed its faith in the working of the courts and the advocacy of lawyers. It emphasized the need for dignity and decorum, even while it reported that the judge, Justice Bloodgood, had cursed the protesters and expressed his desire to shoot and kill them for sport. The paper's disapproval of women's involvement in fugitive rescue attempts is especially surprising in light of the fact that less than two years before, in the summer of 1835, a gang of kidnappers had seized a number of New York's free black children, shipped them south, and sold them into slavery in Mississippi. In fact, children continued to be kidnapped in New York City, and four more had been lost just three or four months before Dickson's trial. At the time of Cornish's reproach, officials were trying to locate captured children, apprehend the culprits, and return the young people to their parents.[13]

An increasing determination marked the organized antislavery movement during the 1840s, and a more strident tone characterized many abolitionist pronouncements. In 1841 David Ruggles, a black New Yorker, urged his colleagues to action, saying that more than words were required. He also revived a call to slave revolt uttered more

than ten years before by the militant free black writer David Walker. Two years later a new generation took up the cry as black minister and former fugitive slave Henry Highland Garnet spoke before the meeting of the National Negro Convention in Buffalo, New York. Garnet vehemently rejected Garrison's principles. He excoriated blacks for submitting to slavery and urged them to resist. Although addressed to faraway slaves, his words perhaps carried a message to his fellows close at hand. "There is not much hope of Redemption," he asserted, "without the shedding of blood . . . Rather die freemen than live to be slaves." The convention was by no means united behind Garnet's call for slave resistance. Black Garrisonians, including Charles Lenox Remond, William Wells Brown, and Frederick Douglass, spoke strongly against resolutions endorsing Garnet's fiery speech.[14]

By the 1840s African Americans in Northern communities left no doubt that slave catchers would be dealt with violently if necessary. In Utica, New York, in 1840 a judge upheld the claim of white Virginians to two black men. A group of black men then overcame the captors using physical force, freed the fugitives, and imprisoned their claimants. In 1847 African Americans met the threat of violence with overwhelming numbers. When slave catchers from Kentucky apprehended accused runaway Christopher Webb, who was working as a waiter in a saloon in Buffalo, New York, a large crowd faced down the armed slave catchers and freed Webb. The slaveholder's agents found themselves arrested for assault and battery as well as false imprisonment. In Boston that same year, several black women, including teacher Nancy Prince, left no doubt about their determi-

In "The Sale," sold slaves are transported south from Richmond, Virginia, ca. 1850s.

nation to rid the community of slave catchers. They physically confronted one slave catcher near the African Meeting House, threw stones at him, and chased him from their Beacon Hill neighborhood. The next year black women in Cincinnati confronted slave catchers who were pursuing a group of eight or ten fugitives. Armed with shovels, rolling pins, and washboards, the women led a crowd of local residents and put to flight the much more heavily armed slave catchers.[15]

Although crowds of blacks confronted slave catchers, black abolitionists and their white allies also used nonviolent strategies in their attempts to protect fugitives. The case of George Latimer illustrates the wide variety of techniques they employed. Latimer was arrested in Boston in October 1842 and accused of belonging to James B. Gray of Norfolk, Virginia. A group of African Americans attacked the officers who were transporting Latimer from the courthouse to the jail. They seriously injured one of the officers, but the rescue attempt was unsuccessful, and eight of the attackers were arrested. The community then pursued legal avenues to free Latimer. First, abolitionists sought a writ of habeas corpus to gain his release, and when this failed, they turned to organizing public protests. They posted broadsides denouncing the Boston police as kidnappers, and they issued a special protest newspaper, called the *Latimer and North Star Journal*, every other day. Antislavery forces formed Latimer aid committees throughout Massachusetts, they circulated petitions, and they held mass protest meetings. At the African Meeting House in Boston, protesters endorsed all methods to gain the fugitives' freedom. Their announcement of a meeting to be held in Lynn in early November was published in Garrison's *Liberator*, and its tone was far from nonviolent. "Let the New 'Cradle of Liberty' rock on Friday evening," the writer declared, "as the Old one did, in the days of Hancock and Adams. If our present Government fails to protect us from the blood-hounds of the South," the announcement continued, "it is high time to fall back upon our reserved rights! LIBERTY BEFORE CONSTITUTIONS!! The times demand a second revolution!!!" Such language dispelled all thoughts of compromise. Although Latimer asserted that his freedom had already been purchased, abolitionists finally raised funds and bought his freedom from Gray. Following his release, Latimer aid committees presented to the Massachusetts legislature a 150-pound petition containing 64,526 signatures. The following year Massachusetts passed a Personal Liberty Act that forbade state officials or facilities from being used to capture fugitive slaves.[16]

Congress made another fateful attempt at compromising the interests of slaveholding and free states in 1850. In an effort to prevent a threatened secession by Southern states and to settle the slavery issue once and for all, Congress passed a series of resolutions that included the admission of California as a free state, provided for popular sovereignty regarding the existence of slavery in the territories of New Mexico and Utah, and protected slavery itself while abolishing the slave trade in the District of Columbia. With this com-

promise, Illinois senator Stephen A. Douglas decided that he would make no more speeches on slavery. "Let us cease agitating, stop the debate, and drop the subject," Douglas said. "If we do this, the Compromise will be recognized as a final settlement." Most importantly, the compromise also included the passage of a new federal Fugitive Slave Law that strengthened the power of slaveholders to retrieve runaways. The new law made it easier to claim a person as a fugitive slave and provided harsh penalties for bystanders who failed to aid in a fugitive's capture. The fact that presiding officials were paid double if the accused was found to be a fugitive slave placed the federal government squarely on the side of the slaveholder and seemed to the abolitionists to encourage the kidnapping of free blacks. The Fugitive Slave Act of 1850 infuriated African Americans and convinced many white abolitionists that nonviolence alone could not thwart the power of slaveholders. The reaction of the antislavery forces was clear even before the bill became law. In the summer of 1850 they held a Convention of Fugitive Slaves in Cazenovia, New York, where they defiantly pledged to protect fugitives. In an open letter, they urged slaves to rise up against their masters and to do anything necessary to escape. The open participation of at least thirty fugitive slaves guaranteed the convention would attract the attention of the media and of Congress.[17]

At the end of August, just a few days after the bill passed the US Senate, slave catchers accosted Henry "Box" Brown on the streets of Providence, Rhode Island. Brown was a fugitive from Virginia who, a year and a half before, had shipped himself in a crate via overland express to abolitionists and freedom in Pennsylvania. He and a friend, James C. A. Smith, presented "Box" Brown's story on the antislavery lecture circuit by displaying and performing a narrative panorama. Called *The Mirror of Slavery*, it depicted Africa, slavery, and Brown's harrowing escape. After one such performance in Providence, a group of men attacked Brown and beat him, but he managed to get away. The men then waylaid him a second time and tried to force him into a carriage, but they could not overpower him. Brown attributed the bold daylight attack to the new fugitive slave law. Shortly thereafter, on the advice of antislavery friends, Brown and Smith left the country and took their panorama to England.[18]

Immediately after President Millard Fillmore signed the new law on September 18, 1850, Northern communities mobilized in protest. African Americans held meetings in churches all over the North to organize their resistance. Abolitionists also held integrated mass meetings in churches and halls, vowing to redouble their efforts to defend fugitives from the most recent federal assault on freedom. The first capture of a fugitive under the new law came just a week later. On September 26, 1850, a US marshal arrested James Hamlet while he was working as a porter in New York City. Hamlet, a fugitive slave from Baltimore, had lived in New York for three years and had settled there with his wife and two children. He claimed that, as the son of a free mother, he had been illegally enslaved. The commissioner refused to entertain his claim, since under the law an alleged fugitive was prohibited from testifying in his own defense. The authorities immediately returned Hamlet to Baltimore, where his owner, who intended to sell him farther south, had him imprisoned.[19]

At a mostly black meeting held at the African Methodist Episcopal Church in Boston four days after Hamlet's arrest, William Lloyd Garrison read aloud the Fugitive Slave Law and provided a heated commentary on its provisions. The densely packed meeting took the new law's threat seriously, declaring that it "[put] in imminent jeopardy the lives and liberties of ourselves and our children." Meanwhile, African Americans in New York City confirmed that James Hamlet's owner was willing to sell him. Fifteen hundred people

met at a black church there to protest the injustice of the law and to pledge their support. The black community raised $500, white merchants and abolitionists contributed another $300, and they purchased Hamlet's freedom.[20]

Black leaders' anger exploded at another meeting held in Boston on October 4 at the Belknap Street Church. Although Garrison was there, African American abolitionists spoke openly of their determination to use violence, if necessary, to protect

Broadside announcing the capture of Anthony Burns on May 25, 1854, and deploring his "mock trial."

fugitives and other community members. Joshua B. Smith, armed with a revolver and a knife, showed the gathering how to run a slave catcher through and advised every fugitive to arm himself. William G. Allen urged listeners to defend their families "to the death." Once again, women took an active role in defending fugitives. Robert Johnson called upon women whose work took them to hotels and boardinghouses to watch for slave catchers, whereupon he was loudly assured that the spirit that had animated the rescuers of Polly Ann Bates and Eliza Small was still alive among the women of Boston. Johnson asserted that Boston's blacks would not be aggressors searching for a slave hunter, but if they were attacked they would "kill him." Many black men in Boston armed themselves and fortified their homes as a precaution.[21]

Ellen Craft, from the *Illustrated London News*, April 19, 1855.

The following day, New Yorkers celebrated the return of James Hamlet from slavery. Four to five thousand people, both blacks and whites, gathered in the park across from city hall to greet him as he was reunited with his family and friends. So strong was community feeling, according to a report in the *Liberator*, that when six female fugitives from Baltimore arrived in New York City the day after Hamlet's triumphant return, the police refused to aid the slave catchers who were attempting to recover them. Northern abolitionists maintained a full calendar of protest meetings throughout the months that followed the Fugitive Slave Law's passage. They called upon the laws of God, the principles of the American Revolution, and decent moral standards as they urged people to disobey this federal law. The published call for a meeting in Boston's Faneuil Hall on October 14 was signed by 336 prominent citizens to illustrate their growing defiance. At this meeting, Frederick Douglass addressed the overflowing crowd and denounced the law for over an hour. Another meeting held at the Brick Wesley AME Church in Philadelphia called the law "Anti-Republican, Anti-Christian [and] Anti-human." The first of the ten resolutions passed at this meeting of African Americans captured the outrage and determination of black communities throughout the North:

> Resolved, That while we have heretofore yielded obedience to the laws of our country, however hard some of them have borne upon us, we deem this law so wicked, so atrocious, so utterly at variance with the principles of the Constitution; so subversive of the objects of all law, the protection of the lives, liberty, and property of the governed; so repugnant to the highest attributes of God, justice and mercy; and so horribly cruel in its clearly expressed mode of operation, that we deem it our sacred duty, a duty that we owe to ourselves, our wives, our children, and to our common nature, as well as to the panting fugitive from oppression, to resist this law at any cost and at all hazards; and we hereby pledge our lives, our fortunes, and our sacred honor so to do.[22]

This resolve was quickly put to the test. On October 26, 1850, a warrant was issued in Boston for the arrest of William and Ellen Craft. The Crafts were fugitives from slavery in Georgia, where William had been mortgaged to a local bank to cover his master's debts. Ellen, the slave and daughter of her owner, had been given as a wedding present to her white half-sister. The Crafts had made a daring escape nearly two years before, setting out on the day after Christmas and traveling by train and boat. Light-skinned Ellen had dressed as a young gentleman, bandaged her face and feigned a toothache to disguise her lack of a beard, and put her arm in a sling so as not to expose her illiteracy if asked to sign a hotel register. In this disguise she had passed for white, with William accompanying her as the young man's personal servant. They reached Philadelphia, where they met abolitionists and were recruited by William Wells Brown as touring antislavery speakers. The Crafts spent a year lecturing in the Boston area and six months in Great Britain, unaware that their owner was following their speaking career in the abolitionist press. Upon their return to Boston in the fall of 1850, the Crafts attended meetings to protest the new Fugitive Slave Law. At the same time, their owner sent two agents to Boston to recover his property.[23]

The entire abolitionist community in the Boston area leapt into action with the threat to William and Ellen Craft. It kept the slave catchers under constant surveillance and had them arrested several times for slander against William and conspiracy to kidnap him. The fugitives were moved frequently from house to house to avoid capture. Angry meetings in the black community vowed to protect the fugitives at all costs. The slave catchers confronted ardent abolitionist Lewis Hayden at his barricaded home where he was sheltering William. Hayden, himself a fugitive slave, was accompanied by a number of armed black men and stood on his front steps with a lighted torch. He would explode the gunpowder he had placed there, he warned, blowing up himself, his house, and every-

one nearby, rather than surrender the fugitive. Unprepared for this level of violence, the slave catchers left the city. One of theme, Mr. J. Knight of Macon, Georgia, later gave a very different report. He admitted that "Abolitionists and Negroes [were] very numerous" in Boston, but he expressed his confidence that the Crafts would eventually be recovered. As for his reason for leaving Boston, he said, "My only regret is, that my own private business compelled me to return home. . . . Had I leisure and means to spare, I should return with pleasure even at the risk of gratifying certain gentlemen of Macon by rotting in a Boston jail." Working together, black as well as white abolitionists had saved the Crafts from being captured and sent back to slavery, but their future safety remained uncertain. The Boston Vigilance Committee arranged for the Crafts to travel to England, where they remained until after the Civil War.[24]

Attempts to enforce the new Fugitive Slave Law led many fugitives, some of whom had lived in the North for a generation, to leave for the safe havens of Canada, Mexico, or Britain. Many free blacks, feeling even more vulnerable to kidnapping, left the country as well. The exodus began almost immediately after the passage of the law. According to one report, in just a few weeks "nearly all the waiters in the hotels" in Cincinnati, an estimated three hundred persons, had "fled to Canada." During the same time, the city of Columbia, Pennsylvania, lost more than four hundred fifty people, more than half of its black residents. Similar situations occurred all over the North, and by mid-December the Anti-Slavery Society of Canada estimated that as many as four to five thousand African Americans had arrived since the law's passage. Ironically, the new law and the publicity attending the fugitive slave cases also seemed to stimulate more escapes from slavery. On October 18, 1850, white abolitionists Samuel May Jr. and Robert Wallcut advertised in the *Liberator*, seeking employment and clothing for the increasing number of fugitives in Boston. Federal authorities made their determination clear that month when they used three military companies to guard a single fugitive captured in Detroit.[25]

In late December, about a month after the Crafts escaped from Boston, Henry Long was arrested in New York City. A twenty-five-year-old fugitive from Richmond, Virginia, Long was living in New York with his wife and working as a waiter in a hotel tavern. In this case, the Union Safety Committee, a group of conservative businessmen, prominent lawyers, and those with ties to Southern commerce, represented the proslavery forces. The Manhattan Anti-Slavery Society, presided over by black abolitionist William P. Powell, led the slavery opponents. When the judge declared that Long should be returned to slavery, an angry crowd of African Americans gathered at the house where they believed he was being held. An altercation broke out when a black man struck a white man. The fight ended when a Southerner who had been a witness at the trial "drew a six-barrelled revolver, and threatened to blow away" anyone who interfered with Long's return. Emotions were running high throughout the North. Just the day before Henry Long was sentenced, abolitionist John Brown took what might be seen as his first step on the road to martyrdom at Harpers Ferry. He formed a new organization, called the US League of Gileadites, in Springfield, Massachusetts.

At the league's initial meeting, forty-four black men and women stepped forward to pledge themselves to self-defense.[26]

The extended trial in New York cost Long's owner $300 and the Union Safety Committee $500, but the owner rebuffed abolitionist efforts to purchase Long's freedom. A Southern congressman urged that "every effort should be made to prevent the owner of Henry from selling him into the hands of the abolitionists." In this way, he believed, slaves might be discouraged from escaping. One Southern newspaper jubilantly declared Long's arrest and return to be a test case for the enforcement of the Fugitive Slave Law, saying that it showed "Boston tricks cannot long be successfully practiced." Officials placed Henry Long in chains, and two hundred policemen escorted him to the wharf where he would begin his return to slavery. Frederick Douglass was infuriated by reports that no African Americans had tried to impede Long's return. If true, he lamented, "it is humiliating in the extreme, that, in a city with a colored population of more than twenty thousand, such a high-handed and daring atrocity could be perpetrated without any intervention on the part of any among them." In late January the *Liberator* reported that Long and about twenty others had been sold at auction in Richmond. A slave dealer from Georgia had purchased him for $750 and posted a $3,000 assurance to guarantee that he would take Long farther south. In the same issue, the *Liberator* reported the safe arrival of William and Ellen Craft in England.[27]

Less than a month after Henry Long's return to slavery from New York, abolitionists in Boston had another opportunity to prove their antislavery credentials. On February 15, 1851, Shadrach Minkins (also

known as Frederick Wilkins) was arrested by US marshals as he was waiting on tables at Taft's Cornhill Coffee House. (Minkins, a fugitive from slavery in Norfolk, Virginia, had made his way to Boston about nine months earlier.) The arrest was handled quietly, and the nine marshals and their deputies stationed in and around the restaurant managed to avoid the attention of the city's abolitionists. Once Minkins was in custody and taken to the courthouse, the authorities could no longer keep the affair quiet. News spread quickly through the community, and in half an hour about two hundred people converged on the courtroom. Antislavery lawyers from the Vigilance Committee and African Americans from Beacon Hill turned out in force, and the committee hired former fugitive slave George Latimer to keep Minkins's owner under surveillance. Although many cases were concluded by a simple confirmation of the fugitive's identity, the judge in this case granted Minkins's lawyers a postponement of three days to prepare their case.[28]

Minkins's lawyers did not need the extra time, however, because another plan was immediately put into action. A large group of black men led by Lewis Hayden forced their way into the courtroom that served as a jail, picked up Minkins, and carried him out of the room, down the stairs, and out of the building. With the

Thomas S. Noble, *Last Sale of Slaves on the Courthouse Steps,* 1860. On the eve of the Civil War, such scenes were still common in the American South.

crowd trailing behind them, the rescuers bore Minkins a quarter mile into the black community and hid him for a short time in the attic of the widow Elizabeth Riley's home near Hayden's house. That afternoon Hayden took the fugitive out of the city by carriage; six days later he arrived in Montreal, Canada. Just three days after Shadrach Minkins's rescue, President Fillmore issued a special proclamation ordering federal charges be brought against the rescuers. Those accused of taking a direct role were a broad cross-section of antislavery forces in the city: black lawyer Robert Morris; black clothing dealers Thomas Paul Smith, James Scott, and John P. Coburn; white lawyer Charles G. Davis; white newspaper editor Elizur Wright; black laborer John Foye; Joseph K. Hayes, the white superintendent of Tremont Temple; Alexander P. Burton, a black barber from Salem; and Lewis Hayden.[29]

The euphoria from the speedy rescue of Shadrach Minkins in mid-February was tempered by another fugitive's capture in Boston on April 4, 1851. On that day Thomas Sims, a seventeen-year-old fugitive from Savannah, Georgia, was arrested and incarcerated in the federal courthouse, which was now secured with chains. During Sims's nine-day imprisonment and trial, police and federal marshals were determined to prevent another rescue. They guarded him heavily, installed bars on the window of the room where he was being held, and conducted random searches of the crowds that gathered outside the courthouse. Abolitionists' legal defense of Sims failed, and planned rescue attempts were thwarted by security precautions, white abolitionists' concerns about violence, and the depleted forces of the diminished black population. A crowd of men

and women kept watch at the courthouse, "occasionally hooting at the officers," during the night before Sims was to be sent back to Georgia. In the early hours of the morning on April 11, about 150 guards armed with clubs, hooks, and swords marched Sims to the wharf. An escort of at least 100 abolitionists followed this procession. The government's determination to enforce the Fugitive Slave Law can be measured by the fact that the recovery of Sims cost the federal government $10,000, and the city of Boston about the same amount.[30]

In the eyes of the antislavery forces, the return of Thomas Sims shamed the city of Boston and tarnished its claim as the cradle of liberty. The mainstream press, however, celebrated the decorum with which the law had been upheld. The *Boston Courier* expressed great relief that no riot had ensued and the mob behavior that had freed Shadrach had not been repeated in the Sims case. "The country will learn with infinite gratification," it reported, "that all fears of a forcible resistance to the law in this city are at an end." Even so, the paper's pronouncement was premature and greatly underestimated African Americans' determination to resist the Fugitive Slave Law. With these highly publicized returns of fugitives to bondage, the general public in Boston and elsewhere in the North expressed increasing sympathy for the slave. Additionally, the antislavery cause gained an important new voice just a few months after the cap-

J. S. Covant, "Lewis Hayden," 1859.

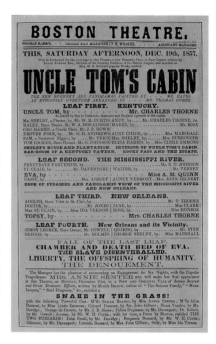

ABOVE: *The Sale of Uncle Tom.*

MIDDLE: A German edition of *Uncle Tom's Cabin,* 1852.

RIGHT: Playbill for *Uncle Tom's Cabin,* **Boston Theatre, 1857.**

OPPOSITE: Little Eva in heaven.

Each from Theodore Johnson, *Uncle Tom's Cabin* theater scrapbook.

ture of Thomas Sims, when a novel by Harriet Beecher Stowe, called *Uncle Tom's Cabin,* began its serialization in the antislavery newspaper, the *National Era,* published in Washington, DC. When published in book form in March 1852, Stowe's novel created a sensation. It sold ten thousand copies in the first week and three hundred thousand in the first year. *Uncle Tom's Cabin* converted many to the antislavery cause both in America and abroad.[31]

During the 1850s more than eighty well-publicized rescues and rescue attempts were made, and each one infuriated slaveholders, garnered increasing Northern sympathy for antislavery, and intensified the determination of abolitionists to fight the Fugitive Slave Law. Members of the Boston Vigilance Committee were especially busy aiding runaways to escape in 1850 and 1851. Their meticulous records describe the forty-nine fugitives they helped to freedom in 1850, including Shadrach Minkins and William and Ellen Craft. In 1851 they

reported Thomas Sims's return to Savannah, but they also listed eighty-four people who had been spirited out of the city successfully. In reviewing these records, historian Stanley W. Campbell also found an upsurge in the number of fugitives arrested in 1851, the vast majority of whom were returned to slavery. The prospects for fugitives who were caught in the North grew dismal, even if black abolitionists were willing to use direct action and the threat of violence to rescue them. Of the 330 fugitives arrested in the decade from 1850 to 1860, Campbell discovered 296 of them, or almost 90 percent, were returned to slavery. This seems a very high success rate for slave owners, but it does not factor in the number of slaves who managed to elude arrest and escaped to freedom. Only some of these runaways were aided by formal committees of the Underground Railroad. In Boston alone, the vigilance committee aided 407 fugitives from 1850 to 1858, only three of whom

(Sims in 1851, Sandy Swan in 1853, and Anthony Burns in 1854) were returned to slavery. Although relatively few of those arrested were rescued, it was the rescues themselves that particularly irritated Southern slave owners and made them demand greater and greater efforts on the part of the federal government.[32]

Fugitive slaves were most in danger of recapture in the states of Pennsylvania and Ohio, free states located just over the border from slavery. From 1850 to 1860, Campbell found, eighty-six slaves were arrested in Pennsylvania and ninety-six in Ohio, compared to only seventeen in New York and seven in Massachusetts. African Americans in lower Pennsylvania were organized and armed for self-defense. William Parker, who had escaped from slavery in Maryland at age seventeen, led the blacks in Christiana in Lancaster County, Pennsylvania. Under Parker's direction, they had organized themselves to thwart the efforts of the Gap Gang, a group of notorious kidnappers. In early September 1851, when the Fugitive Slave Law had been in force for just under a year, Edward Gorsuch, a Maryland slaveholder, set out with a group of his relatives to recover two fugitives who were staying at Parker's home. There, Gorsuch's party, led by a federal marshal, confronted the seven armed and forewarned African Americans who were inside and demanded the fugitives' return. The adversaries exchanged shots, Mrs. Parker sounded an alarm, and a large group of black defenders armed with guns and farm implements emerged from the surrounding houses and fields. A few of the white neighbors came as well, but they refused to respond to the marshal's commands that they aid in recovering the fugitives. In the ensuing struggle with an esti-

mated seventy-five to one hundred fifty blacks, Gorsuch was killed and his son, nephew, and cousin were wounded. According to some reports, several black women attacked the slave owner after he was shot. Parker later remembered it differently. Samuel Thompson, Gorsuch's former slave, struck his owner with a gun, he recalled. Then three or four people attacked Gorsuch, and finally "the women put an end to him." Two African Americans were also wounded in what became known as the Battle of Christiana or the Christiana Riot.[33]

William Parker and two other men left for Canada via the Underground Railroad before they could be arrested. On the way they were sheltered in Rochester, New York, by Frederick Douglass, whom Parker had known in slavery in Maryland. Douglass considered the men heroes, despite the violence of their actions. He reprinted an article from Henry Bibb's Canadian newspaper, *Voice of the Fugitive*, in *Frederick Douglass' Paper* after the fugitives were safely in Canada. Parker, Bibb wrote, deserved "the admiration of a Hannibal, a Toussaint L'Ouverture, or a George Washington. A nobler defence was never made in behalf of human liberty on the plains of Lexington, Concord or Bunker Hill than was put forth by William Parker at Christiana." Apparently, the British government agreed, and it refused to honor the American government's request that

During the Christiana Riot, William Parker and other free blacks routed slave catchers in Christiana, Pennsylvania, in 1851.

the fugitives be extradited. The grand jury in Philadelphia returned indictments against thirty-six people in connection with the Christiana Riot, including five whites, some of whom had simply refused to aid in apprehending the fugitives. At the instigation of the US district attorney, a jury charged the participants with treason against the government of the United States, murder, and riot, as well as with violating the Fugitive Slave Law. When they failed to obtain a conviction in the first test case, the government dropped the charges against the others.[34]

The next widely publicized confrontation between the federal government and antislavery forces occurred in Syracuse, New York, about a month after the Christiana Riot. The agent for a slaveholder in Missouri apparently had been in Syracuse for at least a month, but he chose October 1 to have William McHenry, known as Jerry, arrested as a fugitive from slavery. It was an inauspicious time for

such an arrest, though, since the city was hosting both the county fair and the Liberty Party convention at the time and was crowded with visitors, many of them prominent abolitionists. At first McHenry was told that he was being arrested for theft, a common ruse to avoid resistance. When it became clear that he was charged with being a fugitive, he fought back, and the abolitionist convention was immediately notified. A large crowd, estimated at four to five thousand people, gathered outside the hearing room, and some threw stones at the windows. A small group broke in and carried McHenry out just as the hearing was adjourning for lunch, but he was soon recaptured by the police. Abolitionists then determined to take him back by force, believing this would clearly declare popular opposition to slavery and the Fugitive Slave Law. While the crowd outside provided moral support, a group of forty or fifty blacks and whites (disguised in blackface) broke into the room in back of the police office where McHenry was being held. They pried away the bolts and bars holding the door and chased away the deputy marshals. One marshal jumped out of a second-story window, breaking his arm and spraining his ankle. They freed McHenry and hurried him into a waiting carriage that eventually rushed him out of the city on his way to Canada.[35]

The Jerry Rescue indicated that not only were African Americans willing to use violence in defending themselves against kidnapping or recovery under the law, but now many whites were also willing to employ force to rescue and defend fugitive slaves. Twelve blacks, including ministers Jermain Loguen and Samuel Ringgold Ward, and fourteen whites, among them philanthropist Gerrit Smith, were indicted for what became known as the Jerry Rescue. All but three of the African Americans escaped to Canada. About a month after the rescue, a grand jury indicted a US deputy marshal for attempting to kidnap McHenry. The following June his trial became a suit against the Fugitive Slave Law itself, as Gerrit Smith, one of the attorneys for the prosecution, gave a seven-hour disquisition designed to prove the law's unconstitutionality. The jury needed no time for deliberation to acquit the deputy. Only one of the rescuers, a black man named Enoch Reed, was convicted of violating the law. His case was separated from the others, it was suspected, because officials believed his history might make it easier to convict him. Some time before, a group of Irishmen had assaulted Reed, but he killed one of his attackers in what had been ruled self-defense. Reed, then in his early thirties, was convicted of "resistance of process" under a 1790 law, but he died in 1853 before he could be sentenced. The tri-

als associated with the Jerry Rescue kept the antislavery and proslavery ranks agitated for more than two years. In the end, with only one conviction for a relatively minor infraction, the results seemed to support Southerners' claim that the North was not serious about enforcing the Fugitive Slave Law. Even more threatening to slaveholders' power was a ruling handed down at the time by a judge in Illinois, who released a fugitive on the grounds that the Fugitive Slave Law was unconstitutional.[36]

The arrests of fugitive slaves in the North throughout the decade before the Civil War commonly attracted crowds of defenders and always carried with them the threat of violence. In the case of Washington McQuerry in Cincinnati, for example, only heavy police presence averted violence. At the trial held in August 1853, lawyers once again argued the unconstitutionality of the Fugitive Slave Law, but the judge reject-

Poster advertising an "anti-slave-catchers' mass convention" in Milwaukee, Wisconsin, on April 13, 1854. Organizers of the meeting hoped to prevent "having the free soil of Wisconsin be made the hunting ground for human kidnappers."

The Oberlin rescuers, arrested and photographed in front of the jail in Cuyahoga County, Ohio, in April 1859.

ed their plea and returned McQuerry to slavery in Kentucky. Two cases in the West, however, posed a greater threat to the law and to the compromise over slavery. In March 1854 fugitive Joshua Glover was arrested in his home in Racine, Wisconsin, and taken to jail in Milwaukee. The following day a company of blacks and whites broke down the jail's doors, wrested the captive from his guards, put Glover in a wagon, and rushed him off to Canada. At the trial of Sherman Booth, the editor of the *Milwaukee Free Democrat* and one of Glover's rescuers, the state supreme court judge declared the law unconstitutional because its denial of a jury trial violated the due process of law. Upon appeal, the Wisconsin supreme court concurred with the judge's opinion. Southern slaveholders' concerns were exacerbated by favorable coverage of these rulings in Northern newspapers, which they saw as proof of general antislavery sentiment. One Democratic Wisconsin

paper, the *Ozaukee County Times*, expressed an incendiary opinion.

> The spirit which incited and effected the rescue of Glover is the same which incited and effected our national liberties. The revolutionary fathers rose in arms against unjust and oppressive laws . . . ; the citizens of Milwaukee arose in their might against a law which deprives human beings of personal liberty, and tore from its relentless grasp a victim. That spirit, wherever it manifests itself, we honor. We honor the revolutionary fathers, so do we honor the citizens of Milwaukee.[37]

Congress took up the question of slavery in the territories again in early 1854 and by the end of May had passed the Kansas-Nebraska Act. This act established the principle of popular sovereignty over the question of slavery in the territories of Kansas and Nebraska, and in doing so repealed the hard-won agreement of the Missouri Compromise. Thus, the federal government once more seemed to take the side of Southern slaveholders by potentially opening Northern territories to slavery. That same month, black abolitionists and their white allies again demonstrated their willingness to resort to violence if necessary. One famous case was that of Anthony Burns, a fugitive who was arrested in Boston in May 1854. In attempting to rescue Burns, an integrated band of protestors killed a US marshal while storming the courthouse. Burns's trial attracted a throng of seven to eight thousand people, and it took the efforts of a large volunteer militia, an artillery company, a city militia of at least fifteen hundred men, and a company of Marines to assure the return of Anthony Burns to slavery in Virginia. When John Price, a fugitive from Kentucky, was arrested in Oberlin, Ohio, in the early fall of 1858 and taken to nearby Wellington, an armed crowd of students and townspeople followed him and his captors. After negotiations failed, the crowd surrounded the hotel where he was being held, threatened the police, and removed Price from custody. Price was successfully transported to freedom in Canada, but thirty-seven of the Oberlin-Wellington rescuers were indicted and at least twenty were jailed. Nearly a year later, when all were finally freed, the abolitionist heroes were given a "welcome home" parade and a ceremony replete with defiant speeches and triumphant songs.[38]

The Fugitive Slave Law of 1850 began a decade of increasing anger and disillusionment for African Americans. With each new action by the federal government to uphold slaveholders' rights to their "property," blacks became more determined that compromises over slavery would not stand. After four years of struggling against the law, and after Anthony Burns was captured

in Boston and sent back to slavery, their anger was apparent. A writer reporting on a meeting of black men in Philadelphia urged, "Let all the colored people of the free States declare, once and for all, we will not ingloriously retreat from the land in which our fathers' bones lie buried, but will, if need be, die, though we die struggling to be free." The Kansas-Nebraska Act brought open conflict to the plains of Kansas, and that turmoil was accompanied by violence in Congress itself. In 1856 heated discussion turned into a bloody assault when Representative Preston Brooks of South Carolina brutally beat Senator Charles Sumner of Massachusetts, an abolitionist, on the Senate floor. African Americans' disillusionment was complete with the decision of the United States Supreme Court to deny Dred Scott's appeal for freedom in 1857 and with Chief Justice Roger B. Taney's pronouncement that blacks had "no rights which the white man was bound to respect." Free blacks had little hope that the federal government would protect their freedom or any of the rights they enjoyed. Some agreed with Robert

Winslow Homer, "Arguments of the Chivalry," 1856. Preston Brooks is about to beat Charles Sumner in the United States Senate.

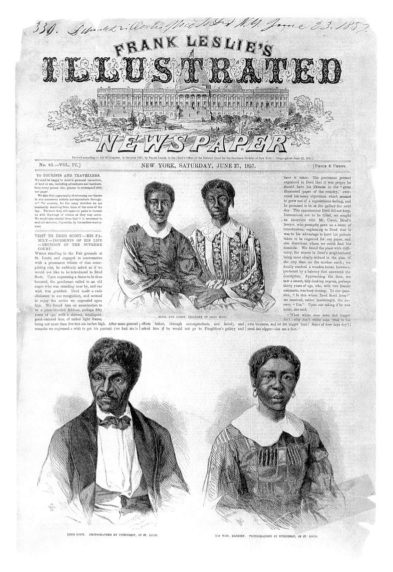

FRANK LESLIE'S
ILLUSTRATED
NEWSPAPER

No. 82.—VOL. IV.] NEW YORK, SATURDAY, JUNE 27, 1857. [PRICE 6 CENTS.

Dred Scott, his wife, Harriet, and their two daughters, Eliza and Lizzie, from *Frank Leslie's Illustrated Newspaper*, June 27, 1857. The *Scott v. Sanford* Supreme Court decision had been handed down that April.

Virginia, in 1859, many African Americans saw the failed effort as the first salvo in the revolution to abolish slavery that Purvis had anticipated. For blacks and their white allies, John Brown became a martyr to the antislavery cause and an inspiration to further efforts. Many of the fugitive African Americans who were most active in the Underground Railroad and in rescue attempts faced another risk: they themselves could be arrested and sent back to slavery. This threat forced some to abandon their homes in the North and flee to a more secure freedom in Canada. Lewis Hayden in Boston, William Parker in Christiana, and Jermain Loguen in New York State, all of them fugitives, were among the well-known activists who risked their own freedom. Another was Harriet Tubman, a confidant of John Brown, who became a legendary conductor on the Underground Railroad and grew quite famous for her forays into the South to rescue slaves. She was also involved in the rescue of a fugitive in Troy, New York, in 1860, just a year before the start of the Civil War.

When Charles Nalle was arrested in the early spring of 1860, Tubman had stopped in Troy on her way to Boston. Nalle, accused of being the slave of B. W. Hamsborough of Culpepper, Virginia, was around thirty years old. He had been in New York State about a year and lived there with his wife and three children. Alerted to Nalle's arrest, a large crowd numbering into the thousands gathered at the building where the commissioner was hearing the case. Harriet Tubman, in her typical guise as a crippled old woman, pleaded with the guards to admit her to the second-floor hearing room. Nalle was held in the hearing room while abolitionists went to obtain a writ of habeas corpus.

Purvis, a black leader in Philadelphia, who saw hope in the possibility that the government would be "overthrown and a better one built up in its place."[39]

The increasing militancy of the fugitive slave rescues during the 1850s did offer some hope. They showed that many white abolitionists were willing to join with blacks, risking jail or worse, to help slaves to freedom. When John Brown, along with thirteen whites and five blacks, attacked the federal arsenal at Harpers Ferry,

During this tense interlude, someone in the crowd offered to buy his freedom. An agent for the owner gave his price as $1,200, and that amount was promptly collected from members of the crowd. Upon seeing this, the agent raised the price to $1,500.[40]

As a lawyer returned with the order for the fugitive to appear before a supreme court judge, and officials began to escort Nalle from the room, Tubman rushed to the window and yelled down to the crowd, "Here he comes! Take him!" She then ran down the stairs, grabbed Nalle by the wrists, and held on tenaciously while policemen beat her over the head with their clubs. The crowd escorted Nalle to the river, where they placed him in a waiting rowboat. He was deposited on the other side of the river, but he did not get very far before he was arrested again. Meanwhile, about four hundred people had crossed the river on the ferry. When they discovered the fugitive had been rearrested, they stormed the judge's office to which he had been taken. The rescuers, armed with brickbats and clubs, faced defenders wielding pistols. In two assaults, they were repelled by more than twenty shots fired from the top of the stairway. Tubman and other black women, followed by more bullets, climbed over a fallen male comrade and brought Nalle out to a commandeered farmer's wagon. The wagon promptly broke down. Nalle and his rescuers continued on foot until two black men with a fast horse overtook them and accompanied them out of town and on to freedom. Remarkably, no one was seriously injured in the melee that freed Charles Nalle.[41] Today, this episode demonstrates the zeal of black communities and some abolitionists to thwart the capture of fugitive slaves.

At the end of this militant decade, the compromise over slavery broke down completely as open conflict over the issue evolved into civil war. Black men and women risked the dangers of capture, injury, and death to save fugitives from bondage or kidnapping. They braved the dangers of war to bring freedom to others of their race. Once the war began, Frederick Douglass argued, the only ways to end it were to grant freedom to the entire nation and to arm blacks to accomplish this task.

Fire must be met with water, darkness with light, and war for the destruction of liberty must be met with war for the destruction of slavery. *The simple way, then, to put an end to the savage and desolating war now waged by the slaveholders, is to strike down slavery itself*, the primal cause of that war.[42]

An African child rescued from an illegal slave ship off the coast of Florida, from *Harper's Weekly*, June 2, 1860.

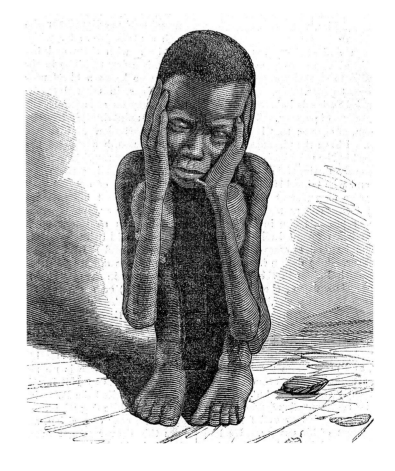

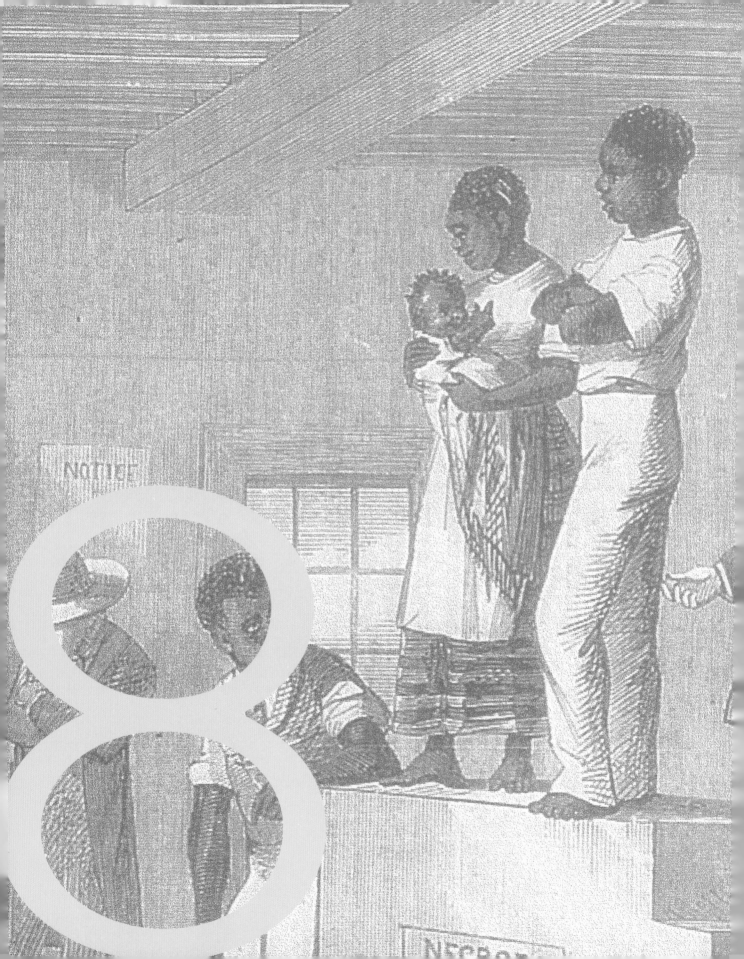

JAMES OLIVER HORTON

A CRUSADE FOR FREEDOM

William Still and the Real Underground Railroad

The story of the Underground Railroad is the story of American ideals in action. The Underground Railroad was as American in its values and goals as slavery was un-American in its consequences and rationalization. Despite many specific definitions, the term Underground Railroad is generally used to describe the movement, most widespread during the three decades before the Civil War, that sought to assist slaves as they attempted to escape from bondage. In reality, of course, the movement was not a railroad and generally did not run underground, but it did endeavor to move fugitives from one safe place to another, and it was largely secretive in its activities. Since any effort to assist a slave to escape might technically be included under this general description, it could be argued that the Underground Railroad actually started before the nineteenth century. When Quakers in the mid-eighteenth century condemned slavery and offered aid to fugitives, their efforts fell under this definition. When, during the American Revolution, guerrilla bands of whites, Native Americans, and free blacks fighting for the British army raided Southern plantations and freed slaves from American masters, their actions might also qualify. And certainly when free people, black, white, or red, took in fugitives who fled by the thousands during the disruption of the Revolution, they were acting in the spirit of the Underground Railroad, although the term had not yet been coined.

Although many, sometimes contradictory, tales exist about how the term first came into general usage, it almost certainly arose in part as a response to the advent of the railroad train during the 1830s and 1840s. As the newest technology of the day, the railroad introduced words and gave new meaning to older terms. Antislavery groups dedicated to assisting runaway slaves used these code words, calling routes of escape "rails" and safe houses "stations." Fugitives themselves were the "passengers" or "packages," and those who assisted fugitives were referred to as "conductors." From the mid-nineteenth century onward into the twentieth century, the folklore that grew up surrounding the Underground Railroad has become one of the most romanticized aspects of American history. According to popular legend, organized groups of reformers, generally pictured as white and often Quaker, guided passive victims of slavery to freedom in the Northern states and beyond in Canada.

In reality, fugitives were not usually passive in their escape. Among the true heroes was Harriet Tubman, a fugitive from slavery in Maryland who, once free, slipped back into the South approximately twenty times and guided more than three hundred slaves to freedom during the 1850s. Yet, for every Tubman who actually brought slaves out of the South, there were thousands of slaves who planned and executed their own escapes, alone or with the aid of friends and family. Their accomplices were frequently slaves themselves. Most of their names have been lost to history, yet their determination to be free in spite of almost overwhelming odds remains a symbol of the most fundamental human impulse for freedom.

The number of slaves who were able to escape is in dispute. Some estimates climb to a hundred thousand or more in the decades before the Civil War. The vast distances involved, the hardships of unpredictable weather, the general ignorance of distant regions, and the ever-watchful, ever-present authority of slaveholders made escape difficult. The unspeakable consequences of failure made attempted

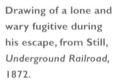

Drawing of a lone and wary fugitive during his escape, from Still, *Underground Railroad*, 1872.

escape frightening. Substantial numbers of runaways were recaptured or returned voluntarily when their chances of successful escape appeared slim. Sometimes slaves used temporary escape as a bargaining point for better treatment or extended privileges to visit family members on neighboring plantations.[1]

When fugitives did strike out for freedom, their destinations varied, depending on their starting point. In the Lower South, Mexico, which had abolished slavery in 1829, offered a tempting haven, as did Native American areas in Florida and elsewhere. Black sailors and river men in port towns along the Mississippi or on the Atlantic Coast became legendary for their willingness to assist fugitives who might stow away on vessels bound for the North, Latin America, Europe, or other freedom ports.[2] Slaves held in the Upper South—as in Kentucky, just across the Ohio River from the freedom of Ohio, or in Maryland or northern Virginia, within a few days' travel from Pennsylvania—had the best opportunity for escape to the Northern states. There, they could often find aid from the organized Underground Railroad groups that have become a part of American folklore. Once in Cincinnati or Ripley, Ohio, or in New York, Boston, or Philadelphia, a fugitive could find various kinds of aid, from food and clothing to medical attention, legal assistance, or sometimes a job. The runaway might also secure protection from slave catchers, those bounty hunters who were employed by slaveholders to recover and return fugitives. Blacks and whites in abolitionist groups established vigilance committees that hid and defended runaways when needed. Since fugitives often were forced to leave loved ones behind, one of their most

pressing needs was communicating with those still in slavery. Here is where the organized underground, with its interregional contacts and its ability to move messages from slavery to freedom and back again, performed a major service.

Successful escape was never easy, and even those who actually made it to freedom often experienced heartache mixed with happiness. "I arrived safe into Canada on Friday last," wrote one Virginia fugitive. He was almost delirious to be "in this glorious land of liberty. . . ." His next thoughts, however, were less joyous. His wife had not escaped but remained in bondage. His hope was to "make short her time in Virginia." Another fugitive also expressed the heartsick feeling of having to leave loved ones behind in order to gain freedom. He too had made it to Canada, but his sadness was obvious. "What is freedom to me when I know that my wife is in slavery?"[3]

For these and other runaways, communication with family and friends, many of whom remained in slavery, was almost as precious as freedom itself. These fugitives depended on the men and women of the underground as a life line to their past. Although they placed their faith in hundreds of underground operatives, the work of one man—William Still—has become legendary in the history of abolition and the Underground Railroad. Still was one of Philadelphia's most effective and most widely known abolitionists and Underground Railroad leaders. He never experienced slavery personally, but he understood the horrors of the institution all too well and served as a conduit between bondmen in the South and those who had escaped north or fled on to Canada. Reputedly, he knew almost everything and everyone of significance in the Eastern underground movement. Still was born in Burlington County, New Jersey, in 1821, after slavery had been outlawed from that state in the early decades of the nineteenth century, but his parents and older siblings had been slaves. Levin Steel, his father, managed to purchase his freedom. His mother, Sidney, had escaped from bondage in Maryland and was a fugitive when William was born. In freedom she changed her first name to Charity, and the family adopted the name Still to help disguise her identity.

Portrait of William Still, frontispiece of Still, *Underground Railroad,* 1872.

William Still's childhood was relatively secure, despite his mother's status as a runaway. He was the youngest of eighteen children, living on the family farm in New Jersey. In 1844 he moved to Philadelphia, a city of over a quarter million people, almost twenty thousand of whom were black. There he joined two of his older sisters, Mary and Kitturah, who earlier had moved to the city. Still accepted a variety of odd jobs, at one point waiting tables and working in a brickyard. Eventually he made contact with members of Philadelphia's antislavery community; his association with J. Miller McKim became especially important. McKim, the editor of the abolitionist newspaper *Pennsylvania Freeman,* encouraged Still's interest in abolition work and helped him learn to read and write. Then, in 1847, Still's life took a momentous turn. He met and married Letitia George—the couple eventually had four children—and he answered an

employment ad for a clerk's position at the office of the Pennsylvania Anti-Slavery Society on North Fifth Street in Center City, Philadelphia. His initial job as mail clerk and janitor evolved into a fourteen-year association during which Still served as the organization's clerk and corresponding secretary.

Although the legend of the Underground Railroad is filled with unsubstantiated folklore about stations where fugitives were sheltered and conductors who risked life and property to usher runaways to safety, Still's role as one of the most effective workers for freedom is indisputable. From the offices of the abolition society and from his home at 832 South Street, Still coordinated the activities that made Philadelphia one of the nation's strongholds of abolition. He was also one of the Underground Railroad's most significant historians, maintaining meticulous records of the 649 fugitives who were sheltered in the city prior to the Civil War and the end of slavery. These records contained dates, names, and details of fugitives and those who assisted them, as well as routes and locations of safe houses throughout the East. They also provided information on abolition agents and collaborators in the slave South. Had these records fallen into the wrong hands, they would have endangered many lives and might well have caused the destruction of the movement. Acutely aware of their importance, Still was always careful to hide these documents. At one point he concealed them in a building in an old cemetery and did not unearth them until well after the Civil War, when slavery had been abolished. In 1872 he published his records, along with the personal stories and the correspondence of hundreds of runaways, in *The Underground*

Railroad, a collection that modern historians of slavery and antislavery have found invaluable.[4]

Here are stories of determination and ingenuity, of a willingness to endure almost any hardship to find freedom. These fugitives loved freedom in the most Jeffersonian sense of liberty—as a natural human right. In this context, William Still was as much an advocate of American principles as any who fought at Lexington or Concord, and perhaps more so, for he sought the completion of freedom's revolution. If a fugitive could find the way to Philadelphia, Still and his fellows were prepared to offer safety. Of course, escaping the South was often the most challenging and dangerous part of the trip. It required careful planning and a good deal of luck. The fugitive who could make contact with abolitionists in Philadelphia had a much better chance of successfully eluding slave catchers. Members of the city's black community and their white abolitionist allies stood ready to protect fugitives in need even at the peril of personal danger.

Still tells the story of Henry Brown, a slave in Richmond, Virginia, who hit upon a most novel means of escape. Brown worked in his master's tobacco factory in the city along with one hundred fifty other slaves and free blacks. Urban slavery often afforded slaves the opportunity to associate with free blacks and even to become part of the free black community. Brown joined the First Baptist Church and sang in the church choir. There, he met James C. A. Smith, a free black dentist—Brown referred to him as "the doctor"—and the owner of a cake shop. Smith's shop often doubled as a clandestine meeting place where slaves could buy liquor. (The *Richmond Daily Dispatch* called it a "rendezvous for negroes.") When Brown's wife and children were sold and shipped away from Richmond, he determined to escape. One day while he was praying over his situation, Brown reported, "There darted into my mind these words, 'Go get a box and put yourself in it.'" With the help of James C. A. Smith and a white shoemaker, Samuel Smith, he planned to do just that. Samuel Smith traveled to Philadelphia and contacted members of the antislavery society. Still was present at the meeting where Smith set out the unlikely plan. Brown was to be shipped to Philadelphia from Richmond in a box aboard a rail car. Further, Brown was willing to pay $100 to anyone in Philadelphia who would assume responsibility for

Drawing of a fugitive running from slave catchers, from Still, *Underground Railroad*, 1872.

receiving the box. At first the abolitionists were skeptical that such an audacious plan could work, but Smith was persuasive. Abolitionist James McKim offered to be the addressee, but he refused to accept the money. The box was to be shipped on Tuesday, March 13, 1849.[5]

Still and the Philadelphia abolitionists considered this a dangerous scheme for the

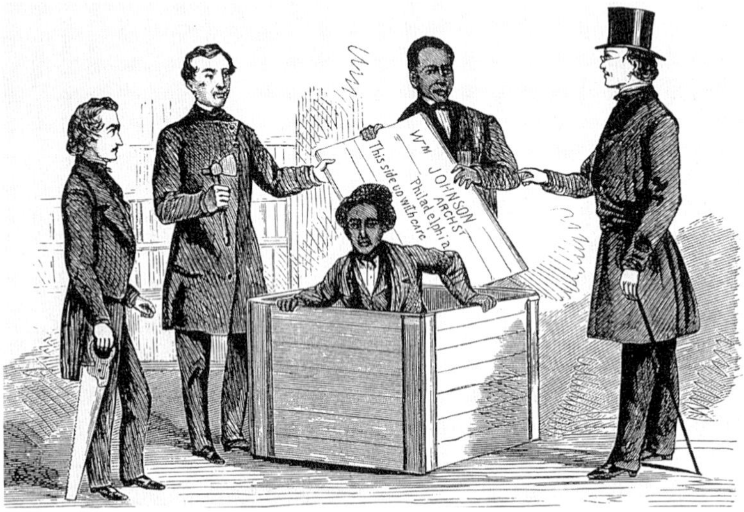

Henry "Box" Brown emerging from his crate in Philadelphia, from Still, *Underground Railroad,* 1872. Still prominently holds the box's lid.

movement. With little air in the box and the ever-present chance of an accident, Brown might be injured or killed. Of course, there was also the chance of discovery, and should the plan be exposed, all involved be arrested and prosecuted. If Brown should arrive dead, the antislavery society in Philadelphia would surely be criticized for its participation in such a far-fetched plan. All those participating would be liable to Brown's master for the loss of his property, and the movement could be discredited. Obviously, the risks were substantial. In the end, McKim backed out of the agreement and refused to allow the box to be shipped to him. Another addressee had to be found. Finally, after several delays, including one that resulted in a severe and painful injury to his finger, Brown met with James C. A. Smith and Samuel Smith and climbed into a hickory box that was then nailed shut for shipment. The box was addressed to James Johnson, 131 Arch Street, Philadelphia, shipped freight due, and marked, "This side up with care." Brown's desperation was obvious. Later he recalled, "I laid me down in my darkened home of three feet by two, and like one about to be guillotined, resigned myself to my fate."[6]

Despite the instructions printed on its side, the box was not handled with care. Brown had a rough trip and turned on his head as the box was tossed about violently. He carried with him a beef bladder filled with water, a hat to fan himself, a small drill with which he bored several small air holes in the box, and some crackers. He was hot, short of air, hungry, in pain, and frightened all the way. "My eyes were almost swollen out of their sockets . . . a cold sweat covered me from head to foot . . . every moment I expected to feel the blood flowing over me, which had burst from my veins."[7]

Finally, at six in the morning, twenty-six hours after it had been sealed shut in Richmond, the box was delivered to the antislavery office in Philadelphia. William Still was one of four abolitionists present when it arrived. This must have been a frightening moment for all outside the box, not sure of what would emerge when it was opened. Inside the box, Brown was equally concerned, not knowing who awaited his emergence. As Still described the scene, "All was quiet. The door had been safely locked. . . . Mr. McKim rapped quietly on the lid of the box and called out, 'All right!' Instantly came the answer from within, 'All right sir!'"[8]

Brown stepped from the box, Still reported, "as wet as if he had come up out of the Delaware [River]." The fugitive extended his hand, bidding the group, "Good morning gentlemen," and then favored them with an "arrival-hymn" that he had chosen before he left Richmond and had vowed to sing on his safe arrival into freedom. The words were touching, but they were not quite an accurate description of the process by which Brown had become free: "I waited patiently for the Lord, and He heard my prayer." Henry "Box" Brown, as he was then christened, had not waited patiently at all. As McKim wrote to a friend, "I had supposed that the white man who made the arrangements with me was the principle in devising and executing the project." Later, however, he learned that "this was not the fact. The whole plan was conceived and nearly the whole of it executed by the slave." Brown had been the

prime mover, an active participant in acquiring his freedom. Members of the Underground Railroad movement often provided critical assistance to fugitives after they had escaped, but typically, runaways took the initiative, fashioned the plans, and made the escape north on their own or with the assistance of friends and family in the South.

William Still and other abolitionists in Philadelphia found housing for Brown and nursed him to health. Soon he recovered from his ordeal, and it was time to resume his journey northward to a safer place. Carrying a letter of introduction to abolitionists in New York, Brown rode the train from Philadelphia in accommodations—a passenger seat—far more comfortable than his box. Still and others from the black community saw him off on his trip first to

"Heaving Weights— Arrival of a Party at League Island," from Still, *Underground Railroad*, 1872.

New York City and then on to Boston, where they had made arrangements for him to find work. Still sent a telegraph to his contacts in New York, possibly to his brother John N. Still, who was also active in antislavery work and was then living in Brooklyn. Other telegrams were sent to abolitionist friends in Boston. As Brown left Philadelphia, he had every reason to believe that he would be well received and sheltered as he traveled north.

Brown's escape garnered great notoriety, but it also made other rescue efforts involving railway shipments doubly dangerous for the Philadelphia group. McKim wrote to Samuel Smith and discouraged similar attempts, but Brown was not the last fugitive who used an express box as a vehicle for escape. Samuel Smith assisted at least two others but with less success. As feared, the fugitives were caught. Although Still and others in Philadelphia were not implicated, Smith was arrested in Richmond and imprisoned for eight years for his part in the attempted escape. As a "prisoner of injustice," Smith became a hero among African Americans and the abolitionist community for his efforts on behalf of fugitives. Upon his release from prison, he traveled to Philadelphia, where the black community held a mass meeting in his honor. Still was one of the organizers of the meeting, and subsequently Smith was a guest at Still's home until he finally left the city, bound for western New York.

As the story of Henry "Box" Brown makes clear, the Underground Railroad movement was both formally organized with regular operatives, such as William Still and the vigilance committee in Philadelphia, and the product of coincidence and individual effort, as in the initial development of Brown's plan. Friends and acquaintances, slave and free, worked together and demonstrated the importance of interracial cooperation. Dedicated white abolitionists often joined blacks in this dangerous business, and sometimes, as the case of Samuel Smith illustrates, they paid a heavy price for their efforts. Blacks and whites shared the philosophical commitment to human freedom that was so rhetorically American, but for black Americans the motivation was often much more personal. Even for those who had never been slaves, slavery was an ever present and very personal enemy. Free black people were the most dedicated members in the movement, and for many with family ties to slavery, as Still did, the work was more than a philosophical stand against evil.

After 1850 the job of sheltering fugitives became more difficult and more dangerous. In that year the United States Congress passed five individual bills collectively known as the Compromise of 1850, and President Fillmore signed them into law. Among them was the infamous Fugitive Slave Law. More harsh than the earlier 1793 fugitive slave legislation, this law all but assumed the guilt of any black person charged with being a runaway. A jury trial or the presence of a lawyer or a judge were not required. The accused was not even guaranteed the right to speak in self-defense. Any African American could be declared a fugitive by any federal commissioner and delivered to an alleged owner on the flimsiest of evidence. The commissioner received a payment of ten dollars for every accused found to be a fugitive, but only five dollars for those freed as nonfugitives.

Nowhere was a black person safe in America. Kidnapping was an omnipresent danger for free blacks, and fugitives could never feel secure, not even in the far northern cities of New England. Within days of the passage of the Fugitive Slave Law, Henry Brown, who by then was working with an antislavery group in Providence, Rhode Island, was attacked in the street by two men. Brown fought them off, and the two were arrested for assault. Although they might not have been slave catchers, a Providence newspaper reported that Brown's friends believed the pair was attempting to capture him and return him to slavery in the South. If true, the Fugitive Slave Law would have endorsed their action as completely legal. Abolitionists arranged for Brown to leave the country after this close call. Within a few weeks Brown sailed for England, where he continued his antislavery activities, lecturing and presenting a panorama abolitionist exhibition to the delight of audiences in Liverpool and other British cities. He regaled audiences with the story of his escape from slavery and of those who helped him.

A part of Brown's exhibition was an engraving depicting his emergence from the mahogany box into the freedom of Philadelphia. Of those pictured in the gathering of abolitionists who received him was one black man, William Still. Several renderings of the scene of Brown's arrival were created. Although each included a black man in the receiving group, one Boston artist, unfamiliar with Still's appearance, substituted the face and form of Frederick Douglass, then the most recognizable black abolitionist in the country. Thus, ironically, although Still is always present in the illustrations, in the Boston version he looks very much like Douglass. Perhaps this was a fitting substitution after all.[9]

While Brown was rallying support for the American antislavery movement in Britain, African Americans and their white abolitionist allies struggled to cope with the repercussions of the new Fugitive Slave Law at home. They saw this law as evi-

"The Resurrection of Henry Box Brown at Philadelphia," Boston, 1854. In this interpretation of the story, the artist replaced William Still with the figure of Frederick Douglass, who was not present at the actual event.

dence of the growing power of slave own-ers and their ability to control the federal government. African Americans regarded it as a direct assault on the basic citizenship rights of all free black Americans. It struck a blow at what they called the "manhood of our race" and raised the anger of black peo-ple everywhere. Reaction was particularly strong in Philadelphia. The city, with its long history of antislavery activity, boasted the nation's first formally organized anti-slavery society. It was formed in 1775 and incorporated in 1789 under an unwieldy name: The Pennsylvania Society for the Promoting the Abolition of Slavery, the Relief of Free Negroes Unlawfully Held in Bondage and for Improving the Condition of the African Race.

Quakers and other whites in Philadelphia had augmented black efforts to convince state officials to pass the Gradual Abolition Act of 1780, which slow-ly reduced the numbers of slaves in Pennsylvania. Philadelphia's slave popula-tion fell from 387 in 1790 to 85 by 1800, even as the number of free African Ameri-cans grew from almost 2,500 to 7,000 over that same period. Yet, the last vestiges of slave labor continued in the state until long after William Still was born. A new genera-tion of free black leaders was coming to power by the time Still migrated to the city. The early leaders of Philadelphia's African American community had been born into slavery. Some had supported the plan of the American Colonization Society to encourage abolition by establishing Liberia as a West African colony where emancipat-ed slaves might be transported. Enthusiasm for this idea diminished quickly during the 1820s, however, as Philadelphia blacks refused to leave the United States or endorse any plan that would demand "deportation" as the price of freedom. By the mid-nineteenth century a new, more militant black leadership came to promi-

The Fugitive Slave Law of 1850 did little to deter fugitives. Instead, it only made their escapes more desperate, as slaves here abscond on stolen horses. From Still, *Underground Railroad,* 1872.

nence. Born into freedom, these African Americans demanded immediate abolition throughout the country. They found white allies among those who were shaped by the militant abolition movement that emerged during the 1830s with the rise of white radical abolitionist William Lloyd Garrison and his Boston-based newspaper, the *Liberator*. Garrison, in turn, received some of his most substantial support from the black community of Philadelphia.[10]

William Still entered this diverse city in the mid-1840s. Slavery had disappeared from Philadelphia, and an increasingly militant activism, supported by an organized community determined to carry on the struggle against slavery, had taken its place. Philadelphia's strong and long-standing interracial antislavery alliances provided fertile ground for Still's leadership in the underground activity that proved so important during the 1850s. Not surprisingly, Philadelphia blacks were outraged by the Fugitive Slave Law that attacked their rights as free people and supported slavery so directly. As they argued, "The bill strips us of all manner of protection. . . ." Philadelphia blacks agreed that "it throws us back upon the natural and inalienable right of self-defense—self-protection." For these blacks, violence against slave catchers was a clear option.[11] They were not alone in their rage. In October 1850 a large gathering of blacks in Boston denounced the new law. They resolved to resist "unto death" any assault on their freedom. "No man will be taken from Massachusetts," they vowed, and when informed of President Fillmore's determination to enforce the law at all costs, they replied, "Let him try!"[12]

This sentiment was echoed in Philadelphia. The formation of the Philadelphia Vigilance Committee in 1852 came about in partial response to the Fugitive Slave Law. Still served as secretary and executive director of this group, a spin-off of the Pennsylvania Anti-Slavery Society that had formed to protect and assist fugitives seeking shelter in the city. Over the next few years Still and his committee organized an extensive network of safe houses and conductors as the foundation of one of the most effective Underground Railroad systems in the country. The group raised money to assist fugitives and kept a watchful eye on the movements of slave catchers throughout Pennsylvania. Still also acted as an agent for two black newspapers published in Canada. One, *Voice of the Fugitive,* was edited by Henry Bibb, and the other, *Provincial Freedman,* was edited by Mary Ann Shadd Cary, formerly of Philadelphia. In this way he maintained valuable contacts in several black Canadian settlements. In conjunction with his efforts to provide information to fugitives in the United States, Still also traveled to Canada to assess the situation there for those seeking to emigrate. Information gathered from these newspapers and his reports was invaluable to runaways bound north from Philadelphia. Still's reputation as a major leader of the underground movement spread far beyond Pennsylvania, and he became a well-known member of the national antislavery movement. He knew and worked with Frederick Douglass, William Lloyd Garrison, Harriet Tubman, and most of the important abolitionist leaders of the day. Indeed, Still became perhaps the nation's most active and effective grassroots organizer for the shelter, protection, and resettlement of fugitive slaves.

The 1850s posed difficult times for Still, the Vigilance Committee, and all those dedi-

Jane Johnson and
Passmore Williamson,
from Still, *Under-
ground Railroad*, 1872.

cated to the protection of fugitives. Clearly the law was on the side of slaveholders. Despite the strong antislavery sentiment in the city, many in Philadelphia demanded that the Fugitive Slave Law be enforced. In the summer of 1854, after one city newspaper criticized Philadelphia blacks for what it called their "disrespect" for the law, Still led a mass meeting to express opposition to what African Americans regarded as the nation's unjust racist laws. "Those who without crime, are outlawed by any government," the meeting resolved, "can owe no allegiance to its enactments. . . ." As blacks often did during these times, they recalled the rhetoric of Revolutionary America with the words "Liberty or Death." They vowed to resist the unjust law and to protect fugitives at all cost. "Let all the colored people of the free States declare, once and for all, we will not ingloriously retreat from the land in which our fathers bones lie buried, but will, if need be, die, though we die struggling to be free."[13]

These were not idle words, and events of the following summer tested their resolve. In July 1855 the US minister to Nicaragua, John H. Wheeler, traveled to New York from Virginia and brought with him three slaves, Jane Johnson and her two young sons. En route, the party stopped in Philadelphia. Their brief stay was long enough for Jane to get word to local blacks that she and her sons needed help. With five other blacks and Passmore Williamson, a white abolitionist in the city, Still confronted Wheeler as he and his slaves were about to leave by boat. Still and Williamson informed the slaves that they could legally walk away from Wheeler as free people. Under Pennsylvania law, any slave voluntarily brought into the state was legally entitled to claim freedom. Since these slaves had not come as runaways, their situation was not covered by the Fugitive Slave Law. A lively debate ensued, with Still and Williamson arguing against Wheeler and another white passenger. Finally, despite Wheeler's protests, the slaves were escorted from the boat to a waiting carriage and were driven away by a group of black men. At one point Wheeler attempted to resist the removal of his slaves but was discouraged from doing so. The exact sequence of events is not clear.

Still recalled that someone yelled, "Knock him down," but he claimed not to know who. Later he expressed his hope that no black person had threatened violence, as "there was not the slightest cause for such language." Another source, however, claimed that two black men warned Wheeler that if he attempted to interfere with the freeing of his slaves, they would "cut his throat from ear to ear." Whatever the truth, the slaves departed the boat and fled the scene.[14]

Less than a month after losing his slaves, Wheeler brought charges against Still, Williamson, and five others involved in the rescue. All were arrested on charges of robbery, inciting to riot, and assault and battery. Wheeler argued that his slaves had been taken by force and had not wanted to go with the defendants—in effect, they had been kidnapped. At a critical moment in the trial, Jane Johnson gave her most dramatic testimony. Immediately after the incident she and her sons had been taken to New England, where it was believed they would be safer than in Philadelphia. She had returned to the city, however, to bear witness in support of those who had rescued her and her family from slavery. On hearing Wheeler testify that she and her sons had been contented slaves, Jane rose from her seat in the courtroom gallery to contradict his claim. Her message was clear: she and her sons desired freedom and had no wish to remain in slavery. "Never before had such a scene been witnessed in Philadelphia," Still later wrote. "It was indescribable."[15]

The jury acquitted the defendants of all charges, except the two men who had threatened Wheeler were convicted of assault and sentenced to a week in jail. Williamson was found guilty of contempt of court for refusing to deliver the slaves to the judge immediately after their rescue. He served just over three months. Although the verdict of the court was mixed, abolitionists viewed it as a victory. The entire incident, including the trial, served to raise the consciousness of the general public. The *Philadelphia Daily Sun* commented that it "has made more 'abolitionists' and excited a more rancourous feeling against slavery than all the debates, feuds, and broken compromises of the past."[16]

These stories illustrate the complexity of the Underground Railroad during the increasingly volatile years before the Civil War. It was a mixture of well-planned and spontaneous events, as well as organized and individual clandestine actions. Vigilance committees used their contacts, and William Still and other leaders placed themselves in personal danger to outwit slave catchers and thwart the law, moving

This slave jail, or "pen," in Alexandria, Virginia, near Washington, DC, was owned by the firm of Price, Birch, and Company around 1862. Government complicity with slavery was most apparent in the existence of such slave jails and auctions.

fugitives from place to place under cover of darkness or in inventive disguise. Moments of high drama focused public attention on the injustice of human bondage. Abolitionists would not allow Americans to ignore the inhumanity of slavery or the fact that the federal government itself was deeply implicated in its existence and continued expansion. The presence of fugitives in northern communities gave a human face to what otherwise might have remained an abstraction. For free blacks, coming into contact with these fugitives and participating in the work of the Underground Railroad were often extremely affecting and personal experiences.

One of the most unforgettable stories Still recorded about his antislavery work involved his own family and a chance encounter that conveys the intimate nature of slavery to him and to almost all African Americans of the time. In early August 1850, just as the Fugitive Slave Law went into effect, two men seeking information visited Still's office at the antislavery society. As Still remembered it, "One . . . I recognized, the other was an entire stranger. My acquaintance introduced the stranger to me by the name of Peter Freedman of Alabama." Freedman was trying to find members of his family who had come north as fugitives some years before. He related a long heartrending tale of his being "stolen away" from some place near Philadelphia when he was six years old. His memories of his parents were dim, but he and a brother named Levin had lived in slavery in Kentucky and then in Alabama, where they were sold and resold until finally Levin died. After several years Freedman convinced a white man to buy him and to allow him to work so he could earn enough money to acquire his freedom. Working at

night and extra hours during the day, Peter became a free man.[17]

Determined to find his family after more than forty years, Freedman worked until he accumulated enough money to finance his search. He had traveled fifteen hundred miles north and finally arrived in Philadelphia. He told Still that he intended to post notices and to have messages read in the city's black churches to aid in his search. At this point Still asked Freedman if he knew the names of his parents. Suddenly there was no need for further notification. He did not know their last names, but their first names were Levin and Sidney. Still continued asking questions, but as he said, "By this time I perceived that an almost wonderful story was about to be disclosed"—and so it was.

Years earlier Levin Steel, William Still's father, had purchased his freedom from slavery. He then turned his attention to securing freedom for his wife, Sidney, and their children, but they soon concluded that escape was the only way to free the family. Sidney and the children were initially successful in getting to New Jersey, but their liberation was short-lived. Slave catchers overtook them, captured Sidney and all four of the children, and returned them to Maryland. This was the childhood memory that Peter had of being kidnapped near Philadelphia. For months Sidney's master watched closely to ensure that she would not attempt another escape. After several months she finally found her chance, but it was clear that a second attempt with all of the children would be impossible. At this point Sidney faced one of the most difficult decisions any mother can make. Leaving the two older boys in slavery, she struck out for freedom a second time, taking only the two younger girls with her. On the night she left in 1807, she went to her sons' bed, and while they slept she "kissed them—consigned them into the hands of God and took her departure again for the land of liberty."[18] This time the slave woman and her two daughters made good their escape and joined her husband, Levin. After they changed their last name to Still, and Sidney changed her first name to Charity, they settled in Burlington, New Jersey, years before William was born.

After his mother and sisters escaped, Peter and his brother, Levin Jr., were sold to the owners of a brickyard in Lexington, Kentucky. The brothers were sold again

plan worked. Peter then took the last name Freedman.

William listened attentively as Peter told his story and their relationship became clear. We can hardly imagine the emotions these two men shared when they realized that they were brothers. William perceived it first. "My feelings were unutterable," he explained. "I could see in the face of my newfound brother, the likeness of my mother." At first William considered not telling Peter what he had discovered. He wanted to speak first to their sister, who lived in Philadelphia and who, coincidentally, William had planned to meet that

Peter and Charity Still, William Still's brother and mother, from Still, *Underground Railroad*, 1872.

and moved to Alabama, where Levin Jr. died. Peter, then twenty-five-years old, married a slave named Lavinia, and the couple had three children. He was allowed to hire out his spare time, and he began saving money to emancipate himself and his family. When he became friends with Joseph Friedman, a Jewish merchant, Peter hit upon the plan to gain his freedom. Friedman would buy him and then allow him to purchase his own freedom. The

evening, but the emotion of the moment proved too great. William asked others in the office to leave, then he turned to Peter. "I told him I could tell him all about his kinfolk," and he did just that. The next day Peter was reunited with his mother. Their father, Levin Sr., was deceased, but Peter met five brothers and three sisters he had never known. "I shall not attempt to describe the feelings of my mother and the family on learning the fact that Peter was

"A Slave Auction in
Virginia," from
*Illustrated London
News*, February 16,
1861.

one of us; I will leave that for you to imagine," William wrote. Indeed, it is nearly impossible for us today to imagine those feelings or a time when the separation of families and the bondage of human beings was constitutional and supported by the full force of the federal government. Yet, as a central social and economic feature of the South and a legal and political fact of American life, slavery routinely created these and other hardships for families.[19]

The Still family's ordeal of separation was not yet over. When Peter departed Alabama, he left behind his wife and children. Although he was determined to free them, William reminded his brother of how difficult this would be. Peter answered that he "would as soon go out of the world

as not go back and do all he could for them."[20] For five years he struggled to free his family. He worked with members of the Underground Railroad, who at one point secured their escape to Indiana. The arm of slavery, however, reached out from the South, and they were recaptured and taken back. When Peter attempted to purchase their freedom, their master demanded the almost impossible sum of five thousand dollars. At this point, William's network of Underground Railroad contacts became the source of salvation for Peter and his family. With the assistance of many of his brother's abolitionist friends, Peter undertook a lecture tour, telling his story and that of his enslaved family in order to raise the necessary money for their freedom. It took four years of fund raising for Peter to gather the money, but in October 1854 he accomplished his goal. Finally, Peter Still and his family were reunited in freedom. They settled on a ten-acre farm in Burlington, New Jersey, where they lived until Peter died of pneumonia in 1868.

Meanwhile, William Still continued his Underground Railroad activities throughout the 1850s and beyond. By the late 1850s the fight against slavery took on a more militant and urgent tone. In 1857 the Supreme Court, in the infamous Dred Scott decision, limited congressional power to curtail the expansion of slavery and declared black Americans noncitizens of the United States. Black anger flared immediately, simmered, and then boiled over in Philadelphia a month after Roger B. Taney, the chief justice of the Supreme Court, read the verdict to the public. At a crowded meeting held in Israel Church, Still and hundreds of others listened to Philadelphia black abolitionist Robert Purvis declare that the court's "atrocious" decision confirmed that the US Constitution was in fact a slave owner's document and supported slaveholder notions of black inferiority. Charles Lenox Remond traveled from Boston to attend the gathering. Remond, the first African American to be a paid speaker for the American Anti-Slavery Society, had worked with Still on many underground activities. He was even more direct in denouncing what he called a racist government. "We owe no allegiance to a country which grinds us under its iron hoof and treats us like dogs. The time has gone by for colored people to talk of patriotism. . . ."[21]

African Americans did more than pass resolutions condemning the federal assault on their rights. In many cities they formed militia units and readied themselves for what many, by the mid-1850s, saw as the coming war on slavery. "Captain" J. J. Simmons of New York City's black militia unit prophesied that soon Northern black military units would be called to march through the South with "a Bible in one hand and a gun in the other."[22] Still collaborated in one of the most significant "military actions" against slavery. In March 1858, a year before John Brown's raid on Harpers Ferry, Brown, Henry Highland Garnet, a black abolitionist from New York, and Frederick Douglass traveled to Philadelphia to raise money and to confer with Still and others. The turnout for the meeting disappointed Brown, but he was encouraged to have Still, an important community leader, there. Still did not join the Harpers Ferry raid, although he probably knew a good deal about the timing of the plan. One historian has speculated that Still was too committed to his underground work in Philadelphia to strike out with Brown to western Virginia. Four days before the raid, Still received a letter from John Kagi, one of Brown's followers who took part in the venture. It likely contained word of Brown's intentions.[23]

The raid on Harpers Ferry failed, however, and most of Brown's men were killed or captured. Brown himself was arrested and tried for treason. He was found guilty and sentenced to hang. On the day of his execution, John Brown's wife, Mary, stayed at the home of the Still family. William Still did not attend meetings held in honor of John Brown so he could remain with Mary, who "grew paler" as the time of her husband's execution came closer. "Folding her hands across her breast she looked straight ahead for nearly an hour," Still

Maria Weems, alias Joe Wright, was a fifteen-year-old slave girl from Washington, DC. She disguised herself in male attire and, with the assistance of William Still and others, escaped to freedom in 1855. From Still, *Underground Railroad*, 1872.

reported, "as if in reverie." Later, Mary Brown sent William and Letitia Still a lock of her dead husband's hair.[24]

During the 1850s and throughout the Civil War, Still continued his alliance with the Underground Railroad and worked on a wide range of social justice issues. He was both an abolitionist and a civil rights leader. Like most blacks of the period, he saw little distinction between the two. Indeed, African Americans encouraged all antislavery organizations to combine abolitionism with what was often called "racial uplift." Many responded positively. In its constitution, the New England Anti-Slavery Society set out its aim not only to rid the nation of slavery but also to secure for black Americans "equal civil and political rights and privileges with the whites."[25] William Still's career illustrates the close connections between antislavery work and civil rights activity during this pre–Civil War era. As he led the struggle for freedom, he also fought for equality. When Philadelphia's first streetcars began operation early in the summer of 1858, for example, they were open to whites only. Throughout the 1860s African Americans were banned from the seats, and at best, they were allowed to ride on the outside, sometimes perched atop the cars. Still took up the cause, pursuing the fight for civil rights with the same vigor he had summoned in protecting fugitives. He

Louise Minks, *Rifle, Harpers Ferry*, 2002.

directed a petition campaign demanding equal treatment on the streetcars, brought litigation against the streetcar company's segregationist practices, and lobbied the state legislature to outlaw racial discrimination on public transportation. The Pennsylvania legislature finally passed a law in the spring of 1867 forbidding discrimination on streetcars.

During the Civil War, Still prominently supported black troops, and he served on the Freedmen's Aid Commission by raising funds to assist former slaves in their new freedom. On the home front, his efforts were tireless as well. In the fall of 1860 he helped organize and finance the Social, Cultural, and Statistical Association of the Colored People of Pennsylvania in an effort to collect social data that could be used to demonstrate the extent of racial injustice in the city. While he participated in social activism, Still acquired bits of real estate and established a number of profitable businesses. During the Civil War he sold new and used stoves, and later started a successful coal business. He became one of the city's most prominent African American businessmen and served on Philadelphia's Board of Trade. In addition, he helped manage homes for aged blacks and destitute black children as well as an orphan asylum for the children of soldiers and sailors. He served on many boards for local charities, and in 1880 he helped open a Young Men's Christian Association (YMCA) for the city's blacks. (The founding meeting was held in the living room of the Still home at 244 South 12th Street.) He was also the first president of Philadelphia's oldest black-owned banking institution, the Berean Savings Association, founded in February 1888 by his son-in-law, the Reverend Matthew Anderson of the Berean Presbyterian Church.

Eastman Johnson, *A Ride for Liberty*, 1862.

William Still continued to hold the position of president of the Pennsylvania Anti-Slavery Society until a year before his death in 1902. He died at home of heart disease, leaving behind a widow, two daughters, and two sons. Caroline Virginia was a medical doctor, Frances Ellen became one of Philadelphia's first kindergarten teachers, William Wilberforce worked as a public accountant, and Robert George earned his living as a journalist and the owner of a print shop. The day after his death, an obituary in the *New York Times* described Still as a man of wealth, one of the best-educated members of his race, and the "Father of the Underground Railroad."[26]

Many descendants of the Still family continue to live in southern New Jersey, where they hold regular family reunions. The story of the William Still family illustrates the intimate nature of the antislavery movement and the Underground Railroad to African Americans in the decades before the Civil War. It also demonstrates the wide range of activities black leaders pursued in service to their communities. All African Americans, even free blacks such as William Still, had a personal stake in ending slavery, and they were generally committed to the twin issues of abolition and achieving civil rights for themselves. The Stills understood that running away from slavery was no easy decision. It sometimes forced women to leave behind children and men to be separated from their families. Even though it often took years, African Americans struggled to maintain their families and to reunite those torn apart by slavery. The story of William Still, like that of the Underground Railroad and the abolition movement, is a tale of freedom, an all-American story of the many who refused to accept the denial of liberty. The commitment of Americans, blacks and whites, determined to guide the nation toward fulfilling its stated goals of human freedom and equality powered the Underground Railroad. The courage of those patriots and their cause can inspire Americans in the twenty-first century to complete their struggle.

CATHERINE CLINTON

"SLAVERY IS WAR"

Harriet Tubman and the Underground Railroad

On April 27, 1860, authorities in Troy, New York, arrested Charles Nalle, a light-skinned fugitive slave. Eighteen months earlier, in October 1858, Nalle had fled Culpepper County, Virginia, to find his wife and three children, who were emancipated and living in Columbia, Pennsylvania. By the spring of 1860 he had moved to Troy, "where he was employed as a coachman."[1] His luck ran out when a Virginia bounty hunter, the Southern agent of Nalle's owner, appeared to reclaim him. The slave catcher was none other than Nalle's own brother, a free black who was paid to do a slave master's dirty work. Nalle was being held at the Mutual Bank Building at the corner of First and State Streets when a large antislavery mob began to gather. As a precaution, observers were barred from the commissioner's second-floor office.

In a significant twist of fate, Harriet Tubman was also in Troy, visiting a cousin. A former fugitive slave herself, she had served as an extraordinarily successful conductor for the Underground Railroad since 1850. When she heard that Nalle had been taken into custody, she decided to help him and made her way to the closed proceedings. Wrapped in a shawl and carrying a food basket, she climbed the steps to the hearing room. Her props helped her to appear elderly and innocuous, which eased her entrance into the crowded chamber.[2] Tubman was standing at the rear of the room when it was announced that Nalle would be shipped back to Virginia.

When he heard the damning decision, Nalle bolted. He scrambled out onto a window ledge, but bailiffs were able to haul him back into the room before he could jump. The presiding judge commanded others to keep a tighter hold on the prisoner until transportation South could be arranged. The crowd

ness reported, "She was repeatedly beaten over the head with policeman's clubs, but she never for a moment released her hold."[4]

A rescue party hauled the bleeding and half-conscious Nalle down to the river and rowed him across the water on a skiff. Authorities lay in wait on the opposite bank. Once Nalle's boat reached the other side, he was taken back into custody and hurried to a judge's chamber. A ferry carrying nearly four hundred abolitionists, all determined to protect the fugitive, followed Nalle's boat across the river.

When Tubman landed, she rallied followers to storm the building where Nalle was being held. Bent on liberation, the human battering ram wreaked havoc. According to one reporter, "At last, the door was pulled open by an immense Negro and in a moment he was felled by the hatchet in the hands of Deputy Sheriff Morrison; but the body of the fallen man blocked up the door so that it could not be shut. . . ."[5] This tactical error gave the antislavery mob an opportunity to retake the fugitive.

Nalle's attorney, who had joined the melee, remembered, "When the men who led the assault upon the door of Judge Stewart's office were stricken down, Harriet and a number of other colored women rushed over their bodies, and brought Nalle out, and putting him into the first wagon passing, started him for the West." The Troy *Times* described the events: "Rescuers numbered many of our most respectable citizens,—lawyers, editors, public men and private individuals. The rank and file, though, were black, and African fury is entitled to claim the greatest share in the rescue."[6]

Tubman was accustomed to this leading role in the liberation of slaves, but Nalle's rescue was the first public battle she led. She had earned the name Moses for her activi-

below, whipped into a frenzy by witnessing Nalle's escape attempt, began to swell.[3]

Harriet Tubman knew she must seize the moment. She would test the good people of Troy. Would they rise to the occasion and help her strike a blow for freedom? She planned to whisk the fugitive to safety on a boat, but she worried about getting Nalle down to the riverside without incident. Shortly after Nalle was manacled, Tubman maneuvered herself into position where she could take swift action.

In the blink of an eye, the "frail old woman" surprised the guards by firmly grabbing hold of Nalle and wrenching him free from their grasp. She dragged him down the stairs and into the waiting arms of comrades assembled below. An eyewit-

ties on the Underground Railroad, but clearly she was a Joshua—both a fighter and a leader—as well. Tubman later recalled that during Nalle's rescue, the "shot was flying like hail above her head," but she knew what most Americans would soon discover and what John Brown had tried to demonstrate several months earlier: slavery was war.

As one of the most exceptional figures associated with the Underground Railroad, Tubman became an icon of the movement. Her historical legacy lost momentum at the end of the nineteenth century, and it is only beginning to reclaim its rightful place within American history at the dawn of the twenty-first century.

Little is known about the details of Tubman's life, and some of the most basic information about her remains a matter of speculation. She was born in Dorchester County, Maryland, but when remains uncertain. When Tubman gave her age during sworn testimony, she claimed her birth year was 1825, but her death certificate indicates she was born in 1815. Perhaps this is why her birth is most often recorded as "circa 1820" and why "1820" is carved on her tombstone.[7]

Her enslaved parents, Benjamin Ross and Harriet Green, gave her the name Araminta when she was born. The slave couple was owned by different masters, but they managed to build a home together on Maryland's Eastern Shore. Although she was one of eleven children born to loving

Lewis Miller, "Slave Trader, Sold to Tennessee," 1853.

and devoted parents, Tubman's early years were full of misery. She was hired out as a domestic at a very young age, and she frequently returned to her parents in a debilitated state, bearing the scars of beatings given by a harsh mistress. While an adolescent, Tubman was hit in the head with an iron weight thrown by an angry overseer. Consequently, she was bedridden for several weeks and was plagued by headaches and sick spells stemming directly from this injury. As a teenager, she recovered her strength and excelled at plowing and heavy labor, including clearing timber. She preferred outdoor work and learned to love the woods and fields where she chose to spend her time. Around 1844 she married a free black named John Tubman. Five years later, in 1849, she fled Maryland for freedom in the North, and took the name Harriet. When she feared that a niece with two children would be sold and moved South (as others of her siblings, including this girl's own mother, had been before), Tubman boldly returned to Maryland in 1850 to smuggle them out of slavery.

Tubman crossed back into slave territory several more times. At first she rescued family members, but soon she was recruiting other runaways, and she eventually earned a well-deserved reputation as Moses while working with the Underground Railroad. For over a decade she was involved with two key "stationmasters": Thomas Garrett in Wilmington, Delaware, and William Still in Philadelphia. Tubman reportedly made nearly twenty trips into the South between 1850 and her final Underground Railroad foray in December 1860. She is credited with rescuing more than two hundred slaves.[8]

In 1857 Tubman returned to her former home in Maryland to guide her elderly parents—both were in their eighties—all the way north to Ontario, Canada, where five of her siblings had resettled after she had conducted them to freedom. Tubman eventually moved her parents into a house she purchased from William Seward in his hometown of Auburn in Upstate New York on the Finger Lakes between Rochester and Syracuse. This would become her permanent home after the end of slavery and the close of the Civil War.

During her association with the Underground Railroad, she accomplished numerous amazing feats. Tubman became especially adept at mass escapes. Her indefatigable efforts to liberate and guide fugitive slaves gained her an international reputation, as abolitionists in Scotland and England heralded her exploits and donated funds to support Moses's operations.[9]

The role of "first fugitive" might well be awarded to Harriet Tubman. Due to the uniqueness of her career and the fact she was a black woman who achieved notoriety and respect, we might expect that lavish descriptions of her role and accomplishments appear in historical literature on the period, but her Underground Railroad achievements have not received the attention they merit. Until the 1940s only a handful of books and articles were available on Tubman; and most of those were tributes written by friends and admirers, such as James B. Clarke, who published "An Hour with Harriet Tubman" in 1908.[10] In the 1950s a growing number of books and articles began to re-examine her heroic life, most notably juvenile biographies by Dorothy Sterling and Ann Petry.[11] By the 1960s a steady stream of children's books and juvenile novels reflected the growing interest in her accomplishments: six were published in the 1960s, five in the 1970s,

and another six in the 1980s. In the 1990s, however, a whopping twenty-one children's and young adult books focused on Tubman. With twenty published or in the works from 2000 to 2003, the revival flourishes.

Even though she has been mythologized and maternalized by her star turn as one of the most popular heroines of the elementary school set, Tubman has not been given her scholarly due. Only two biographies of Tubman have been produced: one, written by her friend and patron Sarah Bradford, appeared in 1869, and another by journalist Earl Conrad was published in 1943. This is a considerable injustice to the complexity of Tubman's achievements: she was illiterate, black, and female, and yet she rose to prominence within a movement dominated by elite white males. The sheer force of her personality, combined with her ability to let her

actions speak louder than any others' words, transformed her into a heroine of biblical proportions.[12]

Tubman was a larger-than-life figure whose exploits drew attention to antislavery militance. By the end of the 1850s, just a decade after her fateful escape, this Moses was as revered a figure in the North as she was vilified in the South. In the summer of 1859 she stumped across New England, raising funds for John Brown's campaign and promoting the Underground Railroad. Following Brown's disastrous raid in October 1859 and execution in December, he became an antislavery martyr. For many involved in the antislavery cause, Brown was more valuable in death than in life—but not to Harriet Tubman.

Although many have questioned Brown's sanity, and even those who admired him might have condemned his

Paul Collins, "Harriet Tubman's Underground Railroad."

methods, Tubman never wavered in her support of him. Franklin Sanborn, an abolitionist, described that many years after Brown's death, when Tubman encountered a bust of Brown in Sanborn's parlor in Concord, Massachusetts, she was transported into a rapturous state marked by her "ecstasy of sorrow and admiration."[13] Her esteem of Brown remained with her all her life and withstood the barrage of criticism this antislavery martyr provoked. Both his death and his dream galvanized her commitment to liberation by any means.

Brown and Tubman spent very little time together, but after their first, brief meeting, they formed an abiding mutual bond. They shared an intense and impassioned hatred of slavery, and both were willing to act on personal beliefs. Brown always called Tubman "general," which signaled his high esteem for her accomplishments with the Underground Railroad and her role as a warrior against slavery. Tub-man, unlike Frederick Douglass, was willing to join Brown on his raid to incite a slave uprising in the South. Brown's repeated postponements of the date and poor communication channels prevented Tubman from joining him for the actual attack on Harpers Ferry.[14] Once she witnessed the explosive consequences on both sides of the Mason-Dixon line following Brown's failed raid, Tubman understood that at long last, white Americans might also recognize slavery as a state of war.

After her dramatic participation in Nalle's rescue in April 1860, Tubman headed east to Boston, where she was greeted as a celebrity. She moved among the literati, visiting the home of Ralph Waldo Emerson, meeting the family of Louisa May Alcott, and taking tea with the wife of Horace Mann. Tubman mixed with the antislavery intelligentsia, who were as awed by her actions as she might have been by their erudition. She was now willing to play a more public role if it would incite more

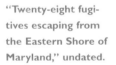

"Twenty-eight fugitives escaping from the Eastern Shore of Maryland," undated.

than sympathy and provide a call to arms for her antislavery brethren.

Tubman attended the New England Anti-Slavery Society Conference, which opened in Boston on May 27, 1860, as an honored guest, and she addressed a special session on women's suffrage on June 1. The *Liberator* reported on the "Moses" speech, declaiming that her "quaint and amusing style won much applause."[15] She spoke to the group from the same platform as other invited speakers, such as abolitionist Wendell Phillips, but Tubman alone was compelled not to use her real name for fear bounty hunters might be prowling the Massachusetts capital. She took the pseudonym Harriet Garrison, an homage to the great Boston abolitionist William Lloyd Garrison.

By this time, Tubman's fame was such that her colleagues feared it would interfere with her Underground Railroad work—and her safety. By the summer of 1860 slaveholders throughout Maryland gathered in Baltimore to push for changes in slave laws, a movement spearheaded by Eastern Shore delegates. Notices in Maryland papers indicated the heightened alarm Chesapeake slaveholders felt.

> *Stampede of SLAVES*—On the night of the 24th ult., twenty-eight slaves made their escape from Cambridge, Md. A reward of $3,100.

The exodus of valuable property out of the region reflected deep disturbances in the slave society of Maryland. A proposal to ban free blacks from the state was defeated. Even if free blacks could not be eliminated, these Maryland slaveholders hoped perhaps this "Moses" could be. They increased rewards for the capture of anyone aiding and abetting fugitives, and they inflated the price on Tubman's head to the astronomical figure of $40,000.[16]

Tubman's friend and admirer, Thomas Wentworth Higginson, feared for her safety, yet she persisted in leading rescues even after Maryland slaveholders debated the "various threats of the different cruel devices by which she would be tortured and put to death" if she were caught.[17] Higginson viewed her as a modern-day Joan of Arc who repeatedly risked being burned at the stake. Since Nat Turner's head was allegedly put on a pike in 1831 for his role in slave uprisings, and more recently, John Brown had swung from the gallows, there was every reason to believe Tubman would meet an equally harsh fate in the hands of her enemies.

Proslavery advocates were especially vehement in vowing vengeance against Tubman. One vituperative critic, Philadelphian John Bell Robinson, read about Tubman's appearance at the Boston abolitionist convention in 1860 and included an aggressive attack on her in his book *Pictures of Slavery and Anti-Slavery* (1863). "What could be more insulting after having lost over $50,000 worth of property by that deluded negress," Robinson warned, "than for a large congregation of whites and well educated people of Boston to endorse such an imposition on the Constitutional rights of the slave States."[18]

Robinson's invective grew when he addressed Tubman's removal of her aging parents from Maryland. His attack reflected quintessential proslavery apologism.

> Now there are no old people of any color more caressed and better taken care of than the old worn-out slaves of the South. . . . Those old slaves had earned their living while young, and a home for themselves when past labor, and had sat down at ease

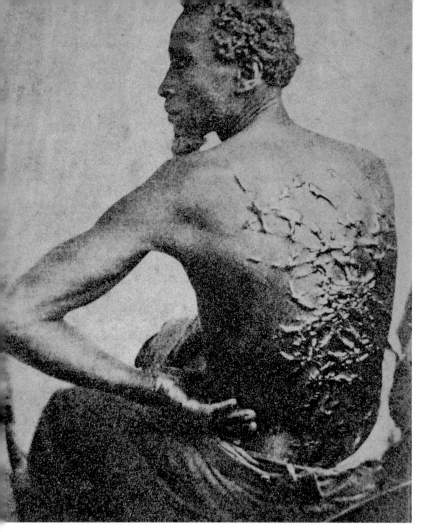

"Gordon" showing scars he received from savage beatings while in slavery.

they have nearly six months of severe winter out of twelve" and "no master's woodpile to go to." His ludicrous complaint continued with his observation that Tubman's parents will have "no rich white man or woman to call them 'Uncle Tom, and Aunt Lotta.'" Robinson insisted that, considering her crime, life imprisonment would be "inadequate" punishment for Tubman. Seemingly obsessed with her success at spiriting away slaves from their masters, Robinson concluded that Tubman's deed was "as cruel an act as ever was performed by a child toward parents."[20]

From the first edition of Frederick Douglass's autobiography (1845), to Harriet Beecher Stowe's *Uncle Tom's Cabin* (1852), to *The Boston Slave Riot and Trial of Anthony Burns* (1854), to James Redpath's authorized biography of John Brown (1860), abolitionist propaganda hammered home messages about the evils of slavery. Although Stowe's fiction outsold all these books combined, the most powerful genre during this period was the "slave narrative." The abolitionist Theodore Parker suggested that autobiographical tales produced by the slaves themselves were America's only indigenous and original contribution to world literature. A reviewer of Henry Bibb's narrative reported in 1849, "This fugitive slave literature is destined to be a powerful lever. . . . Argument provokes argument, reason is met by sophistry; but narratives of slaves go right to the heart of men."[21]

around the plentiful board of their master whose duty it was to support them through old age, and see them well taken care of in sickness, and when dead to give them a respectable burying.[19]

Like many proslavery firebrands, Robinson painted slavery as a "cradle to grave" welfare system that whites shouldered for the benefit of blacks.

Robinson's portrait of Harriet railed against her "diabolical" and "fiendish" powers. Tubman should have allowed her parents to remain behind, he argued, where the "laws of the State compelled him [their master] to give them that support righteously due them the balance of their days." He lamented that the elderly couple must have been spirited off to Canada, "where

These eyewitness accounts were intended to move readers—preferably into the abolitionist camp. Such propaganda spoke loudly and clearly to a Northern audience, just as white Southerners feared. One abolitionist claimed, "This growing sympathy for the slave is more to be dreaded by the South

I Sell the Shadow to Support the Substance.
SOJOURNER TRUTH.

Southerners were forced to fight back. In 1856 the *Southern Literary Messenger* suggested that "as literature has been the most powerful weapon which the enemies of African slavery have used in their attacks . . . let Southern authors, men who see and know slavery as it is, make it their duty to deluge all the realms of literature with a flood of light upon the subject."[24] This call for counterliterature evidently did not inspire a successful flow of material, but some propaganda was published nevertheless.

One example of a "counternarrative" appeared in Philadelphia in 1860. This volume, like many books in the nineteenth century, had an overly long title.

DISCLOSURES AND CONFESSION
OF
FRANK A. WILMOT

With An Accurate Account of the
UNDER-GROUND RAILROAD!
WHAT IT IS, AND WHERE LOCATED!
BY A LATE CONDUCTOR ON THE
SAME.
ALSO—FULL PARTICULARS OF THE
PLANS ADOPTED FOR RUNNING OFF
SLAVES

FROM THE
Southern States to the Canadas
ADDED TO WHICH IS A HISTORY OF
THE

Abduction of Miss Lucille Hamet,

THE PLANTER'S DAUGHTER,
AND A TRUE DESCRIPTION OF
SLAVE LIFE ON A PLANTATION

In a nutshell, Wilmot claimed to have been recruited into a ring of slave stealers that had only goal: to make money. He suggests in his exposé that most slaves opposed Underground Railroad activities because their kindly masters took care of them. Wilmot personally regretted his role in

than bullets and guns combined."[22]

Several of these personal accounts of slavery became bestsellers. Douglass's autobiography sold five thousand copies during its first four months of publication, and by the time of the Civil War more than thirty thousand copies—in several editions—had been sold in the United States and abroad. Solomon Northup's *Twelve Years a Slave,* an account of a free black sold into slavery and his ordeal until he regained his freedom, appeared in 1853. Northup sold more than twenty-five thousand copies of his memoir in two years. In addition, William Wells Brown, Josiah Henson, Henry "Box" Brown, and Sojourner Truth, as well as William and Ellen Craft, proved the most successful of the nearly sixty narratives published between 1840 and 1860.[23]

Faced with the popularity and prevalence of fugitive slave literature, white

encouraging one particular slave to flee, as this black man later kidnapped his own master's virginal daughter (a child by his white wife) and tried to violate her. In a fantasmagoric scene in a cave, Wilmot rescues the captive woman and the slave-rapist dies in the struggle. In addition, the book offers a string of unflattering portraits of the "nefarious" business of the Underground Railroad.[25]

A note from the publisher, Barclay and Company, addresses the ludicrous quality of this confessional tale. "We were at first disposed to disbelieve the whole affair," declared the publisher, "but on making the inquiry we found that Wilmot was not a *myth*, but a reality; and further that it was well known in this city that he was engaged in running off slaves."[26]

Wilmot's tale opens when, as a young man, he is induced into working for the "Aiding and Abetting Society." He does not possess strong views for or against slavery at the outset, and he confesses he is in it for the money. He paints for the reader an extremely sympathetic portrait of slave-

holding. From first contact with plantation life, Wilmot is impressed by the "scenes of beauty and good order" he encounters. "I saw the slaves during their every-day life," Wilmot argues, "a happy, contented and careless race; well fed, as their looks testified; well lodged, and not overtasked." By contrast, Northern laborers are "shut up in their narrow and filthy dens, where vice and depravity stalk abroad."[27] (Wilmot describes murder and incest among Northern laborers for good measure.) His idyllic description of plantation life rivals that of George Fitzhugh and other proslavery ideologues, and demonstrates how desperate some white Southerners were to defend slavery as benign against growing antislavery resistance.

According to Wilmot, his Underground Railroad secret society purchased a series of farms along an escape route that provided safe houses for slaves in flight from Alabama to Ohio and on to Canada. The "station house farmers" held slaves and treated them worse than any of their neighbors in order to thwart suspicion. The entire system, Wilmot suggests, "worked to a charm," and this group assisted thirty-two hundred slaves to freedom from 1856 to 1858.

Wilmot offers a series of thrilling tales of Underground Railroad mishaps and misdeeds. At one point his lecherous compatriots had "dishonorable" designs on a trio of Creole women slaves they planned to "rescue." They tried to storm the planter's household to capture these women, but a mob from the slave quarters ran them off.

In another incident, Wilmot finds himself on a sinking ship when "old black Sam" saves him from drowning. Wilmot tries to buy the man's freedom to show his gratitude, but his master replies, "Sam wouldn't leave me for the world. If he had

"Escaping with master's carriages and horses," 1872, from Still, *Underground Railroad*, 1872.

wanted his freedom he would have long since had it. I have offered repeatedly to set him free, but he would never accept the boon." Wilmot closes with the tale of a misguided antislavery man who marries a wealthy slave owner's daughter in Louisiana. The enterprising young man emancipates his wife's slaves and sets them up on land in Illinois, but the experiment turns into a disaster, with desertion, indolence, and ingratitude abounding.[28]

Wilmot confides that thousands of slaves were railroaded out of slavery only because mercenaries wanted to bilk funds. As he lamely explains, "The only way we can do it is to actually run the slaves off to Canada." He echoes John Bell Robinson's lament about blacks being sent from "the sunny climes of the Southern tropic to the frigid regions of Canada," where they end up "poor, degraded, pilfering wretches." Blacks in freedom, he complains, could only

be found in hospitals and grog shops. Wilmot then takes a final swipe at the Underground Railroad. "All, I may say, or nearly all, who are actually engaged in the practical operation of running off the slaves, care no more for their future benefit and welfare, than did I. And those who, the charitableness of their hearts, advance or subscribe money for such purposes, are simply filling the pockets of a mischievous set of men, too lazy to work, and who wish to live easy, having but few scruples as to the manner whereby they obtain that living."[29]

Wilmot's wholesale discrediting of the Underground Railroad and his promotion of the notion that African Americans preferred slavery were direct attempts to subvert increasing public sympathy for those held in bondage and especially for the plight of fugitive slaves seeking freedom. His book conjured up the black rapist (featured in the title with "the abduction of Miss Lucille Hamet"), and the text played upon the worst fears of white readers by trying to intimate that any hint of disorder (self-emancipation) not only would upset the stability of slavery but also would threaten all whites and leave them prey to barbaric black desires.

Harriet Tubman's career and those of countless others contradicted this libel, but this freedom fighter rarely let herself be drawn into a war of words. In her world, actions spoke louder than language. She eagerly anticipated a time when resistance would overtake rhetoric.

Tubman's fame before and during the Civil War coincided with the emergence of the daguerreotype and the popularity of *cartes de visite*. This was a fortunate coincidence for the Underground Railroad

Studio portrait of Harriet Tubman from the Civil War era.

leader, as photographic images became instrumental to protecting her identity. Being illiterate, letters of introduction from others were not appropriate for her. It could be a costly mistake if Tubman revealed her Underground Railroad agenda to anyone but a fellow traveler. Her collection of photos helped to prevent such mishaps. When she made initial contact with strangers, Tubman's treasured pack of images became her insurance policy. To test their credentials, she showed them her collection of photos and asked them to name the sitters. If they could identify her antislavery friends from the *cartes de visite*, then she felt secure, knowing she was dealing with someone who had face-to-face acquaintance with her comrades.[30]

An early studio portrait of Tubman provides an excellent likeness of the woman at the height of her career as Moses. It provides an imposing image of Tubman, freedom fighter against the slave power. Her white ruff, along with her hat and coat placed neatly on a tasseled chair, challenged those who chose to portray her,

and women of color in general, as slatterns. Her hands neatly folded, her gaze direct, Tubman conveys a dignified demeanor respectable appearance.

Tubman was a mistress of disguises during this period. On one return trip to Maryland, she used a sunbonnet and a few flapping chickens to help her pass undetected within a few inches of a former master. On another mission, she used a shawl and a basket, and she stooped to disguise herself as an elderly woman in order to fool local lawmen in Troy, New York.[31] Such exploits and daring stoked the public's imagination.

Although thousands of Americans had heard of this famous conductor, relatively few saw her in person. She became a minor sensation on the New England antislavery circuit late in the 1850s, swaying her audiences with powerful tales of the Underground Railroad. In June 1859, when Tubman spoke in Worcester, Massachusetts, her friend Thomas Higginson introduced her as Moses. Later she addressed a large crowd at a Fourth of July celebration in Framingham. An observer reported, "The mere words could do no justice to the speaker, and therefore we do not undertake to give them; but we advise all our readers to take the earliest opportunity to see and hear her."[32]

A later portrait of Tubman, sketched during the Civil War, has become somewhat infamous in recent years. Tubman was both instrumental and inspirational when war broke out, throwing herself into the fray by attaching herself to the Union army. Governor John Andrew of Massachusetts sponsored Tubman's passage to the Union-occupied Sea Islands of South Carolina in late May 1862. Once the soldiers at Port Royal learned they were dealing with Moses, the famed conductor of the Underground Railroad, due deference was paid. Indeed, former fugitive slave and author William Wells Brown reported that Union officers "never failed to tip their caps when meeting her."[33]

During her time in South Carolina, Tubman repeatedly stole behind Confederate lines while armed enemies patrolled. Under direction from the War Department, she made contact with slaves within the region and built up a network of agents and scouts. Tubman engineered a daring raid in late spring 1863. On the night of June 2, more than seven hundred fifty blacks were spirited onto Union gunboats that had silently made their way up the Combahee River from the coast. These blacks were whisked away from plantations owned by the Heyward and the Lowndes families and other Carolina dynasties. Tubman's plan was triumphant, as scores of irreplaceable laborers and their families were snatched from under the nose of Confederate troops. News of Tubman's success traveled through the Union military grapevine. The War Department crowed over this significant victory. A full account of these exploits appeared in Northern papers, although at first Tubman was identified only as "a black woman." By mid-July an article in Franklin Sanborn's *Commonwealth* exposed her by name, offered both a biographical sketch and details of her lead role as scout in the operation, and paid tribute to her heroism.[34]

An infamous image of Tubman appeared on the frontispiece of the first edition of her authorized biography, *Scenes in the Life of Harriet Tubman* (1869). Today, this iconic portrait generates enormous controversy. Purveyors of political correctness are concerned that Tubman holds a rifle. She typically carried a musket during raids with the Union army. In this particular portrait, her hair is covered with a headscarf, she wears a jacket and a striped skirt, and a canvas satchel is draped over her shoulder. This outfit was presumably her "uniform."

The gun included here reinforces her status as a warrior. At the same time, the image itself is not particularly warlike, or military, or even militant. Instead, Tubman is a "warrior in repose." The rifle butt clearly rests on the ground; Tubman holds the gun's barrel and leans on the weapon as if it were a prop, in both senses of the word.

Portrait of Harriet Tubman, Auburn, New York, ca. 1900.

Since this image has not yet been traced to any known photograph, it is difficult to determine if it is an authentic image, or even if Tubman knew about this portrait before it was published. Trying to tie it to gun culture or including it in debates over firearms seem futile exercises, although they occur in numerous Internet exchanges.[35]

Stories from others as well as her own testimony confirm that Tubman did have a gun during her Underground Railroad treks, but she never carried a *rifle* during her days as a conductor. Quite naturally, she was concerned about secrecy and disguise. A black woman toting a musket in the slaveholding South would attract attention. Further, the pistol Tubman kept concealed was not intended to fight off bounty seekers. She testified that she used her gun to prevent panicked fugitives from turning back. One person losing nerve could endanger an entire group. She once threatened to fire her weapon when a frightened runaway tried to run home. Again, descriptions of her language and the intent of her threat remain folkloric: Did she tell him to "move or die"? Did she really use the word "nigger," as some accounts indicate? We have no firm evidence confirming details from this scene.[36]

Maybe she did, as any desertion would have put Tubman and all her recruits in jeopardy. In one recorded instance when she used her gun to maintain control, she kept the frightened man with the party and shepherd her entire flock to safety—as she did time and time again. She testified with great pride that she never lost a passenger.[37]

During the final phase of her career in the postwar years, Tubman took on an unlikely role—that of philanthropist. For African Americans, the goal of economic self-sufficiency seemed as elusive as political self-determination after the Civil War. Tubman redirected her energies, working within her local community for better conditions for blacks. She spent nearly five decades collecting funds and struggling to establish a charitable home in her upstate community of Auburn, New York.

Tubman opened her own household to the aged, the orphaned, and disabled veterans—people of color who were otherwise forgotten. She dedicated her time, money, and talents to a dream of building an institution for the needy and calling it the John Brown Home. In addition, she purchased land in Auburn at auction in 1896 and, with assistance from the African Methodist Episcopal Zion Church (who took over the property in 1903), a home bearing Tubman's own name opened in 1908. The charitable home closed in the 1920s, but a refurbished structure on the original property is now an historic site available for tours. A portrait of Tubman during this era shows that her mesmerizing dignity never deserted her, even though she was confined to a wheelchair in her final years.

Although Tubman may have languished in obscurity following her death in 1913, she nevertheless gained notoriety as an "underground" figure in the African American community. Ladies' auxiliaries of

Portrait of Harriet Tubman, ca. 1910.

the AME Zion Church formed Harriet Tubman clubs to keep her memory and name alive. In 1937 the Empire State Federation of Women's Clubs erected a tombstone over Tubman's grave in celebration of her life's accomplishments. Schools and centers throughout the country—even in Canada—bear her name and honor her memory yet today.[38] In the 1990s parks in Cambridge, Maryland, and in Wilmington, Delaware, were dedicated in Tubman's honor. At the end of the decade not only was ground broken for a Harriet Tubman Park in Boston's South End, but city leaders also later dedicated a ten-foot-tall bronze statute, *Step on Board*, that depicts Tubman leading five fugitives to freedom.

Black artists have long celebrated her notable contributions as well. Jacob Lawrence's magnificent thirty-one panel series, "The Life of Harriet Tubman," begun in 1939 and completed in 1940, reflects this enduring fascination. A 1945 portrait by William H. Johnson, now in the collection of the Smithsonian American Art Museum, shows Tubman in her soldier's garb, guns stacked nearby, juxtaposed with the haunting image of her as an elderly, veiled woman—a compelling "double" vision of her legacy.

Harriet Tubman symbolizes the most powerful and purest elements of the Underground Railroad movement, namely, righteous self-determination and the defeat of unjust laws through collective resistance.

William H. Johnson,
Underground Railroad,
ca. 1945.

Those who fought the slave power only with words or at a comfortable distance were scarcely exposed to the dangers Tubman faced repeatedly on the paths to freedom. During her Underground Railroad career, she risked her own life and her own freedom again and again, making daring rescues to liberate others. Her aggressive agenda helped bring the war against slavery above ground and paved the way for its ultimate downfall and defeat.

BRUCE LEVINE

FLIGHT AND FIGHT

The Wartime Destruction of Slavery, 1861–1865

Successful escapes from slavery in the first half of the nineteenth century never posed a mortal threat to "the peculiar institution." During the 1850s, moreover, new laws and practices reduced the annual incidence of effective flight from just over a thousand down to about eight hundred slaves. According to the federal census, escape was freeing the African American population from bondage "at the rate of one fiftieth of one per cent" per year by the time of Abraham Lincoln's election. Frederick Douglass later reflected that "as a means of destroying slavery," the Underground Railroad "was like an attempt to bail out the ocean with a tea-spoon."[1]

As a political factor, however, antebellum escapes did help to bring on full-scale emancipation precisely by accelerating the coming of war. They did this, above all, by sharpening planters' concerns about their ability to control their labor force. Each successful escape encouraged those who remained behind to dream of an end to their own bondage and to reject their owners' assurances that bondage was absolute and permanent. Such hopes under-mined labor discipline. Successful escapes also eroded the white South's sacred myth that slaves accepted and were satisfied with their station in life. Debunking that myth strengthened antislavery sentiment in the North. Reciprocally, each case of flight into the free states stoked slave owner anger at "outsiders" (i.e., Northerners) who were doubtless fomenting and materi-ally assisting such escapes.

Planters and their political allies responded by demanding greater and greater federal protection for chattel slavery. They called for and obtained the Fugitive Slave Law of 1850, which required citizens of free states to assist

Enslaved Africans aboard an illegal slave ship seized off the coast of Florida in 1860, from *Harper's Weekly,* June 2, 1860.

in capturing alleged escapees. That law provoked a hostile political response in the North. The Kansas-Nebraska Act of 1854, designed in part to block flight from the neighboring slave state of Missouri, triggered an even bigger and angrier reaction in the free states.[2]

These and other measures intended to prevent slaves from escaping bondage (including the Supreme Court's Dred Scott decision of 1857) severely aggravated the sectional antagonisms that produced the Republican Party and led to Lincoln's election and later Southern secession. South Carolina, the first state to depart the Union, complained that the states of the North had "permitted the open establishment among them of societies, whose avowed object is to disturb the peace" and which have "encouraged and assisted thousands of our slaves to leave their homes." Secessionist advocates from other states stressed the same and kindred themes.[3]

Secession and the war it provoked, in turn, radically transformed the possibilities for and impact of slave flight. In the new context created by military conflict, escape to freedom could for the first time assume truly huge proportions. It liberated hundreds of thousands of individuals and undermined the institution of slavery as a whole by emboldening those still in bondage; sharpening tensions among different groups of white Southerners; weakening the Confederacy militarily, economically, and diplomatically; strengthening the Union war effort; and speeding the evolution of Union war policy in the direction of general and immediate emancipation.

At first, however, the Lincoln administration emphasized that its sole aim in war was to preserve rather than to transform the Union: to defeat secession rather than to abolish slavery. The newly elected president despised human bondage, and his electoral platform pledged to outlaw slavery in the federal territories and thereby stop its expansion beyond its existing confines. Lincoln also shared the nearly universal belief that the federal government had no constitutional power to act against slavery within states where it already existed. "Do the people of the South really entertain fears that a Republican administration would, *directly*, or *indirectly*, interfere with their slaves, or with them, about their slaves?" he asked Georgia's Alexander Stephens. "If they do, I wish to assure you . . . that there is no cause for such fears." He made the same point in countless speeches during the winter of 1860–61 and forcefully reiterated it on March 4, 1861, in his first inaugural address.[4]

Lincoln also hoped that, by adhering to a circumspect policy toward slavery even during wartime, he could keep the rest of the Union solidly behind him. Caution was especially necessary, he believed, in order to hold on to the four slave states that remained within the Union (Delaware, Maryland, Missouri, and especially militarily crucial Kentucky). Yet even in the free states of the North, as Lincoln was well aware, 45 percent of the electorate had cast their presidential votes in 1860 not for him but for one of his three more conservative opponents. Eight months after the war's outbreak, Lincoln once again pointedly forswore the employment of "radical and extreme measures," much less any kind of "remorseless revolutionary struggle."[5]

Congress underscored its support for this policy in July 1861 when it overwhelm-

"A Slave Auction at the South," from *Harper's Weekly*, July 13, 1861.

ingly endorsed the Crittenden-Johnson Resolution, which flatly denied any intention "of overthrowing or interfering with the rights of established institutions of those States" currently in rebellion. The Senate approved these words by a vote of thirty to five; the House of Representatives, by an even more lopsided one hundred nineteen to two.[6]

In the last analysis, however, the character of the developing situation overshadowed what Lincoln or the Congress initially wished or said. A correspondent of New York's *Anglo-African,* the country's premier free-black newspaper, wrote, "The friends of universal emancipation are enabled to see by the impending difficulties that their [previous] labors have not been thrown away, for [that] agitation has driven the South mad. . . . He that is able to read this nation's destiny, can see and decipher the handwriting on the wall." Confederate leaders had explicitly boasted that the South's core strength lay in its access to slave labor. Surely, it followed that breaking the Confederacy's power required depriving it of its labor force. The *Anglo-African* foresaw that "public opinion purified by the fiery ordeal . . . will rightly appreciate the cause of its political disquiet and apply the remedy."[7]

No one framed this matter more clearly or eloquently than the former fugitive slave and abolitionist leader Frederick Douglass. "Any attempt," Douglass warned during the second month of war, "to separate the freedom of the slave from the victory of the Government, . . . any attempt to secure peace to the whites while leaving the blacks in chains . . . will be labor lost." Yes, Douglass knew, "the American people and the Government at Washington may refuse to recognize it for a time," but ultimately "the 'inexorable logic of events' will force

it[self] upon them," compelling recognition that at bottom "the war now being waged in this land is a war for and against slavery; and that it can never be effectually put down till one or the other of these vital forces is completely destroyed."[8]

Slaves, free black and white abolitionists, and Republicans all played crucial roles in leading the Union government and public to acknowledge this central strategic fact. Of these, unfree African Americans played the first, most consistent, and most compelling roles. More than one of every three residents of the Confederacy (3.4 million out of a total 9.1 million) was a slave. They attended as closely as they could to the political events unfolding in the secession season of 1860–61, seeking opportunities to benefit from the novel and volatile situation. "The slaves, to a man, are on the alert," the black newspaper correspondent George E. Stephens reported in the war's early months. They "are watching the events of the hour, and . . . hope lights up their hearts."[9]

Making sense of these events was a complex, difficult undertaking, especially for a slave population that had been successfully maintained in a state of near-total illiteracy. Slave owners did their best to mislead bondspeople about the war's nature and its implications for them. They assured slaves that the North had no chance to defeat the Confederacy militarily. Even if they did win, a Union victory would leave them worse off than before, for in that case they would share the doleful lot of wretched blacks in the North. "The white folks would tell their colored people not to go to the Yankees," the former slave Susie King Taylor later remembered, "for they would harness them to carts and make them pull the carts around, in place of

horses." If not that, masters warned, the Republicans would sell slaves away from their homes, friends, and family members and send them to New Orleans or, even worse, to the reputed hell hole of Cuba. One former slave typically recalled (in the Gullah accents of the Carolina Sea Islands), our masters "tell we dat de Yankees would shoot we, or would sell we to Cuba, an' do all de wust tings to we, when dey come." At the very least, slaves were told, the Yankees would simply return them to their vengeful owners. The often hostile treatment of fugitives in the hands of Union troops, particularly during the first year of the war, lent credence to admonitions such as these. "So many fugitives have been returned by them [Union troops] that the slaves are almost their enemies," George E. Stephens discovered in the Chesapeake in November 1861. In light of all this, it is hardly surprising that some slaves and Southern free blacks made ostentatious displays of loyalty to the Confederacy, thereby hoping to improve their own conditions marginally or, at least, avoid the wrath of aroused Southern whites.[10]

Slaves soon heard their owners say contradictory things. Since the 1850s, masters and their spokesmen not only had been loudly equating Republicans and abolitionists but also had been depicting the ascendancy of the Republican Party as the overture to mass emancipation. Ultimately, the accumulated weight of such pronouncements made a deeper impression on Southern blacks than did the masters' more recent attempts to frighten their chattels.

Timothy H. O'Sullivan photographed slaves on J. J. Smith's plantation near Beaufort, South Carolina, in 1862.

Shortly after the fall of Fort Sumter on April 12, 1861, William H. Lee, a small farmer in Alabama, warned the Confederate regime that "the Negroes is very Hiley Hope up that they will soon be free." From Athens, Georgia, came word that "numbers of them believe that Lincoln's intention is to set them all free." Eventually, most slaves decided quite literally that the enemy of their known enemy must be their friend. "Massa hates de Yankees, and he's no fren' ter we, so we am de Yankee bi's fren's." Another reasoned, "Dem 'Blue-coats' was devils but de 'gray-coats' wuz wusser." A group of slaves on South Carolina's Combahee River, advised to fear approaching Yankee gunboats, watched their master flee instead. "Good-by, ole man," they later remembered calling after him. "That's right. Skedaddle as fas' as you kin. When we cotch you ag'in, I 'specs you'll know it. We's gwine to run sure enough; but we knows the Yankees, an' we runs that way," gesturing toward the Union ships.[11]

Some slaves began to act even before Fort Sumter fell. A month earlier, on March 12, 1861, eight Florida slaves escaped from their masters and appeared at the gates of Fort Pickens, one of the few federal installations in the Deep South that secessionists had not already seized. The fort's amused commanding officer found the fugitives "entertaining the idea" that the garrison's troops "were placed here to protect them and grant them freedom." That officer "did what I could to teach them the contrary," promptly arranging to have them returned to their owners. Two months later, at the end of May, three Virginia fugitives requested sanctuary from General Benjamin Butler, the Union commander of Fort Monroe on the Yorktown peninsula. "We had heard it since last Fall, that if Lincoln was elected, you would

"Negroes Leaving Their Home," from *Harper's Weekly*, April 9, 1864.

come down and set us free," one slave explained. Therefore, "the colored people have talked it all over; we heard that if we could get in here we should be free, or at any rate, we should be among friends."[12]

A Democratic politician from Massachusetts, General Butler had no previous military experience and no abolitionist sympathies, but he was a shrewd tactician with a legal background. He found it illogical to return valuable laborers to masters who had taken up arms against the US government, especially slaves who had been laboring (as they claimed to be) on the enemy's fortifications. When a Confederate officer bearing a flag of truce sought to return these fugitives to their owners, Butler refused. "I shall hold these negroes as contraband of war," he announced, "since they are engaged in the construction of your battery and are claimed as your property. The question is simply whether they shall be used for or against the Government of the United States." He subsequently expanded upon the point: "Property of whatever nature, used or capable of being used for warlike purposes, and especially when being so used, may be captured and held . . . as property contraband of war." Butler put the fugitives to work under the direction of his own quartermaster—and under the general's protection.[13]

News of that decision spread rapidly along the slave grapevine in the region surrounding Fort Monroe. Two days later, eight more runaways made their way to what came to be called "Freedom Fort." Another fifty-nine black men and women joined them the following day. By the end of July 1861, the number of such fugitives had reached nine hundred.[14]

Simply by reacting to the initiative of the slaves themselves and by recognizing how they could serve the military needs of the Union, Butler pragmatically fashioned a policy that would permit Northern forces to use slave labor without formally changing the character of Union war aims. Lincoln recognized the ingenuity of Butler's decision and endorsed it as a legitimate tactic of war. Radical Republican congressmen, such as Charles Sumner of Massachusetts, Salmon P. Chase of Ohio,

"Morning Mustering of the 'Contraband' at Fortress Monroe," 1862.

Owen Lovejoy of Illinois, and Thaddeus Stevens of Pennsylvania, drew the appropriate policy conclusions from these slaves' initiatives and Butler's creative response. In the name of military necessity and to advance the destruction of slavery, they urged one measure after another on their colleagues. Every Confederate victory not only pointed up the need to strengthen Union forces and weaken the enemy, but it also increased Northern anger at the South's planter aristocracy. And every Union advance drove blue-clad troops deeper into slavery's heartland and brought them into closer proximity with Confederate-owned slaves. Such direct confrontation underscored the hopelessness of trying to conquer the slave owners while still respecting their property rights.

At the urging of Illinois Republican congressman Owen Lovejoy, the House of Representatives resolved on July 9, 1861, that "it is no part of the duty of the soldiers of the United States to capture and return fugitive slaves." The next month Congress passed its first Confiscation Act, which provided that any slave owner using a slave (or permitting that slave to be used) in aid of the Confederate war effort "shall forfeit all right" to that slave. In December 1861, an attempt to have the House of Representatives reaffirm the conciliationist spirit of the Crittenden-Johnson Resolution (originally passed just five months earlier) failed. On March 13, 1862, Congress passed into legislation a new article of war that formally prohibited Union soldiers from returning fugitive slaves who had entered their lines.[15]

The Union army was as deeply divided over what to do about slavery as was the North's civilian population. Those Union officers who also saw the value of acquiring additional laborers now followed Butler's lead. Their decisions, in turn, improved conditions for slave escapes and encouraged additional attempts. Two Union commanders tried to step up the pace. In August 1861, General John C. Frémont proclaimed the emancipation of all slaves in deeply divided Missouri. Seven months later, in March 1862, Major General David Hunter utilized his position as commander of the Union's Department of the South to declare all slaves in Georgia, South Carolina, and Florida free. In both cases, the Lincoln administration, unwilling to move so rapidly, countermanded the orders.

"Contrabands" aboard the USS *Vermont*, 1862.

Other Union commanders flatly rejected Butler's welcoming policy toward refugees. On November 20, 1861, Major General Henry W. Halleck, having replaced Frémont as commander in Missouri, issued his General Orders No. 3. He decreed that no fugitive slaves would be "hereafter permitted to enter the lines of any camp, or of any forces on the march; and that any now within such lines be immediately excluded therefrom." Halleck reiterated that order three months later. Generals John A. Dix, Don Carlos Buell, and others acted similarly.[16]

Over time, the argument in favor of a firm antislavery war policy grew steadily more compelling. At the end of the war's first year, in April 1862, a bill to begin the immediate abolition of bondage in the District of Columbia passed into law. That same month Congress authorized diplomatic recognition of the black governments of both Liberia and Haiti. In mid-June, Congress decreed that "there shall be neither slavery nor involuntary servitude in any of the Territories of the United States now existing, or which may at any time hereafter be formed or acquired." A few weeks later, in July 1862, Congress approved the Second Confiscation Act. This law provided that slaves belonging to anyone who supported the rebellion and who for any reason came under the control of Union troops "shall be deemed captives of war, and shall be forever free of their servitude and not again held as slaves."[17]

Despite these changes in official US policy, bondspeople who were considering flight toward Union lines still confronted daunting obstacles. Most refugees had to part from friends and immediate family; they did not know when or if they would ever see their loved ones again. They had good reason to fear that those left behind would feel the wrath of the frustrated master. Meanwhile, the fugitives had to evade not only their own masters and overseers but also mounted slave patrols and Southern troop detachments and pickets. Even those refugees who reached and were accepted into Union-occupied regions could never assume they were free. Rebel attacks could (and did) recapture individuals and groups. The constant movement of the front could (and did) suddenly return whole communities of freed people to Rebel control. Those who were recaptured faced the prospect of severe punishment, including torture and execution on the spot. Still, the number ready to risk these perils continued to grow.[18]

For some time Abraham Lincoln merely seemed to be pulled passively, even haltingly, in the wake of Congress's antislavery initiatives. In reality, as Lincoln later put it, the fact that "slavery is at the root of the rebellion, or at least its *sine qua non*" increasingly dominated his thoughts and plans. Early in March 1862, he urged Congress to provide financial assistance to any state that "may adopt gradual abolishment of slavery," and Congress passed such a bill in April. The president assured leaders of the loyal border states that he intended no coercive interference in their internal affairs, but he also insistently pressed them to accept this financial offer, pointedly advising them that it was the best deal they were likely to get. As the war continued, Lincoln warned, "The institution [of slavery] in your States will be extinguished by mere friction and abrasion—by the mere incidents of war."[19]

Then, on July 22, 1862, five days following passage of the Second Confiscation Act, Lincoln told his cabinet that he intended, in

S. A. Peters and Company, Hartford, Connecticut, "The Reading of the Emancipation Proclamation," 1864.

his capacity as wartime commander in chief, to issue a general proclamation emancipating all slaves in those parts of the South still in revolt. At the urging of cabinet members, the president agreed to postpone a public announcement until a Union victory could cast the measure as an expression of strength rather than weakness. That opportunity came with the Battle of Antietam in September, which stopped Robert E. Lee's raid into Union-held Maryland. Lincoln issued his preliminary emancipation proclamation on September 22, 1862, announcing that on January 1 of the new year, all slaves within the Confederacy would become, in the eyes of the US government, "then, thenceforward, and forever free."[20]

During the following months, Republican losses in the North's 1862 congressional elections, compounded by frustrations and setbacks on the battlefield, led many to expect Lincoln would rescind or at least postpone the New Year's Day deadline. Yet, on January 1, 1863—by which time no Confederate state had responded to the September warning—Lincoln finalized the Emancipation Proclamation, declaring that

"all persons held as slaves within said designated States are, and henceforward shall be, free" and adding that the government and its armed forces "will recognize and maintain the freedom of said persons." The president had by then dismissed the political and juridical hesitations that had previously preoccupied him; recent history had rendered them irrelevant. "We must disenthrall ourselves" of "the dogmas of the quiet past," Lincoln realized, and recognize the imperatives of "the stormy present. . . . We know how to save the Union. . . . In *giving* freedom to the *slave*, we *assure* freedom to the *free*."[21] Union forces soon received thousands of copies of the proclamation for soldiers to distribute as they penetrated further into the Confederacy.

Contemporary critics and many later historians derided the Emancipation Proclamation as a gesture with little practical significance, since it applied only to people over whom federal forces exercised no direct power. It did not touch slaves within the Union (i.e., in Delaware, Maryland, Kentucky, or Missouri), nor did it apply to slaves living in those parts of the Confederacy that had been previously returned to Union control.

Even so, the Emancipation Proclamation's impact was no less real. Coming from the army's commander in chief, it carried far more weight among the soldiers than did the Second Confiscation Act (which formally anticipated much of the proclamation's real content). It sharply reduced ambiguities in official Union policy and made it far more difficult for recalcitrant conservative-minded officers to do as they pleased. In addition, it strengthened pro-Union popular sentiment in Europe, thereby helping to stay the hand of Confederate sympathizers in governments there. Most of all, it clearly encouraged slaves to assist and flee toward Union troops.

Once again, the slave grapevine spread the news. Areas closest to the Union and to Union troop encampments received the word most swiftly. One federal provost marshal asked Confederate prisoners of war in 1863 "what effect the President's Proclamation of Freedom had produced in the South." They replied that "it had played hell with them." The official then expressed surprise, pointing out that few slaves could read the proclamation's text, to which one Confederate prisoner replied "that one of his negroes had told him of the proclamation five days before he had heard it in any other way." Some of this man's colleagues agreed that "their negroes gave them their first information of the proclamation." A South Carolina fugitive supplied the solution to the apparent mystery: "We'se can't read, but we'se can listen."22

In 1863–64, as Union forces completed the conquest of the Mississippi Valley and then drove from southeastern Tennessee down through Georgia to the Atlantic Coast, the earlier stream of individual (usually young, male) slave fugitives turned into a cascade and then a flood of refugees, now including whole family groups and even the entire labor force of plantations. The best modern estimates suggest that by war's end between one-half and three-quarters of a million people, or from 15 to 20 percent of the Confederacy's entire slave population, had taken advantage of the proclamation's promise. "See how much better off we are now dan we was four years ago," one refugee explained in a reference to Underground Railroad imagery. "It used to be five hundred miles to git to Canada from Lexington, but now it's eighteen miles! *Camp Nelson* is now *our* Canada!"23

Typical was the scene that greeted General William T. Sherman's troops as they entered the town of Covington, Georgia. Sherman harbored little love for African Americans, and his army treated

In "The Effects of the Proclamation," former slaves travel toward safety from New Bern, North Carolina.

"General Sherman's Rear-Guard," from *Harper's Weekly*, April 12, 1864. Freedpeople followed the Union armies in Georgia during Sherman's "March to the Sea."

slaves callously at best. Nevertheless, Sherman later recalled, "The negroes were simply frantic with joy. Whenever they heard my name, they clustered about my horse, shouted and prayed in their peculiar style, which had a natural eloquence that would have moved a stone." He recalled the sight of "a poor girl, in the very ecstasy of the Methodist 'shout,' hugging the banner of one of the regiments and jumping up to the 'feet of Jesus.'" At a nearby plantation, an elderly black man explained the warmth of this reception. "I asked him if he understood about the war and its progress," Sherman wrote in his memoirs. "He said he did; that he had been looking for the 'angel of the Lord' ever since he was knee-high,

and, though we professed to be fighting for the Union, he supposed that slavery was the cause, and that our success was to be his freedom." The general asked the man if "all the negro slaves" there held the same opinion, "and he said they surely did."[24]

The former slaves offered Union forces invaluable assistance. The quartermaster department put men to work at a wide range of tasks, including building fortifications, digging graves, caring for the horses, and driving wagons. Women cooked, washed clothes, and nursed the sick and wounded. Men and women alike tilled the soil. They also pressed the emancipation process further forward. Soon after reaching federal lines, some fugitives began laying plans to return home in order to liberate friends and family members. One Georgia fugitive named Nat reportedly helped seventy to a hundred other bondspeople reach freedom during the war before a Confederate soldier shot and killed him. Such expeditions could carry former slaves hundreds of miles back into the Confederate interior, and sometimes included Union troops as well. "A negro brought the Yankees from Pineville," a South Carolina Confederate reported grimly, "and piloted them to where our men were camped, taking them completely by surprise, capturing Bright and killing two of his men." Protestant evangelist and Georgia planter Charles Colcock Jones Sr. warned his family members, "They are traitors who may pilot an enemy into your *bedchamber!* They know every road and swamp and creek and plantation in the county, and are the worst of spies."[25]

During most of the war, proslavery newspapers—like Confederate nostalgics ever since—printed and reprinted comforting stories about loyal slaves standing by beloved masters, both on the plantations and in the storm of battle. Those who cherished and lovingly repeated such stories "needn't have done that," an old black man later reflected, since "every now and then we were falling behind a stump or into a corner of the fence and praying for the Union soldiers." Some slave owners began facing these discomfiting truths. Catherine Edmonston of North Carolina wrote, "[A]s to the idea of the *faithful servant, it is all a fiction.* I have seen the favorite and most petted negroes the first to leave in every instance." Ella Clanton Thomas of Georgia came to the same conclusion: "Those we loved best, and who loved us best—as we thought—were the first to leave us."[26]

During the last half-year of the war, such bitter realities were forcing their way into even the Confederate press. The

Freedmen laborers on the Union quartermaster's wharf, Alexandria, Virginia, ca. 1864.

Lynchburg Virginian now confessed that "wherever the enemy goes, our slaves follow him in droves." A Georgia editor reported, "Instead of manifesting the loyalty for which some give them credit, the men, women and children, prompted by abolition emissaries, rushed to the Yankees from every quarter." A North Carolinian observed resentfully, "Vast numbers of them have voluntarily gone over to the enemy whenever a favorable opportunity presented itself to them, and, in many instances, joined their army of their own free choice." A prominent Richmond editor conceded that Union vessels "proceeding up our rivers" have had to do "little more . . . than display their colors" before "the negroes at once threw down their hoes, axes and spades, and quitted their plows, and flocked to the Yankee steamers and other craft by tens of thousands."[27]

The wartime breakdown of slavery became apparent beyond those Southern districts actually penetrated by Union troops. In still-unoccupied parts of the Confederacy, masters, army officers, and government officials clashed repeatedly over which of them had the greater need for and claim to the labor of remaining slaves. This process eroded the real power of Rebel masters—and emboldened those still under their formal control. A South Carolina overseer bemoaned the "goodeal of obstanetry" he faced among "Some of the Peopl" working on his plantation, "mostly amongst the Woman a goodeal of Quarling and disputing and telling lies." James Alcorn, a Mississippi planter, found that Union raids in his area had "thoroughly demoralized" his slaves. (This phrase was common planter parlance for saying that power over a slave—and a slave's fear

"Negroes Escaping Out of Slavery," from *Harper's Weekly,* May 7, 1864.

of a master—had faded.) That change, moaned Alcorn, had rendered his human property "no longer of any practical value." Even among those field laborers who had not fled, a Louisiana overseer reported to his employer, "but very few are faithful— Some of those who remain are worse than those who have gone." In one district after another, bondspeople began to call for improvements in their conditions as well as implicit but no less momentous alterations in their status—and they withheld their labor until such demands were met. Owners thus found themselves forced to bargain, more and more openly, for the services of those who were still viewed as property. "Their condition is one of perfect anarchy and rebellion," Georgia plantation mistress Mary Jones confided in her journal. "They have placed themselves in perfect antagonism to their owners and to all government and control. We dare not predict the end of all this, if the Lord in his mercy does not restrain the hearts and wills of this deluded people."[28]

The wartime crisis of slavery left a deep imprint not only on southern whites but also on Union troops. As Lincoln and others had feared, and as the 1862 elections made clear, the decision to add the destruction of slavery to the North's war aims at first provoked fierce opposition in parts of the Union. Few Union soldiers had gone to war committed to abolition, and the emancipation proclamations of the fall and winter of 1862–63 triggered heated discussions and considerable resistance to black freedom in army camps across the land.

Over time the Union soldiers' firsthand exposure to the real nature of slavery did much, however, to change minds and soften hearts. Soldiers' letters told of hiding fugitives in camp and jeering at the impotent fury of owners sent home empty-handed. One group of New York soldiers, observing the whipping of recently returned fugitives, freed the slaves and flogged the masters. "There is quite an audible murmur here about the return of fugitives," soldier George Stephens reported from the Chesapeake in February 1862. "I expect to see the time very shortly when more than one slave hunter will bite the dust. An officer of high rank told one of them [slave hunters] some time ago that in a very short time he would not guarantee his life five minutes in the lines on a slave hunt." In the fall of 1863 Union soldier James T. Miller concluded with satisfaction, "These two years of war have made more Abolitionists than the lectures of Wendell Phillips and Gerrit Smith and Wm Lyod Garison [*sic*] would have made in a hundred years." As if in corroboration, Sergeant Eli Pickett of Minnesota wrote home early that same year. "I have never been in favor of the abolition of slavery," but "this war has determined me in the conviction that it is a greater sin than our Government is able to stand—and now I go in for a war of emancipation and I am ready and willing to do my share in the war." A Union officer from Chicago, previously a staunch Democrat, wrote home from Louisiana, "Since I am here, I have learned what the

"Contrabands" with white officers, Camp Brightwood, near Washington, DC, 1863.

horrors of slavery was . . . and I am glad that the signs of the times show, towards closing out the accursed institution." As if writing in agreement, a Michigan farmer stated from Georgia in 1864, "The more I learn of the cursed institution of Slavery, the more I feel willing to endure, for its final destruction."[29]

Experiences and lessons of war also transformed federal policy concerning African Americans serving in Union uniforms. At first, the government bluntly and sternly rebuffed attempts by Northern free blacks to enlist. Lincoln and his advisors feared that allowing blacks into the army would be interpreted as a Republican move to overturn white supremacy—and so send the "loyal border states" into the Confederacy's open arms. Strong doubts also existed that blacks had either the courage or the intelligence to make good soldiers. "This Department," announced Secretary of War Simon Cameron on April 29, 1861, "has no intention to call into the service of the Government any colored soldiers." Local political authorities drove home his point by flatly prohibiting black recruitment meetings, calling them "disorderly gatherings." The widespread belief that this would be a short, relatively bloodless "gentlemen's war" bolstered this attitude. If the South would be subdued easily, why inflame the racial animosities of Northern whites by asking them to serve in uniform beside blacks? Racist mobs attacked some Northern free blacks who organized recruitment meetings at their own initiative. The Cincinnati police warned would-be soldiers in that city, "We want you d—d niggers to keep out of this; this is a white man's war!"[30]

In December 1861, Secretary of War Cameron hesitantly suggested the Lincoln administration reconsider its policy. "If . . . the men who have been held by the rebels as slaves are capable of bearing arms and performing efficient military service," he wrote, "it is the right, and may become the duty, of this Government to arm and equip them, and employ their services against the rebels. . . ." Lincoln balked, and Cameron soon found himself replaced by the seemingly more conservative Edwin M. Stanton. Union commanders in South Carolina and Kansas nevertheless created units composed of former slaves; in both cases, Lincoln ordered them to stand down.[31]

In time, the same reasoning that eventually counseled emancipation also led to placing freedmen under arms. The Second Confiscation Act (July 1862) authorized the president to "employ as many persons of African descent as he may deem necessary and proper for the suppression of this rebellion, and . . . in such manner as he may judge best." The Militia Act, passed the same day, provided for the employment of blacks in "any military . . . service for which they may be found competent" and granted freedom to all so employed. The War Department, in August 1862, authorized the formation of the First South Carolina Volunteers, the first official Union regiment of this type. Lincoln's final Emancipation Proclamation reiterated his decision to see "such persons, of suitable condition, . . . received into the armed forces of the United States."[32]

Over the course of the war, more than 180,000 African Americans donned Union blue, with some 80 percent of them recruited in the slave states. "My present position in reference to the rebellion," Abraham Lincoln told critics in September 1864, is "the only position upon which any Executive can or could save the Union."

> Any different policy in regard to the colored man deprives us of his help, and this is more than we can bear. We can not spare the hundred and forty or fifty thousand now serving us as soldiers, seamen, and laborers. This is not a question of sentiment or taste, but of physical force which may be measured and estimated as horse-power and Steam-power are measured and estimated. Keep it and you can save the Union. Throw it away, and the Union goes with it.

The war's final year saw more than 120,000 African American soldiers serving in the Union army. That number approximated the total number of Confederate soldiers still present for duty anywhere by that time. In the spring of 1865, when Ulysses S. Grant's forces besieged Petersburg, his troops included thirty-three black regiments, or about one out of every eight Union soldiers there.[33]

Black troops guarded crucial but vulnerable supply lines and performed many other essential support tasks. They also distinguished themselves in combat, which played an important role in transforming Northern opinion about both slavery and African Americans. All told, black soldiers took part in some 450 military engagements, about 40 of which were major battles, and provided the Union with 120 infantry regiments, 12 heavy artillery regiments, 10 batteries of light artillery, and 7 cavalry regiments. Colonel Thomas Wentworth Higginson, commander of the First South Carolina Volunteers, summarized the blacks' most striking qualities as soldiers. "They know the country, which White troops do not," he noted, but their

Freedmen as teamsters for the Union armies, near Bermuda Hundred, Virginia, 1864.

motives and incentives were also unique. "Instead of leaving their homes and families to fight, they are fighting for their homes and families; and they show the resolution and sagacity which a personal purpose gives. . . . It would have been madness to attempt with the bravest White troops what I have successfully accomplished with Black ones." General David Hunter informed Secretary of War Stanton that black troops under his command were "hardy, generous, temperate, strictly obedient, possessing remarkable aptitude for military training, and deeply imbued with that religious sentiment (call it fanaticism, such as like) which made the soldiers of Oliver Cromwell invincible." A black sergeant put it more directly: "We are fighting for liberty and right, and we intend to follow the old flag while there is a man left to hold it up to the breeze of heaven. Slavery must and shall pass away."[34]

As early as October 1862, black troops mustered in Kansas saw action in neighboring Missouri. "The men," a Northern journalist reported, "fought like tigers, each and every one of them." Black soldiers participated in their first major engagement seven months later in May 1863 and displayed conspicuous valor in an unsuccessful assault at Port Hudson, Louisiana. Two weeks later, five hundred former slaves bore the brunt of an attack by five times that number of Confederate troops at nearby Milliken's Bend. A report to the Union War Department noted that "sentiment in regard to the employment of negro troops has been revolutionized by the bravery of the blacks. . . . Prominent officers, who used in private to sneer at the idea, are now heartily in favor of it." The Southern commander that day acknowledged that his charge "was resisted by the negro portion of the enemy's force

with considerable obstinacy, while the white or true Yankee portion ran like whipped curs almost as soon as the charge was ordered." Another soldier reminded Confederate president Jefferson Davis that Secretary of State William H. Seward "has boldly laid down the proposition of an irresistible conflict between free and slave labour. Well," the man continued sourly, since "the protracted duration of the war" owed so much to the slaves' support for the Union, Seward "no doubt often recalls this, as the most sage remark of his life." The black soldier, a Confederate newspaper editor summarized, "fights willingly and

RIGHT: Broadside issued by Frederick Douglass calling "men of color to arms" and recruiting black troops, 1863.

fiendishly for his own freedom." The fruits of that effort could be especially sweet, as one slave-turned-soldier exclaimed when he discovered his former owner among the Confederate prisoners he was guarding. "Hello, massa," the man sang out. "Bottom rail [on] top dis time!"[35]

By the final months of the war, slavery had collapsed in key parts of the South and had been drastically undermined in others. Millions, however, had yet to achieve their freedom when Robert E. Lee surrendered in April 1865. Eradicating these last vestiges of slavery continued long after the formal end of hostilities. In places Union troops had bypassed, masters were more successful in keeping slaves unaware of the word—and the full reality—of freedom. An African Methodist Episcopal missionary discovered that in parts of Georgia in August 1865, four months after Appomattox, "the people do not know really that they are free, and if they do, their surroundings are such that they would fear

to speak of it." In the loyal slave states of Delaware and Kentucky, which had been formally exempted from the Emancipation Proclamation's terms, many blacks remained legally enslaved until the Thirteenth Amendment's ratification in December 1865. Elsewhere in the former Confederacy, masters reportedly managed to conceal the fact of emancipation from their laborers for two years following the war's end.[36]

Over the next decades, the condition of African Americans fluctuated radically. Southern planters in 1865–66 sought to reassert their power, but an alliance of freedpeople and white Republicans turned back that attempt with a program of Reconstruction. In response, foes of racial equality launched a campaign of terror that overthrew Reconstruction in the 1870s and still later imposed the system of Jim Crow segregation.

Colonel Thomas Wentworth Higginson knew in the 1860s that "revolutions may go backward." This one did. Years later, author W. E. B. Du Bois wrote, "The slave went free; stood a brief moment in the sun; then moved back again toward slavery."[37] Descendants of these freedpeople and the nation as a whole continue to grapple with the legacy of America's tragically incomplete second revolution.

None of this, however, signified that the Civil War had been fought in vain. In the late nineteenth century, the revolution against the planter elite was driven backward but not completely undone. To use Du Bois's words, black Americans' forced retreat back *toward* slavery never drove them back *into* slavery. The ineradicable fact remained that in the 1860s slaves, soldiers, and the Union government together had put an end to the legal ownership of one human being by another. Thereafter, millions of human beings in the United States could not again be bought and sold like cattle, nor could their rights as family members be arbitrarily ignored. The former slave Charlie Barbour and others now knew

"dat I won't wake up some mornin' ter fin' dat my mammy or some ob de rest of my family am done sold." Jacob Thomas, another former slave, could note with satisfaction that "I has got thirteen great-gran' chilluns, an' I knows whar dey ever'one am. In slavery times dey'd have been on de block some time ago."[38]

Other important gains also survived. As exploitative and impoverishing as the postwar sharecropping system became, it never equaled antebellum gang labor in severity or brutality. Nor were African Americans—in contrast with black South Africans in the twentieth century—formally barred from national citizenship, herded into geographically isolated labor reserves, or prohibited by law from moving from one part of the country to another.

These and other lasting results of the Civil War helped black people to forge stronger families and to build tenacious church and community organizations, all of which assisted them to mobilize in self-defense far more effectively than had ever been possible under slavery. In later decades, when conditions became more favorable, African Americans would use those and other hard-won gains of the Civil War era to carry forward the struggle for equality.

GO FREE

PART THREE
THE STORY ENDURES
IN HISTORY AND LEGEND

DAVID W. BLIGHT

WHY THE UNDERGROUND RAILROAD, AND WHY NOW? A LONG VIEW

In certain regions of the northern United States, especially Ohio, but also in many other areas of the Midwest and New England, Underground Railroad sites, or "stations," are hallowed ground, places crucial to local heritage tourism and identities. I cannot count the times, without even asking a leading question, I have been told of places predating 1860 that local citizens claim was a "depot" on the Underground Railroad. They include: the friend who swore her house, located on the common in a lovely western Massachusetts town, was "really" a "station," based solely on local lore; the student working at the circulation desk of an Ivy League university library who, when observing that I was checking out several books related to the Underground Railroad, immediately told me, a total stranger, that her grandparents in Iowa lived in a house with secret hideaways where fugitive slaves were once hidden; the occasional teacher in summer institutes that I lead who tells of annual field trips to the local Underground Railroad house, as though every American town needs one, and believes the experience is a rite of passage for young people; the restaurant in a famous Pennsylvania historic town that allows patrons waiting for a table to see the special crawl space where a few half-lit dummy fugitive slaves lay in hiding; the remarkable growth of the Underground Railroad as one of the most popular themes in children's literature (one fifth-grade drama instructor in Columbus, Ohio, annually teaches ten plays based on the Underground Railroad, and as of February 2003 was searching for more); and the realtor in New Haven, Connecticut, who told me, without knowing I am a historian, that some of the old houses backing up to the river in town were connected to recently discovered tunnels that could not have been used for any other purpose than harboring and transporting

A scene from *Along the Tracks*, Jeff Chastang's play about escaped slaves traveling through Washtenaw County, Michigan, 2001.

runaway slaves. Is there a realtor in the Northern or border states selling old or historic homes, largely to white people, who has not contemplated the market value of space that might have been used in the nineteenth century to hide black people who were fugitives from slavery?

Moreover, Web sites on this topic proliferate on the Internet almost daily. Some of them represent legitimate historic sites and others promote the commerce of historical tourism, conferences, workshops, and annual "teaching summits." A "National Underground Railroad Family Reunion Festival" now occurs every year.[1] Everyone interested in this topic has come across the same local tales and observed the same passion for this American story of the pursuit of freedom. Indeed, despite all the changes in historical education related

to the teaching of slavery that have occurred in recent decades, it is still likely that the average American encounters the subject first, and most often, through the *lore* of the Underground Railroad.

This is not a new phenomenon. When the pioneering researcher and collector of Underground Railroad material, Charles L. Blockson, first traveled the byways of America in search of these stories some forty years ago, he found that wherever he went, "people pointed out some home, barn, church, or cave that allegedly was part of the Underground Railroad system." And in the early 1980s, as Blockson spent three years touring the country to prepare an article on the Underground Railroad for *National Geographic* magazine, he "met many descendants of slaves and their helpers, black and white, who delved deeply into their memories in order to help me."[2] Admittedly, exploring a story that involved so much secrecy and clandestine action as did the process of fugitive slaves seeking freedom in the North or in Canada must rely to some extent on oral history. Folklore, narratives, interviews, and testimonies from over a century and a half are crucial to this enterprise of historical recovery. Intergenerational transfer of such stories is an integral part of our access to the past. Although extremely valuable in aggregates and as a reflection of memory, oral history should be used with caution if it is the only source for retelling human experience or for judging the legitimacy of events in historic places.

Academic historians tend to privilege written documents, the archaeologists surviving objects, the folklorists tales or songs that open the secrets of a culture. All of these approaches are essential to developing both a general picture and a detailed comprehension of the past. Caution especially must be applied to determine just how much we fashion usable pasts, histories that reflect our desire for a particular kind of lineage, individual or collective. When it comes to the Underground Railroad, we need a healthy skepticism about local lore, but we should also study the lore, respect it, and examine where it can lead in understanding just why slavery was such a fundamental problem in America. The oral source and the written source should be employed to a common, if not always comfortable, end—an interpretation of resistance to slavery in all its successes and failures. Desire and knowledge walk hand in hand in any search for the past; the challenge is to keep them in a balance that serves the purpose of historical truth, as close as we can come to that holy, if elusive, grail.

Why do so many Americans want to claim a piece of this story? Why the

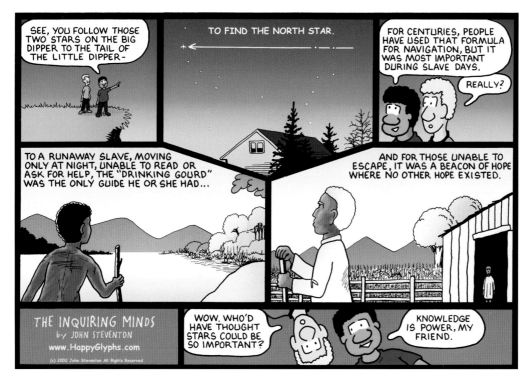

John Steventon's comic strip *The Inquiring Minds*, "Salute to the Underground Railroad," 2002.

Charles T. Webber,
*The Underground
Railroad,* 1893.

Underground Railroad, and why now, at the turn of the twenty-first century? To answer these questions we must look back at least a century, to the 1890s, and examine the remarkable work of Wilbur H. Siebert, a historian at Ohio State University. Siebert was born in Columbus, Ohio, in 1866, and as a young professor in 1892, he launched his personal quest to collect and record the story of what he called "the Road." His inspiration came from the tales he heard in his youth, as well as from his visit in 1893 to the World's Columbian Exposition in Chicago, where he first viewed C. T. Webber's painting *The Underground Railroad*. Siebert was hooked for life as a researcher, and for over forty years he wrote more about the networks for escaping slaves than anyone else. In Siebert's work it becomes apparent how a legend can grow from real history, and how that real history becomes so reliant on legend.

Siebert's passion for the Underground Railroad materialized in the thousands of circular letters he mailed all over the Northern states, soliciting recollections of or information about the trafficking of fugitive slaves. In these form letters Siebert asked for names, routes, incidents of escapes, and general reflections on the character of the system. From the beginning, Siebert's central assumption was that the Underground Railroad was a "great system," a "widespread institution," a series of hundreds of interlocking "lines," a "chain of stations leading from the Southern states to Canada."[3] His classic book, *The Underground Railroad*, published in 1898, is still an essential source both for the reality of the process by which fugitive slaves achieved freedom, as well as for how and why so much mythology has flourished around this story.

Siebert's work leaves no doubt that hundreds of Northerners were engaged in helping fugitive slaves on their way to safety and that thousands of blacks made their way to Canada and into Northern communities from 1830 to 1860. He documented numerous genuine heroes of abolitionism,

Wilbur Siebert, "'Underground': Routes to Canada," 1896, from Siebert, *Underground Railroad*, 1896.

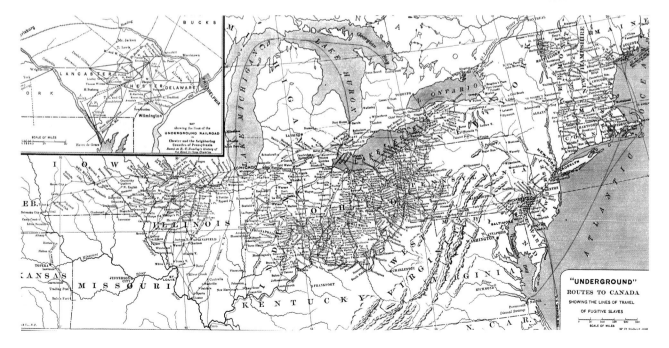

white and black, among them Levi Coffin, Thomas Garrett, William Still, Harriet Tubman, Calvin Fairbank, Charles Torrey, and many others. His research also demonstrated how much any understanding of fugitive slaves' prospects depended on what he called "local conditions," a lesson for all future researchers.[4] Fascinated by routes, Siebert produced his own "Underground Routes to Canada" map in his book, a creation that has been reproduced numerous times since 1898 as an allegedly authoritative source. Like the real railroads in the mid-nineteenth century, which created and sustained the economies of many a new town, old communities in the twentieth and early twenty-first centuries have needed to find their own connection to Siebert's vast network of "depots" as they seek historical prestige and ply the market for nostalgia about how America overcame slavery. No one did more to expand the geographic imagination for the Underground Railroad than Siebert.

Siebert wrote with clarity about the many methods and directions by which a fugitive might escape: by water, by wagon, on foot, eventually on real railroads, on ships in the coastal maritime trade, or out to sea as a stowaway. Other than the network of conductors, one of his principal subjects was how Canada was the "one real refuge" for American slaves. Indeed, he conducted numerous interviews with former slaves living north of the United States border and wrote informatively about the communities and productive lives of the "refugees" in Canada. Finally, Siebert showed the important role the Underground Railroad played, as reality and symbol, in the political crises over slavery in the decade before the Civil War. He quoted Southern congressmen in 1860 and 1861,

bitterly complaining in floor debate that Northerners had created "underground railroads . . . [and] secret societies . . . to steal away slaves."[5] A striking irony survives in that congressman's choice of words, since "Steal Away to Jesus" became one of the most famous Negro spirituals based on the idea of an Underground Railroad. Theft of human property and of liberty did help cause the Civil War.

All students of the Underground Railroad are forever in Siebert's debt. He collected existing literature from local newspapers and county histories, which proved to be a trove of reminiscences in the late nineteenth century. Then he assembled the material in thirty-eight scrapbook volumes, most of them organized by states. They include twelve volumes for Ohio, five for Illinois, three each for New York, Pennsylvania, and Iowa, two for Massachusetts, and one each for Michigan, Maine, Kansas, Missouri, and New Jersey. These volumes preserve the 1890s origins of both the history and the memory of the Underground Railroad. Siebert received many handwritten maps, countless stories about routes and escapes, plenty of names of alleged conductors, and a host of tall tales. The Ohio historian relied heavily on oral testimony from participants and their children; interviews were the basis of his analysis. He requested and received from respondents a great deal of sentimental retrospection.

Siebert defended the use of reminiscence as a historical source, especially when such material was collected from abolitionists. He believed that the work of "old time abolitionists," helping fugitive slaves flee to freedom, was too dramatic to be forgotten. "Not only did repetition serve to deepen the general recollections of the average operator," wrote Siebert, "but the strange and romantic character of his unlawful business helped to fix them in his mind."[6] Relying on this dubious theory of memory, Siebert cultivated the soil of Northern memory and fashioned a popular story of primarily white conductors helping generally nameless blacks to freedom. Repetition undoubtedly leads to deeper memory—the reliability of such memory is another matter—but the forms of such melodrama often provide a reliable and popular narrative in which we so often prefer to find ourselves. Over and over again in our popular culture, and especially in the movies, it becomes apparent that Americans love the story of heroes who do not play by the rules in order to resist and serve a higher cause.

Siebert received more stories than he could possibly use, and to his credit, he did not recycle some of the most bizarre cases. Nevertheless, he stirred up a nest of recollection and invention. In one escape after another, "valuable pieces of ebony" were hidden in caves, attics, garrets, haymows, and cellars. Heroic station keepers repeatedly pointed out the North Star at midnight to helpless fugitives, and duped slave catchers were always sent off course. Siebert gave many people the chance to place themselves, and their ancestors, in precisely the kind of narrative they desired. And thus, the legend of the Underground Railroad, just waiting to bloom, burst from its roots. One Iowa correspondent sent a long handwritten account proclaiming the Underground Railroad as the new source of romance, one sure to "furnish a rich field in which to delve for genuine material with which to adorn the historic page." The story, said the Iowan, as though writing a promotional advertisement, would "thrill the heart and quicken the pulse of the eager student of the grand progressive movement of human liberty in the past" and provide "hairbreath escapes, perilous journeys by land and water, incredible human suffering for a wide readership."[7] Today's broad fascination with the Underground Railroad in teaching, local history, and children's literature may still be rooted in just such a view of history as a progressive adornment, a journey of risk and success that lifts our spirits and makes us proud.

Reminiscence is a valuable source, but Siebert treated it uncritically, more like artifacts to be judged for their accuracy rather than as a mass of creative cultural memory. Sometimes people reminisce because they truly do want to relive part of their past. At other times objects or places induce a rush of remembrance or nostalgia where none may have been intended. Often reminiscence takes the form of wistfulness, a melancholy contemplation of the sheer transience of human experience—time just seems lost. Reminiscence can also be communal, stimulated by an audience of like-minded rememberers. Whatever the stimulus, we reminisce not merely to render the

Historian and writer Wilbur Siebert.

"The Bloodhound Business," from *Suppressed Book of Slavery*, 1864.

past retrievable but also to serve present interests and our own needs. At stake in reminiscence, therefore, are the dual needs of personal understanding and personal recognition, an urge to know "how I/we got here," as well as an appeal to others to look at "how far I/we have come."

As Siebert primed the pump of reminiscence among ordinary people, several motivations or themes seemed to emerge from his correspondents, especially the needs to express filial piety toward the exploits of parents and ancestors, to declare that slavery and race problems had been permanently eradicated in America (especially by the good works of abolitionists and Underground Railroad operatives), to express antislavery memory through racist and melodramatic tales of helpless black fugitives and their heroic white rescuers, and to imagine stories that evaded the social memory of conflict over race and sectionalism and

served the ends of national reconciliation. "My father's house was always a hiding place for the fugitive from slavery," wrote an Illinoisan in 1896. "Many were the . . . hardships these abolitionists endured and narrow escapes in carrying fugitives from one place to another." Siebert got what he wanted, namely, repeated stories about good and true souls helping their fellow humans. Much truth is embedded in these scores of tributes, but tall tales abound as well, particularly in yearnings to bask in the glory of the old abolitionist generation. A seventy-three-year-old man wrote from Nebraska, rejoicing in the "memories of a holy life left by our godly parents" and thanking Siebert for the chance to declare his "fascination about the 'UGRR' biz. that fires me up."[8] We must keep asking why this story so inspires the American historical imagination. Why does it intrigue us now even more than in Siebert's era?

In the 1890s Siebert tapped into a vast reservoir of Northerners eager to claim their places, or that of their parents, in a legacy, not so much as soldiers in the Civil War but as veterans of the "old liberty life line," as one Connecticut man called his father. For many women and civilian men, sharing lore about the Underground Railroad may have given them an alternative veteranhood in an age of Blue-Gray reunions of old soldiers and the widespread building of Civil War monuments. It may have allowed them to say they too had served in a great cause. Old stationmasters or their descendants recited their victories over slave catchers and remembered virtually no defeats. One Ohioan sent a copy of a term paper he had written for a history class in college in which he claimed "there were men and women there who would have burned at the stake rather than refuse aid to fugitives." Living martyrs abounded in the story of the Underground Railroad as Siebert collected it. An article from 1897 sent to Siebert from Marysville, Ohio, described a "fearless and uncompromising abolitionist" who "was not a soldier" in the late war but had two sons who "fought clear through it." The elder man, argued the author, deserved "a recompense as so many of our brave boys in blue are so deservedly receiving today."[9]

Siebert struck deep chords of nostalgia. He also elicited many stories that seem to reflect common racial attitudes of the era. Some correspondents enjoyed telling their own versions of what people in the late nineteenth century called "darky stories"— tales of helpless black vagabonds, rescued in comic, Keystone Kops-style from hapless slave hunters. Others wrote as though mimicking the routines of blackface minstrel shows. One writer sent his version of

comic relief in a tale of a neighbor who, "disguised with burnt cork as a fugitive," tries to gain admittance to a house hiding four real fugitives. As he washes his hands and face, all could enjoy a laugh, or so the story went. Another writer from Hillsboro, Ohio, delivered a tale of "conductors and brakemen" who "managed to get some amusement" in the midst of their "serious business" by reversing roles. They would "play the Kentuckian" on a "new found abolitionist," accusing their neighbor of "stealing niggers" and "abolition lies" until just the right moment to reveal the trick.[10]

To his credit, Siebert did not exploit the racist elements of the many such stories he received. The minstrel show character "Jim Crow," however, ragged, grotesque, even barbaric, seems to have dominated the Underground Railroad memories of many white Northerners. In the perceived natural innocence of nameless fugitive slaves and in fables of white heroism, tempered with occasional comic relief, some white Americans endeavored to establish their place in the story of black freedom. They seemed to desire a kind of nostalgia that one scholar of blackface minstrelsy called a "pleasurable escape into naturalness."[11] By converting the realities of the Underground Railroad into romantic adventure stories—about themselves— people could turn reminiscence into a welcome alternative to the complicated and conflicted race relations plaguing the United States at the turn of the twentieth century. One wonders how much our own culture has needed just such a romantic fix at the turn of the twenty-first century.

In light of such sentimentalism, it is remarkable how many of Siebert's correspondents declared that their efforts and those of abolitionists in general had *perma-*

nently destroyed slavery and its related problems. In some Underground Railroad reminiscences, it was as if the victory had long been won and emancipation had banished the question of race. After providing a tale of a black woman who had "passed in my care," who swam the Mississippi River avoiding "alligators" because "they thought she was one" of them, and who exuded "African heathenism," Willis Boughton, a professor at Ohio University, concluded his letter with, "I thank God it's all over now." In her letter of 1896, Mrs. Levi Monse Gould of Illinois remembered for Siebert how "our hearts have ached" so many times over "the terrible revolting things connected with American slavery." She concluded with a flourish and a sense of finality: "But thank God we have lived to see the curse removed from our fair land. . . . Thank God too for the Emancipation Proclamation of our devoted Abraham Lincoln, which struck the shackles of slav-ery from four million human beings, and now they no more need an Underground R. R. to liberty—*they are free.*"[12] The disturbing present can always be avoided by finding the right place to reside in the past, or simply by declaring that past dead. Only rarely in Siebert's research was the Underground Railroad depicted as a struggle over race that endured into a new time. Masked in this comforting haze was the real history of Underground Railroad heroism and tragedy.

In his landmark study published in 1961, *The Liberty Line: The Legend of the Underground Railroad*, Larry Gara tried to bring historical clarity out of the haze of mythology. With excellent research, Gara treated the story as both "melodrama" and "reality," and he fully acknowledged that "folklore" trumped "history" in the popular imagination. Working extensively with Siebert's collections, Gara

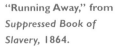
"Running Away," from *Suppressed Book of Slavery,* 1864.

demonstrated how the Underground Railroad had been "accepted on faith as part of America's heritage." He did not scorn the "legend"; it was the result of "repetition and exaggeration rather than pure fabrication"— and perhaps it has ever been thus. The legend of a vast network of aid to fugitives emerged well before emancipation as both sides, abolitionists and antiabolitionists, found great propaganda value in "fostering a popular belief in the conspiracy of organized slave abductors." In reality, Gara showed, running away was a frightening and dangerous proposition for slaves, and the overall numbers who risked it, or for that matter succeeded in reaching freedom, were "not large."[13] Gara further argued, and subsequent scholarship has agreed, that much of what we call the Underground Railroad was actually operated clandestinely by African Americans themselves through urban vigilance committees and rescue squads that were often led by free blacks. Perhaps above all, Gara redirected historical attention to the fugitive slave as an individual who required a stunning degree of courage and self-reliance in order to seek or achieve freedom.

Moreover, from Gara, and especially from a newer work, *Runaway Slaves: Rebels on the Plantation* by John Hope Franklin and Loren Schweninger, we now know that far more slaves ran away within the South than ever made it to liberty in the North or Canada. By examining planters' records, runaway advertisements, and county court petitions for the period 1790 to 1860, Franklin and Schweninger have shown that most planters (defined as those who owned twenty or more slaves) experienced the escape of a number of their bondspeople at some point. Among the 385,000 slave owners in 1860, of whom about 46,000 were planters, Franklin and Schweninger suggest the

"extremely conservative" estimate of more than 50,000 runaways *within* the Southern states annually during the late antebellum period.[14] Undoubtedly, even a single runaway from a plantation or farm could cause considerable social havoc in the tense relations between masters and slaves. Even if the overall numbers of slaves who successfully escaped to Northern freedom were only a tiny fraction of the whole, the fugitive slave represented a tremendous contradiction to the slaveholders' fiction of loyal and contented black people serving in the benign and protective institution of slavery.

While slavery itself changed markedly from one generation to the next in the American South, one thing remained essentially a constant: the profile of the average runaway slave. Among two thousand slaves advertised in some twenty Southern newspapers in two time periods—1790 to 1816 and 1838 to 1860—Franklin and Schweninger compiled a database in which approximately 80 percent of these fugitives were young males in their teens and twenties who generally absconded alone. Indeed, in the later period, 95 percent fled alone. Young slave women were much less likely to run away because of their family and child-rearing responsibilities. Entire families with children did attempt flight to freedom, but such instances were rare.[15]

Contrary to so many of the stories Siebert received from white respondents, real fugitive slaves had actual names and identities—they had real stories. In runaway advertisements, slave owners often included descriptions of physical appear-

Columns of advertisements about runaway slaves commonly appeared in Southern newspapers.

ance, scars, gender, age, laboring and language skills, color, and even country of origin. In 1816 a North Carolina farmer ran a notice in a Raleigh newspaper offering a reward of $25 for his "NEGRO MAN, named FRANK, pretty stout, one straight scar on his cheek passing from the under part of the ear towards the corner of the mouth, of a common dark color, something of a flat nose, a short, round chin, and a down look, about 26 or 27 years of age." Frank had been wearing "brown yarn homespun pantaloons, striped homespun waistcoat, and a white yarn roundabout" when he fled. In 1838 an Alabama planter advertised for his "negro man named JIM or ARMSTEAD, aged about 22 years, about five feet ten inches high, very likely, and when spoken to has a pleasing appearance." This Alabama slave was wearing fine clothes, "a fur cap, brown cloth frock coat, boots, &c." Remarkably, he also made off on a "large bay horse." His owner pleaded for help to "apprehend him and commit him to jail." A runaway slave with boots on and riding a horse, symbols of status and freedom of movement, was a dangerous threat to the meaning of slavery. And in 1857 a South Carolina planter announced a reward of $25 for his absent "Negro Man Toney," who was "about 5 feet 6 inches in height; stoutly built, is very black, has a broad, full face, black eyes, and when he laughs, shows a very white set of teeth."[16] Slave owners were keen observers of their property, especially when it exercised such human impulses as fleeing from bondage. Armstead's "pleasing appearance," Toney's white teeth, and Frank's scar were all vivid testimonies to how well slave owners did and did not know the people they enslaved.

One of the most active operators of the Underground Railroad was William Still, a free black in Philadelphia. His "committee" helped hundreds of fugitives to freedom, and he recorded most of their names and narratives in his remarkable book, *The Underground Railroad* (1872). In interviews and letters, Still provided real story after real story of fugitives who stowed away on steamers out of Virginia or Maryland ports, and of slaves who traversed hundreds of miles on foot. He also described all manner of lonely, usually young, blacks who left behind spouses, children, and parents. Still's collection is replete with the elation and heartbreak so many former slaves experienced when they found new lives through this crucible of sacrifice and dislocation.

"Arrivals" came through Still's office or notified his network of contacts almost daily. On one day alone, June 1, 1855, Still noted in his record book the arrival of some sixteen fugitive slaves. Among them was Emory Roberts, who hailed from Talbot County, Maryland, and had been the slave of Edward Lloyd, one of Frederick Douglass's former owners. Roberts fled to "avoid a terrible flogging" and left behind his wife, parents, and brothers and sisters. An elderly man, Daniel Payne, "infirm and well-nigh used up," sought to die on "free land." Harriet Mayo also arrived that June day, a "tall . . . intelligent young woman" of twenty-two years, who left behind her "poor old mother" and "three brothers who kindly aided her to escape." John Judah was a mulatto who was "fond of nice clothing" and had saved money from being hired out by his mistress. Due to her unfair dealings with his money, Judah had fled to the North and looked forward to being reunited with his free wife, who would join him in Canada. Still indicated that Judah seemed to succeed in gratifying "this love" of fancy clothes. And finally, among those arrivals in June 1855 was an entire family. Daniel Bennett, his wife, Martha, and their two children somehow liberated themselves from a cruel master in Loudon County, Virginia, who had flogged Martha mercilessly. She appeared before Still's committee, "a woman poorly clad with a babe just one month old in her arms, and a little boy at her side, who could scarcely toddle . . . a most painfully touching picture."[17]

Still provided description after description of humanity on the move, of a mass of individuals seeking to re-create their lives, and of a slave system that bred a steady flow of resistance by flight. As though fully aware of the potential mythology that might surround the story of the Underground Railroad, Still assured his readers that he had exercised the "most scrupulous care" with his mass of documentation in order to "furnish artless stories, simple facts,—to resort to no coloring to make the book seem romantic." His work is anything but artless, for he sought to inspire the reading public during the Reconstruction years and beyond with an epic story of agony and transcendence, of survival, and of affirmation of the human spirit that the "prison house of bondage" could not destroy.[18] Still assembled a treasure trove of history that we can fold into our ever-replenished memory of the Underground Railroad.

What does the story of the Underground Railroad promote or displace today? How does it affect our dilemmas with race relations, our yearning for a vibrant civic life, our lack of political engagement, or our need to be entertained? Are we another generation or two of latter-day Siebert correspondents, choosing the past that serves our present? Or are we more informed about our racial past and eager to know its consequences? As we confront the presence of slavery in our past, are we seeking to view it through the most positive and progressive lens possible? The answer is probably a complex mixture of all these motives, manipulated by a marketplace that exploits the lucrative power of "heritage."

As historians, curators, teachers, and concerned citizens, we must hold our ground in this proliferation of Underground Railroad enthusiasm and in the sometimes friendly, sometimes contentious, battle between learning and lore, between knowledge and wish-fulfillment. We will hold our ground by keeping a long view. Beyond the phenomenon of the Internet and interactive Web sites, little is truly new in this mixture of public history and memory. As early as 1885, the editor of the *Weekly News* of Oberlin, Ohio, invited readers to submit material on the storied background of that town, calling it "the grand central station on the line" of the Underground Railroad. Without a doubt, Oberlin, a town with a strong and active free black community and an abolitionist tradition well before the Civil War, was an important sanctuary for fugitive slaves. In addition, the Oberlin-Wellington rescue of the fugitive John Price in 1858 reflects the town's commitment to protecting ex-slaves from bounty hunters. Yet even today, as Oberlin College historian Carol Lasser has demonstrated, the town of Oberlin struggles with a "blurred line" between myth and history, between what residents can "know" of this story and what they "like to remember."[19]

In black heritage tourism today, pil-

grimages are being made to Harriet
Tubman sites and local Freedom Trails are
being researched and founded in nearly
every Northern state. These efforts are
actually part of a long tradition of discovery and legend. In 1902 the *Baltimore Afro-
American Ledger* reported that Dr. E. M.
Matson in Brookville, Pennsylvania, had
"discovered a closed passageway leading
from the cellar to a good sized underground room some distance from the
house" while "making improvements in his
home." Since Judge Heath, who was known
to have been prosecuted for aiding fugitive
slaves before the Civil War, had originally
owned the house, the renovator's discovery, "it is supposed," wrote the *Ledger*, "was
used as a hiding place for escaped slaves."
This shows perfectly the ambiguous but
fascinating relationship that has endured
for more than a century among physical
spaces, circumstantial evidence, and lore.

The nature of evidence is so often the
rub in determining whether a site can be
authenticated as part of the real Underground Railroad. In an extensive study conducted for the Connecticut Historical
Commission in 2000, historian Peter Hinks
employed eight varying criteria—from lore
to written records, autobiographies to oral
history, and rumors to newspaper articles—to investigate the credibility of
alleged Underground Railroad sites in that
state. When all or a majority of his criteria
were reasonably met, Hinks declared the
site merited "accreditation" on Connecticut's Freedom Trail. In only seven
of some twenty-seven towns examined did
Hinks find sites that met his criteria of
authentification.[20] Hinks is a practicing,
university-trained historian, and his
approach to evidence is no doubt not the
same as the more than twenty custodians
of local lore he interviewed. The nature

and reliability of evidence will perhaps forever remain a point of contention in all such cases of public history intermixed with memory.

Learning and lore have to be companions in order for us to understand the hold of the Underground Railroad on Americans' historical imagination. When possible, learning should gracefully lead in this enterprise, not suffering fools, but listening intently to the lore. Lore can also direct willing scholars into worlds that nurture an abiding, exciting sense of the past. Sometimes scholars and the keepers of local lore are one and the same, drawing from similar wells of imagination and the same toolboxes of methodology. Only by continuing to find common ground in the pursuit of this great American story will we attain trustworthy histories and comprehend the power of memory. Determining exactly what constitutes reliable evidence about Underground Railroad sites and stories is an important endeavor. Even more important is understanding why American society, with its long history of racial conflict, needs this story, and whether feel-good narratives of escape and cooperation alone meet the need, or serious confrontations with the realities and legacies of slavery are still required in a land founded on the ideas of consent, liberty, and equality.

JANE WILLIAMSON

TELLING IT LIKE IT WAS AT ROKEBY

The Evolution of an Underground Railroad Historic Site in Vermont

Few themes in our history fascinate Americans like the Underground Railroad—especially now. A surge of interest in recent years has resulted in the identification and documentation of new historic sites, cooperative research projects, major exhibitions, interactive Web sites, and the opening of the National Underground Railroad Freedom Center in Cincinnati, Ohio. Few themes in American history rely so heavily on stories and myths, mixing them with history in a sometimes confusing stew. Historian David Blight has referred to this mix as the "vexing relation-ship" between history and memory, and it can be difficult indeed to disen-tangle the two—but that is what I propose to do here: separate the strands of history and memory in one very specific case.

Rokeby Museum, a ninety-acre historic site located in Ferrisburgh, Vermont, was designated a National Historic Landmark in 1997 based on its considerable Underground Railroad history. From 1793 to 1961 it was home to four generations of Robinsons, a remarkable family of Quaker farmers, abolitionists, artists, and authors. During the 1830s and 1840s Rokeby was a prosperous sheep farm and an "unshackled space" that provided refuge to many who had escaped from bondage.

Rowland Thomas Robinson was born at Rokeby in 1796 shortly after his parents had emigrated to Vermont from Newport, Rhode Island. He and his wife, Rachel Gilpin Robinson, were devout Quakers, religious perfectionists, and radical abolitionists. Rowland and Rachel believed that slavery was a sin, and every acceptable means should be used to oppose it. Not only were they active in local and national antislavery societies, but they also boycotted slave-made goods, operated an interracial school at their farm, and offered

Quaker abolitionists Rowland Thomas Robinson and Rachel Gilpin Robinson sheltered fugitive slaves on their farm in Vermont.

work and shelter to enslaved African Americans who sought freedom in the North. They were part of overlapping networks of abolitionists and Quakers who demanded an immediate end to the despised institution. Luckily for us, the Robinsons were also pack rats who saved everything. Literally thousands of letters and other documents span the generations and relate how the Robinsons put their abolitionist beliefs into action, and how their efforts were remembered by their children and grandchildren. This trove of documents provides a marvelous twenty-first-century window into the broader nineteenth-century story of the Underground Railroad.

A significant place to start is with a document created decades after the Underground Railroad had ceased to operate. In 1896 historian Wilbur H. Siebert sent a questionnaire to the descendants of

Rowland Thomas and Rachel Gilpin Robinson. Siebert, then a young professor of history at Ohio State University, used this modern and rather novel approach to gather data for what became his magnum opus on the Underground Railroad, published in 1898.[1] Since the Robinsons had been dead for more than twenty years, Siebert sent this request for information to their son, George Gilpin Robinson, but he had died two years earlier, in 1894. Thus, the task of responding fell to Rowland and Rachel's youngest child, Rowland Evans Robinson, who was then sixty-three years old.[2]

A naturalist, artist, and author, Rowland Evans Robinson was temperamentally the opposite of his parents, and he had little interest in their causes. Nevertheless, he respected their dedication to principled action and took this opportunity to record their work seriously.[3] His lengthy reply was clear, thoughtful, and concise. Although he had been a child during the 1830s and 1840s, his detailed recollections rang true. He recalled "seeing four fugitives at a time in my father's house and quite often one or two harboring there."[4] His memory of the four was still vivid because one "carried the first pistols I ever saw and the other the first bowie knife." Robinson's effort to remember and record his experience as clearly as possible is almost palpable. He said nothing of concealing fugitives at Rokeby, but he did mention that they sometimes stayed for months, working on the farm.

Siebert returned to this subject forty years later for his research on the Underground Railroad in Vermont, and he contacted the Robinsons again in 1935.[5] Now yet another generation removed, the abolitionists' *grandson* and namesake, Rowland Thomas Robinson, answered Siebert's request. His response, though brief, included an important piece of information in its last line: "You can get the book *Out of Bondage* in your local library."

Published in 1905, *Out of Bondage* is a collection of some dozen stories by Rowland Evans Robinson, a successful and popular author who has been compared to his more famous contemporaries Sarah Orne Jewett, Mary Wilkins Freeman, and Joel Chandler Harris.[6] Like them, Robinson employed a variety of dialects in folktales that romanticized and yet expressed his admiration for the early residents of the Green Mountain State.[7] He clearly understood the market for literary fiction at the time, and during the last few years of his life, he turned his pen (or actually, pencil) to writing stories of the Underground Railroad.

Siebert obviously located a copy of *Out of Bondage*, for these stories are related in some detail in his book on Vermont. He presented them as fact, however, explaining that Robinson "had actually heard most of the anecdotes he wrote and published, but he made use of fictitious names for his characters."[8] Although Robinson included some real people and events in *Out of Bondage* (for example, the near mobbing of Samuel J. May in Montpelier) and incorporated his own

Wilbur Siebert used this questionnaire to gather data on the Underground Railroad in the mid-1890s.

Rowland Evans Robinson wrote *Out of Bondage* and other stories about the Underground Railroad in Vermont.

experience, these stories are clearly works of fiction and not of history. As such, they should not have confused a serious reader, let alone a professional historian.

Rowland Evans Robinson died in 1900, shortly after his Underground Railroad stories were first published.[9] As his generation passed on, these stories were what remained to inform future generations of Vermonters. Today, the Underground Railroad is one of the most familiar and popular themes in American history, with its tales of how enslaved African Americans, under cover of darkness, fled in search of freedom in Canada, guided by the North Star and aided by sympathetic white Northerners. These much-loved stories regale readers with daring and altruism, as well as hidden doors, loose floorboards, and attic hideaways. Visitors to Rokeby, like those to many other sites across the northeastern and midwestern United States, come seeking precisely that—and until the mid-1980s

they found it. They were conducted into a small upstairs chamber in the oldest part of the house. It had been dubbed the "slave room" in the early years of the twentieth century, since runaway slaves were thought to have been hidden there. How this room came to represent the Underground Railroad at Rokeby can be traced in both written records and oral traditions, but it originated with Rowland Evans Robinson's stories.

Although written at the same time as his response to Siebert, two stories—"Out of Bondage" (the title story) and "The Mole's Path"—paint a strikingly rosy picture of fugitive slaves. The aging author may have readily recalled the fugitives of his youth, particularly those who arrived at Rokeby bearing pistols and bowie knives, but these brave men made no appearance in his fiction. Instead, he described John. Seriously ill, incapacitated, and easily terrified ("I was dat skeered I's jus' shook to pieces"), John's main contribution to the plot is to cough at the most unfortunate moments. Milly of "The Mole's Path" is even more of a cipher, and like John, she does little more than expose her hiding place by peeking out the window. John coughs and Milly peeks. How two such ineffectual characters could have escaped the slave South and journeyed to northern Vermont is a mystery Robinson chooses not to address. Admittedly, these two stories are superficially like others of the genre, yet Robinson was not interested in the plight of the fugitive slaves, nor the righteousness of the cause, nor the altruism of Vermont abolitionists. As ever, he focused on common Vermonters, whose range of attitudes he recorded in "Out of Bondage." The abolitionist Barclay family represents one end of the spectrum, while

Jehiel James, who complains of "nigger-stealin' Aberlitionists a-interferin' wi' other folks' prop'ty," anchors the other. Most of his characters share the perspective of the stage driver, who confides, "Ownin' other folks kin' o' goes agin my Yankee grain."[10]

"Out of Bondage" is a much longer, more detailed, and serious story than "The Mole's Path," but they share the same rough outline. A fugitive from slavery hiding in a Quaker household is about to be discovered. Insurmountable circumstances force Friends to depend on someone outside their usual circle for aid—someone not "in sympathy with the cause" and therefore not entirely trustworthy. Although from opposite ends of the social and economic spectrum, Robert Ransom ("Out of Bondage") and Joe Bagley ("The Mole's Path") each fulfills his mission and experiences a transformation of character in the process.

The Quaker home of the Barclay family in "Out of Bondage" bears an undeniable resemblance to the house at Rokeby. Robinson obviously took specific features,

such as the poles suspended from iron hooks in the kitchen ceiling, as well as more generic ones—the open hearth—from his own home. A master of authentic and telling detail, Robinson enlivened his fiction by borrowing from life.[11] It is one of the chief reasons his work was so popular with Vermonters: it was instantly recognizable and real to them.

His description of two chambers, one housing John the runaway slave and the other serving as the sleeping quarters of Jerome, the traitorous hired man, is also based on the house at Rokeby. John's hiding place is vaguely described as "back of the great warm chimney," while Jerome's room is specifically called the kitchen chamber. In the Robinson home, these adjoining rooms (the kitchen and east chamber) are separated by a wall containing the massive central chimney and are connected by a plank door. Their close proximity is not made altogether clear in "Out of Bondage"—and for good reason. It would have made little sense in the context of the story to place John, who was ill and

In "Shooting Scene," the violence and horror fugitives faced in their flight differ greatly from the pleasing stories Robinson told in *Out of Bondage*.

Rowland Evans Robinson's pencil sketch of the kitchen chamber at Rokeby, showing the doorway to the alleged "slave room."

unable to control his cough, so near the "snaky-eyed Canuck" no one dared trust with a secret.[12]

The east chamber is mentioned again in a biographical sketch of Rowland Evans Robinson written by his daughter, Mary Robinson Perkins, in 1921 and published in the centennial edition of *Out of Bondage* fifteen years later. "The Robinson home was a 'station,' and there is a room in it—the 'east chamber'—which was often called the 'slave room.' It is not a hidden room, but the doorway is inconspicuous and at the far end of another bedroom."[13] This description is fairly accurate, except for its characterization of the doorway as "inconspicuous." A pencil sketch of the kitchen chamber (misidentified as the "slave room") was printed in the centennial edition and clearly shows that the doorway would be impossible to miss.

The story of the Rokeby slave room had blossomed by the 1930s. The last Rowland Robinson described it in a letter to Wilbur H. Siebert in 1935. "In a chamber of this house, there was in one corner, a built out clothes press, which to persons not knowing the secret looked innocent enough, but to we uns the back opened into a room beyond, where the slave was kept and where a slave was hiding once when the house was searched by the slave's master and the County sheriff. After they had gone the slave told Grandfather, 'I suah thought I was kotched.'"[14] (Where does a fourth-generation Vermont farmer come up with "we uns," "suah," and "kotched"? Straight from the pages of *Out of Bondage* is the answer.)

Visitors to Rokeby were told this story after the house became a museum in the early 1960s. Although embellished, this version at least recognized that the doorway to the east chamber had to be obscured. Even so, the story retains an aura of absurdity. The notion that blocking a door with a clothes press could make a room go unnoticed—despite the fact that it occupies fully one-third of the second-floor area and contains two windows and a dormer—represents the triumph of wishful thinking over reason.[15]

This interpretation of the Underground Railroad at Rokeby changed dramatically when staff and volunteers began to plumb the museum's collection of correspondence in the late 1980s. More than fifteen thousand letters spanning the decades from 1760 to 1960 document the site and the Rowland family as well as form the basis of current interpretation. Letters to and from Rowland Thomas and Rachel Gilpin Robinson from the 1830s and 1840s describe abolition, nonresistance, the evils of slavery, and the necessity of taking action. Several document fugitives from slavery in some detail, among them Simon, Jesse, John and Martha Williams, Jeremiah Snowden, and unnamed others. These letters dictated a revised interpretation of the site and a fresh understanding of how the Underground Railroad actually operated in Vermont.[16]

Letters from abolitionists Oliver Johnson and Charles Marriott provide a different but remarkably consistent story. First, these letters verify that Vermont was truly an unshackled space—a safe haven for those who had escaped from bondage. In 1837 Johnson wrote from western Pennsylvania, where he was traveling as an agent of the American Anti-Slavery Society. He explained that the area near Maryland "had at all times no small number of runaway slaves, but they are generally caught unless they proceed further north." Johnson wrote on behalf of one of those runaways, Simon, who had "intended going to Canada in the spring, but says he would prefer to stay in the US if he could be safe. I have no doubt he will be perfectly safe with you."[17]

Charles Marriott thought it best to send John and Martha Williams north from his home in Hudson, New York, after the US Supreme Court struck down state personal liberty laws in 1842. He explained that "the recent decision of the Supreme Court as to the unconstitutionality of jury trial laws for them has decided us to send them further north either to you or to Canada. If they can be taken in by thee, we should think them safer."[18] Even though the decision in *Prigg v. Pennsylvania* would have rendered personal liberty laws in Vermont just as null as those in New York, Marriott seemed to believe John and Martha Williams would not be pursued into Vermont.[19] Note that Johnson and Marriott both made explicit comparisons between Vermont and Canada and found in favor of Vermont.

The main house at Rokeby, a ninety-acre site and National Historic Landmark

Among the most fascinating letters in the Rokeby collection are those exchanged in the spring of 1837 between Rowland Thomas Robinson and Ephram Elliott, a slave owner in Perquimans County, North Carolina. Robinson wrote on behalf of Jesse, a runaway slave, to negotiate the cost of a freedom paper that was "the most anxious wish of his heart." In doing so, of course, he revealed Jesse's precise whereabouts. Surely this indicates just how confident Robinson (and Jesse!) must have been that Elliott would not take action and try to retrieve his property. In his reply Elliott admitted that "Jesse's situation at this time

Oliver Johnson, a native Vermonter and an agent for the American Anti-Slavery Society, arranged for Simon, a fugitive slave, to travel to Rokeby in 1837.

places it in his power to give me what he thinks proper" for the freedom paper, but he named his price of $300, "which is not more than one-third what I could have had for him before he absconded if I had been disposed to sell him." Robinson presented a counter offer. "Since leaving thy service he has by his industry and economy laid up $150 & he is willing to give the whole of this sum for his freedom . . . if Jesse was in possession of a larger sum he would freely offer it all for his freedom." Robinson urged Elliott to accept Jesse's offer, noting that "considering his present circumstances & location, it must be ackgd liberal." Elliott conceded that "at this time [Jesse] is entirely out of my reach," but he held firm on his price. He apparently considered the prospect of reclaiming a fugitive slave in Vermont then out of the question.[20]

Just what were conditions in antebellum upper New England? Vermonters were (and are) proud to claim a string of antislavery firsts. Theirs was the first state to outlaw slavery in its constitution of 1777, the first to form a state branch of the American Anti-Slavery Society in 1834, and its senator, William Slade, was the first to call for immediate emancipation from the US Senate floor. The Vermont legislature counteracted the fugitive slave laws of both 1793 and 1850 with personal liberty laws that were designed to protect African Americans from kidnapping and to guarantee due process to fugitives from slavery. Thousands of Vermonters joined the abolitionist ranks in the 1830s, forming dozens of town and county societies.[21] It is easy to see how Vermont came to be known as "the most abolitionist state in the Union," but it is more difficult to judge how much any of these factors contributed to the safety of fugitive slaves.

Probably the most important factor in making Vermont a safe haven for runaways was simply its geography. The sheer physical distance from the slave South to Vermont was just too great to make capture economically feasible. Historians John Hope Franklin and Loren Schweninger have shown that the cost to the slave catcher could exceed the value of the fugitive if the search extended too far or took too long.[22] In addition, the proximity of the Canadian border made the proposition of retrieving a fugitive slave highly uncertain, if not already too expensive.

In fact, research on the Underground Railroad in Vermont has so far revealed only one documented case of successful recapture. The case of Colonel S. T. Bailey of Georgia was reported in the *Green Mountain Freeman* in August 1844. Colonel Bailey was visiting relatives in Hartford, Vermont, accompanied by a female slave. He left her behind when he traveled to Canada and found her missing on his return. Aided by Samuel Nutt, a Windsor County justice of the peace, Bailey had no trouble locating her at a house "a few miles distant." Together, the two men "proceeded to bind their fellow being hand and foot, in open day, in the presence of several females, threw her into a wagon, and the slaveholder drove off with his victim." Bailey was arrested and tried for kidnapping, but he was acquitted for lack of evidence that the woman had been taken by force.[23] Vermont's personal liberty laws and abolitionist reputation notwithstanding, local officials did not protect *this* fugitive from slavery. Whether Colonel Bailey would have tracked her as far as Vermont had she run away from Georgia is another question.

The second clear and consistent message derived from the Robinson letters is that fugitive slaves needed work, and they were sent to Rokeby for that reason. (The Robinsons had grown prosperous raising Merino sheep, and they relied heavily on hired help.) In this light, the Johnson and Marriott letters read like employment references. Simon, according to Oliver Johnson, "appeared to me to be an honest, likely man. . . . I was so well pleased with his appearance . . . that I could not help thinking he would be a good man for you to hire. Mr. Griffith says that he is very trustworthy, of a kind disposition, and knows how to do almost all kinds of farm work. He is used to teaming, and is very good to manage horses. He says that he could beat any man in the neighborhood where he lived at mowing, cradling, or pitching." Charles Marriott assured Robinson that John Williams was "a good chopper and farmer" and his wife, Martha, was "useful and well conducted in the

A slave catcher or owner pursuing a fugitive at gunpoint, from *Antislavery Record*, January 1836

house." He also expressed his concern that in Canada "they [fugitive slaves] are too numerous to obtain profitable employment."[24] Jesse, of course, proposed to pay for his freedom paper with $150 he had saved while working on the farm, a sum that would have taken at least a year to accumulate.

Writing from New York State in 1844, Quaker Joseph Beale addressed the issues of work and safety. Concerned that the

Robinsons welcomed African Americans into their home, hired them to work on their farm, and provided a measure of safety and security in a hostile world. In delving beyond the melodrama to the real human story, we provide visitors to Rokeby Museum with a much more complex and meaningful understanding of the actual people involved in these easily sensationalized events. There are no secret rooms, no slave catchers, no subterfuges here—just individu-

A depiction of "paid" and "unpaid" labor, from *Anti-Slavery Almanac*, 1839. This kind of comparison must have been a frequent reality at Rokeby.

fugitive slave Jeremiah Snowden had been discovered, he concluded it would be "safer for him to be in Massachusetts or Vermont *if* [emphasis added] work is to be had for him." Beale continued: "We were unwilling to risk his remaining, although we had abundance of work for him at this busy season."[25]

Discovering these letters was a museum director's dream, much like finding an original copy of the Declaration of Independence behind an old painting or a Gutenberg Bible in the attic. Their information has transformed our interpretation of the Underground Railroad. Instead of stowing fugitives for a night on their way to Canada, the

als from vastly different circumstances who met, incredibly enough, across boundaries of geography, race, law, class, and social convention. This is an interracial story of resistance and of refuge, of enslaved African Americans who resisted their own subjugation by risking everything in a run for freedom, and of privileged white Vermonters who also resisted the powerful institution of chattel slavery by offering refuge to those in flight from it. It is a story of justice and of hope, and one that hopefully will continue to inspire visitors today.

The Robinsons deserve the last word. Rachel Gilpin Robinson penned this postscript to an absent family member in 1844.

This passage hints at the personal concern and interaction that is at the heart of this story.

> Oh, before I forget it, thee must be told that we have had *two* of the fugitive slaves who fled from bondage in a whale-boat, and were pursued by an *American* vessel of war! Noble work! They have gone on to Canada, for they were afraid to remain anywhere within our glorious republic lest the chain of servitude should again bind soul and limb. They tarried with [us] only one night & were very anxious to journey on to Victoria's domain. Poor men! They left wives behind, and deeply did they appear to feel the separation: they felt it so keenly that one of them said he would not have come away, had he not supposed he could easily effect the escape of his wife also when he was once away. Both seemed very serious, as though grief sat heavy on their hearts.[26]

Laden with this combination of courage and grief, the actual Underground Railroad operated through Vermont and elsewhere. The drama in such real stories is more potent than the pleasing legends we sometimes invent about America's struggle against slavery.

Farm buildings at Rokeby in Ferrisburgh, Vermont.

MILTON C. SERNETT

READING FREEDOM'S MEMORY BOOK

Recovering the Story of the Underground Railroad in New York State

New York State claims Harriet Tubman, the most widely known conductor of the Underground Railroad, as one of its historic treasures. The Tubman property in Auburn (located in Cayuga County) is touted as a heritage tourism gem, and a movement is under way to have Tubman's death date, March 10, declared a state holiday. Yet a few decades ago, when issues about rewriting America's "memory book" to include the African American experience dominated public discourse, the Harriet Tubman Home for the Aged was dark and silent. In 1971 vandals broke in, smashed a glass showcase, tore down posters of "Black Moses," and spattered glue about the room.[1] Lacking a resident manager for more than two years, Tubman's home "slumbered," to use Bishop William J. Walls's apt description.[2]

Bishop Walls had reason for concern. In the 1940s he had spearheaded a movement to save the white frame structure on the twenty-five-acre parcel then owned by the African Methodist Episcopal Zion (AMEZ) Church. He challenged his denomination, which hails itself as "the Freedom Church," to rebuild the house that Tubman used as a home for the elderly and indigent. Located at 180 South Street, the Harriet Tubman Home for the Aged was at the time widely believed to have been Tubman's personal residence. Time and neglect had reduced it to a mere shell.[3] The campaign succeeded, and the restored building was dedicated on April 30, 1953. By the early 1970s, however, the Harriet Tubman Home again was in danger of slipping into history's dustbin, a victim of benign neglect and inadequate financial resources. Then in 1975, the Tubman Home was declared a National Historic Landmark, and slowly, but with ever-increasing determination, supporters of the effort to foster greater recognition of Tubman's legacy worked to enhance the memory of "Black Moses" in Auburn. Fifteen years later, in 1990, the AMEZ Church finally obtained control of the brick house where Tubman actually lived until a few years before her death in 1913. First Lady Hillary Rodham Clinton visited the combined Tubman properties on her "Save America's Treasures" tour in 1998.[4] The brick house at 182 South Street was designated a National Historic Landmark in 2001, and as of late spring 2002 state and federal officials had pledged more than a million dollars for the restoration of Tubman-related properties in Auburn. Their goal is to inspire visitors to reflect on the life and legacy of this legendary conductor of the Underground Railroad.[5]

The revival of interest in Tubman and her Auburn connections mirrors the general renaissance of enthusiasm in the Underground Railroad, most noticeably since 1990 when Congress authorized the National Park Service to conduct a resource study with the goal of establishing a National Freedom Trail. Author and researcher Charles L. Blockson may rightly be called the father of this revival, for with conviction and passion

he argued on behalf of national legislation to commemorate the Underground Railroad.[6] Blockson—whose paternal great-grandfather, James Blockson, had sought freedom and had been aided by the famous stationmaster William Still—also helped inspire New York's Freedom Trail Act of 1997. In addition, Blockson galvanized Auburn's Harriet Tubman Boosters Club to reconvene after many years of inactivity.[7]

Though the rebirth of interest in the Underground Railroad in New York State is not due to a single agent, Blockson's pioneering work demonstrates that preserving any historical legacy depends on committed individuals. Authors and researchers who took an early interest in the state's connections to the Underground Railroad also made significant contributions. Arch Merrill, a journalist and collector of regional lore based in Rochester, garnered stories in full measure for his book *The Underground: Freedom's Road and Other Upstate Tales*, published in 1963.[8] Merrill utilized accounts of Underground Railroad personalities, sites, and events passed by word-of-mouth as well as those mentioned in assorted documentary materials. Unfortunately, Merrill's slender but engagingly written

The Harriet Tubman Home in Auburn, New York, before restoration, 1990s.

RIGHT: The Harriet Tubman Home, 2002.

narrative lacks footnotes and references. He depended upon a journalist's instinct for which oral sources were crucial, although few claims can be verified today. Helene C. Phelan's book, *"And Why Not Every Man?": An Account of Slavery, the Underground Railroad, and the Road to Freedom in New York State's Southern Tier* (1987), also appeared prior to the current revival.[9]

Much earlier than either Merrill or Phelan, of course, was the pioneering work of Wilbur Siebert. When Siebert, a professor of history at Ohio State University, compiled *The Underground Railroad from Slavery to Freedom* (1898), he was still able to interview veterans of the abolition movement and others who were alive when fugitives were coming into New York State before the end of the Civil War. Siebert's chronicle has drawn criticism for slighting African American participants as helpers and for sometimes uncritically accepting the stories that had been told and sent to him. Nevertheless, Siebert's classic can still be mined for links to the New York story, a task made easier by the availability on microfilm of his research collections.[10]

The paucity of scholarly studies about the history of the Underground Railroad in New York State demands explanation. Why did the topic fail to attract significant interest among professional historians until the last decade of the twentieth century?[11] We can only speculate. Historian Larry Gara debunked the myths surrounding the Underground Railroad. His criticisms contributed to the notion that the topic was not one to which serious researchers and academics should devote their careers.[12] Gara primarily wrote during the early 1960s, before American history was written in a more inclusive way to recognize the struggles and contributions of African Ameri-

cans. One hallmark of the current revival is the emphasis on African Americans as active participants in liberating themselves and shaping their life stories. In hindsight, some people were drawn to reexamining the Underground Railroad as an extension of their interest in telling the story of the quest for freedom in America more inclusively and, therefore, more accurately. The moral imperative to interpret the Underground Railroad as a form of African American resistance to slavery drives many of the recent efforts to recover the stories of freedom seekers and their allies.

New scholarship aside, the "romance" of the Underground Railroad still attracts individuals to the topic. They are inspired by stories about ancestors running to freedom, braving the bounty hunters and bloodhounds, or by accounts of how a great-grandfather helped his parents shelter a poor, scared runaway in the family barn. Many white Americans take pride in being numbered, by right of heritage, among the righteous who helped fugitives. Black New Yorkers who claim kinship with a slave who followed the North Star to freedom also find honor in such acts of bravery. New Yorkers who have no family ties to the Underground Railroad express pleasure in discovering a freedom house or like structure still standing in their community.

"Fugitive Slaves," from Theodore Johnson, *Uncle Tom's Cabin* theater scrapbook.

Miguel Covarrubias, "Simon Legree" with slave-hunting dogs, illustration in *Uncle Tom's Cabin*, from Theodore Johnson, *Uncle Tom's Cabin* theater scrapbook.

Some of what motivates the contemporary revival falls under the label of community self-promotion. Officials now direct funds to research and preservation efforts, persuaded by the argument that identifying Underground Railroad sites will promote tourism. Local historian George M. Sands, who grew up in Harlem and was schooled in African American history long before it became a topic of popular interest in the 1990s, early recognized the tourism potential in commemorating the Underground Railroad in New York. An advocate of the notion that "great stuff is made locally," Sands utilizes the Internet in his "Forging the Freedom Trail Project," an attempt to develop a network of Freedom Trail coordinators throughout the state who have similar interests in heritage tourism.[13]

Public officials who seeded local efforts and expected large financial windfalls are probably not pleased with the immediate returns from the tourism trade. As Underground Railroad enthusiasts across New York have learned since passage of the Freedom Trail Act in 1997, the task of locating and marking relevant sites has been difficult. If those of us involved with the Freedom Trail Commission have learned one important lesson, it is that the recovery and retelling effort must be grounded in local communities. A flood of expertise, not to mention money, out of Albany did not materialize to the extent that many had anticipated when the statewide Freedom Trail Commission was first organized.

The effort to establish a Freedom Trail in the Empire State began when the New York Department of Education authorized a preliminary survey of personalities, sites, and events associated with the Underground Railroad. The study, conducted under the auspices of the Schomburg Center for Research in Black Culture and completed in 1999, was meant to guide the work of the state's commission.[14] It eventually became clear, however, that the Freedom Trail Commission was not going to be the central and commanding "station" of the Underground Railroad renaissance in the state.[15] In 2001, for example, one aspect of the original mandate given to the Freedom Trail Commission—marking and linking Underground Railroad sites—was turned over to the Heritage New York Program, a state agency that benefited from Governor George E. Pataki's announcement that one million dollars in matching grants would be awarded for capital projects to aid municipalities and nonprofit organizations in preserving structures associated with the Underground Railroad.[16]

The Underground Railroad revival in New York contained an inherent contradiction in that the desire for local autonomy clashed with a concurrent need for some kind of centralizing and incorporating organization. The Freedom Trail Commission was seriously short of funds by 2001, due probably to the necessary reallocation of state resources in the aftermath of the attacks on New York City's World Trade

Center on September 11. The state may also have lacked enough official commitment to match the agenda of the Freedom Trail Commission. This suggests that the pulse of the revival can best be felt not in details about political struggles in the state capital to fund and establish the trail, but rather in what individuals and groups have accomplished at local and regional levels.

One pioneer, Onondaga County, established a Freedom Trail commission on December 15, 1997. The commission did not go much beyond proclaiming its good intentions until 2001, when Samuel Gruber of the Preservation Association of Central New York publicly asked, "Where is our Freedom Trail?"[17] An intensive effort then began to conduct research in primary sources and to nominate sites worthy of historic recognition. Judith Wellman, a historian with extensive experience in public history, led the way. She had successfully directed a similar effort in Oswego County, making it the first county in the state to establish a Freedom Trail, and it was enhanced by a map for tourists and a well-designed and informative Web site. Other counties, especially Madison, subsequently organized their own Freedom Trail commissions.[18] In other parts of the state, individuals from adjoining counties formed cooperative alliances. The Southern Tier Underground Railroad Commission, based in Binghamton and representing eleven counties, successfully created an Underground Railroad exhibition that opened at the Roberson Museum in Binghamton in February 2002.[19]

On the individual level, enthusiasts of the Underground Railroad in New York have met on many occasions, formally and informally, to share information and to plan strategies for developing Freedom Trails and obtaining funding for historical markers, tourist brochures, and the preservation of at-risk properties. At these meetings, participants generally emphasized the importance of having all Americans appreciate the historical, as opposed to the mythical, Underground Railroad, yet they struggled to agree upon a common definition of the subject at hand, its scope, and a chronological framework. New enthusiasts tended to accept at face value every story they heard about the Underground Railroad, while old hands—veterans of the public and local history circuit and academics specializing in African American history or nineteenth-century American reform history—seemed pleased by the sudden ground swell of interest. They were, however, protective of their knowledge, wary lest the new converts claim the veterans' stories as their own discoveries or disseminate misinformation. Myth and history are very much in contention in New York's revival.

At their discussions familiar topics emerged, freighted with subtexts that in and of themselves are weighty matters. Some of the questions stemmed from social and historical contexts of more recent times, certainly since the 1960s. How did the term "Underground Railroad" originate? How was the Underground Railroad organized and what kind of timeline can

The African Methodist Episcopal Zion Church in Rochester, New York. For a brief time Frederick Douglass published his newspaper, *North Star*, in the church's basement. The church allegedly housed fugitive slaves, since Douglass himself actively participated in moving runaways through Rochester to the docks on Lake Erie and on to Canada.

AFRICAN CHURCH,
ROCHESTER, NY.

be ascribed to it? Should those who followed the North Star be called a "runaway slave," "freedom seeker," or "self-liberated"? How many of the enslaved escaped, went to Canada, stayed in New York, or returned at various times from safety north of the forty-ninth parallel? Should African resistance to bondage, even while aboard the slave ships, fall within the purview of the Freedom Trail? Should the story of the Underground Railroad be told primarily from the viewpoint of those seeking freedom, stressing their agency rather than that of white benefactors? What was the role of free blacks? Who has the right to call the topic "their story"? How valid are oral recollections, and how do we deal with the paucity of documentary evidence? Since many structures that served as hiding places or harbored runaways in New York State were of the vernacular nature and either have been taken down or altered substantially, how can they meet the requirements of state and national registries for historical or landmark status? And what about those persistent stories of tunnels and secret passages?

Some of these questions stem from moral passions reminiscent of those that motivated abolitionists and civil rights activists. The current campaign to memorialize nineteenth-century freedom seekers and those who helped them asks Americans to honor them by striving to fulfill the dream of an egalitarian society. More attention has been paid to recovering the stories of those who opposed slavery, black and white, than to telling the history of slave owners, their agents, and their political allies. When a researcher discovers that an existing home may have once been the residence of a slaveholder, the current owners

"Talking Over Old Times—'How We Won the Day,'" from *Harper's Weekly*, September 14, 1867. In the wake of the Civil War, reminiscence became a widespread pastime and the basis of a publishing industry in the North.

usually view the news with embarrassment.[20] This revival stresses the positive as it endeavors to fill in the blanks on the honor roll of those who resisted slavery, directly or indirectly. In this respect, it follows paths of research and interpretation trod by earlier generations of Underground Railroad historians and enthusiasts, but the call to memorialize the positive appears to be louder in this revival than in earlier ones.

Recovering important events, places, and people associated with the Underground Railroad may lead to a more civil and just America—let us hope so—but historians will be better able to evaluate the social goods born of this revival a generation from now. While the renaissance is in full swing, we must exercise a measure of caution, lest present needs distort the representation and interpretation of the past. A bland and celebratory history that is palatable to all political constituencies will not pass close scrutiny in the years ahead.

Like those who advocated marked Freedom Trails at local and county levels in the 1990s, educators in New York took an interest in the Underground Railroad. Critics of what children were being taught about the state's history faulted the existing curriculum for failing to give adequate attention to minority communities and their stories. Various racial and ethnic groups competed for space in textbooks and for time in public school classrooms during debates about multiculturalism in the 1980s.[21] For example, New Yorkers of Irish descent wanted their history to be represented. In response, the Famine Curriculum was introduced to teach children about the potato crop failure in Ireland, attendant social problems, emigration, and changes in Irish culture as expressed, for instance, in "The Famine

Song," which students compared to the slave spiritual "Nobody Knows the Troubles I've Seen." The *New York State Freedom Trail Program Study* included examples from the Famine Curriculum to inform Underground Railroad advocates about how to design their curriculum materials. These educators and their political allies in Albany operated on the assumption that knowledge about New York's Freedom Trail would foster a more civic-minded and egalitarian society.[22]

Social history became popular when professional historians began to embrace the concept of writing America's story "from the bottom up." Students took courses in how to use oral sources, and advocates of black studies demanded revisions in high school and college curricula. This augured well for a revived Freedom Trail movement. The phenomenal interest in genealogy, or more broadly, family history, generated during the last quarter century has also fostered fascination with the Underground Railroad. Alex Haley's best-selling book *Roots*, published in 1976, and the subsequent television miniseries that aired a year later, inspired many Americans to investigate their ancestral stories. Haley spent twelve years and traveled an estimated half-million miles in search of his ancestors.[23] Today, genealogical researchers can take advantage of technology Haley did not

Malvina ("Viney") Russell seated on the back stoop of the Smith-Miller mansion in Peterboro, New York. She was a child when Gerrit Smith purchased her family's freedom in 1841 from a Mississippi slaveholder. Malvina lived in Peterboro the rest of her life and did domestic work for the Smiths and other families.

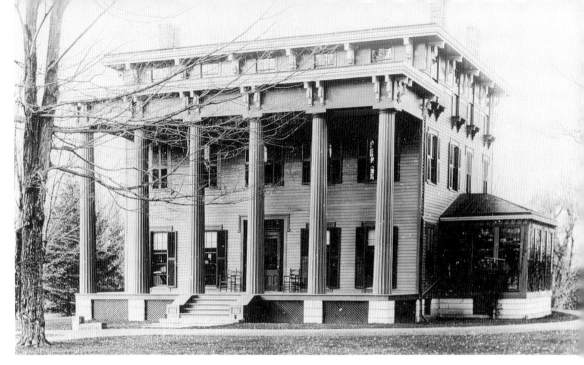

The Gerrit Smith mansion in Peterboro, New York, was built from 1804 to 1806 and later was extensively remodeled. The Smith mansion harbored numerous fugitive slaves and was host to many abolitionists. The structure burned in 1936.

have. Underground Railroad enthusiasts in New York hope to develop an online, centralized database, operated under the auspices of the Freedom Trail Commission, but that aim has not yet been realized.[24]

Researching the Underground Railroad can be personally rewarding. Investigators report a "find" with as much enthusiasm as a family genealogist might do when discovering a long-forgotten ancestor. Newcomers to the topic soon realize, however, that conducting research can be difficult and time-consuming. Once the easier subjects have been handled, the harvest of good results must be gleaned from patient and diligent examination of primary sources, such as old legal records, handwritten manuscripts, and census materials. Soon the law of diminishing returns sets in, and early enthusiasm wanes. Politicians, community boosters, and those in the tourism business tend to grow impatient waiting for stories about a "depot" in their jurisdiction. The burden then falls to the individual researcher who, in the company of informed peers, must mine the sources, often at personal expense.

In New York, as elsewhere across the nation, Underground Railroad enthusiasts have created a virtual community via the Internet. Historian Christopher Densmore, whose interest in radical reform and the Society of Friends led him to primary sources about freedom seekers, used the Internet to post valuable information about the Underground Railroad on the Web while he was an archivist at the University at Buffalo. He continues this effort as curator of the Friends Historical Library at Swarthmore College, and he strongly advocates telling the Underground Railroad story as accurately as possible rather than succumbing to a new mythology born of a desire for "feel good history."[25] Hadley Cruczek-Aaron agreed. While a graduate student in Syracuse University's archaeology program in 2002, she was intensively involved in research at the Gerrit Smith property in Peterboro. She observed with some concern that the public accepts without critical reflection a "shiny and happy" version of Underground Railroad history in their communities, yet she hoped that interest in what is now a popular topic can be transformed into widespread support for well-documented historic preservation efforts and tourism attractions.[26]

Fortunately, the story of the Underground Railroad in New York State does exist, regardless of who manages the storytelling or how difficult it is to retrieve reliable evidence. Geography and history have conspired so that New York can make significant contributions to any national recovery of the legacy of the Underground Railroad. Strategically located with the Canadian provinces to the north, the Empire State was well positioned to harbor runaways or to serve as a threshold they crossed on the way to freedom. Strong centers of abolitionist sentiment emerged in the 1830s, particularly in the "Burned-Over District" of Upstate New York. Safe havens for runaways developed in many localities. The abolitionist and wealthy landowner Gerrit Smith helped transform the village of Peterboro in Madison County into one of the most racially integrated communities in the North. Henry Highland Garnet, an African American clergyman and political abolitionist, remarked in 1848, "There are yet two places where slaveholders cannot come—Heaven and Peterboro."[27]

New York's contribution to Underground Railroad lore has been especially strong because Garnet and other African Americans took leadership roles in advancing the cause of freedom. Some of them have become icons, such as Auburn's Harriet Tubman and Rochester's Frederick Douglass, as well as William Wells Brown in Buffalo. Thanks to the ground swell of interest in the Underground Railroad, names of more African Americans who rendered assistance to escapees from slavery have been added to the honor roll.

Examples include John W. Jones of Elmira, Austin Steward of Rochester, Stephen Myers of Albany, the Reverend Thomas James of Rochester, the Reverend Jermain W. Loguen of Syracuse, and David Ruggles of New York City. Researchers driven to examine primary sources have also discovered the names of long-forgotten African Americans, among them, Tudor Grant of Oswego and Catherine Harris of Jamestown. White helpers, hitherto obscure, have also surfaced as a result of the diligence of modern researchers. Tom Calarco, a self-declared Railroad buff, recovered the story of Abel Brown, a Baptist minister with a congregation at Sand Lake. Brown published the *Tocsin of Liberty*, a newspaper in which he listed the first names of freedom seekers he had assisted along with the identities of their former slave masters.[28]

Daniel Huntington, *Gerrit Smith*, 1874. Smith, an immediatist abolitionist by 1836, gave liberally of his wealth to the antislavery and other reform movements.

The Cazenovia
Anti-Fugitive Slave
Act Convention,
August 22, 1850.
Among the abolition-
ists in attendance
were Frederick
Douglass (seated to
right of table), Gerrit
Smith (standing with
outstretched left arm
behind Douglass), and
the Edmondson sis-
ters: Mary, age seven-
teen (to right of
Smith), and Emily, age
fifteen (to Smith's
immediate left). The
Edmondson sisters
were escaped slaves
from the Washington,
DC, area.

LEFT: Portrait of
Austin Steward. Born
a slave in New York
State in 1793,
Steward sued for his
freedom with the help
of the New York
Manumission Society
in 1815. He settled in
Rochester and
became one of the
city's first black busi-
ness owners, operat-
ing a grocery and dry
goods store.

While investigating the involvement of blacks in aiding others along the road to freedom, researchers have become more aware of the alliances that were forged between black and white abolitionists. Among them are Amy and Isaac Post of Rochester, members of the Society of Friends who helped Frederick Douglass; Susan B. Anthony, who cooperated with Harriet Tubman in aiding fugitives; and of course, Gerrit Smith, who seems to have received solicitations for aid from most of the African American activists of the antebellum period. Smith and Douglass issued a joint call for an interracial public protest of the 1850 Fugitive Slave Law. Their appeal resulted in the Great Fugitive Slave Convention, held in Cazenovia, New York, on August 21 and 22, 1850. Abolitionists, black and white, along with close to fifty fugitives, openly defied and condemned what some then called the "bloodhound bill." Those at the convention drafted a public letter "to the American Slaves," calling upon them to stage an insurrection, if necessary, in order to obtain their freedom. Such interracial ties, born of efforts to thwart slave catchers, contributed to the successful effort on October 1, 1851, to free the runaway William McHenry, better known as Jerry, after his arrest in Syracuse.[29]

The principal focus of the current revival's research agenda has been to find as many people, places, and events associated with the Underground Railroad as possible. Communities have engaged in rituals of celebration when history's memory book can be amended to include another name, place, or event exemplifying the crusade against American slavery. During the last few years, several sites in New York have undergone a rigorous review process

5000 Men & Women
WANTED,
To attend the Meetings in

Canastota, *Wednesday, Oct. 23d,* 10 a.m.
Cazenovia, *Friday, Oct. 25th.* "
Hamilton, *Wednesday, Oct. 30th,* "
Peterboro, *Friday, Nov. 1st,* "

None but *real* Men and Women are wanted. The sham Men and Women, who can stick to the Whig and Democratic parties, are not wanted. These parties made the accursed law, under which oppressors and kidnappers are now chasing down the poor among us, to make slaves of them. Hence, there is no hope of good from persons, who can stick to these Devil-prompted parties.

We want such men and women to attend these Meetings, as would rather suffer imprisonment and death than tolerate the execution of this man-stealing law. We want such, as would be glad to see William L. Chaplin, now lying in a Maryland prison on account of his merciful feelings to the enslaved, made Governor of the State of New-York. We want, in a word, such noble men and women, as used to gather under the banners of the good old Liberty Party.

Let us, then, get together again to speak the truth, and to sing the truth. Those were good times, when we came together to hear warm-hearted speeches for the slave, and to hear Otis Simmons' daughters, and Rhoda Klinck, and Miss Cook, &c. &c., sing

"*Come join the Abolitionists.*"
"*What mean ye, that ye bruise and bind?*"
"*The Yankee Girl.*"
"*There's a good time coming, boys.*"

October 10, 1850.

and achieved National Historic Landmark status. For example, the Gerrit Smith estate in Peterboro earned landmark recognition in 2001, which likely would not have happened without the national resurgence of interest in the Underground Railroad. The revival has stimulated many new research endeavors and resulted in a plethora of stories in the public media, but a comprehensive account of the Underground Railroad in New York has yet to be written.

Whoever takes on this challenge will benefit from the good work done by individuals who have participated in the current revival largely out of personal interest. Commitment, beyond ordinary curiosity, characterizes the refueled Freedom Trail movement. For example, researcher Rebecca Schwarz-Kopf developed a passion for history while growing up on Long Island. To nurture her keen interest in the past, her parents provided her with books, including Charles L. Blockson's *The Underground Railroad: First Person Narratives of*

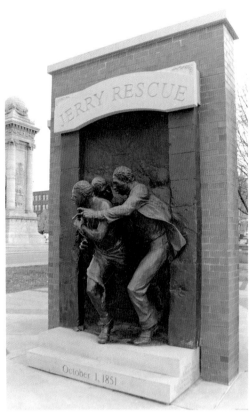

The Jerry Rescue memorial in Syracuse, New York, was dedicated on August 10, 1990. Chester Whiteside, a retired African American fireman, led the campaign to erect the monument to William "Jerry" McHenry, Jermain Loguen, and Samuel J. May.

RIGHT: The Bristol Hill Congregational Church in Volney, New York.

Escapes to Freedom in the North, which she read at age twelve. Schwarz-Kopf's personal odyssey began in the summer of 2000, when she and her husband, Chris, came across a historical marker at Northern Orchards farm in Peru, New York. Intrigued by the inscription—"A barn on this property was one of the stations on the Underground Railroad, where runaway slaves were concealed and protected on their way to freedom in Canada"—Schwarz-Kopf eventually learned that the farm had once belonged to Samuel Keese Smith, a Quaker and a known Underground Railroad operative. She wrote about her investigations throughout the North Country of New York State in a four-part series printed in the *Lake Champlain Weekly*, a newspaper based in Plattsburgh. Overwhelmed by requests for reprints, offers of more stories, and queries for additional information, Schwarz-Kopf published the results of her Underground Railroad investigations in booklet form.[30] She is one of hundreds of New Yorkers who have climbed on board the refueled freedom train out of a deeply felt passion for local history.

While the general public has enthusiastically embraced the Underground Railroad renaissance, scholars at New York universi-

ties have followed rather than led the revival. Professor Judith Wellman is a notable exception. In the years she served as coordinator of the Oswego County Freedom Trail Commission, she encouraged volunteers to work cooperatively and to donate hundreds of hours of research time, always with the goal of finding credible evidence and developing publicly accessible information about the Underground Railroad in Oswego County. Results included a driving tour brochure, public workshops, notebooks of primary sources for distribution to local libraries, a research guide, a curriculum unit, a well-designed Web site, and fifteen nominations to the National Park Service's National Network to Freedom. In addition, Wellman and others developed a multiple-property nomination for "Historic Sites Relating to the Freedom Trail, Abolitionism, and African American Life in Central New York, 1820–1870."[31]

Among the many strengths of Professor Wellman's commitment to the refueled freedom train has been her ability to piece together human interest stories from sundry details scattered in obscure records and oral recollections. One such story involved the Bristol Hill Congregational Church, a small, Federal-style struc-

ture in Volney, New York. While researching Hiram Gilbert, an Oswego County abolitionist mentioned in oral traditions,
Wellman received a call from George Wise,
the historian for the town of Volney. Wise
suggested that Gilbert might have been a
deacon of the Bristol Hill Church. He and
Wellman, along with the church's pastor,
the Reverend Jim Hinman, examined the
church's records dating back to 1817. To
their surprise and delight, the records contained the names of many African American members that Wellman recognized
from her previous research. The Bristol Hill
Congregational Church, now on the National Register of Historic Places, had been
both biracial and abolitionist. To celebrate
this discovery, the Reverend Hinman's congregation held a special service with representatives of Syracuse's Bright Chapel African Methodist Episcopal Church, an event
that expressed the spirit of biracial cooperation many hope to achieve from the current revival.[32]

Paul and Mary Stewart, a husband-and-
wife team, have become particularly knowl-
edgeable about Underground Railroad activities in the Albany area. Mary, a fifth-grade
teacher, became involved after her students
expressed interest in the Underground
Railroad when they read about Harriet
Tubman. Paul, who had already been writing articles on local African American history, soon joined in, and much of the couple's
free time has been devoted to researching
the Underground Railroad. They have
developed a Web site, organized conferences and workshops, made public presentations, and given tours. Paul, an African
American, has said about himself, "The
details of the history story, and its relationship to my past, and the use of it in our
family as an activity have all combined to

make it a lasting and stimulating
personal adventure." Mary, who
notes with some puzzlement that
those who attend the couple's
public presentations predominantly have been whites, such as
herself, is inspired by the stories
she and Paul have uncovered,
especially tales about individuals.
"I do believe that for some folks,
me included, UGRR history
stands with dignity against the
wars and warriors and states-
men's retelling of history."[33] The
challenge for the Stewarts, as it is
for everyone who develops a
strong personal interest in this
topic, is to move from a celebration of the recovered past to a
more critical perspective of historical
events.

Underground Railroad enthusiasts in
Elmira (Chemung County) have enjoyed a
noteworthy supportive relationship with
community leaders and the general public
in their efforts to memorialize John W.
Jones, a runaway slave. Jones escaped in
1844 at the age of twenty-seven from Ellzey
Plantation in Leesburg, Virginia, and made
his way north to Elmira, where he served as
the sexton of the predominantly white First
Baptist Church for forty-three years. He
assisted hundreds of fugitives, many of
whom found refuge in his house next door
to the church. The house was demolished in
1890. Barbara and William Ramsdell, longtime members of the First Baptist church,
helped galvanize community interest in preserving a small frame structure located on a
sixteen-acre farm where Jones lived after
the Civil War, with the intent of restoring it
as the John W. Jones Museum.[34]

Lucy Brown, a retired nurse and a

A former fugitive
slave who escaped
from a plantation in
Leesburg, Virginia, in
1844, John Jones was a
major figure in fugi-
tive slave escapes
through Elmira, New
York.

descendant of a fugitive who escaped from Maryland in 1861, served as president of the John W. Jones Museum. She, along with the Ramsdells, committed themselves to preserving the Jones house after Southside High School's Diversity Group provided a proper marker for Jones's grave in 1997. Jones lies buried in Elmira's Woodlawn Cemetery, not far from Mark Twain's final resting place. Brown has said that her interest in Jones and the Underground Railroad "runs deep in my blood lines. We lived and breathed it, and survived." She claims direct descent from Mary Ann Cord, the former slave who worked as a cook at Quarry Farm, which was owned by Twain's father-in-law, Jervis Langdon, an abolitionist in his own right. Twain credited Cord with sensitizing him to the plight of the slave, and her storytelling inspired him to write about racial prejudice.[35]

While public understanding of the history of New York State and the Underground Railroad has been broadened and deepened, troublesome undercurrents also persist. Close attention to the language in recent newspaper accounts and other reports about Underground Railroad stations reveals an alarming use of phrases such as "reputed to be," "alleged," "thought to be," "it is said that," and "[unidentified] sources say." Additionally, historical accuracy is compromised when writers, often in popular media formats, cite as evidence "soft" sources where little or no documentation can be independently reviewed and assessed. In some efforts to preserve at-risk properties, exaggerated or unproven claims have been generated during campaigns to win public support and funding. An agreed-upon rating system should be established so suspected sites can be ranked on the basis of documentation, the credibility of oral traditions, and archaeological evidence. Much work needs to be done to educate Underground Railroad enthusiasts, the public, and the custodians of state and national registries on the merits and proper use of oral sources as well as to foster more precise language and evaluation criteria. In spite of all the progress made in recent years to recover the legacy of New York's Underground Railroad, historian Carol Kammen's cautionary note is worth remembering. "About no other local topic, except possibly the weather, are there more legends, more hearsay or more dubious claims; about no other topic is there more to question."[36]

An informed and critical perspective, tantamount to historical agnosticism, is all the more important when interest in the Underground Railroad reaches a fever pitch. We must guard against embracing unsubstantiated claims. The preservationist dollar is not well spent, nor are heritage trails likely to stand the test of time, if verification is not the researcher's first priority. Historians demythologized the older romantic interpretation of the Underground Railroad. A new myth bolstered by unsubstantiated claims should not take its place. Overzealous enthusiasts who promote unproven

Lucy Brown standing in front of the John Jones Museum in Elmira, New York.

Underground Railroad stories may not intend to deceive the public, as did the perpetrators of what came to be called the Great American Hoax in the years after the Civil War, but the will to believe is strong.[37] We must guard against accepting as fact many stories about the Underground Railroad that are currently in circulation, no matter the well-meaning intentions of their promoters, until sound historical research has proven their truth.

Stories of alleged Underground Railroad "finds" in New York State have circulated widely. While researchers close to these sites were careful not to say more than the evidence warranted, the public may have been led to believe otherwise. The discovery in the late 1980s of seven sculpted "faces" on the clay walls of a tunnel-like basement beneath the Wesleyan Methodist Church in Syracuse received widespread press coverage. Some accounts were written as if researchers had found convincing proof that fugitives had made the clay "faces," although the principal investigators reported only circumstantial evidence, such as they were probably of nineteenth-centu-

ry origin. Several of the best-preserved "faces" were removed, stabilized, and eventually made centerpieces of an exhibition on the Underground Railroad, despite the lack of knowledge as to who created them and when, or even who the sculpted reliefs were meant to represent. Journalists outside Syracuse referred to the "faces" as if they were indeed artifacts of the Underground Railroad, an indication that the "faces" story had taken on a life of its own.[38] It is noteworthy that efforts in Syracuse to preserve the "faces" and interpret them as symbols of the Underground Railroad developed in response to their possible removal and placement in the then-proposed National Underground Railroad Freedom Center in Cincinnati.

Another instance where enthusiasm ran ahead of evidence occurred in Buffalo. In 1997 New York State's Freedom Trail Act was signed in a public ceremony at the Michigan Street Baptist Church. Although documentary evidence confirms antislavery meetings were held in the church, convincing proof that the structure served as a hiding place for runaways has yet to be found.

"Clay faces," believed by some to have been made by fugitive slaves, were found in the Wesleyan Methodist Church in Syracuse, New York.

The Michigan Street Baptist Church in Buffalo, New York, was built in 1845 by an African American congregation.

In its absence, oral traditions, of indeterminate origin and constant evolution, assert that fugitives hid in a crawl space in the church's basement, slept in pews, and took refuge in a rear stairwell behind a false wall. Kevin Cottrell, a grants specialist with the New York State Office of Parks, Recreation, and Historic Preservation, has been a leading participant in a community effort to preserve the historic church. His interest in the Underground Railroad resulted in the formation of his own company, Motherland Connextions, which conducts tours of Underground Railroad stops located along the Niagara frontier from Buffalo to Niagara Falls and into Canada.[39]

Preservationists were interested in obtaining control of the church property at 511 Michigan Avenue (formerly Michigan Street), but they came into conflict with the small, black Pentecostal congregation, led by Bishop William Henderson, that held the title to the red brick building. In explaining his unwillingness to release the property to the preservationists, Bishop Henderson told the press, "I think the congregation felt things were slipping out of our hands. Even though it is a historical landmark, we want to maintain it as a place of worship."[40] By

mid-summer 2002, Buffalo's Planning Board had endorsed a proposal to transform the block in which the Michigan Street Baptist Church is located into a heritage tourism corridor, anchored by the historic church and the home of the Reverend J. Edward Nash, the church's pastor from 1892 to 1953. The Michigan Street Preservation Corporation, headed by Cottrell, presented the plan and emphasized linking the theme of the Underground Railroad (via the Michigan Street Baptist Church) to that of the civil rights movement (through restoration of the Nash home). When asked about the way promoters of the project continually referred to the church as a Underground Railroad stop, Cottrell responded that he was a preservationist and would leave the question of evidentiary proof to the historians.[41]

These two examples, among others, point to the need for additional conversations about methodology and sources among Underground Railroad researchers. Oral history techniques and standards have become quite sophisticated in the last quarter century, yet many Underground Railroad enthusiasts have not been trained in them. They often invoke oral history in a compensatory way because of the dearth of written records pertaining to the Underground Railroad, especially records compiled by African Americans. All Underground Railroad researchers need to become more familiar with the historical context of their topic of interest. One helpful resource is the *Journal of Afro-Americans in New York Life and History*, whose January 2001 issue focused on the Underground Railroad.

Enthusiasts in New York State have a full agenda. While selected areas of the state have been intensively researched "from the ground up," others await a systematic investigation. Local research must be compiled or linked so patterns and connections can emerge. Due to funding considerations, much of the research done to date has been organized along existing political boundaries, yet the freedom seekers who followed the North Star did not care about county lines or legal jurisdictions. Students of the Underground Railroad in the Empire State need to forge stronger alliances with those who are similarly interested in neighboring states, notably Pennsylvania and Vermont, as well as in Canada. Education is also a priority. If this renaissance is to have an enduring legacy, every possible means must be used to educate the public (school children in particular) about the significance of this important chapter in state history and the national struggle over slavery.

Underground Railroad enthusiasts, at least those who want to know the whole record, must also candidly relate stories that convey the power and persistence of racism. The kidnapping of free blacks and alleged runaways, the actions of antiabolitionist mobs, community involvement in government-sponsored efforts to recapture freedom seekers, and similar manifestations of the inhumanity of racism belong in any honest reexamination of the Empire State's past.

Sometimes the results of such research can be surprising in their ability to break down presuppositions. Not every black person claiming to be a fugitive was indeed a true freedom seeker. Primary sources speak of the problems blacks caused when they posed as runaways and laid claim to the money, food, and clothes that had been contributed to aid fugitives. Sometimes individuals who received support for their efforts to aid freedom seekers used the con-

tributions for their own ends. For example, James Watkins Steward, a young black man from Oswego who became an antislavery agent after escaping from slavery, fell in with the wrong crowd, so to speak, and turned to crime.[42]

While the dream of a New York State Freedom Trail has not yet materialized, the revival has fostered increased recognition of the multicultural humanitarianism New Yorkers displayed when they aided fugitives. We have witnessed a bountiful harvest in stories about the Underground Railroad as a result of the refueled freedom train. We have had many converts to the crusade to remember, research, and restore, but the wheat has yet to be winnowed from the chaff. When we have accomplished this, a trustworthy legacy can be given over to future generations. Each generation of Americans goes to the well of memory to quench a thirst for meaning and identity. Through its fascination with the Underground Railroad, this generation seeks a time when Americans, black and white, worked together for the cause of freedom. Moralistic appeals to set history right by celebrating the "true" heroes and heroines of the Underground Railroad resound throughout the current revival. We long for a redemptive history, but we can achieve true redemption only through a history that stands on a foundation of truth that will survive the tests of time.

The Frederick Douglass Memorial Monument in Rochester, New York, was dedicated in 1898, three years after the antislavery leader's death and burial there. The monument originally stood at Saint Paul Street and Central Avenue, but it was moved to Highland Park in 1941.

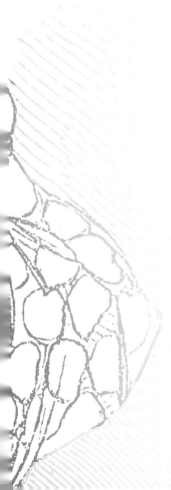

DIANE MILLER

THE PLACES AND COMMUNITIES OF THE UNDERGROUND RAILROAD

The National Park Service Network to Freedom

S ome history will never be forgotten. For thousands of people involved in the Underground Railroad, that activity was a life-changing event. It marked the start of new lives as free people for many. For others it symbolized their core values and declared their stand as people of conscience against an oppressive, though legal, system. Momentous as these events were for the people who lived them, they often were not recorded as historic episodes. While in some areas people openly supported the Underground Railroad, most participants maintained a certain level of secrecy. And, as the story of enslaved people and ordinary citizen-activists, the dealings of the Underground Railroad have not been given the level of attention commonly lavished on public figures.

Despite this, the story lives on in the families and communities of those who were involved. Often it is carefully passed from one generation to the next as an important piece of family or local heritage. In his seminal article on the Underground Railroad for *National Geographic* magazine in 1984, Charles Blockson observed, "Though forty years have passed, I remember as if it were yesterday the moment when the Underground Railroad in all its abiding mystery and hope and terror took possession of my imagination." The moment Blockson relates came while "listening to my grandfather tell stories about our family."[1] Others dedicated to preserving this history are convinced that understanding the institution of slavery and American resist-ance to it is critical to comprehending our national history. As Cathy Nelson, founder and president of the Friends of Freedom Society and state coordina-tor for the Ohio Underground Railroad Association, eloquently observed in her congressional testimony in 1997, "We are also joined this morning by

279

Oberlin Underground
Railroad quilt made
by senior citizens of
Neighborhood House,
1982.

National Park Service (NPS) involvement with the Underground Railroad actually began in response to Public Law 101-
628. Enacted in November 1990, it directed
the agency to study alternatives for commemorating and interpreting the Underground Railroad. As specified in the legislation, the NPS completed a Special Resource
Study in 1995 with the guidance of an advisory committee.[3] Several alternatives for
commemorating the Underground Railroad
were evaluated, including: establishing a
commemorative and interpretive center,
improving and expanding interpretive programs, aiding visitor interaction with a
concentration of Underground Railroad
resources over a broad geographic area,
developing a single commemorative monument, and creating a series of trails. The
advisory committee recommended that "all
the alternatives . . . be pursued with equal
vigor and simultaneously as appropriate."[4]

Three findings of the study were especially important in preparing for the
National Underground Railroad Network to
Freedom Act of 1998, which established the
framework for an ongoing NPS program.

• No single site or route completely
reflects and characterizes the Underground
Railroad. The story and related resources
involve networks and regions rather than
individual sites and trails.

• A tremendous amount of interest in
the subject exists, but it lacks organized
coordination and communication among
interested individuals and organizations.

• A variety of partnership approaches
would most appropriately protect and
interpret the Underground Railroad. These
partnerships could include federal, state,
and local governments, along with involvement from the private sector.

thousands of people whose faces you cannot see but voices we hear, those of our
ancestors. They are the voices of the past
whose determination, courage, and sacrifices have spoken to us so we could bring
their story to you."[2] Ultimately this ground
swell of community support led to the
enactment of the National Underground
Railroad Network to Freedom Act of 1998
as Public Law 105-203.

From its inception, the Network to Freedom Program was conceived as a unique effort to honor and commemorate the people of the Underground Railroad, past and present. A three-pronged program emerged from planning sessions. NPS first created educational materials, with the program's Web site serving as a primary vehicle for presenting information on the history of the Underground Railroad and slavery.[5] The second component was for NPS to provide technical assistance to local efforts related to the Underground Railroad. While some of this assistance is site specific in the areas of documentation, preservation, or interpretation, much of this technical support helps local advocates and researchers share information and coordinate commemorative efforts. As a story of migration, the Underground Railroad is best studied by examining connections among historic individuals, sites, and communities, rather than focusing on each story in isolation. Volunteers working at the grass roots level, such as the Friends of Freedom Society in Ohio, recognized the importance of this approach before the Network to Freedom legislation was passed, and they organized themselves on a statewide basis to collect and share information. NPS works to develop organizations in other states and to coordinate efforts among state groups. Members of the public can use the Network's Web site to post information about upcoming Underground Railroad events and to share pertinent history they have researched. This allows individual researchers to place the people and events in their communities within a broader context as well as follow geographically distant connections.

The heart of the legislated program, however, was the establishment of a net-work of sites, interpretive and educational programs, and research and educational facilities with a verifiable connection to the Underground Railroad. Consulting with community advocates and local researchers was an essential ingredient in formulating the program. If the Network to Freedom was to represent the significance of the Underground Railroad, its role as the manifestation of community memories had to be respected. Questions about what types of sites, programs, and facilities should be included and, more importantly, what constitutes a "verifiable" association had to be defined. NPS invited community representatives to participate in several meetings and focus on these issues. The prevailing sentiment expressed was that the Network to Freedom should be as inclusive as possible in the types of sites, programs, and facilities that could qualify, but it would maintain clear standards for documenting a verifiable association. Most of the participants, having

African-born "Princess Madia" was captured aboard an illegal slave ship off the coast of Florida. From *Harper's Weekly*, June 2, 1860.

"Act of Sale" for slave Sophia Godman at a price of $1,400 in Howard County, Missouri, dated March 3, 1857.

researched the history of the Underground Railroad for many years, were keenly aware of the perception that accurate information is not available and many claims for association are rooted in myth. Above all, community researchers were concerned with the importance of this history and the need for credible claims to association with the Underground Railroad.

With this in mind, however, oral traditions must be respected as a legitimate source of information. The NPS Network to Freedom Program acknowledges the centrality of oral traditions in learning about the Underground Railroad. Even so, the NPS requires additional documentation to substantiate details before oral traditions (or written evidence) may be used to validate site associations. As with all historical research, more than one source of information, written or oral, is generally required for corroboration. This issue is so critical that the Network to Freedom Program has developed a publication describing methodologies for documenting Underground Railroad associations and working with oral traditions. This publication also addresses the question of what evidence is sufficient to verify Underground Railroad connections.

As the story of the Underground Railroad continues to unfold, it is clear that the traditional image—white Quakers helping fugitives from safe house to safe house on the way to Canada—represents only a portion of the entire picture. Not all roads led to Canada. Those who sought freedom made their way to any secure place. They might settle in maroon communities in remote areas or in territories beyond established settlements. Some fugitive slaves went to Spanish Florida, California, Mexico, the Caribbean, or Central America. The Network to Freedom Program focuses on the act of self-liberation, rather than the act of assistance, when defining the Underground Railroad. Consequently, the program acknowledges events and persons dating from the colonial period through the passage of the Thirteenth Amendment in 1865. In addition to safe houses where shelter and sustenance were provided, NPS recognizes sites where escapes, rebellions, rescues, or kidnappings occurred, maroon communities, sites related to legal cases involving the various fugitive slave acts, churches associated with active congregations, destination sites, landscape features such as caves or swamps, properties linked to prominent participants, military sites (including contraband encampments), and cemeteries. This list remains fluid to incorporate and encourage new and original investigations, interpretations, and commemorative activities around the country.

While the Underground Railroad existed in the context of slavery, abolitionism, and antislavery thought, those associations alone are not sufficient reason to include a site, facility, or program in the Network to Freedom. Participating in the Underground Railroad was a direct violation of the federal Fugitive Slave Acts and hence illegal. Supporting its activities involved sheltering fugitives, raising money, sewing clothes for runaways, passing information, or "conducting" freedom seekers between safe houses. Through such actions, these individuals demonstrated an exceptional level of commitment to the principles of freedom and self-determination. It is this higher level of commitment that the Network to Freedom recognizes.

Congress envisioned an ongoing program when it passed the Network to Freedom Act. Still in its infancy after four rounds and 182 applications, the Network has accepted 117 sites, programs, and facilities representing 24 states and the District of Columbia (a 64 percent acceptance rate). The primary criteria for acceptance are a verifiable, documented association with the Underground Railroad and written consent from the owner or manager of the site, program, or facility. Each year NPS staff reviews applications in two rounds and votes on recommending inclusion at public meetings, where comments and input on candidates are invited. The variety of list-

ings at this early stage indicates that the future of the Network will become a tool for reevaluating knowledge and understanding the complexities of the Underground Railroad.

One of the more unusual sites listed in the Network to Freedom is Forks of the Road Enslavement Market Terminus in Natchez, Mississippi. It marked the terminus of major routes of the internal trade in enslaved Africans coming from the Upper South, Georgia and the Carolinas, Florida, and New Orleans. Ads about runaways in the *Natchez Weekly Courier* document escapes from Forks of the Road. This site allows the Network to Freedom to address the untold story of the Underground Railroad in the Deep South and its connection to slavery in the Upper South. When the Union army arrived in Natchez in May 1862, the town was converted into a contraband camp. Enough people among the local enslaved population emancipated themselves and then joined the Union army camped at this location that they eventually formed four regiments.

Freedom Monument in front of the Customs House, Saint Croix, Virgin Islands. The statue commemorates the 1848 slave rebellion and the Emancipation Declaration.

Local advocates view current efforts to preserve, commemorate, and interpret this site as part of achieving a balanced history in Natchez, Mississippi. Through partnerships among private organizations and local, state, and federal agencies, efforts are under way to recognize the significance of the site, raise funds, purchase it, and then develop its tourism potential. Advocates in the area use their listing in the Network to Freedom as a tool to accomplish these tasks.

> We are new and maintain publicly, the UGRR Network to Freedom Program is a great common denominator opportunity for all of us to overcome past historical inequities with regards to Africans in America . . . and [we] now work together to tell the whole history. Remember, we are in the deep south where fear, pain, racial discrimination and prevailing southern pride have kept the slavery story much hidden and laying [sic] dormant. . . .[6]

Farther north along the Mississippi River, the Mary Meachum Freedom Crossing marks the location above Saint Louis where a party of fugitive slaves and their free conductors launched a skiff to cross from Missouri to Illinois. Met by police officers and slave owners when they landed in Illinois, five fugitives were caught, others were shot at, and Mary Meachum was arrested for assisting the escape. Freeman, an African American "abolitionist agent" from Illinois, may have later died of his wounds, and Esther, a enslaved woman owned by Henry Shaw, a business magnate in Saint Louis, was sold "down river." Today, the Mary Meachum site is located adjacent to some of the lowest

income communities in Saint Louis, where over 90 percent of the citizens are African Americans, 36 percent of the households are headed by females, more than 42 percent of the people earn an income of less than ten thousand dollars per year, and over half of the adults have not graduated from high school.

The Grace Hill Settlement House, a social service organization in Saint Louis, is leading efforts to develop the site as "an anchor of pride for the community" that can contribute economically to residents involved in the local tourism industry. To foster a sense of community ownership and involvement, Grace Hill, supported in part by a Network to Freedom grant, has embarked on Neighborhood Pride, a project intended to educate neighboring communities about the Underground Railroad and the story of the Mary Meachum site as well as issues of development and the potential impact of tourism. Grace Hill AmeriCorps Trail Rangers, young neighborhood adults who serve their community, lead the presentations and gather input from community members. From these contacts, three residents are identified to serve on the site advisory group. The completed site development, targeted for 2005, is expected to include venues for community events, antebellum landscaping, art and historical signage related to the 1855 event, visitor amenities, and opportunities for local entrepreneurs.

Many of the sites listed in the Network to Freedom represent the more commonly recognized safe houses where freedom seekers were given shelter. Sites in Iowa, such as the Hitchcock House and Todd House, played an important role during the Bleeding Kansas period, when these antislavery strongholds were also active Underground Railroad safe houses. Throughout the Midwest and the Northeast, in Ohio, Illinois, Michigan, New York, and Massachusetts, homes that sheltered fugitives from slavery have been recognized in the Network to Freedom. Notable examples include the Gerrit Smith estate in New York, the Levi Coffin House State Historic Site in Indiana, and Wayside, Louisa May Alcott's childhood home in Massachusetts.

Homes associated with important Underground Railroad participants have also been included in the Network. The Frederick Douglass National Historic Site in Washington, DC, and the Harriet Tubman Home in New York State represent two well-known fugitive slaves who became conductors. The John Parker House, on the banks of the Ohio River in Ripley, Ohio, was the home of a formerly enslaved African American who purchased his freedom and went on to obtain several patents based

on his skill as an ironmaster. Parker frequently patrolled the river at night, ferrying hundreds of fugitives from Kentucky to freedom in Ohio, though he only briefly sheltered one person in his home.

While many of the places listed in the Network to Freedom are privately owned and not accessible to the public, several play prominent parts in the community's tourism. Heritage tourism can bring much needed economic development to surrounding areas as it helps the public learn about the untold stories of the Underground Railroad. Since educating the public is so critical to preserving this nearly lost history, the Network includes programs and facilities of an educational, research, or interpretive nature. Approximately 20 percent of the Network to Freedom listings are programs, and 12 percent are facilities.

The types of interpretive and educational programs listed range from driving

Landscaping designed by architecture students at Washington University in Saint Louis and installed with the assistance of Grace Hill AmeriCorps Trail Rangers provides visitors with a view of the Mary Meachum Freedom Crossing site.

Ripley, Ohio, as seen from the Kentucky side of the Ohio River. The Reverend John Rankin's house, a safe haven now designated as a National Historic Landmark, stands at the top of the hill.

The restored Parker House, Ripley, Ohio. Following reorganization of its significant Underground Railroad connections, local community advocates in the John P. Parker Historical Society were able to restore the building with grants.

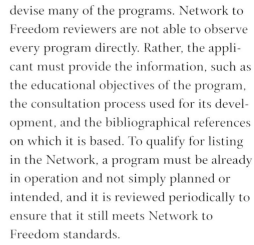

or walking tours, traveling trunks (for school programs), exhibitions, and house tours, to living history reenactments, lecture series, annual conferences or celebrations, and research programs. Communities and individuals develop the programs based on local needs and their own creative and interpretive visions. A number of programs have been initiated since the Network to Freedom was established, although many had been conducted for years prior to that time.

In developing the criteria for including programs in the Network, the need for accurate information and professional presentation was balanced with the reality that volunteers, who perhaps are not trained educators, interpreters, or historians,

devise many of the programs. Network to Freedom reviewers are not able to observe every program directly. Rather, the applicant must provide the information, such as the educational objectives of the program, the consultation process used for its development, and the bibliographical references on which it is based. To qualify for listing in the Network, a program must be already in operation and not simply planned or intended, and it is reviewed periodically to ensure that it still meets Network to Freedom standards.

The range of programs listed in the Network reflects the public's enthusiasm and interest in learning about the Underground Railroad. While the programs fall into a few broad categories, almost every one is unique in its implementation, employing different techniques, objectives, stories, and messages. Such variety indicates the profound ways that the meaning of the Underground Railroad has inspired these projects and in turn has touched people today.

In San Bernardino County, California, the Footsteps to Freedom Study Tour developed from the effort of the superintendent of schools' office to educate teachers on the history of slavery and the Underground Railroad. Collaborating with the Riverside County superintendent of

schools, the San Bernardino County super-intendent, and county curriculum specialists, Cheryl Brown, publisher of *Black Voice News*, designed the tour route and its content. The tour, which covers a possible route from Kentucky through Ohio to Canada, is intended to preserve, document, and teach participants—primarily educators—about the Underground Railroad as it focuses on the struggle for human freedom and cooperation among people of all types. Through this program participants have gained a strong belief in the importance of these events in American history as well as confidence in their ability to share these ideas in the classroom. As leaders in their schools and communities, they advocate curricula and programs that teach about freedom.

Another example is the Indiana Freedom Trails (IFT), which was created as a result of a "gathering" sponsored by the National Park Service and the Indiana State Historic Preservation Office (ISHPO). IFT follows the model established by the Friends of Freedom Society in Ohio and is dedicated to researching, interpreting, and commemorating Indiana's Underground Railroad heritage. Through its Educational and Research Program, which was listed in the Network to Freedom, volunteers work within their home regions to research local sites and to convey information to the public through presentations, conferences, meetings, and educational materials. As a direct result of a cooperative effort among IFT, NPS, and ISHPO, seven researchers were granted funds to complete further study of the Underground Railroad in Indiana. These grants resulted in more than six hundred hours of historical research and generated seven new public reports. Based on IFT

research, trails illustrate possible routes freedom seekers traveled from Kentucky to Michigan. Where trails are fragmented because of insufficient information for some counties, the IFT Educational and Research Program has received a Network to Freedom grant to investigate sources further.

At the initiative of the Convention and Visitors Bureau in Clermont County, Ohio, research was conducted on Underground Railroad connections just east of Cincinnati along the Ohio River. Prior to this project, Clermont County was thought to have few significant Underground Railroad associations. Through an innovative research approach, nineteen sites related to the Underground Railroad and an additional fourteen sites associated with abolitionism have been identified and developed into a tour with an accompanying publication. The nineteen Underground Railroad sites, as well as the tour itself, have been recognized through the Network to Freedom. Located close to Kentucky and to Cincin-nati's transportation hub, Clermont County has proven a fertile terrain for Under-ground Railroad discoveries.

California educators pause outside the Hamilton County Library in Cincinnati, Ohio, while on a Footsteps to Freedom study tour in 2000.

As with these programs, criteria for facilities focus on accuracy, professionalism, and operation. Volunteers who may not be formally trained operate many of the houses and sites. In response, technical assistance and the application process emphasize professional practices rather than formal qualifications. Accepted facilities must either center on the Underground Railroad, as expressed in their mission statement, or have significant materials related to the topic. Facilities listed in the Network to Freedom tend to be small community-based museums with permanent exhibitions, community libraries with local history rooms, or large state institutions.

Indicative of a small museum listed in the Network to Freedom is the River Road African American Museum and Gallery. Established in 1994 as a repository for African American history, art, and artifacts in Louisiana, it is dedicated to telling the history of the enslaved people who labored on area plantations. The diverse collection includes original documents, photographs, maps, shackles, farm tools, and associated buildings. A portion of the permanent exhibition addresses the Underground Railroad. Additionally, a database and a Web site make information from the archival collection more accessible.

Large institutions, such as historical societies, state libraries, or state archives, are also eligible for inclusion in the Network to Freedom, although they have a much broader mission than just the Underground Railroad. An excellent example is the Maryland State Archives in Annapolis, which holds records of permanent value for the state and local governments of Maryland. Original materials crucial for researching the Underground Railroad are found in its government records and its special collections of newspapers and private, corporate, and religious records. Underground Railroad associations also can be documented through its variety of records—property, estate, tax, church, court, manumission—and its nineteenth-century journals, photographs, and maps. The large number of potentially relevant records and the institutional commitment to Underground Railroad research qualified these archives for inclusion in the Network to Freedom.

Louise Minks, *Breaking the Chains*, 2002.

The Maryland State Archives is working on a collaborative project with the Commission to Coordinate the Study, Commemoration, and Impact of Slavery's History and Legacy in Maryland, along with Morgan State University, Goucher College, and Maryland Public Television, to study the Underground Railroad in a Southern border state. Aided with a Network to Freedom grant, those involved in this collaboration are researching court dockets, slave jail records, pardon records from the secretary of state, census data on the African American population, and local newspapers. Support from several partnerships has reinforced the institutional commitment of the Maryland State Archives to this work. Maryland's location and history make it an especially strong example for other states to conduct similar research, not only because of its pivotal geography on the border between slavery and freedom, but also because so many famous black abolitionists, including Frederick Douglass, Harriet Tubman, Henry Highland Garnet, and many others, escaped from bondage on its boundaries and shores.

The Underground Railroad offers a primary example of cooperation across racial, ethnic, socioeconomic, gender, and religious lines in the pursuit of individual freedom and self-determination. Relevant now more than ever, this connection to our shared heritage is vital to forging a shared goal of self-identity, community, and national unity. As communities work to document, preserve, and celebrate this history, they look to the Underground Railroad as a model of inclusiveness, perseverance, and the human will for freedom and survival. In these efforts, the important, hard work is being done at the local level.

Frederick Douglass ca. 1848. Douglass escaped from slavery on Maryland's Eastern Shore in 1837 and lived in Rochester, New York, from 1848 to 1872. He assisted many fugitive slaves to freedom through his own home.

Projects commonly involve partnerships among diverse organizations and individuals. The National Park Service's National Underground Railroad Network to Freedom Program supports activities that create an environment of collaboration. Through these efforts the Network to Freedom helps Americans better understand, with credible evidence, this anguished but rich and important part of our national history.

15

EDDIE S. GLAUDE JR.

A SACRED DRAMA

"Exodus" and the Underground Railroad in African American Life

On October 20, 1838, the front page of the *Colored American* contained a dialogue between Moses and Pharaoh. The exchange recounted the events of the Exodus story in ways that approximated the contemporary context of slavery and freedom in America. Pharaoh declares that freeing the Israelite slaves was impractical because "they cannot take care of themselves." His secretary warns of possible insurrection, and Pharaoh's advisor fears the possibility of the two groups mating. "Oh King, there would be an amalgamation of the Egyptians and Hebrews, utterly destructive of honor and happiness. We never can come upon such grounds of equality with them. The question is settled." Moses counters with the oft-quoted passage from Acts 17: "Hath God made of one blood all nations?" He also invokes such liberal notions as liberty and rights, emphasizing that the slaves are God's chosen people. The column ends simply with God ordering Moses, "Go tell Pharaoh to let my people go."[1]

With no explanation, the column presupposed a prior knowledge among its readers of the Exodus story and its application to the experiences of African Americans. They knew for whom Moses spoke and on whose behalf God acted. Moments such as this demonstrate how the Exodus story captured the political and existential imaginations of African Americans prior to the Civil War. The story's account of bondage, the trials in the wilderness, and the Israelites' final entrance into the Promised Land resonated with a people who experienced the terror of slavery and the hardships of racial discrimination.

291

In fact, the story has been central to most political efforts in African American history. The events of the Civil War and the mass migrations of the late 1870s have been described as reenactments of the Exodus story. Thomas B. Wester, a black Union soldier, wrote in December 1864 "that he and his comrades were overthrowing 'Pharaoh' as 'in the days of old.'"[2] Sojourner Truth described the magnitude of efforts to relocate African Americans to Kansas in terms of the biblical narrative: "I have prayed so long that my people would go to Kansas, and that God would make straight the way before them. Yes, indeed, I think it is a good move for them. I believe as much in that move as I do in the moving of the children of Egypt [*sic*] going out of Canaan [*sic*]—just as much."[3]

The legend of the Underground Railroad is also inextricably connected to the metaphors of the Exodus story. Harriet Tubman is described as her people's Moses, and the repeated journeys of slaves to freedom are depicted as escapes to the Promised Land. A quick survey of songs associated with the Underground Railroad reveals the importance of Exodus symbology. For example, Harriet Tubman sang as she plotted her escape from slavery:

> When dat ar ole chariot comes,
> I'm gwine to lebe you,
> I'm boun' for de promised land,
> Friend's, I'm gwine to lebe you.

From "Go Down Moses" to "Now Let Me Fly," travelers on the Underground Railroad deployed the images of the Promised Land, crossing the river Jordan, and of God's activity in history to nurture a faith that helped them to circumvent the brutality and potential hopelessness of life on the plantation. Such efforts were memorialized in historical accounts that took the analogy of the plight of the Jews as the interpretative template to present the courage of Underground Railroad operatives and the righteousness of their mission. Despite this, rarely has the use of Exodus been critically examined in light of the broader set of meanings that the story represents.

Exodus is central to the symbolic construction of the United States. Puritans in New England imagined their voyage from the Old World to the New as an exodus to a New Canaan and as "an errand into the wilderness." This religious aspect of their journey aided in their efforts to shed the burdens of European custom and habit and in its place to imagine a limitless future sanctioned in the promises of the Bible. Here in the "Promised Land," inherited titles meant little, and economic success was virtually guaranteed if one simply comported with the will of God. The Puritans' efforts elevated our country's beginnings to

"Have We Not All One Father?" from *Legion of Liberty***, 1847. The kneeling slave appealing to the natural rights tradition became a common symbol of abolitionism.**

HAVE WE NOT ALL ONE FATHER?

biblical drama and bequeathed to us a rich source of metaphors not only to explain our unfolding history but also on which to base a national identity. Americans are the New Israelites. This land is the "shining city on the hill"—both paradise and a world of travail. As Jeffrey Mason notes, "This is the myth of the New Eden, the fantasy of the middle class come to America: a prelapsarian, sentimental garden where the natural state of humanity is virtuous domesticity, where industry produces happiness, where sensible people conform to established belief, and where property is the emblem and evidence of moral and worldly success . . . as well as the raison d'etre of the new society."[4] In short, this is the stuff of American melodrama.

Of course, melodrama involves sentimental and romantic plots, as well as characters whose virtue or vice are readily apparent. At the heart of the genre is the triumph of virtue over villainy and the idealization of the moral views assumed to be held by the audience. Overdrawn characterizations and appeals to sentiment reaffirm a world of "virtue" that is often threatened by evil but never supplanted by it.

"John Bull's Monarchy a Refuge from Brother Jonathan's Slavery," from *Anti-Slavery Almanac*, 1839.

America's religious myth takes place within this "democratic drama," where virtuous Puritans (or Western pioneers or European immigrants) struggle mightily to live up to the dictates of God as they forge a life out of this inheritance. God's chosen people continuously face challenges that threaten their way of life. The inevitable resolution of these situations, however, only solidifies a form of life through the reproduction of an ideological consensus sanctioned in the Bible and given a distinctive melodramatic shape. In this story, race and other problems are confronted and eventually banished from the "New Eden," reaffirming for all to see the nation's inherent goodness.

"En Route to Kansas," from *Harper's Weekly*, August 16, 1879. Several thousand Southern blacks migrated in the Kansas Exodus of 1879, driven both by religious motivation to find a new Promised Land and by violence and famine in their former homes.

"Hail Columbia,
Happy Land!" from
Legion of Liberty, 1847.

This particular narrative of America obscures the inherent conflicts that shaped our nation's beginnings. The enslavement of Africans and American Indians by a people who were committed to freedom and "chosen" by God contradicted the fantasy of a New Eden and the belief that the United States was the New Canaan. The structure of melodrama (in this instance) is not indicative of a fundamental inner conflict, say, between a nation committed to democracy *and* undemocratic practices, but rather it reaffirms the wholeness of the nation in the face of obstacles, incidents, and situations. The problem arises not by way of some inherent conflict that cuts to the core of the nation and its principles. Instead, melodramatic resolutions are always ready at hand.[5]

Within this uplifting and confident narrative, the legend of the Underground Railroad functions as a place of redemption. Here, somewhat hidden from view, heroic white men and women conquer the evil of slavery and, in turn, absolve the nation of the sins of its racist past. The legend fits neatly within the myth of America as a nation of progress, able to solve its problems, because the actions of these righteous men and women helped ensure the coming of the new millennium in the bounty that was America, and yet the fundamental conflict of American democracy endures. The incompleteness of this fragile experiment in pluralistic liberty remains off stage. If we turn our attention to the nation's darker children, however, and particularly their use of the Exodus story, the tragedy of America comes into full view. Indeed, African American uses of the story, in my view, destabilize the melodramatic plot structure of the legend of the Underground Railroad by disclosing for all to see the basic inner conflict of race that still haunts the nation.

EXODUS WITH A DIFFERENCE

To invoke Exodus in an account of the Underground Railroad is to highlight the distinctive religious dimension of the slave's journey to freedom—that is, to give particular attention to the individual pilgrimage (internal and external) for self-determination bound up in a religious faith. This pilgrimage involved, to some degree, a rejection of the hypocrisy of white Christianity. Descriptions of this rejection are found in many of the letters and articles in William Still's *The Underground Railroad*. In an account of Peter Petty's journey from slavery to freedom, Still deftly demonstrates the hypocrisy of slaveholding Christians by recounting Petty's description of white Christian preaching.

> Peter's master was quite a devoted Methodist, and was attached to the same Church with Peter. While on the subject of religion, Peter was asked about the kind and character of preaching that he had been accustomed to hear; whereupon he gave the following graphic specimen: "Servants obey your masters; good servants make good masters; when your mistress speaks to you don't pout out your mouths; when you want to go to church ask your mistress and master," etc., etc.[6]

This account comes on the heels of Petty's description of his "pious" master and an invocation of the Exodus story as justification for traveling on the Underground Railroad. "Mr. B. was rowdyish in his habits, was deceitful and sly, and would sell his slaves any time. Hard bondage—something like the children of Israel, was his simple excuse for fleeing."[7]

In 1862 Charles Thompson echoed the sentiment that white Christians were hypocrites. When asked what he thought of slavery, Thompson replied, "I think it's a great curse, and I think the *Baptists* in *Richmond* will go to the deepest hell, if there is any, for they are so wicked they will work you all day and part of the night, and *wear cloaks and long faces*, and try to get all the work out of you by telling you about Jesus Christ. All the extra money you make they think you will give to hear talk about Jesus Christ."[8] One could assume that Thompson generally lacked faith. He is not certain that hell exists, and his remarks about Jesus Christ seemingly cut a bit deeper than simply a rejection of the theology of white Baptists in Virginia. Members of the vigilance committee must have sensed this as well, for they asked Thompson if he believed that he had ever heard the true Gospel. Thompson responded, "One part of it, and one part burnt me as bad as ever insult did."[9]

This ability to distinguish between "good" and "bad" preaching of the Gospel points to the interpretative dimension of African American appropriations of Christianity. They did not simply accept the teachings of the master's Christianity; they formed and shaped it to speak to their particular circumstances. As a result, the form of Christianity that emerged often constituted a stinging rebuke of *white* Christianity. As George Rhoads of Perryville, Maryland, noted, "A horrid example professed Christians set before the world, while holding slaves and upholding Slavery."[10] This view can be seen in African American uses of the Exodus story, where

America—the "shining city on the hill"—is depicted as Egypt and slaveholding Americans are figured as a people acting against the will of God.

The invocation of Exodus drew on a theology of history that framed African American actions in light of God's will. God delivered the Israelites from Egyptian bondage, and as historian Albert Raboteau writes, God would send "Moses to tell 'ol' Pharaoh to let my people go. Once again the mighty wind of God parted the Red Sea so the Hebrew children could cross over dry shod. Once again Pharaoh's army 'got drowned.'"[11] The convergence of theology and history within the story provided, to some degree, the courage *and* the language needed to risk oneself and to resist subordination. Author Sarah Bradford's description of Harriet

Tubman's account of God's agency in relation to her own comes to mind.

> She expected deliverance when she prayed, unless the Lord had ordered otherwise, and in that case she was perfectly willing to accept the Divine decree. When surprise was expressed at her courage and daring, or at her unexpected deliverances, she would always reply: "Don't, I tell you, Missus, 'twan't me, 'twas de Lord! Jes so long as he wanted to use me, he would take keer of me, and when he didn't want me no longer, I was ready to go; *I always tole him, I'm gwine to hole stiddy on to you and you've got to see me trou.*"[12]

Here is a splendid example of what Jean Humez describes as Tubman's "essential spiritual transformation plot," which shows the connection between her politics and her spiritual life.[13] Tubman's faith and her political choices were bound together; indeed, her special relationship with God gave her the courage to act.

Tubman's passage exemplifies the way black religious language infused the political choices of many black travelers on the Underground Railroad, making their journey simultaneously a spiritual *and* a political one. For example, slaves George Solomon, Daniel Neall, Benjamin Fletcher, and Maria Dorsey drew on the language of Exodus when they decided to escape from slavery in Washington, DC. In this 1856 account, Solomon stated, "In thus opening his mind to his friends, he soon found a willing accord in each of the hearts, and they put their heads together to count up the costs and to fix a time for leaving Egypt and the host of Pharaoh to do their own 'hewing of wood and drawing of water.'"[14] Slave Cordelia Loney understood God's presence in history and "was persuaded that, *by industry and assistance of the Lord,* a way would be opened to the seeker of Freedom even in a strange land and among strangers."[15] In each instance, agency is made possible ironically by a dependence on what John Henry Hill, a slave who escaped the auction block in Richmond, Virginia, called "an unshaken confidence that God was on the side of the oppressed, and a strong hope, that the day was not far distant, when slave power would be suddenly broken and without remedy."[16]

Obviously, attention to the Exodus story offers a compelling rereading of the legend of the Underground Railroad (and the American experience in general) by demonstrating how a story so central to America's national imagination can be used *with a difference.* More specifically, African American uses of the story point out that

the Underground Railroad, romantic and redemptive to so many, can also be understood within a narrative about the American nation conceived as a land and a time of "Egyptian" bondage. In this view, the central protagonists do not offer redemption in the same way as the legend suggests, with historical examples of white Americans acting justly and righteously, but rather they provide the stuff of black prophetic utterance—what has been called the black jeremiad.[17] As Edmund Turner, an escaped slave from Petersburg, Virginia, warned in 1858,

> Stop, poor sinner, stop and think
> Before you further go;
> Think upon the brink of death
> Of everlasting woe.[18]

African American invocations of the Exodus story turn attention away from the heroic sacrifices of white Quakers and abolitionists as examples of the triumph of good over the evil of racism. Instead, they focus on the efforts of black agents to secure freedom in a world structured by racism and, by extension, on the possibility of salvation for the nation. Of course, melodrama remains—villains and heroes still exist––but the basic internal conflict of race that infests the

nation—the unreconciled impulses that threaten to tear the nation apart—remains in view.

SHINING CITY ON THE HILL

Americans have often understood themselves through religious language. New England Puritans drew on this language as they sought to escape persecution in Europe and elevated to biblical drama their journey from the Old World to the New. John Winthrop's famous sermon, "Modell of Christian Charity" (1620), well exemplifies the use of religious language in this way. Winthrop, the leader of the expedition to the Massachusetts Bay Colony, described in his sermon the "convenantal" obligations to God of those who were making the journey across the Atlantic, linking them to the original covenant of Israel. Here, obligation to God formed the basis for a corporate identity. Through their figural participation in the biblical narrative, the Puritans, in effect, became the biblical antitypes of ancient Israel—a nation persecuted by the enemies of God. Their transatlantic voyage, then, was interpreted as a new exodus, "their mission as an errand in the wilderness, and their role as that of a chosen people."[19]

At the conclusion of his sermon Winthrop even paraphrased Moses's last instructions to the Israelites.

> Beloved there is now sett before us life, and good, deathe and evil in that wee are Commaunded this day to the Lord our God and to love one another, to walke in his ways and to keepe his Commanundements . . . and the Articles of our Covenant with him that wee may live and be multiplied,

and that the Lord our God may blesse us in the land whither we goe to possesse it: But if our heartes shall turne away soe that wee will not obey, but shall be seduced and worship . . . other Gods . . . it is propounded unto this day, wee shall surely perishe out of the good Land whither wee passe over this vast Sea to possesse it.[20]

Here, the ideas of migration, pilgrimage, and progress, so central to the religious construction of American national identity, come together to exhort the faithful to recognize that their success and, eventually, the success of the New World are contingent upon their obligations to God. These three notions—migration, pilgrimage, and progress—were critical elements in the creation of an American ideological consensus. They were also important tools in the characterization of an American destiny linked to divine Providence, and as such they form a powerful connection between the imagery of the Exodus story and the idea of an Underground Railroad.

Migration suggested not simply the movement from one place to another but the journey from the Old World to a New Canaan. In this sense, migration was prophetic: it signaled the coming of the new millennium in the bounty that was America (an event sanctioned, it was believed, in the promises of the Bible). Pilgrimage was generally conceived as a march through the wilderness of one's soul to God, or as the literary historian Sacvan Bercovitch puts it, "the believer's pilgrimage through the world's wilderness to redemption."[21] This aspect of the "errand" connected individual action to a broader community of concern by promoting individualism without anarchy, grounding community in the private acts of the will, and rooting personal identities in the social

Timothy H. O'Sullivan
photographed former
slaves fording the
Rappahannock River
in Virginia in August
1862.

enterprise. Finally, "errand" as progress referred to the teleology (pattern of development) inherent in these biblical dramas. Colonial New England "was movement from sacred past to sacred future, a shifting point between migration and millennium."[22]

To be sure, this Puritan inheritance bequeathed to us a religious language for the symbolic construction of an American national identity. America, with the success of its revolution and the power of its capitalist economy, represents the complete break with the Old Israel and the prophetic creation of the New Israel. According to Bercovitch, "With the Revolution, God has shown that 'the United States of America are to be His vineyard'—'the principal Seat of [His] glorious kingdom'—wherein the promises of the past 'are to be brought to harvest,' for the benefit of the whole world.'"[23] America then is the Redeemer Nation, a beacon of freedom and the principal carrier of liberty. The religious construction of this national identity brings together in powerful ways issues of history and memory, shaping interpretations of our nation's cultural beginnings and our sense of national cohesion.[24]

Of course, the ubiquitous use of the Exodus story in the early era of the Republic affected African American appropriations of it. In many ways, African American interpretations of Exodus cannot be understood apart from this broader conception of the American nation. Such use of the story signals the fact that African Americans are quintessentially American. For them, however, the image of the nation as the New Canaan was reversed: the United States was Egypt. As historian Vincent Harding notes,

"One of the abiding and tragic ironies of our history [is that] the nation's claim to be the New Israel was contradicted by the Old Israel still enslaved in her midst."[25] Like the United States in general, African Americans saw themselves as the children of God and linked the freeing of the Israelites with their own eventual liberation. Even so, their appropriation of the Exodus story stood, among other things, as a form of critique of American society for betraying its ideals.

The concepts of migration, pilgrimage, and progress remained important elements in African American uses of the story. Migration was more than simply moving from one place to another. It represented a religious journey from bondage to freedom—from Egypt to Canaan—and conveyed God's promise to his chosen people. Migration was also prophetic, for blacks' special relationship with God suggested that the coming of the new millennium in the bounty of America required that African Americans be free.

Pilgrimage was broadly perceived as an inward journey through the travails of worldly temptation to redemption and grace. This spiritual journey did not, however, stand apart from the worldly realities that shaped the lives of the slaves. Indeed, the march through the wilderness of "the slave's soul" to God represented a journey during which a new self was made. As such, pilgrimage constituted a technique of self-making in which the "slave" within a person died, and the renewed individual, fashioned in the image of God, was now capable of acting freely in the world. Pilgrimage also linked the individual to a particular community of experience. Personal identity was shaped by and within a broad common concern shared by those who were struggling to end slavery and racial discrimination. Thus, migration involved the activity of God in history, and pilgrimage aided in the construction of a self and a community that acted within this sacred drama.

In 1829, for example, the free black author David Walker argued in his *Appeal* that redemption required not only the will of God but also the strenuous activity of the slaves themselves.

> We believe that, for thy glory's sake,
> Thou wilt deliver us;
> But that thou may'st effect these things,
> Thy glory must be sought.[26]

In Walker's view, the duty of every black Christian was to fight (even if it meant to the death) against the scourge of slavery and racial discrimination, for submission to such evils was tantamount to a sin against God. And indeed, because God was active in history and was on the side of the oppressed, Walker and others believed that progress involved the inevitable destruction of slavery and would bring about God's will in the world: they stood between a sacred past and a sacred future.

Drawing on the images of Exodus, Walker offered a vision of hope to African Americans and, on that basis, exhorted them to freedom. "Though our cruel oppressors and murderers," wrote Walker, "may (if possible) treat us more cruel as Pharaoh did the Children of Israel, yet the God of the Ethiopians, has been pleased to hear our moans in consequence of oppression, and the day of our redemption from abject wretchedness draweth near."[27] This is theological history at its most compelling. He relates the brutalities of African American life to biblical narrative and makes African Americans over in the image of Hebrew slaves. Walker also had a message for white Americans: "How cunning slave-holders think they are!!!—How much like the king of Egypt who, after he saw plainly that God was determined to bring out his people, in spite of him and his, as powerful as they were. He

was willing that Moses, Aaron and the Elders of Israel, but not all the people should go and serve the Lord. But God deceived him as he will Christian Americans, unless they are very cautious how they move."[28] Walker called on white Americans to humble themselves before God and to live up to the nation's promise or suffer the consequences of their sins. His was a black jeremiad—a warning—in which African Americans, envisioning themselves as Hebrew slaves crying for freedom in Egypt, reminded the nation of its principles and served as the prophetic voice of the United States.

Walker presupposed that this biblical story was widely known. In fact, such famil-

iarity helped make his passionate plea more powerful. In some ways Walker was striking the chord of the central religious myth of America. His use of the story was somewhat different—perhaps a blue note—given that he spoke for slaves, yet it was ambivalently tied to the religious symbolism of the nation and to what Walker's biographer, Peter Hinks, calls "the values of liberty and equality that formed the hope that was America."[29]

The importance of the Exodus story to the symbolic construction of America and its distinctive appropriation by African Americans form the backdrop for a remarkable moment in William Still's book *The Underground Railroad*. A letter from Edmund Turner draws on the Exodus narrative to issue a warning to slaveholders. In a startling example of the black jeremiad, Turner wrote:

> Well may the Southern slaveholder say, that holding the Fellow men in Bondage is no (sin), because it is their delight as the Egyptians, so do they; but nevertheless God in his own good time will bring them out by a mighty hand, as it is recorded in the sacred oracles of truth, that Ethiopia shall soon stretch out her hands to God. . . . And my prayer is to you, oh slaveholder, in the name of that God who in the beginning said, Let there be light, and there was light. Let my people go that they may serve me; thereby good may come unto thee and to thy children. . . . As one that loves your soul repent ye, therefore, and be converted, that your sins may be blotted out when the time of refreshing shall come from the presence of the Lord.[30]

Turner's remarks, like those of Walker, signaled a country divided against itself. His words drew on the languages so central to the nation, but they also called America to come to terms with the urgency of its unreconciled impulses—one toward democracy and freedom, the other toward slavery. His invocation of Exodus then was not to confirm the goodness of America but rather to call attention to the nation's sins. Turner as well as others involved with the Underground Railroad understood the tragedy of race in America, the underside of the story of progress in which most Americans wish to find themselves, generation after generation.

UNDERGROUND RAILROAD, EXODUS, AND REDEMPTION

Attention to the Exodus story and its varied uses in the United States lends insight into the aggregate of beliefs sufficiently at odds with one another to yield distinctive accounts of our nation's cultural beginnings.[31] How we remember those beginnings and struggles, and how those memories can justify opposite kinds of conduct or overburden present efforts to respond to the problems of race warrant more careful consideration.

The Underground Railroad is well suited to this sort of analysis. The Exodus story provides a particularly interesting point of entry into examining what is at stake in continuing to circulate tales of elaborate networks of "conductors" and "depots" manned by benevolent and heroic white people. Many white abolitionists indeed risked their lives to aid fugitive slaves, but the story's significance extends beyond brave acts of heroism. The *need* for this interracial effort as well as its *scope* go to the heart of a certain way of imagining the

"The black exodus— The old style and the new," from *Harper's Weekly*, May 1, 1880.

nation—that of redeeming the soul of the Redeemer Nation.

David Blight offers an insightful account of the "use" of the legend of the Underground Railroad by focusing on the audience for romantic memory of the Civil War era. He engages in a close reading of the reminiscence material William Siebert collected for his popular book, *The Underground Railroad*, published in 1898. Blight demonstrates quite convincingly that Siebert's collection of reminiscences must be understood within a larger context of reconciliation between the North and South, which required forgetting the past of slavery and the realities of racial proscription so prevalent in the late nineteenth century. Here, remembering the efforts of white family members engaged in the battle to rid the nation of the evil of slavery and to help hapless slaves to freedom enables their descendants to see themselves as the inheri-

tors of an antislavery past or, at least, as the inheritors of a nation capable of righting an egregious wrong.

Typical of melodrama, once the battle was joined, however violent the conflict, resolution was inevitable. The sin of slavery was abolished and, as Mrs. Levi Monse Gould remarked in 1896 with an air of accomplishment, "the shackles of slavery [were removed] from four million human beings, and now they no more need an Underground R.R. to liberty—*they are free*." The fact that the foundations of American apartheid were being laid mattered little to Mrs. Gould. Virtue triumphed over villainy. The battle had to be declared a victory, or America's inherent goodness could be called into question. As Blight puts it, "All of this adds up to a mythos of accomplished glory, a history of emancipation completed. . . . Not only had reunion trumped race, but the war itself had bludg-

Leaving behind generations of slavery in the South, these refugees wait on a Mississippi River levee in 1879 for a steamboat to take them to freedom.

eoned the problem of slavery out of history. . . . Masked in this comforting haze was a real history of Underground Railroad heroism, as well as the deteriorating condition of American race relations."[32] What is interesting here is that the forgetting that is requisite for reunion also fortifies the religious myth of the nation. America, without the stain of slavery, was redeemed.

The legend of the Underground Railroad stands as a paradigm of the burden of America's melodrama of race. The heroic efforts of black and white alike to escape and fight against slavery are overshadowed by the sins of the nation. Somehow the actions of these brave souls were supposed to free us from the terror of our own history. I suppose the virtue of interracial cooperation is all too often weighed down by the expectation that it will banish the evil of racism forever. I have attempted to show how the voices of those African Americans traveling on the Under-ground Railroad disrupt such accounts. When we listen to them, America is hardly the "shining city on the hill," and racism is not "bludgeoned . . . out of history." Instead,

we hear the sounds of joy for reaching the banks of Jordan, cries of praise to God who has carried them over, and moans for family members left behind. If we listen closely, the tragedy of America can be heard.

To be sure, African American appropriations of the Exodus story lend themselves to melodrama. References to Pharaoh and the Israelites reinforce sentimental and romantic representations of the inherent virtues of suffering black servants and the apparent vices of evil whites. In some ways, to be American is to be melodramatic about race. Nevertheless, such accounts of race—in which the complexity of our nation's racial past and present are obscured—must be cast aside if we are to grapple seriously with the challenge racism poses to our democracy. This requires, I believe, interracial cooperation to be freed of its historical burden and understood for what it is: fragile efforts by fragile human beings to make real the promises of American democracy. If we act together, like many of those travelers on the Underground Railroad, redemption *is* possible, but it is never guaranteed.

SUGGESTIONS FOR FURTHER READING

BOOKS

Abzug, Robert B. *Cosmos Crumbling: American Reform and the Religious Imagination.* New York: Oxford University Press, 1994.

Aptheker, Herbert. "Maroons Within the Present Limits of the United States." 1939. Reprinted in *Maroon Societies: Rebel Slave Communities in the America.* Edited by Richard Price. Garden City, N.Y.: Anchor Books, 1973.

Bay, Mia. *The White Image in the Black Mind: African-American Ideas about White People, 1830–1925.* New York: Oxford University Press, 2000.

Berlin, Ira. *Many Thousands Gone: The First Two Centuries of Slavery in North America.* Cambridge: Harvard University Press, 1998.

———. *Slaves Without Masters: The Free Negro in the Antebellum South.* New York: Pantheon Books, 1974.

Bibb, Henry. "Narrative of the Life and Adventures of Henry Bibb." In *Puttin' On Ole Massa: The Slave Narratives of Henry Bibb, William Wells Brown, and Solomon Northup.* Edited by Gilbert Osofsky. New York: Harper and Row, 1969.

Blackett, R. J. M. *Building an Antislavery Wall: Black Americans in the Atlantic Abolitionist Movement, 1830–1860.* Baton Rouge: Louisiana State University Press, 1983.

Bland, Sterling Lecater, Jr. *Voices of the Fugitives: Runaway Slave Stories and Their Fictions of Self-Creation.* Westport, Conn.: Praeger, 2000.

Blassingame, John W. *The Slave Community: Plantation Life in the Antebellum South.* New York: Oxford University Press, 1972. Rev. and enl. ed. New York: Oxford University Press, 1979.

Blight, David W. "The Confluence of History and Memory." Introduction to *Beyond the Battlefield: Race, Memory, and the American Civil War.* Amherst: University of Massachusetts Press, 2002.

———. *Race and Reunion: The Civil War in American Memory.* Cambridge: Harvard University Press, 2001.

Blockson, Charles L. *The Underground Railroad: First-Person Narratives of Escapes to Freedom in the North.* New York: Prentice Hall, 1987.

Bolster, W. Jeffrey. *Black Jacks: African American Seamen in the Age of Sail.* Cambridge: Harvard University Press, 1997.

Botkin, B. A., ed. *Lay My Burden Down: A Folk History of Slavery.* Chicago: University of Chicago Press, 1945.

Bradford, Sarah H. *Scenes in the Life of Harriet Tubman.* Auburn, N.Y.: W. J. Moses, 1869.

Brundage, Fitzhugh, ed. *Where These Memories Grow: History, Memory, and Southern Identity.* Chapel Hill: University of North Carolina Press, 2000.

Buckmaster, Henrietta. *Let My People Go: The Story of the Underground Railroad and the Growth of the Abolition Movement.* Boston: Beacon Press, 1959.

Cecelski, David C. *The Waterman's Song: Slavery and Freedom in Maritime North Carolina.* Chapel Hill: University of North Carolina, 2001.

Coffin, Levi. *Reminiscences of Levi Coffin.* 1876. Reprint, New York: Augustus M. Kelly, 1968.

Cover, Robert. *Justice Accused: Antislavery and the Judicial Process.* New Haven: Yale University Press, 1975.

Douglass, Frederick. *Life and Times of Frederick*

Douglass: His Early Life as a Slave, His Escape from Bondage, and His Complete History. 1892. Reprint, New York: Collier Books, 1962.

———. *My Bondage and My Freedom.* 1855. Reprint, New York: Dover Publications, 1969; New York: Penguin, 2003.

———. *Narrative of the Life of Frederick Douglass, An American Slave.* 1845. Reprint, Boston: Bedford Books, 2003.

Drew, Benjamin. *The Narratives of Fugitive Slaves.* 1856. Reprint, Toronto: Prospero, 2000.

Egypt, Ophelia S., J. Masouka, and Charles S. Johnson, eds. *Unwritten History of Slavery: Autobiographical Accounts of Negro Ex-Slaves.* Vol. 18 of *The American Slave, A Composite Autobiography.* Edited by George Rawick. 1945. 19 vols. Westport, Conn.: Greenwood, 1972.

Eldridge, Carrie. *Cabell County's Empire for Freedom.* Huntington, W.V.: Marshall University, 1999.

Ernest, John, ed. *Running a Thousand Miles for Freedom, Or the Escape of William and Ellen Craft from Slavery.* Acton, Mass.: Copley Publishing, 2000.

Essig, James D. *The Bonds of Wickedness: American Evangelicals Against Slavery, 1770–1808.* Philadelphia: Temple University Press, 1982.

Franklin, John Hope, and Loren Schweninger. *Runaway Slaves: Rebels on the Plantation.* New York: Oxford University Press, 1999.

Frey, Sylvia R. *Water from the Rock: Black Resistance in a Revolutionary Age.* Princeton: Princeton University Press, 1991.

Gara, Larry. *The Liberty Line: The Legend of the Underground Railroad.* Lexington: University of Kentucky Press, 1961. Reprint, Lexington: University of Kentucky Press, 1967, 1996.

Geggus, David Patrick. "Slavery, War, and Revolution in the Greater Caribbean, 1789–1815." In *A Turbulent Time: The French Revolution and the Great Caribbean.* Edited by David Barry Gaspar and David P. Geggus. Bloomington: University of Indiana Press, 1997.

Genovese, Eugene D. *Roll Jordan Roll: The World the Slaves Made.* New York: Random House, 1972.

Glassie, Henry. *Pattern in the Material Folk Culture of the Eastern United States.* Philadelphia: University of Pennsylvania Press, 1968.

Goodman, Paul. *Of One Blood: The Abolitionists and the Origins of Racial Equality.* Berkeley: University of California Press, 1998.

Hadden, Sally E. *Slave Patrols: Law and Violence in Virginia and the Carolinas.* Cambridge: Harvard University Press, 2001.

Hagedorn, Ann. *Beyond the River: The Untold Story of the Heroes of the Underground Railroad.* New York: Simon and Schuster, 2002.

Hall, Gwendolyn Midlo. *Africans in Colonial Louisiana: The Development of Afro-Creole Culture in the Eighteenth Century.* Baton Rouge: Louisiana State University Press, 1992.

Harding, Vincent. *There is a River: The Black Struggle for Freedom in America.* New York: Harcourt Brace Jovanovich, 1981.

Harrold, Stanley. *The Abolitionists and the South, 1831–1861.* Lexington: University Press of Kentucky, 1995.

———. *Subversives: The Antislavery Community in Washington, D.C., 1828–1865.* Baton Rouge: Louisiana State University Press, 2002.

Henson, Josiah. *An Autobiography of the Reverend Josiah Henson.* 1881. Reprint, Reading, Mass.: Addison-Wesley Publishing, 1969.

Higgins, Chester, Jr., and Orde Coombs, eds. *Some Time Ago: A Historical Portrait of Black Americans from 1850 to 1950.* Garden City, N.Y.: Anchor Books, 1980.

Hinks, Peter. *To Awake My Afflicted Brethren: David Walker and the Problem of Antebellum Slave Resistance.* University Park: Pennsylvania State University Press, 1997.

Horton, James Oliver, and Lois E. Horton. *Black Bostonians: Family Life and Community Struggle in the Antebellum North.* New York: Holmes and Meier, 1979. Rev. ed. New York: Holmes and Meier, 2000.

———. *In Hope of Liberty: Culture, Community and Protest Among Northern Free Blacks, 1790–1860.* New York: Oxford University Press, 1997.

Jacobs, Harriet A. *Incidents in the Life of a Slave Girl.* Edited by Jean Fagan Yellin. Cambridge: Harvard University Press, 1987.

James, C. L. R. *Black Jacobins: Toussaint L'Ouverture and the San Domingo Revolution.* New York: Harcourt, Brace, 1938.

Jamieson, Annie Straith. *William King: Friend and Champion of Slaves.* 1925. Reprint, New York: Negro Universities Press, 1969.

Johnson, H. U. *From Dixie to Canada: Romances and Realities of the Underground Railroad.* 1896. Reprint, Westport, Conn.: Negro Universities Press, 1970.

Johnson, Walter. *Soul by Soul: Life Inside the Antebellum Slave Mart.* New York: Cambridge University Press, 1999.

Kammen, Michael. *In the Past Lane: Historical Perspectives on American Culture.* New York: Oxford University Press, 1997.

———. *Mystic Chords of Memory: The Transformation of Tradition in American Culture.* New York: Knopf, 1991.

Klees, Emerson. *Underground Railroad Tales: With Routes Through the Finger Lakes Region.* Rochester: Friends of the Finger Lakes Publishing, 1997.

Kolchin, Peter. *American Slavery: 1619–1877.* New York: Hill and Wang, 1993.

Kraditor, Aileen. *Means and Ends in American Abolitionism: Garrison and His Critics on Strategy and Tactics, 1834–1850.* New York: Pantheon Books, 1969. Reprint, New York: Ivan Dee Publishers, 1989.

Landers, Jane. *Black Society in Spanish Florida.* Urbana: University of Illinois Press, 1999.

———. *Colonial Plantations and Economy in Florida.* Gainesville: University Press of Florida, 2000.

Litwack, Leon. *North of Slavery: The Negro in the Free States, 1790–1860.* New York: Oxford University Press, 1965.

Loguen, Jermain W. *The Rev. J. W. Loguen, as a Slave and as a Freeman: A Narrative of Real Life.* Syracuse: J. G. R. Thuair and Company, 1859.

Lowenthal, David. *Possessed by the Past: The Heritage Crusade and the Spoils of History.* New York: Free Press, 1996.

Lyght, Ernest. *Path of Freedom: The Black Presence in New Jersey's Burlington County, 1659–1900.* Cherry Hill, N.J.: E and E Publishing, 1978.

Mabee, Carleton. *The Non-Violent Abolitionists from 1830 through the Civil War.* New York: Macmillan, 1970.

Matthews, Essie Collins. *Aunt Phebe, Uncle Tom and Others: Character Studies Among the Old Slaves of the South, Fifty Years After.* Columbus, Ohio: Champlin Press, 1915.

McLaurin, Melton. *Celia, A Slave.* Athens: University of Georgia Press, 1991.

Melish, Joanne Pope. *Disowning Slavery: Gradual Emancipation and Race in New England.* Ithaca: Cornell University Press, 1998.

Miller, William Lee. *Arguing About Slavery: The Great Battle in the United States Congress.* New York: Oxford University Press, 1996.

Morgan, Edmund S. *American Slavery—American Freedom: The Ordeal of Colonial Virginia.* New York: Norton, 1975.

Morgan, Philip D. *Slave Counterpoint: Black Culture in the Eighteenth-Century Chesapeake and Lowcountry.* Chapel Hill: University of North Carolina Press, 1998.

Mullin, Gerald W. *Flight and Rebellion: Slave Resistance in Eighteenth-Century Virginia.* New York: Oxford University Press, 1972.

Mulroy, Kevin. *Freedom on the Border: The Seminole Maroons in Florida, the Indian Territory, Coahuila, and Texas.* Lubbock: Texas Tech University Press, 1993.

Newman, Richard S. *The Transformation of Abolitionism: Fighting Slavery in the Early Republic, 1790–1835.* Chapel Hill: University of North Carolina Press, 2002.

Nichols, Charles H. *Many Thousand Gone: The Ex-Slaves Account of Their Bondage and Their Freedom.* Bloomington: Indiana University Press, 1963.

Northup, Solomon. "Twelve Years a Slave: Narrative of Solomon Northup." In *Puttin' On Ole Massa: The Slave Narratives of Henry Bibb, William Wells Brown, and Solomon Northup.* Edited by Gilbert Osofsky. New York: Harper and Row, 1969.

Nye, Russel B. *Fettered Freedom: Civil Liberties and the Slavery Controversy.* East Lansing: Michigan State College Press, 1949.

Oates, Stephen. *To Purge This Land with Blood: A Biography of John Brown.* New York: Harper and Row, 1974.

Osofsky, Gilbert, ed. *Puttin' On Ole Massa: The Slave Narratives of Henry Bibb, William Wells Brown, and Solomon Northup.* New York: Harper and Row, 1969.

Parker, John P. *His Promised Land: The Autobiography of John P. Parker, Former Slave and Conductor on the Underground Railroad.* Edited by Stuart Seely Sprague. New York: W. W. Norton, 1996.

Pease, Jane H., and William H. Pease. *Black*

Utopia: Negro Communal Experiments in America. Madison: State Historical Society of Wisconsin, 1963.

———. *They Who Would Be Free: Blacks' Search for Freedom, 1831–1861.* New York: Oxford University Press, 1974.

Perdue, Charles L., Jr., Thomas E. Barden, and Robert K. Phillips, eds. *Weevils in the Wheat: Interviews with Virginia Ex-Slaves.* Charlottesville: University Press of Virginia, 1976.

Porter, Kenneth W. *The Black Seminoles: History of a Freedom-Seeking People.* Gainesville: University Press of Florida, 1996.

Price, George R., and James Brewer Stewart. *To Heal the Scourge of Prejudice: The Life and Writings of Hosea Easton.* Amherst: University of Massachusetts Press, 1999.

Quarles, Benjamin. *Allies for Freedom: Blacks and John Brown.* New York: Oxford University Press, 1974.

———. *The Black Abolitionists.* New York: Oxford University Press, 1965.

Rael, Patrick. *Black Identity and Black Protest in the Antebellum North.* Chapel Hill: University of North Carolina Press, 2002.

Rawick, George P. *The American Slave: A Composite Autobiography.* Vol. 17, pt. 1. Westport, Conn.: Greenwood Publishing, 1972.

Redpath, James. *The Roving Editor or Talks with Slaves in Southern States.* New York: Burdick, 1859.

Refugees from Slavery in Canada West: Report to the Freedman's Inquiry Commission. 1864. Reprint, New York: Arno Press, 1969.

Richards, Leonard L. *The Slave Power: The Free North and Southern Domination.* Baton Rouge: Louisiana State University Press, 2000.

Ripley, C. Peter, ed. *Witness for Freedom: African American Voices on Race, Slavery, and Emancipation.* Chapel Hill: University of North Carolina, 1993.

Ripley, C. Peter, Roy E. Finkenbine, Michael F. Hembree, and Donald Yacovone, eds. *The Black Abolitionist Papers.* Vol. 4, *The United States, 1847–1858.* Chapel Hill: University of North Carolina Press, 1991.

Roediger, David. *The Wages of Whiteness: Race and the Making of the American Working Class.* New York: Verso Press, 1997.

Rosenzweig, Roy, and David Thelen. *The Presence of the Past: Popular Uses of History in American Life.* New York: Columbia University Press, 1998.

Sernett, Milton C. *North Star Country: Upstate New York and the Crusade for African American Freedom.* Syracuse: Syracuse University Press, 2002.

Siebert, Wilbur H. *The Underground Railroad from Slavery to Freedom.* New York: Macmillan, 1898. Reprint, New York: Arno Press, 1968.

Smedley, Robert C. *History of the Underground Railroad in Chester and the Neighboring Counties of Pennsylvania.* Lancaster, Penn., 1883.

Stauffer, John. *Black Hearts of Men: Abolitionism and the Transformation of Race.* Cambridge: Harvard University Press, 2001.

Sterling, Dorothy, ed. *Speak Out in Thunder Tones: Letters and Other Writings by Black Northerners, 1787–1865.* Garden City, N.Y.: Doubleday and Company, 1973.

Stewart, James Brewer. *Holy Warriors: The Abolitionists and American Slavery.* New York: Hill and Wang, 1997.

———. *Wendell Phillips: Liberty's Hero.* Baton Rouge: Louisiana State University Press, 1986.

Still, William. *The Underground Railroad.* Philadelphia: Porter and Coates, 1872. Reprint, New York: Arno Press, 1968.

Switala, William J. *Underground Railroad in Pennsylvania.* Mechanicsburg, Penn.: Stackpole Books, 2001.

Upton, Dell, and John Michael Vlach, eds. *Common Places: Readings in American Vernacular Architecture.* Athens: University of Georgia Press, 1986.

Walker, Juliet E. K. *Free Frank: A Black Pioneer on the Antebellum Frontier.* Lexington: University Press of Kentucky, 1983.

Walters, Ronald. *The Antislavery Appeal: Abolitionism after 1830.* Baltimore: Johns Hopkins University Press, 1978.

Ward, Samuel Ringgold. *Autobiography of a Fugitive Slave: His Anti-Slavery Labours in the United States, Canada, and England.* London: John Snow, 1855.

White, Deborah Gray. *Ar'n't I a Woman? Female Slaves in the Plantation South.* Rev. ed. New

York: W. W. Norton, 1999.

Winch, Julie. *Philadelphia's Black Elite: Activism, Accommodation, and the Struggle for Autonomy.* Philadelphia: University of Pennsylvania Press, 1988.

Winks, Robin. *The Blacks in Canada: A History.* New Haven: Yale University Press, 1971.

PERIODICALS AND JOURNALS

Berlin, Ira. "From Creole to African: Atlantic Creoles and the Origins of African-American Society in Mainland North America." *William and Mary Quarterly* 53 (1996): 252–88.

Blockson, Charles L. "Escape from Slavery: The Underground Railroad." *National Geographic* 166, no. 1 (July 1984): 3–39.

Clark, Elizabeth B. "'The Sacred Rights of the Weak': Pain, Sympathy and the Culture of Individual Rights in Antebellum America." *Journal of American History* 82 (1995): 463–93.

Dunn, Richard. "The Tale of Two Plantations: Slave Life at Mesopotamia in Jamaica and Mount Airy in Virginia, 1799–1828." *William and Mary Quarterly* (January 1977): 58.

Fields, Harold B. "Free Negroes in Cass County." *Michigan History* 44 (1960): 378.

Fruehling, Bryan D., and Robert H. Smith. "Subterranean Hideaways of the Underground Railroad in Ohio: An Architectural, Archaeological, and Historical Critique of Local Traditions." *Ohio History* 102 (summer–autumn 1993): 98–117.

Goggin, John M. "The Seminole Negroes of Andros Island, Bahamas." *Florida Historical Quarterly* 24 (1946): 206.

Harrold, Stanley. "The Pearl Affair: The Washington Riot of 1848." *Records of the Columbia Historical Society* 50 (1980): 140–60.

Johnson, Michael P. "Denmark Vesey and His Co-Conspirators." *William and Mary Quarterly* 58, no. 4 (October 2001): 915–76.

Kammen, Carol. "The UGRR and Local History." *Cultural Resource Management* 21, no. 4 (1998): 11.

Kimmel, Ross M. "Free Blacks in Seventeenth-Century Maryland." *Maryland Historical Magazine* 71 (1976): 22–25.

Kulikoff, Allan. "A 'Prolifick' People: Black Population Growth in the Chesapeake Colonies, 1700–1790." *Southern Studies* 16 (1977): 392–93.

Landers, Jane. "Gracia Real de Santa Teresa de Mose: A Free Black Town in Spanish Colonial Florida." *Florida Historical Quarterly* 95 (1990): 9–30.

Morgan, Edmund S. "Slavery and Freedom: The American Paradox." *Journal of American History* 59 (1972): 18.

Siebert, Wilbur H. "Beginnings of the Underground Railroad in Ohio." *Ohio History* 15 (1947): 78.

Snyder, Charles McCool. "Oswego's Abolitionists and Their Tunnels." *New York Folklore Quarterly* 17 (1961): 95–103.

Stewart, James Brewer. "The Emergence of Racial Modernity and the Rise of the White North." *Journal of the Early Republic* (summer 1998): 202–11.

———. "Peaceful Hopes and Violent Experiences: The Evolution of Radical and Reforming Abolitionism." *Civil War History* (December 1971): 293–309.

Wayne, Michael. "The Black Population of Canada West on the Eve of the American Civil War: A Reassessment Based on the Manuscript Census of 1861." *Histoire Sociale/Social History* 28, no. 56 (1995): 472–74.

Yacovone, Donald. "The Transformation of the African American Temperance Movement, 1827–1854." *Journal of the Early Republic* (fall 1988): 282–97.

CONTRIBUTORS

IRA BERLIN teaches history at the University of Maryland, where he is a university professor. He was the founding director of the Freedmen and Southern Society Project and an editor of the project's multivolume *Freedom: A Documentary History of Emancipation.* Among his books are *Slaves Without Masters: The Free Negro in the Antebellum South* (1974), *Many Thousands Gone: The First Two Centuries of Slavery in North America* (1998), and *Generations of Captivity: A History of African American Slaves* (2003).

R. J. M. BLACKETT is Andrew Jackson Professor of History at Vanderbilt University. He is the author of *Building an Antislavery Wall: Black Americans in the Atlantic Abolitionist Movement, 1830–1860* (1983) and *Divided Hearts: Britain and the American Civil War* (2001) Currently he is studying the ways communities reacted to the 1850 Fugitive Slave Law.

DAVID W. BLIGHT is the Class of '54 Professor of American History at Yale University. He is the author of *Frederick Douglass' Civil War* (1989), *Race and Reunion: The Civil War in American Memory* (2001), and *Beyond the Battlefield: Race, Memory, and the American Civil War* (2002), and he has edited several books, including editions of Frederick Douglass's *Narrative* and W. E. B. Du Bois's *The Souls of Black Folk.*

CATHERINE CLINTON is the author or editor of more than a dozen books on American history, including *The Plantation Mistress* (1982) and, most recently, *Harriet Tubman: The Road to Freedom* (2004). Her children's book, *The Battle of Fort Wagner: Hold the Flag High*, will be published in 2005.

SPENCER CREW is the executive director and CEO for the National Underground Railroad Freedom Center. He is the former director of the National Museum of American History, Smithsonian Institution. He has curated numerous exhibitions, including *Field to Factory: Afro-American Migration 1915–1940*, and co-curated *The American Presidency: A Glorious Burden.* He also has published extensively in the fields of African American history and public history. His most recent publication is the collaborative *Unchained Memories: Readings from the Slave Narratives* (2002).

EDDIE S. GLAUDE JR. is associate professor of religion and African American studies at Princeton University. He is author of *Exodus! Religion, Race, and Nation in Early Nineteenth-Century Black America* (2000). He also edited *Is It Nation Time?* (2001) and co-edited *African American Religious Thought: An Anthology* (2003) with Cornel West.

JAMES OLIVER HORTON is the Benjamin Banneker Professor of American Studies and History at George Washington University and director of the African-American Communities Project of the National Museum of American History, Smithsonian Institution. He is the author of *Free People of Color* (1993), editor of the Oxford University Press series "The Landmarks of American History," and coauthor of *Black Bostonians* (1979; reprinted 1999), *In Hope of Liberty* (1997), and *Hard Road to Freedom* (2001).

LOIS E. HORTON is professor of history at George Mason University. She is coeditor of *A History of the African-American People* (1995), a contributing author to *City of Magnificent Intentions: A History of the District of Columbia* (1983), and coauthor of *Black Bostonians* (1979; reprinted 1999), *In Hope of Liberty* (1997), *Von Benin nach Baltimore: Geschichte der African Americans* and *Hard Road to Freedom* (2001).

JANE LANDERS is associate professor of history and associate dean of arts and sciences at Vanderbilt University. She is the author of *Black Society in Spanish Florida* (1999) and editor of *Colonial Plantations and Economy in Florida* (2000). Many of her articles examine the colonial periods of Florida and the Caribbean.

BRUCE LEVINE is professor of history at the University of California, Santa Cruz. He is the former research director at the American Social History Project at the Graduate Center of the City University of New York and is a principal author of *Who Built America?: Working People in the Nation's Economy, Politics, Culture and Society* (3d ed., 2005). His other books include *Half Slave and Half Free: The Roots of Civil War* (1992) and *The Spirit of 1848: German Immigrants, Labor Conflict, and the Origins of the Civil War* (1992). He is currently at work on *Confederate Emancipation: Southern Plans to Free Slaves During the Civil War* (forthcoming).

DIANE MILLER has a master's degree in African American history from the University of Maryland and is the national coordinator for the National Park Service's National Underground Railroad Network to Freedom Program. Since 1984 she has worked extensively on historic preservation for the National Park Service, the National Register of Historic Places, and National Historic Landmarks.

MILTON C. SERNETT is professor of African American studies and history and is adjunct professor of religion at Syracuse University. He is the author of five books, including *North Star Country: Upstate New York and the Crusade for African American Freedom* (2002), and he is working on *Harriet Tubman*

and American Memory: The Forging of an American Icon (forthcoming).

JAMES BREWER STEWART is the James Wallace Professor of History at Macalester College and has published biographies of prominent abolitionists Wendell Phillips, William Lloyd Garrison, Joshua R. Giddings, and Hosea Easton (with George Price). He also wrote *Holy Warriors: The Abolitionists and American Slavery* (1976; reprinted 1996), as well as numerous scholarly articles on abolitionism's history in the United States.

JOHN MICHAEL VLACH is professor of American studies and anthropology and the director of the Folklife Program at George Washington University. He has curated museum exhibitions as well as lectured and written on the tangible aspects of the African diaspora in the Caribbean and across the American South. His books include *The Afro-American Tradition in Decorative Arts* (1978), *By the Work of Their Hands: Studies in Afro-American Folklife* (1991), *Back of the Big House: The Architecture of Plantation Slavery* (1993), and *The Planter's Prospect: Privilege and Slavery in Plantation Paintings* (2002).

DEBORAH GRAY WHITE is Distinguished Professor of History at Rutgers University. She is the author of a study of enslaved women, *Ar'n't I a Woman: Female Slaves in the Plantation South* (1985; reprinted 1999). Among her other publications is *Too Heavy a Load: Black Women in Defense of Themselves, 1894–1994* (1999), a century-long look at black women and their organizing, and *Let My People Go: African Americans 1804–1860* (1996), a study of the trials and tribulations of black people in the immediate years before the Civil War.

JANE WILLIAMSON is the director of Rokeby Museum, a National Historic Landmark Underground Railroad site in Ferrisburgh, Vermont. She holds a master's degree in historic preservation from the University of Vermont and one in library science from Columbia University. She is researching two fugitive slaves, one from Maryland and the other North Carolina, for a permanent exhibition on the Underground Railroad at Rokeby.

NOTES

INTRODUCTION

1. Frederick Douglass, *My Bondage and My Freedom* (1855; reprint, New York: Penguin, 2003), 203–204.
2. Ibid., 233, 207.
3. Wilbur H. Siebert, *The Underground Railroad from Slavery to Freedom*, (1898; reprint, New York: Arno Press, 1968), 44–46; Larry Gara, *The Liberty Line: The Legend of the Underground Railroad* (Lexington: University of Kentucky Press, 1961), 173–74. Also see Robert C. Smedley, *History of the Underground Railroad in Chester and the Neighboring Counties of Pennsylvania* (Lancaster, Penn., 1883). On other folk origins of the term see Henrietta Buckmaster, *Let My People Go: The Story of the Underground Railroad and the Growth of the Abolition Movement* (Boston: Beacon, 1959).
4. Saint Augustine, *Confessions*, trans. Edward Bouverie Pusey (New York: Book-of-the-Month Club, 1996), 240.
5. Abraham Lincoln, "My Childhood's Home," in *The Poems of Abraham Lincoln* (Bedford, Mass.: Applewood Books, 1991), 9–12. George Santyana, from *Reason and Religion*, quoted in Clifford Geertz, *The Interpretation of Cultures* (New York: Basic Books, 1973), 87.
6. John Lukacs, *Historical Consciousness or the Remembered Past* (1968; reprint, New York: Schocken Books, 1985), 33.
7. See David W. Blight, "The Confluence of History and Memory," introduction to *Beyond the Battlefield: Race, Memory, and the American Civil War* (Amherst: University of Massachusetts Press, 2002), 1–7. For an interesting discussion of how one community faces its real and mythic past about the Underground Railroad see Carol Lasser, "The Underground Railroad in Oberlin: History and Memory," paper presented at the symposium "Threads of Freedom: The Underground Railroad Story in Quilts," Oberlin, Ohio, June 23, 2001; copy provided by the author.
8. On public tastes for history and especially how historical memory begins locally and in families see Roy Rosenzweig and David Thelen, *The Presence of the Past: Popular Uses of History in American Life* (New York: Columbia University Press, 1998).
9. For one of the finest introductions to how historians study the problem of memory see Fitzhugh Brundage, "No Deed But Memory," in Fitzhugh Brundage, ed., *Where These Memories Grow: History, Memory, and Southern Identity* (Chapel Hill: University of North Carolina Press, 2000), 1–28. On memory and heritage in American culture see Michael Kammen, *Mystic Chords of Memory: The Transformation of Tradition in American Culture* (New York: Knopf, 1991); Michael Kammen, *In the Past Lane: Historical Perspectives on American Culture* (New York: Oxford University Press, 1997), 161–226; and David Lowenthal, *Possessed by the Past: The Heritage Crusade and the Spoils of History* (New York: Free Press, 1996).
10. Richard Slotkin, *The Fatal Environment: The Myth of the Frontier in the Age of Industrialization, 1800–1890* (New York: Atheneum, 1985), 19; Roland Barthes, *Mythologies* (London: Jonathan Cape, 1957), 143; and Kammen, *Mystic Chords of Memory*, 38.

I. BEFORE COTTON

1. Ira Berlin, "From Creole to African: Atlantic Creoles and the Origins of African-American Society in Mainland North America," *William and Mary Quarterly* 53 (1996): 252–88.
2. Ibid., 272–74.
3. J. Douglas Deal, *Race and Class in Colonial Virginia: Indians, Englishmen, and Africans on the Eastern Shore of Virginia during the Seventeenth Century* (New York: Garland, 1993), 217–50; T. H. Breen and Stephen Innes, *"Myne Owne Ground": Race and Freedom on Virginia's Eastern Shore, 1640–1676* (New York: Oxford University Press, 1980), chap. 1; Ross M. Kimmel, "Free Blacks in Seventeenth-Century Maryland," *Maryland Historical Magazine* 71, no. 1 (1976): 22–25; Alden T. Vaughan, "Blacks in Virginia: A Note on the First Decade," *William and Mary Quarterly* 29 (1972): 475–76.
4. Edmund S. Morgan, *American Slavery—American Freedom: The Ordeal of Colonial Virginia* (New York: Norton, 1975), 108–79, 215–49.
5. Deal, *Race and Class*, 187–88; Breen and Innes, *"Myne Owne Ground,"* 68–69; Edmund S. Morgan, "Slavery and Freedom: The American Paradox," *Journal of American History* 59 (1972): 18 n. 39; Allan Kulikoff, "A 'Prolifick' People: Black Population Growth in the Chesapeake Colonies, 1700–1790," *Southern Studies* 16 (1977): 392–93.

6. The latter point becomes clear in examining the genealogies of seventeenth-century free people of color constructed by Paul Heinegg in *Free African Americans of Maryland and Delaware: From the Colonial Period to 1810* (Baltimore: Johns Hopkins University Press, 2000).

7. Ira Berlin, *Many Thousands Gone: The First Two Centuries of Slavery in North America* (Cambridge: Harvard University Press, 1998), 15–92.

8. Ibid., 93–108.

9. For an overview of the Plantation Revolution in its Atlantic context see Philip D. Curtin, *The Rise and Fall of the Plantation Complex: Essays in Atlantic History* (Cambridge: Cambridge University Press, 1990), chaps. 1–6.

10. Berlin, *Many Thousands Gone*, 93–216, provides an overview of the development of the Plantation Generation. For a detailed account of the changes in the Chesapeake and low country see Philip D. Morgan, *Slave Counterpoint: Black Culture in the Eighteenth-Century Chesapeake and Lowcountry* (Chapel Hill: University of North Carolina Press, 1998). For the lower Mississippi Valley see Gwendolyn Midlo Hall, *Africans in Colonial Louisiana: The Development of Afro-Creole Culture in the Eighteenth Century* (Baton Rouge: Louisiana State University Press, 1992); and Thomas N. Ingersoll, *Mammon and Manon in Early New Orleans: The First Slave Society in the Deep South, 1718–1819* (Knoxville: University of Tennessee Press, 1999).

11. The transformation of the Revolutionary Generation is traced in Berlin, *Many Thousands Gone*, 217–357. Also see Benjamin Quarles, *The Negro in the American Revolution* (Chapel Hill: University of North Carolina Press, 1961); Sylvia R. Frey, *Water from the Rock: Black Resistance in a Revolutionary Age* (Princeton: Princeton University Press, 1991); Winthrop D. Jordan, *White over Black: American Attitudes toward the Negro* (Chapel Hill: University of North Carolina Press, 1968), 269–314; and Ira Berlin and Ronald Hoffman, eds., *Slavery and Freedom in the Age of The American Revolution* (Charlottesville: University Press of Virginia, 1983).

12. Quoted in Philip Foner, ed., *The Complete Writings of Thomas Paine*, 2 vols. (New York: Citadel Press, 1945), 2:15–19; Jordan, *White over Black*, 291–94.

13. Rhys Isaac, *The Transformation of Virginia, 1749–1790* (Chapel Hill: University of North Carolina Press, 1982), chaps. 8–9; James D. Essig, *The Bonds of Wickedness: American Evangelicals Against Slavery, 1770–1808* (Philadelphia: Temple University Press, 1982); Christine Leigh Heyrman, *Southern Cross: The Beginnings of the Bible Belt* (New York: Norton, 1997); and Donald G. Mathews, *Slavery and Methodism: A Chapter in American Morality, 1780–1845* (Princeton: Princeton University Press, 1965), chaps. 1–3.

14. Robin Blackburn, *The Overthrow of Colonial Slavery, 1776–1848* (London: Verso, 1988), 163–264; C. L. R. James, *Black Jacobins: Toussaint L'Ouverture and the San Domingo Revolution* (New York: Harcourt, Brace, 1938); and David Patrick Geggus, "Slavery, War, and Revolution in the Greater Caribbean, 1789–1815," in David Barry Gaspar and David P. Geggus, eds., *A Turbulent Time: The French Revolution and the Great Caribbean* (Bloomington: University of Indiana Press, 1997), 1–50. For a deft summary of how events in France shaped the demise of slavery in Saint Domingue see Carolyn E. Fick, "The French Revolution in Saint Domingue: A Triumph or a Failure?," in Gaspar and Geggus, *Turbulent Time*, 51–75; Carolyn E. Fick, *The Making of Haiti: The Saint Domingue Revolution from Below* (Knoxville: University of Tennessee Press, 1990); and Julius S. Scott, "The Common Wind: Currents of Afro-American Communication in the Era of the Haitian Revolution" (PhD diss., Duke University, 1986), chap. 5.

2. SIMPLE TRUTHS

1. Stated by former slave Sallie Crane, quoted in Mia Bay, *The White Image in the Black Mind: African-American Ideas about White People, 1830–1925* (New York: Oxford University Press, 2000), 168.

2. David Eltis, *The Rise of African Slavery in the Americas* (Cambridge: Cambridge University Press, 2000), 220–23.

3. Kenneth M. Stampp, *The Peculiar Institution: Slavery in the Ante-Bellum South* (New York: Random House, 1956), 61–65.

4. Stated by an antebellum traveler in Mississippi, quoted in Stampp, *Peculiar Institution*, 34; stated by fugitive slave Henry Bibb, quoted in *Narrative of the Life and Adventures of Henry Bibb*, in *Puttin' On Ole Massa*, ed. Gilbert Osofsky (New York: Harper and Row, 1969), 65.

5. John W. Blassingame, *The Slave Community: Plantation Life in the Antebellum South*, rev. and enl. ed. (New York: Oxford University Press, 1979), 251.

6. See, for example, Peter Kolchin, *American Slavery: 1619–1877* (New York: Hill and Wang, 1993), 22–23, 100–101.

7. Deborah Gray White, *Ar'n't I a Woman? Female Slaves in the Plantation South*, rev. ed. (New York: W. W. Norton, 1999), 113; stated by Frances Kemble, quoted in Charles H. Nichols, *Many Thousand Gone: The Ex-Slaves Account of Their Bondage and Their Freedom* (Bloomington: Indiana University Press, 1963), 59.

8. Stampp, *Peculiar Institution*, 141; ibid.

9. B. A. Botkin, ed., *Lay My Burden Down: A Folk History of Slavery* (Chicago: University of Chicago Press, 1945), 85, 75.

10. Stated by former slave Katie Rowe of Arkansas, quoted in ibid., 123.

11. Stampp, *Peculiar Institution*, 180.

12. Leslie Howard Owens, *This Species of Property: Slave Life and Culture in the Old South* (New York: Oxford University Press, 1976), 130–31.

13. Stampp, *Peculiar Institution*, 141–91.

14. Blassingame, *Slave Community*, 257.

15. Ibid.

16. Stampp, *Peculiar Institution*, 207–13.

17. Stated by former slave Clayborn Gantling of Florida, quoted in Botkin, *Lay My Burden Down*, 6–7.

18. Stated by former slave Manda Walker of South Carolina, quoted in ibid., 169; Sally E. Hadden, *Slave Patrols: Law and Violence in Virginia and the Carolinas* (Cambridge: Harvard University Press, 2001), 123, 59–60.

19. Stated by fugitive slave Harriet Jacobs in her narrative *Incidents in the Life of a Slave Girl* (Mineola, N.Y.:

Dover Publishing, 2001), 66.

20. Stated by former slave Mary Reynolds of Louisiana, quoted in Botkin, *Lay My Burden Down*, 122; Melton McLaurin, *Celia, A Slave* (Athens: University of Georgia Press, 1991), 21, 110.

21. Bibb, *Narrative of the Life and Adventures of Henry Bibb*, 120; Solomon Northup, *Twelve Years a Slave: Narrative of Solomon Northup*, quoted in Osofsky, *Puttin' On Ole Massa*, 321.

22. White, *Ar'n't I a Woman?* 31–33. Stated by a former slave, quoted in Ophelia S. Egypt, J. Masouka, and Charles S. Johnson, eds., *Unwritten History of Slavery: Autobiographical Accounts of Negro Ex-Slaves*, vol. 18 of *The American Slave, A Composite Autobiography*, ed. George Rawick (1945; Westport, Conn.: Greenwood, 1972), 92.

23. Ulrich Bonnell Phillips, ed., *Plantation and Frontier Documents, 1649–1863*, 2 vols. (Cleveland: Arthur Clarke, 1909), 1:312; Bay, *White Image in the Black Mind*, 99–101; stated by Kemble and the former slave Lula Cottonham Walker of Alabama, quoted in ibid., 130.

24. Botkin, *Lay My Burden Down*, 160–62.

25. White, *Ar'n't I a Woman?* 101–102; Richard Dunn, "The Tale of Two Plantations: Slave Life at Mesopotamia in Jamaica and Mount Airy in Virginia, 1799–1828," *William and Mary Quarterly* (January 1977): 58; White, *Ar'n't I a Woman?* 102.

26. A former slave, quoted in Bay, *White Image in the Black Mind*, 120.

27. Ibid., 161–69. The best explanations of this can be found in ibid., 117–49, and Lawrence W. Levine, *Black Culture and Black Consciousness: Afro-American Folk Thought from Slavery to Freedom* (New York: Oxford University Press, 1977), 10–55.

28. Stated by former slave Katie Sutton, quoted in Bay, *White Image in the Black Mind*, 153; Stampp, *Peculiar Institution*, 156–62; Jacobs, *Incidents in the Life of a Slave Girl*, 59.

29. Eugene D. Genovese, *Roll Jordan Roll: The World the Slaves Made* (New York: Random House, 1972), 208.

30. Levine, *Black Culture and Black Consciousness*, 34–37, 50. Stated by former slave H. B. Holloway of Arkansas, quoted in ibid., 35.

31. Quoted in ibid., 41.

32. From a slave song, quoted in ibid., 51.

33. From a slave song, quoted in ibid., 39, 51.

34. Ibid., 55–58.

35. Ibid., 66.

36. Ibid.

37. Ibid., 63.

38. Genovese, *Roll Jordan Roll*, 223.

39. Jones and a former slave quoted in Levine, *Black Culture and Black Consciousness*, 74.

40. Former slave Josephine Bacchus of South Carolina, quoted in Genovese, *Roll Jordan Roll*, 227.

41. White, *Ar'n't I a Woman?* 124–25.

42. Daniel C. Littlefield, *Rice and Slaves, Ethnicity and the Slave Trade in Colonial South Carolina* (Baton Rouge: Louisiana State University Press, 1981), 63; James Redpath, *The Roving Editor, or Talks with Slaves in Southern States* (New York: Burdick, 1859), 40–41.

43. Helen T. Catterall, ed., *Judicial Cases Concerning American Slavery and the Negro*, 5 vols. (Washington, D.C.: Carnegie Institute of Washington, 1936), 1:411.

44. White, *Ar'n't I a Woman?* 67–69, 103–104.

45. Former slave quoted in ibid., 110.

46. Botkin, *Lay My Burden Down*, 145; White, *Ar'n't I a Woman?* 143–45.

47. Ibid., 97.

48. Marli F. Weiner, *Mistresses and Slaves: Plantation Women in South Carolina, 1830–1880* (Urbana: University of Illinois Press, 1998), 131.

49. See White, *Ar'n't I a Woman?* 155; Genovese, *Roll Jordan Roll*, 486, 487–90; and Blassingame, *Slave Community*, 179. Former slave Louisa Adams of North Carolina, quoted in Genovese, *Roll Jordan Roll*, 486.

50. White, *Ar'n't I a Woman?*, 155.

51. Botkin, *Lay My Burden Down*, 189.

52. See Levine, *Black Culture and Black Consciousness*, 106.

53. Ibid., 99.

54. Ibid., 81–135.

55. White, *Ar'n't I a Woman?* 151–52.

56. Michael Meyer, ed., *Frederick Douglass: The Narrative and Selected Writings* (New York: Random House, 1984), 75–81, 138–51.

57. Ibid., 151.

58. Nichols, *Many Thousand Gone*, 114–15; former slave quoted in Genovese,

Roll Jordan Roll, 649.

59. Botkin, *Lay My Burden Down*, 123.

60. Brown and the Crafts in Nichols, *Many Thousand Gone*, 115–16; stated by fugitive slave Austin Steward, quoted in Blassingame, *Slave Community*, 194.

61. Nichols, *Many Thousand Gone*, 101, 160.

62. Still and Penn quoted in White, *Ar'n't I a Woman?* 72.

63. Ibid., 72–74.

64. Ibid., 74.

65. Ibid., 74–75; Johnson and an antebellum Virginia planter quoted in Blassingame, *Slave Community*, 248.

66. White, *Ar'n't I a Woman?* 75–77.

67. Ibid., 79.

68. Stated by an antebellum Virginia planter, quoted in ibid., 80; also see ibid., 79–82.

69. Ibid., 64–86.

70. Ibid., 87–88.

71. Blassingame, *Slave Community*, 122–23.

72. Ibid., 126.

73. Historian Michael P. Johnson has recently renewed the debate over the reality of the Vesey conspiracy. His reading of the court documents, including the trial transcripts, leads him to believe that Vesey did not conspire to revolt, but that city and court officials worked together to make Charleston citizens believe there had been a slave conspiracy. Several historians rebut Johnson's thesis. For Johnson's argument see Michael P. Johnson, "Denmark Vesey and His Co-Conspirators," *William and Mary Quarterly* 58, no. 4 (October 2001): 915–76. For responses see the January 2002 issue of the *William and Mary Quarterly* (vol. 59, no. 1), which contains the following relevant articles: Edward A. Pearson, "Trials and Errors: Denmark Vesey and His Historians"; Philip D. Morgan, "Conspiracy Scares"; David Robertson, "Inconsistent Contextualism: The Hermeneutics of Michael Johnson"; Thomas J. Davis, "Conspiracy and Credibility: Look Who's Talking, about What—Law Talk and Loose Talk"; Winthrop D. Jordan, "The Charleston Hurricane of 1833; Or, the Law's Rampage"; James Sidbury, "Plausible Stories and Varnished Truths"; Robert L. Paquette, "Jacobins of the Lowcountry: The Vesey Plot on Trial"; and

Michael P. Johnson, "Reading Evidence."

74. Vincent Harding, *There is a River: The Black Struggle for Freedom in America* (San Diego: Harcourt, Brace Jovanovich, 1981), 66, 72, 65–72.

75. Ibid., 77–81, 94–100.

3. FROM MORAL SUASION TO POLITICAL CONFRONTATION

1. For the biographical treatment of Phillips that informs this essay at numerous points see James Brewer Stewart, *Wendell Phillips: Liberty's Hero* (Baton Rouge: Louisiana State University Press, 1986). For the quotation see Wendell Phillips, "The War for the Union," in *Speeches, Lectures and Letters* (Boston: Higginson and Lee, 1863), 438–39.

2. Stewart, *Wendell Phillips*; also see Richard Hofstadter, "Wendell Phillips: Patrician as Agitator," in *The American Political Tradition and the Men Who Made It* (New York: Alfred Knopf, 1948), 137–63.

3. Stewart, *Wendell Phillips*, 117–76.

4. Descriptions of Phillips's oratory are found in ibid., 177–95. Quotations are found in the *Ohio State Journal*, reprinted in the *Liberator*, April 5, 1861; also see the *Liberator*, December 15, 1850, and February 19, 1855.

5. Vast amounts have been written about the development of antislavery ideology in the free states and secessionist ideology in the South in the 1840s and 1850s. Two fine introductions include Eric Foner, *Free Soil, Free Labor, Free Men: The Ideology of the Republican Party before the Civil War* (New York: Oxford University Press, 1970) and William J. Cooper Jr., *The South and the Politics of Slavery, 1828–1856* (Baton Rouge: Louisiana State University Press, 1978).

6. The fullest recent treatment of the development of immediatist religious sensibility is Robert B. Abzug, *Cosmos Crumbling: American Reform and the Religious Imagination* (New York: Oxford University Press, 1994). See also Bertram Wyatt-Brown, *Lewis Tappan and the Evangelical War Against Slavery* (Cleveland, Ohio: Press of Case Western Reserve, 1969), 78–125, and Ronald Walters, *The Antislavery Appeal: Abolitionism after 1830* (Baltimore: Johns Hopkins University Press, 1978).

7. For the historical contexts that gave rise to these feelings of empathy see Elizabeth B. Clark, "'The Sacred Rights of the Weak': Pain, Sympathy and the Culture of Individual Rights in Antebellum America," *Journal of American History* 82 (1995): 463–93.

8. Garrison quoted in the *Liberator*, August 7, 1832; February 2, 1833; and December 14, 1833.

9. For deeper explanations of these trends see John Ashworth, *Slavery, Capitalism and Politics in the Antebellum Republic*, vol. 1, *Commerce and Compromise, 1820–1850* (New York: Cambridge University Press, 1995); Walter Johnson, *Soul by Soul: Life Inside the Antebellum Slave Mart* (New York: Cambridge University Press, 1999); and Thomas O'Connor, *The Lords of the Loom: The Cotton Whigs and the Coming of the Civil War* (New York: Alfred Knopf, 1968).

10. A full, recent discussion of the Constitution's relationship to slavery is Paul Finkelman, *Slavery and the Founders: Race and Liberty in the Age of Jefferson* (London: M. E. Sharp, 1996). For the broader implications of slavery's relationship to federal governance see Leonard L. Richards, *The Slave Power: The Free North and Southern Domination* (Baton Rouge: Louisiana State University Press, 2000).

11. See John M. McFaul, "A Expedience vs. Morality: Jacksonian Politics and Slavery," *Journal of American History* (1975): 24–39; Michael F. Holt, *The Political Crisis of the 1850s* (New York: Norton, 1978), 17–33; and Leonard L. Richards, "Jacksonians and Slavery," in Lewis Perry and Michael Fellman, eds., *Antislavery Reconsidered: New Perspectives on the Abolitionists* (Baton Rouge: Louisiana State University Press, 1978), 99–118.

12. See David Roediger, *The Wages of Whiteness: Race and the Making of the American Working Class* (New York: Verso Press, 1997); Joanne Pope Melish, *Disowning Slavery: Gradual Emancipation and Race in New England* (Ithaca: Cornell University Press, 1998); Richard S. Newman, *The Transformation of Abolitionism: Fighting Slavery in the Early Republic* (Chapel Hill: University of North Carolina Press, 2002); Patrick Rael, *Black Identity and Black Protest in the Antebellum North* (Chapel Hill: University of North Carolina Press, 2002); and James Oliver Horton and Lois Horton, *In Hope of Liberty: Culture, Community and Protest among Northern Free Blacks, 1790–1860* (New York: Oxford University Press, 1997).

13. In addition to titles in the previous note see Leon Litwack, *North of Slavery: The Negro in the Free States, 1790–1860* (New York: Oxford University Press, 1965).

14. For the fullest statement of white supremacy's multiplying influences on political culture in the early republic see Alexander Saxton, *The Rise and Fall of the White Republic* (New York: Verso Press, 1978), *passim*.

15. For nullification see William W. Freehling, *Prelude to Civil War: The Nullification Crisis in South Carolina, 1816–1836* (New York: Oxford University Press, 1969). For Walker see Peter Hinks, *To Awake My Afflicted Brethren: David Walker and the Problem of Antebellum Slave Resistance* (University Park: Pennsylvania State University Press, 1997). Samuel E. Sewall to Samuel J. May, July 7, 1831, Antislavery Collection, Boston Public Library. For Garrison quote see the *Liberator*, April 16, 1832.

16. For an overview of these activities see James Brewer Stewart, *Holy Warriors: The Abolitionists and American Slavery* (New York: Hill and Wang, 1997), 51–74.

17. Valuable accounts of these developments include Leonard L. Richards, *"Gentlemen of Property and Standing": Antiabolitionist Mobs in Jacksonian America* (New York: Oxford University Press, 1970); William Lee Miller, *Arguing About Slavery: The Great Battle in the United States Congress* (New York: Oxford University Press, 1996); and Leonard L. Richards, *The Life and Times of Congressman John Quincy Adams* (New York: Oxford University Press, 1986).

18. See Richards, *"Gentlemen of Property and Standing,"* and James Brewer Stewart, "The Emergence of Racial Modernity and the Rise of the White North," *Journal of the Early Republic* (summer 1998): 202–11.

19. Ibid. See also George R. Price and James Brewer Stewart, *To Heal the Scourge of Prejudice: The Life and Writings of Hosea Easton* (Amherst: University of Massachusetts Press, 1999), 16–25.

20. For Lovejoy see Merton L. Dillon, *Elijah Lovejoy: Abolitionist Editor* (Champaign-Urbana: University of Illinois Press, 1965). Also see the *Liberator*, December 8, 1837.

21. The fullest, most perceptive analysis of these abolitionist factions and their respective beliefs remains Aileen Kraditor, *Means and Ends in American Abolitionism: Garrison and His Critics on Strategy and Tactics, 1835–1854* (reprint, New York: Ivan Dee Publishers, 1989).

22. This interpretation of the evolution of white abolitionism is developed most fully in James Brewer Stewart, "Peaceful Hopes and Violent Experiences: The Evolution of Radical and Reforming Abolitionism," *Civil War History* (December 1971): 293–309.

23. On this aspect of Phillips's career see Stewart, *Wendell Phillips*, 54–76. For Garrison quote see *National Anti-Slavery Standard*, May 25, 1867.

24. The best and most recent examination of black abolitionists' resistance to colonization, and of their activism prior to the 1830s, is Newman, *Transformation of American Abolitionism*.

25. For these developments, and for excellent recent studies of black as well as white abolitionism, see ibid.; Patrick Rael, *Black Identity and Black Protest*; and Paul Goodman, *Of One Blood: The Abolitionists and the Origins of Racial Equality* (Berkeley: University of California Press, 1998).

26. Goodman, *Of One Blood*, 11–65.

27. The best studies of black abolitionism and its transformation in the 1840s and 1850s are Jane H. Pease and William H. Pease, *They Who Would Be Free: Blacks' Search for Freedom, 1831–1861* (New York: Oxford University Press, 1974); Benjamin Quarles, *The Black Abolitionists* (New York: Oxford University Press, 1965); R. J. M. Blackett, *Building an Antislavery Wall: Black Americans in the Atlantic Abolitionist Movement, 1830–1860* (Baton Rouge: Louisiana State

University Press, 1983); Donald Yacovone, "The Transformation of the African American Temperance Movement, 1827–1854," *Journal of the Early Republic* (fall 1988): 282–97; and Julie Winch, *Philadelphia's Black Elite: Activism, Accommodation, and the Struggle for Autonomy* (Philadelphia: University of Pennsylvania Press, 1988).

28. Carleton Mabee, *The Non-Violent Abolitionists from 1830 through the Civil War* (New York: Macmillan 1970) and Stewart, *Holy Warriors*, 127–49.

29. Donald M. Jacobs, "The Nineteenth Century Struggle over School Segregation in Boston," *Journal of Negro Education* 39 (1970): 76–85; Stewart, *Wendell Phillips*, 99–100.

30. Litwack, *North of Slavery*, 64–112.

31. A fine study of relationships between legal systems and struggles for equality is Robert Cover, *Justice Accused: Antislavery and the Judicial Process* (New Haven: Yale University Press, 1975). See also Litwack, *North of Slavery*, 247–79.

32. A path-breaking account of abolitionist activities south of the Mason-Dixon line, including "slave stealing," are two books by Stanley Harrold, *The Abolitionists and the South, 1831–1861* (Lexington: University Press of Kentucky, 1995) and *Subversives: Antislavery Community in Washington, D.C., 1828–1865* (Baton Rouge: Louisiana State University Press, 2003).

33. James G. Birney to Ezekial Webb and others, October 6, 1836, in Dwight L. Dumond, *The Letters of James Gillespie Birney, 1831–1857*, 2 vols. (Ann Arbor: University of Michigan Press, 1938), 1:363. The fullest discussion of the relationship between civil liberty concerns and antislavery feelings in the North remains Russel Blaine Nye, *Fettered Freedom: Civil Liberties and the Slavery Controversy* (Ann Arbor: University of Michigan Press, 1949).

34. Stewart, *Wendell Phillips*, 120–21.

35. These trends are discussed in greater detail in Stewart, *Holy Warriors*, 151–80.

36. Phillips quoted in Stewart, *Wendell Phillips*, 155.

37. Garrison quoted in the *Liberator*, October 16, 1857. For a good survey of the increasingly militant methods

of abolitionists in the 1850s see Jane H. Pease and William H. Pease, "Confrontation and Abolition in the 1850s," *Journal of American History* (March 1972): 923–37.

38. The literature on John Brown is vast and is effectively introduced by Stephen Oates in his biography of Brown, *To Purge This Land with Blood: A Biography of John Brown* (New York: Harper and Row, 1970) and by Benjamin Quarles, *Allies for Freedom: Blacks and John Brown* (New York: Oxford University Press, 1974). Also see John Stauffer, *Black Hearts of Men: Abolitionism and the Transformation of Race* (Cambridge: Harvard University Press, 2001).

39. Stewart, *Wendell Phillips*, 202–208.

40. Useful analyses of planters' frightened responses to abolitionism and the Republican Party are found in Stephanie McCurry, *Masters of Small Worlds: Yeoman Households, Gender Relations and the Political Culture of the Antebellum South Carolina Low Country* (New York: Oxford University Press, 1997) and Cooper, *South and Politics of Slavery*.

4. ABOVE GROUND ON THE UNDERGROUND RAILROAD

1. Frederick Douglass, *My Bondage and My Freedom* (1855; reprint, New York: Dover Publications, 1969), 323.

2. Samuel Ringgold Ward, *Autobiography of a Fugitive Slave: His Anti-Slavery Labours in the United States, Canada, and England* (London: John Snow, 1855), 161.

3. John W. Blassingame, *The Slave Community: Plantation Life in the Antebellum South* (New York: Oxford University Press, 1972), 112; "Narrative of William Wells Brown" (1848), in Gilbert Osofsky, ed., *Puttin' On Ole Massa: The Slave Narratives of Henry Bibb, William Wells Brown, and Solomon Northup* (New York: Harper and Row, 1969), 217. John P. Parker, *His Promised Land: The Autobiography of John P. Parker, Former Slave and Conductor on the Underground Railroad*, ed. Stuart Seely Sprague (New York: W. W. Norton, 1996), 138. See also Charles L. Blockson, *The Underground Railroad: First-Person Narratives of Escapes to Freedom in the North* (New York: Prentice Hall,

1987) for the accounts of Daniel Fisher from South Carolina (67–70) and Harry Grimes from North Carolina (73–75).

4. Larry Gara, *The Liberty Line: The Legend of the Underground Railroad* (1961; reprint, Lexington: University of Kentucky Press, 1967), 3.

5. Oliver Jensen, *Railroads in America* (New York: Bonanza Books, 1975), 32, 36; Sarah H. Gordon, *Passage to Union: How the Railroads Transformed American Life, 1829–1929* (Chicago: Ivan R. Dee, 1996), 15. On the influence of technology on the formation of American moral values see John F. Kasson, *Civilizing the Machine: Technology and Republican Values in America, 1776–1900* (New York: Penguin Books, 1976).

6. George P. Rawick, *The American Slave: A Composite Autobiography,* vol. 17, pt. 1 (Westport, Conn.: Greenwood Publishing, 1972), 146; Gara, *Liberty Line,* 149; *Narrative of the Life and Adventures of Henry Bibb, an American Slave* (1845), reprinted in Osofsky, *Puttin' On Ole Massa,* 82; John Hope Franklin and Loren Schweninger, *Runaway Slaves: Rebels on the Plantation* (New York: Oxford University Press, 1999), 229; W. H. Lyford in Gara, *Liberty Line,* 42.

7. Franklin and Schweninger, *Runaway Slaves,* 100–101.

8. Rawick, *American Slave,* vol. 2, pt. 1, 1; Frederick Douglass, *Life and Times of Frederick Douglass: His Early Life as a Slave, His Escape from Bondage, and His Complete History* (1892; reprint, New York: Collier Books, 1962), 39.

9. Norman R. Yetman, *Life Under the "Peculiar Institution": Selections from the Slave Narrative Collection* (New York: Holt, Rinehart, and Winston, 1970), 240–41.

10. Franklin and Schweninger, *Runaway Slaves,* 101; Herbert Aptheker, "Maroons Within the Present Limits of the United States," 1939, reprinted in Richard Price, ed., *Maroon Societies: Rebel Slave Communities in the Americas* (Garden City, N.Y.: Anchor Books, 1973), 159, 163.

11. Frederick Law Olmstead, *The Cotton Kingdom: A Traveller's Observations on Cotton and Slavery in the American Slave States,* ed. Arthur M. Schlesinger (New York: Alfred A. Knopf, 1970), 121. Ishreal Massie, in

Charles L. Perdue Jr., Thomas E. Barden, and Robert K. Phillips, eds., *Weevils in the Wheat: Interviews with Virginia Ex-Slaves* (Charlottesville: University Press of Virginia, 1976), 209–10. For a similar hideout used by a Mississippi fugitive see Yetman, *Life Under the "Peculiar Institution,"* 128.

12. Kevin Mulroy, *Freedom on the Border: The Seminole Maroons in Florida, the Indian Territory, Coahuila, and Texas* (Lubbock: Texas Tech University Press, 1993), 9. Also see Jane Landers, "Gracia Real de Santa Teresa de Mose: A Free Black Town in Spanish Colonial Florida," *Florida Historical Quarterly* 95 (1900): 9–30; Thomas S. Jesup in Kenneth W. Porter, *The Black Seminoles: History of a Freedom-Seeking People* (Gainesville: University Press of Florida, 1996), 67.

13. Ibid., 39; see the map of the major battles of the Second Seminole War. William Bartram, *Travels and Other Writings, 1773–74* (New York: Literary Classics of the United States, 1996), 170–71, provides details of the Seminole town of Cuscowilla. See also Peter Nabokov and Robert Easton, *Native American Architecture* (New York: Oxford University Press, 1989), 104–14, for their discussion of town-planning practices of the Creek Indians.

14. Henry Glassie, Pattern in the Material Folk Culture of the Eastern United States (Philadelphia: University of Pennsylvania Press, 1968), 102; Jane Landers, "Free Black Plantations and Economy in East Florida, 1784–1821," in Jane Landers, *Colonial Plantations and Economy in Florida* (Gainesville: University Press of Florida, 2000), 144–45; Fred B. Kniffen and Henry Glassie, "Building in Wood in the Eastern United States: A Time-Place Perspective" (1966), reprinted in Dell Upton and John Michael Vlach, eds., *Common Places: Readings in American Vernacular Architecture* (Athens: University of Georgia Press, 1986), 159–81; see especially figure 28, which charts the dominant use of saddle notching and round logs for buildings in the South. John M. Goggin, "The Seminole Negroes of Andros Island, Bahamas," *Florida Historical Quarterly* 24 (1946), 206;

Rawick, *American Slave,* vol. 5, pt. 4, 2.

15. Douglass, *My Bondage,* 306; Gerald W. Mullin, *Flight and Rebellion: Slave Resistance in Eighteenth-Century Virginia* (New York: Oxford University Press, 1972), 95, 118; Stanley Harrold, "The Pearl Affair: The Washington Riot of 1848," *Records of the Columbia Historical Society* 50 (1980), 140–60. Also see Mary Kay Ricks, "A Passage to Freedom," *Washington Post Magazine,* February 17, 2002, 20–23, 34–36.

16. William Still, *The Underground Railroad* (Philadelphia: Porter and Coates, 1872), 46, 98, 212, 482, 243.

17. W. Jeffrey Bolster, *Black Jacks: African American Seamen in the Age of Sail* (Cambridge: Harvard University Press, 1997), 191, 235–39; C. Peter Ripley, ed., *Witness for Freedom: African American Voices on Race, Slavery, and Emancipation* (Chapel Hill: University of North Carolina, 1993), 93–95.

18. David C. Cecelski, *The Waterman's Song: Slavery and Freedom in Maritime North Carolina* (Chapel Hill: University of North Carolina, 2001), 124.

19. Douglass, *My Bondage,* 147; Cecelski, *Waterman's Song,* 27, 136–37; Harriet A. Jacobs, *Incidents in the Life of a Slave Girl,* ed. Jean Fagan Yellin (Cambridge: Harvard University Press, 1987), 156–58, describes how her uncle, who was a steward aboard a sailing vessel, helped her find passage on a ship bound for Philadelphia.

20. Mary Thomas, as told to Levi C. Hubert, October 2, 1938, Folklore Project, Life Histories (1936–39), Manuscript Division, Library of Congress, Washington, D.C. Charles C. Smiley, *A True Story of Lawnside, N.J.* (Camden, N.J.: Robert J. Wythe, 1921), 17.

21. See John Michael Vlach, "'Not Mansions . . . But Good Enough': Slave Quarters as Bi-cultural Expression," in Ted Ownby, *Black and White Cultural Interaction in the Antebellum South* (Jackson: University Press of Mississippi, 1993), 89–114, especially figures 1–4.

22. The origins of the name Timbuctoo are unknown, but the use of African place names for other black sites in

New Jersey has been noted. Guineatown, for example, is the name of a cluster of ten houses in Upper Alloways Creek Township in Salem County, New Jersey. See Ernest Lyght, *Path of Freedom: The Black Presence in New Jersey's Burlington County, 1659–1900* (Cherry Hill, N.J.: E. and E. Publishing, 1978), 39–40.

23. The story of Pokepatch, Ohio, is summarized on the Web site of the National Forest Service [www.fs.fed.us/r9/wayne/ur_home.html]; Coy D. Robbins, *Forgotten Hoosiers: African Heritage in Orange County, Indiana* (Bowie, Md.: Heritage Books, 1994), 19, 27.

24. See Elizabeth Fuller, "Miller Grove, An African-American Farming Community, Pope County, Illinois (1840–1920)," (master's thesis, Southern Illinois University, 2001).

25. Juliet E. K. Walker, *Free Frank: A Black Pioneer on the Antebellum Frontier* (Lexington: University Press of Kentucky, 1983), chaps. 6–7, and see especially 148–49.

26. Alfred Matthews, *History of Cass County, Michigan* (Chicago: Wareman, Watkins and Company, 1882), 110; Harold B. Fields, "Free Negroes in Cass County," *Michigan History* 44 (1960): 378. Also see Carrie Eldridge, *Cabell County's Empire for Freedom* (Huntington, W.V.: Marshall University, 1999); Marcia Renee Sawyer, "Surviving Freedom: African-American Farm Households in Cass County, Michigan, 1832–1880" (PhD diss., Michigan State University, 1990), 47. A team of students under the direction of Michael Nassaney, an archaeologist in the anthropology department at Western Michigan University, is currently investigating the site of Ramptown. See Lynn Turner, "Town of Freedom Found," *Kalamazoo Gazette*, June 15, 2002, for a report of the promising results of the first field survey.

27. Bryan D. Fruehling and Robert H. Smith, "Subterranean Hideaways of the Underground Railroad in Ohio: An Architectural, Archaeological, and Historical Critique of Local Traditions," *Ohio History* 102 (summer–autumn 1993): 98–117. Also see Charles McCool Snyder, "Oswego's

Abolitionists and Their Tunnels," *New York Folklore Quarterly* 17 (1961): 95–103; Carol Kammen, "The UGRR and Local History," *CRM: Cultural Resource Management* 21, no. 4 (1998), 11, provides comment on tunneling myths in the vicinity of Ithaca, New York. National Park Service, *Underground Railroad* (Washington, D.C.: Department of Interior, 1998), 12, describes how the Western Reserve Historical Society in Cleveland, Ohio, was twice called to inspect Saint John's Episcopal Church for a reputed Underground Railroad tunnel. On both occasions no signs of a tunnel could be found. Gara, *Liberty Line*, 7.

28. Levi Coffin, *Reminiscences of Levi Coffin* (1876; reprint, New York: Augustus M. Kelly, 1968), 112, 301; Douglass, *Life and Times*, 266; James Oliver Horton and Lois E. Horton, *Black Bostonians: Family Life and Community Struggle in the Antebellum North* (New York: Holmes and Meier, 1979), 55.

29. Wilbur H. Siebert, *The Underground Railroad from Freedom to Slavery* (New York: Macmillan, 1898), 76–77; also see the Wilbur H. Siebert Collection, Ohio Historical Society, Columbus, H.U. Johnson, *From Dixie to Canada: Romances and Realities of the Underground Railroad* (1896; reprint, Westport, Conn.: Negro Universities Press, 1970), 107.

30. Wilbur H. Siebert, "Beginnings of the Underground Railroad in Ohio," *Ohio History* 15 (1947): 78; Parker, *His Promised Land*, 86; B. A. Botkin, ed., *Lay My Burden Down: A Folk History of Slavery* (Chicago: University of Chicago Press, 1945), 187.

31. Siebert, "Beginnings of the Underground Railroad in Ohio," 77, and Parker, *His Promised Land*, 156, n. 4; Coffin, *Reminiscences*, 107, 304, 448; Still, *Underground Railroad*, 623–41, 746–47; and Blockson, *Underground Railroad*, 166–68.

32. Emerson Klees, *Underground Railroad Tales: With Routes Through the Finger Lakes Region* (Rochester: Friends of the Finger Lakes Publishing, 1997), 127; Carol Lee and Dan G. Deibler, "National Historic Landmark Nomination for the F. Julius Lemoyne House," United States Department of Interior, National

Park Service, August 13, 1996, 13–14, and William J. Switala, *Underground Railroad in Pennsylvania* (Mechanicsburg, Penn.: Stackpole Books, 2001), 68, 78, who indicates that Tar Adams and Samuel W. Dorsey were two known black conductors on the Underground Railroad operating in Washington County.

33. Horton and Horton, *Black Bostonians*, 101. In Henry David Thoreau, *A Year in Thoreau's Journal: 1851* (New York: Penguin, 1993), 247, Thoreau describes how he purchased a train ticket to Canada for escaping slave Henry Williams, and then made sure the fugitive avoided police surveillance and got safely aboard.

34. Robin Winks, *The Blacks in Canada: A History* (New Haven: Yale University Press, 1971), 234–35; Michael Wayne, "The Black Population of Canada West on the Eve of the American Civil War: A Reassessment Based on the Manuscript Census of 1861," *Histoire Sociale/Social History* 28, no. 56 (1995): 472–74.

35. *Refugees from Slavery in Canada West: Report to the Freedman's Inquiry Commission* (1864; reprint, New York: Arno Press, 1969), 66.

36. Fred Coyne Hamil, *The Valley of the Lower Thames—1640 to 1850* (Ontario: University of Toronto Press, 1951), 117–18, 122–23; Josiah Henson, *An Autobiography of the Reverend Josiah Henson* (1881; reprint, Reading, Mass.: Addison-Wesley Publishing, 1969), 92.

37. William H. Pease and Jane H. Pease, *Black Utopia: Negro Communal Experiments in America* (Madison: State Historical Society of Wisconsin, 1963), 65, 113; Annie Straith Jamieson, *William King: Friend and Champion of Slaves* (1925; reprint, New York: Negro Universities Press, 1969), 143–44, and Winks, *Blacks in Canada*, 217.

38. Pease and Pease, *Black Utopia*, 97; Ripley, *Witness for Freedom*, 190; Franklin and Schweninger, *Runaway Slaves*, 294.

39. Douglass, *Life and Times*, 125; Still, *Underground Railroad*, 215–17, and Coffin, *Reminiscences*, 594; National Park Service, *Underground Railroad*, 50.

40. James Birney, in August Meier and

Elliot Rudwick, *From Plantation to Ghetto* (New York: Hill and Wang, 1970), 127.

41. Gara, *Liberty Line*, 43–44.

5. SOUTHERN PASSAGES

1. National Park Service publications refer to the Underground Railroad as "the effort—sometimes spontaneous, sometimes highly organized—to assist persons held in bondage in North America to escape from slavery." They also acknowledge that early slave escapes to Spanish Florida and several other locations, such as Fort Mose and British Fort, have been designated "precursor sites" to the Underground Railroad. See the NPS Web site [www.cr.nps.gov/nr/travel/underground] and its publication *Underground Railroad*, Handbook 156 (Washington, D.C.: US Department of the Interior, 1997).

2. Jane Landers, *Black Society in Spanish Florida* (Urbana: University of Illinois Press, 1999), chap. 1.

3. Ibid., 12–13.

4. Ibid.; Ira Berlin, *Many Thousands Gone: The First Two Centuries of Slavery in North America* (Cambridge: Harvard University Press, 2000).

5. "William Dunlop's Mission to St. Augustine in 1688," *South Carolina Historical and Genealogical Magazine* 34 (January 1933): 1–30. Royal officials to the king, dated March 3, 1699, cited in Irene Wright, "Dispatches of Spanish Officials Bearing on the Free Negro Settlement of Gracia Real de Santa Teresa de Mose," *Journal of Negro History* 9 (1924): 151–52; "William Dunlop's Mission," 29–30.

6. Royal edict, November 7, 1693, SD 58-1-26, Stetson Collection (hereafter cited as SC), P. K. Yonge Library of Florida History, Gainesville (hereafter cited as PKY). Despite the royal decree of 1693, Governor Laureano de Torres y Ayala returned six newly arrived blacks and an Indian "to avoid conflicts and ruptures between the two governments" in 1697. Joseph de Zúñiga to the king, October 10, 1699, Santo Domingo 844 (hereafter cited as SD), on microfilm reel 15, PKY.

7. Landers, *Black Society*, 25.

8. Report of Governor Robert Johnson, January 12, 1719, cited in H. Roy Merrens, ed., *The Colonial South Carolina Scene, Contemporary Views, 1697–1774* (Columbia: University of South Carolina Press, 1977), 57–66; Peter H. Wood, *Black Majority: Negroes in Colonial Carolina from 1670 through the Stono Rebellion* (New York: Norton Press, 1974), 127–30; and Frank W. Klingberg, ed., *The Carolina Chronicle of Dr. Francis Le Jau, 1706–1717* (Berkeley: University of California Press, 1956), 60–137. The Yamasee had earlier harried Spanish settlements. See John H. Hann, "St. Augustine's Fallout from the Yamasee War," *Florida Historical Quarterly* 68 (October 1989): 180–200.

9. The following year Carolina enacted a new and harsher slave code. Wood, *Black Majority*, 298–99, 304; Memorial of the Fugitives, 1724, SD 844, on microfilm reel 15, PKY.

10. One of the Spanish delegates was the royal accountant, Don Francisco Menéndez Márquez, who was probably already by then the owner of Francisco Menéndez, the man who would be his namesake and the future leader of Florida's first free black town. *Documentos históricos de la Florida y la Luisiana Siglos XVI al XVII* (Madrid, 1912), 252–60. Antonio de Benavides to the king, November 11, 1725, cited in Wright, "Dispatches," 164–66; Consulta by the Council of the Indies, April 12, 1731, cited in Wright, "Dispatches," 166–72. Accord, June 27, 1730, SD 844, on microfilm reel 15, PKY.

11. June 13, 1728, British Public Record Office (hereafter cited as BPRO) Trans., XII, 61–67, cited in Wood, *Black Majority*, 305. Later English visitors to Saint Augustine recognized four former slaves taken from a plantation near Port Royal in 1726. Arthur Middleton, June 13, 1728, BPRO Trans., XIII, 61–67, and John Pearson, October 20, 1727, BPRO Trans., XIX, 127–28, cited in Wood, *Black Majority*, 305. Six years later Governor Benavides advocated sending the runaways north to foment rebellion in Carolina and paying them for English scalps, but the Council of the Indies in Spain rejected this plan. Antonio de Benavides to the king, April 27, 1733, SD 833,

Archivo General de Indias, Seville (hereafter cited as AGI).

12. The Crown actually issued two separate edicts in 1733. The first, dated October 4, 1733, forbade any future compensation to the British, reiterated the royal offer of freedom, and specifically prohibited the sale of fugitives to private citizens (no doubt in response to the auction of 1729). The second, dated October 29, 1733, commended the blacks for their bravery against the British in 1728, but it also stipulated that they would be required to complete four years of royal service as an indentured servant prior to being freed. Royal edict, October 4, 1733, SD 58-1-24, SC, PKY; Royal edict, October 29, 1733, SD 58-1-24, SC, PKY.

13. Memorial of the Fugitives, included in Manuel de Montiano to the king, March 3, 1738, SD 844, microfilm reel 15, PKY. Jorge added that a "heathen" Yamassee, Mad Dog, had betrayed Menéndez and the other black allies and sold them back into slavery, but Jorge did not hold him responsible. Rather, he blamed the Spaniards who, as Christians, should have known better. Memorial of Chief Jorge, included in Manuel de Montiano to the king, March 3, 1738, SD 844, microfilm reel 15, PKY.

14. Montiano's financially strapped predecessors had satisfied government debts to important citizens by giving them incoming fugitives as slaves. They requested reimbursement for their losses, but Montiano ruled that they had ignored the royal determination expressed in repeated decrees and, therefore, all deals were null and void and all the enslaved were free. Petition of Diego Espinosa and reply by Manuel de Montiano, May 5, 1738, SD 845, microfilm reel 16, PKY. King to Manuel de Montiano, July 15, 1741, AGI 58-1-25, SC 5943, PKY.

15. The town's name was a composite of the old Indian place name, Mose; the phrase Gracia Real, which indicates the town was established with the king's permission; and the name of the town's patron saint, Teresa of Avila, who was also the patroness of Spain. Manuel de Montiano to the king, September 16, 1740, SD 2658, AGI. Fugitive Negroes of the English

plantations to the king, June 10, 1738, SD 844, microfilm reel 15, PKY.

16. J. H. Easterby, ed., *Journal of the Commons House of Assembly, May 18, 1741–July 10, 1742* (Columbia: University of South Carolina Press, 1952), 83.

17. Allen D. Candler and Lucien L. Knight, eds., "Journal of William Stephens," *Colonial Records of the State of Georgia* (Atlanta, 1904–16), 358; Manuel de Montiano to Juan Francisco de Guemes y Horcasitas, February 16, 1739, SD 845, microfilm reel 16, PKY; Manuel de Montiano to Juan Francisco de Guemes y Horcasitas, August 31, 1738, and January 3, 1739, "Siege of St. Augustine," *Collections of the Georgia Historical Society,* vol.7, pt. 1 (hereafter cited as Letters of Montiano), (Savannah, 1909), 27; Candler and Knight, "Journal of William Stephens," *Colonial Records,* 357. Claim of Captain Caleb Davis, September 17, 1751, SD 2584, AGI; *Journal of the Commons House of Assembly, November 10, 1736—June 7, 1739,* 595–97. There is no evidence that Davis ever recouped his losses.

18. Some of these men were "cattel-hunters" belonging to Captain Macpherson, whose horses they stole, and who would have had opportunity to know the terrain. Although a large posse failed to recapture them, Indian allies of the English did kill one slave. "Account of the Negroe Insurrection," 232–33, cited in Wood, *Black Majority,* 310–11.

19. Lieutenant Governor Bull to the Duke of Newcastle, May 1739, BPRO Trans., XX, 40–41, cited in Wood, *Black Majority,* 311–12. Also see Representation of President William Bull, May 25, 1739, K. G. Davies, ed., *Calendar of State Papers, Colonial Series, America and West Indies,* vol. 44 (London, 1860–1919), 243–45. *Journal of the Commons House of Assembly, November 10, 1736–June 7, 1739,* 680–81.

20. Manuel de Montiano to Juan Francisco Guemes de Horcasitas, August 19, 1739, Letters of Montiano, 32.

21. *Journal of the Commons House of Assembly, September 12, 1739–May 10, 1740,* 63–67. The most complete analysis of Stono is offered by Wood in *Black Majority.* A more traditional account of the rebellion is found in Eugene Sirmans, *Colonial South Carolina: A Political History, 1663–1763* (Chapel Hill: University of North Carolina Press, 1966). John Thornton argues that the Stono rebels were probably not actually from Angola but from the Kongo, which traders generically referred to as the Angola Coast. See John K. Thornton, "African Dimensions of the Stono Rebellion," *American Historical Review* (October 1991): 1101–13. For more on Kongo war techniques see John K. Thornton, "African Soldiers in the Haitian Revolution," *Journal of Caribbean History* 25 (1991): 58–80.

22. Sirmans, *Colonial South Carolina,* 208. "Extract of a Letter from South Carolina Dated October 2," *Gentleman's Magazine* (London), n.s. 10 (1740): 127–29, in Michael Mullin, ed., *American Negro Slavery: A Documentary History* (Columbia: University of South Carolina Press, 1976), 84–87.

23. Wood, *Black Majority,* 326; Candler and Knight, "Journal of William Stephens," *Colonial Records,* 402–403.

24. *Runaway Slave Advertisements: A Documentary History from the 1730s to 1790,* vol. 3 (Westport, Conn.: Greenwood Press, 1983), 2, 3. Also see Daniel E. Meaders, "South Carolina Fugitives as Viewed Through Local Colonial Newspapers with Emphasis on Runaway Notices, 1732–1801," *Journal of Negro History* 60 (April 1975): 288–317; Philip D. Morgan, "Colonial South Carolina Runaways: Their Significance for Slave Culture," *Slavery and Abolition* 6 (December 1985): 57–78. Landers, *Black Society,* 61–66.

25. British Florida planters described their "new Negroes" as being from the Windward, Grain, Gold, and Guinea coasts of West Africa, from Gambia, and from Angola, and they sometimes identified them by specific "nations," such as the Sulundie or Ibo. Daniel L. Schafer, "Yellow Silk Ferret Tied round Their Wrists: African-Americans in British East Florida, 1763–1784," in *The African American Heritage of Florida,* eds. David R. Colburn and Jane Landers (Gainesville: University Press of Florida, 1995), 82–85, 71–103; and J. Leitch Wright, *Florida in the American Revolution* (Gainesville: University Press of Florida, 1975), 108–109.

26. Treaty of Paris, May 3, 1783, cited in Joseph Byrne Lockey, *East Florida, 1783–1785: A File of Documents Assembled and Many of Them Translated* (Berkeley: University of California Press, 1949), 91. Many exiled Floridians chose to return to their former homeland, but there is no clear evidence that any of the free blacks of Mose returned. Diego Eligio de la Puente died on September 25, 1790, at about age seventy and was buried the next day in the Tolomato cemetery by Father Hassett. His name, his free status, and the fact that he had been born in North America make it possible that he was related to Lieutenant Antonio Eligio de la Puente of Mose. Black Burials, Burial of Diego Eligio de la Puente, Cathedral Parish Registers, St. Augustine, vol. 2, microfilm reel 284 L, PKY. Wilbur Henry Siebert, *Loyalists in East Florida, 1783–1785: The Most Important Documents Pertaining Thereto, Edited With an Accompanying Narrative,* 2 vols. (Deland, Fla.: Florida State Historical Society, 1929), 125, 140.

27. Landers, *Black Society,* 76–82. The governor charged that "not one of them has manifested once here the least inclination to be instructed in and converted to our Holy Faith." Vicente Manuel de Zéspedes to Joseph de Ezpeleta, October 2, 1788, Cuba 1395, AGI. Proclamation of Vicente Manuel de Zéspedes, July 26, 1784, cited in Lockey, *East Florida,* 240–41.

28. Alexander Semple to Commander McFernan, December 16, 1786. "To and From the United States" microfilm reel 41, East Florida Papers (hereafter cited as EFP), PKY.

29. Landers, *Black Society,* 77, 87, 97–98, 101, 122, 148, 220–28.

30. Thomas Jefferson to Juan Nepomuceno de Quesada, December 17, 1790, and August 9, 1791. "To and From the United States," 1784–1821, microfilm reel 41, EFP, PKY.

31. Landers, *Black Society,* 67–68, 235–37; Kenneth Wiggins Porter, *The Black Seminoles,* rev. and ed. Alcione M. Amos and Thomas P. Senter (Gainesville: University Press of Florida, 1996). By the 1790s Chief

Payne was reported to "own" some twenty black slaves, along with large herds of cattle, horses, sheep, and goats. James W. Covington, *The Seminoles of Florida* (Gainesville: University Press of Florida, 1993), 29. Howard F. Klein, *Florida Indians*, vol. 2 of *Provisional Historical Gazeteer and Locational Notes on Florida Colonial Communities* (New York: Garland Press, 1964). Brent R. Weisman argues that the agricultural labor of blacks and their expansion into previously unexploited ecological zones enabled both the creation of a surplus and Seminole entry into a true plantation economy. See Howard F. Klein, "The Plantation System of the Florida Seminole Indians and Black Seminoles During the Colonial Era," in *Colonial Plantations and Economy in Florida*, ed. Jane Landers (Gainesville: University Press of Florida, 2000), 136–49.

32. Canter Brown Jr., *Florida's Peace River Frontier* (Orlando: University of Central Florida Press, 1991), 9–10; Brown, "'Sarrazota' or Runaway Negro Plantations," in ibid.; George Klos, "Blacks and the Seminole Indian Removal Debate, 1821–1835," in *African American Heritage of Florida*, eds. Colburn and Landers, 128–56. Department of Archives, *The Bahamas in the Age of Revolution, 1775–1848* (Nassau, 1989), 16.

33. John K. Mahon, *History of the Second Seminole War* (Gainesville: University Press of Florida, 1967); Mulroy, *Freedom on the Border*.

6. "FREEMAN TO THE RESCUE!"

1. Kathryn Grover, *The Fugitive's Gibraltar: Escaping Slaves and Abolitionism in New Bedford, Massachusetts* (Amherst: University of Massachusetts Press, 2001), 1; George A. Lavesque, "Inherent Reformers—Inherited Orthodoxy: Black Baptists in Boston, 1800–1873," *Journal of Negro History* 60 (1975), 492, 510; *(Pittsburgh) Morning Post*, September, 26, 1850.

2. Wendell Phillips Garrison and Francis Jackson Garrison, *William Lloyd Garrison 1805–1874*, 4 vols. (1885–89; reprint, New York: Arno Press, 1969), 3:323; Samuel J. May,

The Fugitive Slave Law and Its Victims (1861; reprint, Freeport, N.Y.: Books for Libraries Press, 1970) 22; Benjamin Quarles, *Black Abolitionists* (New York: Oxford University Press, 1969), 199.

3. *Liberator*, October 4, 1850; John Blassingame, ed., *The Frederick Douglass Papers*, vol. 2, *1847—1854* (New Haven: Yale University Press, 1982), 294–95; *Pennsylvania Freeman*, October 31, 1850; Angela Murphy, "'It Outlaws Me, and I Outlaw It!' Resistance to the Fugitive Slave Law in Syracuse, New York" (graduate seminar paper, University of Houston, 2000), 5.

4. *Pennsylvania Freeman*, October 31, 1850; *Liberator*, October 11, 1850; Carol M. Hunter, *To Set the Captives Free: Reverend Jermain Wesley Loguen and the Struggle for Freedom in Central New York, 1835–1872* (New York: Garland Publishing, 1993), 112; C. Peter Ripley, Roy E. Finkenbine, Michael F. Hembree, and Donald Yacovone, eds., *The Black Abolitionist Papers*, vol. 4, *The United States, 1847–1858* (Chapel Hill: University of North Carolina Press, 1991), 64; Grover, *Fugitive's Gibraltar*, 218; Blassingame, *Frederick Douglass Papers*, 2:277.

5. Quarles, *Black Abolitionists*, 204.

6. *Liberator*, October 11, 1850. Blacks in Harrisburg and New Bedford took a similar approach. See *Pennsylvania Freeman*, October 31, 1850; Grover, *Fugitive's Gibraltar*, 218–20; Mary D. Houts, "Black Harrisburg's Resistance to Slavery," *Pennsylvania Heritage* 4 (December 1977): 12.

7. Much of this analysis draws upon Charles M. Payne, *I've Got the Light of Freedom: The Organizing Tradition and the Mississippi Freedom Struggle* (Berkeley: University of California Press, 1995).

8. Gary Collison, *Shadrach Minkins: From Fugitive Slave to Citizen* (Cambridge: Harvard University Press, 1997), 82–87; William Still, *The Underground Railroad* (Philadelphia: Porter and Coates, 1872), 635–36; Joseph A. Berome, "The Vigilance Committee of Philadelphia," *Pennsylvania Magazine of History and Biography* 92 (July 1968): 323; Quarles, *Black Abolitionists*, 154; Dorothy Porter, "David Ruggles, An

Apostle of Human Rights," *Journal of Negro History* 28 (January 1943): 32–38; Graham Russell Hodges, *Root and Branch: African Americans in New York and East New Jersey* (Chapel Hill: University of North Carolina Press, 1999), 245–46.

9. Hunter, *To Set the Captives Free*, 113; Jayme A. Sokolow, "The Jerry McHenry Rescue and the Growth of Northern Antislavery Sentiment During the 1850s," *Journal of American Studies* 16 (1982): 430; *Pennsylvania Freeman*, October 31, 1850.

10. Quarles, *Black Abolitionists*, 150; Katherine DuPre Lumpkin, "'The General Plan Was Freedom': A Negro Secret Order on the Underground Railroad," *Phylon* 28 (Spring 1967): 66–67.

11. Victor Ullman, *Martin R. Delany: The Beginnings of Black Nationalism* (Boston: Beacon Press, 1971), 27; Frank A. Rollin, *Life and Public Services of Martin R. Delany* (1883; reprint, New York: Arno Press, 1969), 43; *(Pittsburgh) Morning Post*, March 8, 1855; Edward Raymond Turner, "The Underground Railroad in Pennsylvania," *Pennsylvania Magazine of History and Biography* 36 (1912): 315; Lumpkin, "'The General Plan Was Freedom,'" 71–74.

12. *(Pittsburgh) Gazette*, September 24, 25, and 26, 1850; Roy E. Finkenbine, "Boston's Black Churches: Institutional Centers of the Antislavery Movement," in Donald M. Jacobs, ed., *Courage and Conscience: Black and White Abolitionists in Boston* (Bloomington: Indiana University Press, 1993), 182. Some confusion exists over the number that fled Buffalo. George Weir Jr. of Buffalo wrote to Frederick Douglass, "Not three have left either church and I know that not three have left the whole city." See *(Syracuse) North Star*, March 20, 1851. Quarles, *Black Abolitionists*, 200; Still, *Underground Railroad*, 764–66; Blassingame, *Frederick Douglass Papers*, 2:245. Donald Yacovone has called this "the largest expatriate movement in American history." See Donald Yacovone, *Samuel Joseph May and the Dilemmas of the Liberal Persuasion 1797–1871* (Philadelphia: Temple University Press, 1991), 139.

13. *Anti Slavery Bugle*, February 16, 1850; Grover, *Fugitive's Gibraltar*, 222; *(Pittsburgh) Morning Post*, September 26, 1850.

14. There are different versions of what Delany actually said. See Rollins, *Life and Services of Martin Delany*, 76, and J. Ernest Wright, "The Negro in Pittsburgh," an unpublished manuscript prepared for the WPA (1937), 65–66; anonymous, *The Rev. Jermain Loguen As A Slave and A Freeman. A Narrative of Real Life* (1859; reprint, New York: Arno Press, 1968), 392–93.

15. Still, *Underground Railroad*, 78, 103; Collison, *Shadrach Minkins*, 83; Quarles, *Black Abolitionists*, 202; Hallie Q. Brown, *Tales My Father Told Me and Other Stories* (Wilberforce, Ohio: Eckerle Printing, n.d.), 4–7.

16. Still, *Underground Railroad*, 558–60; Collison, *Shadrach Minkins*, 110–11; Grover, *Fugitive's Gibraltar*, 14; Hunter, *To Set the Captives Free*, 124; *(Pittsburgh) Gazette*, May 30, 1853.

17. James Oliver Horton and Lois E. Horton, *Black Bostonians: Family Life and Community Struggle in the Antebellum North* (New York: Holmes and Meier, 1979), 101; Nina Moore Tiffany, "Stories of the Fugitive Slaves, I: The Escape of William and Ellen Craft," *New England Magazine* 1 (1890): 528–30; Stanley J. and Anita Robboy, "Lewis Hayden: From Fugitive Slave to Statesman," *New England Quarterly* 46 (December 1973): 598–601; *(Pittsburgh) Gazette*, March 8, 1855; R. J. M. Blackett, *Beatings Against the Barriers: Biographical Essays in Nineteenth Century Afro-American History* (Baton Rouge: Louisiana State University Press, 1986), 57–58.

18. *Pennsylvania Freeman*, October, 31, 1850: Collison, *Shadrach Minkins*, 80.

19. Julie Winch, *A Gentleman of Color: The Life of James Forten* (New York: Oxford University Press, 2002), 232; Leonard W. Levy, "The 'Abolition Riot': Boston's First Slave Rescue," *New England Quarterly* 25 (March 1952): 87–89. Paul Gilje estimates New York City blacks rioted four times—in 1801, 1819, 1826, and 1832—as a result of attempts to protect fugitives and free blacks from slavery. See Paul Gilje, *The Road to Mobocracy: Popular Disorder in New York City, 1763–1834* (Chapel Hill:

University of North Carolina Press, 1987), 153.

20. *(Pittsburgh) Gazette*, March 8, 1855; James C. Scott, *Domination and the Arts of Resistance: Hidden Transcripts* (New Haven: Yale University Press, 1990), 150–51; Sokolow, "The Jerry McHenry Rescue," 433; Collison, *Shadrach Minkins*, 116–17; *(Pittsburgh) Gazette*, March 8, 1855.

21. Horton and Horton, *Black Bostonians*, 99.

22. Harold Schwartz, "Fugitive Slave Days in Boston," *New England Quarterly* 27 (1954): 192; *Anti Slavery Bugle*, November 16, 1850. Similar tactics were used in the effort to protect Anthony Burns. See Albert J. Von Frank, *The Trial of Anthony Burns: Freedom and Slavery in Emerson's Boston* (Cambridge: Harvard University Press, 1998), 33.

23. Philip S. Foner, *Business and Slavery: The New York Merchants and the Irrepressible Conflict* (Chapel Hill: University of North Carolina Press, 1941), 34–63; *(Augusta) Republic*, quoted in Austin Bearse, *Reminiscences of Fugitive Slave Days in Boston* (1880; reprint, New York: Arno Press, 1969).

24. Von Frank, *Trials of Anthony Burns*, 59; Yacavone, *Samuel Joseph May*, 141.

25. Leonard W. Levy, "Sims' Case: The Fugitive Slave Law in Boston in 1851," *Journal of Negro History* 35 (January 1950): 40; Foner, *Business and Slavery*, 49, 57–59; anonymous, *Rev. Jermain Loguen*, 397; Ripley et al., *Black Abolitionist Papers*, 4:48–49.

26. Garrison and Garrison, *William Lloyd Garrison*, 324. See Jane H. Pease and William H. Pease, "Confrontation and Abolition in the 1850s," *Journal of American History* 58 (March 1972): 930–31, for a discussion of these approaches.

27. R. J. M. Blackett, *Building an Antislavery Wall: Black Americans in the Atlantic Abolitionist Movement, 1830–1860* (Baton Rouge: Louisiana State University Press, 1983), 5; R. J. M. Blackett, *Thomas Morris Chester: Black Civil War Correspondent* (Baton Rouge: Louisiana State University Press, 1989), 10–11; *(Harrisburg) Borough Item*, February 10, 15, 23, 24, 28, March 10, 1853.

28. Samuel J. May, *Some Recollections of Our Antislavery Conflict* (1869; reprint, New York: Arno Press, 1968), 363–64.

7. KIDNAPPING AND RESISTANCE

1. Thomas Jefferson to John Holmes, April 22, 1820.

2. John Hope Franklin and Loren Schweninger, *Runaway Slaves: Rebels on the Plantation* (New York: Oxford University Press, 1999); Kathryn Grover, *The Fugitive's Gibraltar: Escaping Slaves and Abolitionism in New Bedford, Massachusetts* (Amherst: University of Massachusetts Press, 2001), 68–69.

3. Ira Berlin, *Slaves Without Masters: The Free Negro in the Antebellum South* (New York: Pantheon Books, 1974), 357.

4. Carol Wilson, *Freedom at Risk: The Kidnapping of Free Blacks in America, 1780–1865* (Lexington: University Press of Kentucky, 1994), 105, 83; *National Enquirer and Constitutional Advocate of Universal Liberty*, January 14, 1837, and March 25, 1837.

5. Wilson, *Freedom at Risk*, 88–95.

6. Ibid., 107; James Oliver Horton and Lois E. Horton, *In Hope of Liberty: Culture, Community and Protest Among Northern Free Blacks, 1700–1860* (New York: Oxford University Press, 1997), 237–38.

7. Ibid., 255–56.

8. James Oliver Horton and Lois E. Horton, "The Affirmation of Manhood: Black Garrisonians in Antebellum Boston," in *Courage and Conscience*, ed. Donald M. Jacobs (Bloomington: Indiana University Press for the Boston Athenaeum, 1993), 127–53.

9. James Oliver Horton and Lois E. Horton, *Black Bostonians: Family Life and Community Struggle in the Antebellum North* (New York: Holmes and Meier, 1979), 107; Dorothy Sterling, ed., *Speak Out in Thunder Tones: Letters and Other Writings by Black Northerners, 1787–1865* (Garden City, N.Y.: Doubleday and Company, 1973), 152; *National Enquirer and Constitutional Advocate of Universal Liberty*, August 3, 1836; *Liberator*, August 6, 1836, and August 13, 1836.

10. Robert C. Smedley, *History of the Underground Railroad in Chester and the Neighboring Counties of Pennsylvania* (Lancaster, Penn.: Office of the Journal, 1883), 355.

11. *Liberator*, August 6, 1836.

12. *Colored American*, April 15, 1837.

13. Ibid., April 22, 1837; *Freedom's Journal*, October 24, 1828.

14. Horton and Horton, "Affirmation of Manhood"; "Speech by Henry Highland Garnet Delivered Before the National Convention of Colored Citizens, Buffalo, New York, August 16, 1843," reprinted in vol. 3 of *Black Abolitionist Papers*, ed. C. Peter Ripley, Roy E. Finkenbine, Michael F. Hembree, and Donald Yacovone (Chapel Hill: University of North Carolina Press, 1991), 403–12, quotes on 408 and 410.

15. Paula J. Priebe, "Central and Western New York and the Fugitive Slave Law of 1850," *Afro-Americans in New York Life and History* 16, no. 1 (January 1992): 19–29; Roy E. Finkenbine, "Life in Garrison's Shadow: Boston's Black Abolitionists and the Problem of Violent Means," paper presented at the annual meeting of the American Historical Association, December 1988; *(Syracuse) North Star*, August 11, 1848.

16. Horton and Horton, *Black Bostonians*, 99; Finkenbine, "Life in Garrison's Shadow," 20–23; "Important Meeting," *Liberator*, November 4, 1842.

17. Allan Nevins, *Ordeal of the Union: Fruits of Manifest Destiny, 1847–1852* (New York: Charles Scribner's Sons, 1947), 349.

18. Jeffrey Ruggles, *The Unboxing of Henry Brown: A Biography* (Richmond: Library of Virginia, 2004).

19. Philip S. Foner, *History of Black Americans: From the Compromise of 1850 to the End of the Civil War* (Westport, Conn.: Greenwood Press, 1983), 3:33–34.

20. *Liberator*, October 4, 1850; Foner, *History of Black Americans*, 34; Paul Finkelman, ed., *Fugitive Slaves and American Courts*, series 2 (New York: Garland Publishing, 1988), 1:572.

21. *Liberator*, October 11, 1850; Finkenbine, "Life in Garrison's Shadow," 28.

22. *Liberator*, October 18, 1850; Ripley et al., *Black Abolitionist Papers*, 4:68–69.

23. R. J. M. Blackett, *Beating Against the Barriers: Biographical Essays in Nineteenth Century Afro-American History* (Baton Rouge: Louisiana State University Press, 1986), 90, 92.

24. Horton and Horton, *Black Bostonians*; James Oliver Horton and Lois E. Horton, "A Federal Assault: African Americans and the Impact of the Fugitive Slave Law of 1850," *Chicago Kent Law Review* 68, no. 3 (1993): 1179–97; *(Syracuse) North Star*, December 5, 1850.

25. *Liberator*, October 4, December 13, and October 18, 1850; *(Syracuse) North Star*, October 24, 1850.

26. Foner, *History of Black Americans*, 3:35; *Liberator*, January 17, 1851.

27. *Liberator*, January 17 and January 24, 1851; Foner, *History of Black Americans*, 3:35; *Liberator*, January 24, 1851.

28. Horton and Horton, *Black Bostonians*, 114; Gary Collison, *Shadrach Minkins: From Fugitive Slave to Citizen* (Cambridge: Harvard University Press, 1997), 117.

29. Ibid. In Montreal, Minkins worked variously as a waiter and restaurateur before he opened a small business as a barber. He lived in Montreal with his wife and children until he died in December 1875 at age sixty-three.
    In late February 1851, charges against Charles G. Davis, who had been Minkins's counsel, were dropped for lack of evidence, and Burton was determined to be the wrong Alexander Burton. Robert Morris was finally acquitted in November, and Wright's trial reconvened nearly a year later in October 1852. See *Report of the Proceedings at the Examination of Charles G. Davis, Esq., Boston, 1851*, in Finkelman, *Fugitive Slaves and American Courts*, 573–614; Collison, *Shadrach Minkins*; *Frederick Douglass' Paper*, November 27, 1851, and November 5, 1852.

30. *(Syracuse) North Star*, April 17, 1851; Horton and Horton, *Black Bostonians*, 106–107; Foner, *History of Black Americans*, 3:41–42. After his return, Sims was sold to a slave owner in Mississippi, and Bostonians did not locate him until 1860. Although the community raised about $1,800 to buy his freedom, Sims remained a slave until he escaped to Union lines in 1863 during the Civil War. He finally returned to Boston just in time to see the black regiment, the Massachusetts Fifty-Fourth, leave for war in May 1863.

31. *Liberator*, April 25, 1851; Joan D. Hedrick, *Harriet Beecher Stowe* (New York: Oxford University Press, 1994), 223.

32. "Fugitive Slaves aided by the Vigilance Committee Since the passage of the Fugitive Slave Bill, 1850," Massachusetts Anti-Slavery Society manuscript, in manuscript collection of the New York Historical Society; Stanley W. Campbell, *The Slave Catchers* (Chapel Hill: University of North Carolina Press, 1968), 199–207. Campbell found 21 cases of arrest in 1850, with 19 returned; he found 66 cases, with 58 returned, in 1851. Of the 243 fugitive slave cases that he recorded from 1852 to 1860, all but 24 were returned to slavery: 6 were released, 1 escaped, and 17 were rescued.

33. Thomas P. Slaughter, *Bloody Dawn* (New York: Oxford University Press, 1991); William Parker, "The Freedman's Story," *Atlantic Monthly*, March 1866, in Sterling, *Speak Out In Thunder Tones*, 258–61.

34. *Frederick Douglass' Paper*, June 24, 1852; Foner, *History of Black Americans*; Slaughter, *Bloody Dawn*, 109, 134–35.

35. *Frederick Douglass' Paper*, October 9, 1851. Historians have generally identified Jerry as McHenry, but credible evidence indicates this has been an error. Many contemporary accounts refer to him only as Jerry. William Henry was the man who had owned him and his mother before McReynolds. This makes it likely that he was actually called (William) Jerry Henry. See Milton C. Sernett, *North Star Country: Upstate New York and the Crusade for African American Freedom* (Syracuse: Syracuse University Press, 2002), 311 n.

36. Horton and Horton, *In Hope of Liberty;* also see *Frederick Douglass' Paper*, November 6, 1851, February 12, June 24, and July 1, 1852, February 11, March 4, June 17, and September 30, 1853, and February 26, 1852.

37. Ibid., August 26, 1853; Foner, *History of Black Americans*, 3:80; Horton and Horton, *In Hope of Liberty; Frederick Douglass' Paper*, June 23, 1854; *Provincial Freeman*, April 22, 1854.

38. Horton and Horton, *Black Bostonians*, 118; Horton and Horton, *In Hope of Liberty*, 259–60.

39. *Dred Scott v. Sanford* (1857), 19; Howard, 393; *Frederick Douglass' Paper*, June 23, 1854.

40. *Douglass' Monthly*, June 1860; Earl Conrad, *General Harriet Tubman* (1943; reprint, Washington, D.C.: Associated Publishers, 1990), 135.

41. Ibid., 136–38; *Douglass' Monthly*, June 1860.

42. *Douglass' Monthly*, May 1861.

8. A CRUSADE FOR FREEDOM

1. National Park Service, *Underground Railroad* (Washington, D.C.: US Department of the Interior, 1997).

2. W. Jeffrey Bolster, *Black Jacks: African American Seamen in the Age of Sail* (Cambridge: Harvard University Press, 1997).

3. Dorothy Sterling, ed., *Speak Out In Thunder Tones: Letters and Other Writings by Black Northerners, 1787–1865* (Garden City, N.Y.: Doubleday and Company, 1973), 175.

4. William Still, *The Underground Railroad* (1872; reprint, New York: Arno Press, 1968).

5. Charles Stearns, *Narrative of Henry Box Brown* (Boston, 1849), 59. Cited in Jeffrey Ruggles, *The Unboxing of Henry Brown: A Biography* (Richmond: Library of Virginia, 2004).

6. Ibid., 52; Stearns, *Narrative of Henry Box Brown*, 60.

7. Ibid., 60–61, cited in Ruggles, *Unboxing of Henry Brown*, 54.

8. Still, *Underground Railroad*, 70.

9. Ruggles, *Unboxing of Henry Brown*, 180.

10. Julie Winch, *Philadelphia's Black Elite: Activism, Accommodation and the Struggle for Autonomy, 1787–1848* (Philadelphia: Temple University Press, 1988).

11. "The Impartial Citizen," quoted in the *Liberator*, October 11, 1850.

12. *Liberator*, November 1, 1850.

13. *Frederick Douglass' Paper*, June 23, 1854.

14. See Still, *Underground Railroad*, 77. For the alternative description see Philip S. Foner, *History of Black Americans: From the Compromise of 1850 to the End of the Civil War* (Westport, Conn.: Greenwood Press, 1983), 3:83.

15. Still, *Underground Railroad*, 84.

16. Quoted in Foner, *History of Black Americans*, 85.

17. C. Peter Ripley, Roy E. Finkenbine, Michael F. Hembree, and Donald Yacovone, eds., *The Black Abolitionist Papers*, vol. 4, *The United States, 1847–1858* (Chapel Hill: University of North Carolina Press, 1991), 53–54.

18. Ibid., 4:56.

19. "William Still to James Miller McKim," Philadelphia, August 8, 1850, in ibid., 4:53–58.

20. Ibid., 4:57.

21. *Liberator*, April 10, 1857.

22. Ripley et al., *Black Abolitionist Papers*, 4:319.

23. Benjamin Quarles, *Allies for Freedom: Blacks and John Brown* (New York: Oxford University Press, 1974).

24. Ibid., 128.

25. "Constitution of the New England Antislavery Society," Article I, 1832, 3–4.

26. *New York Times*, July 15, 1902.

9. "SLAVERY IS WAR"

1. From *Antislavery History of the Year of John Brown: American Antislavery Society Annual Report* (1860), 61.

2. It has been suggested that Tubman was mistaken for Mary Hughes, a scrubwoman who was employed by the bank. This may explain why she was admitted to the courtroom. Jean Hoefer, *New York Alive* 6 (May–June 1986): 3.

3. Ibid. One report indicated that a large mob gathered because someone yelled "Fire!" to attract a crowd.

4. Sarah Bradford, *Scenes in the Life of Harriet Tubman* (Auburn, N.Y.: W. J. Moses, 1869), 88.

5. *(Troy, New York) Whig*, April 27, 1860.

6. *Antislavery History of the Year of John Brown* (1860), 61.

7. Tubman was deposed in legal documents to support her pension application in 1890 and 1892. See documents held in the National Archives, Pension Files WC 415288, in Washington, D.C. The Empire State Women's Club Federation erected a tombstone for Tubman in 1937. Mary Talbot, who headed the Buffalo chapter of the Empire State Federation of Colored Women's Clubs and was a personal friend and longtime supporter of Harriet Tubman, led this effort.

8. The number of trips Tubman made and the number of slaves she rescued seem to be a matter of speculation. The totals of "nineteen trips" and "more than four hundred slaves" first appeared in her obituary in Auburn, New York, in March 1913. See, for example, "Death of Aunt Harriet, Moses of her People," *Auburn Daily Advertiser,* March 11, 1913. An article published in 1912 also offered the number of nineteen trips and "over three hundred people"; see "Harriet Tubman," *American Magazine* 74 (1912): 420–22. The number of three hundred slaves rescued also appeared in "The Moses of the Negroes," *Literary Digest* 46 (1912): 913–16.

9. Bradford, *Scenes in the Life of Harriet Tubman*, 52.

10. See ibid. and Sarah Bradford's revised edition, *Harriet Tubman, the Moses of her People* (1886). Also see Earl Conrad, *Harriet Tubman* (Washington, D.C.: Associated Publishers, 1943) and Brenda Bryson, *Harriet Tubman called Moses* (1934).

11. See Dorothy Sterling, *Freedom Train: The Story of Harriet Tubman* (Garden City, N.Y.: Doubleday, 1954) and Ann Petry, *Conductor on the Underground Railroad* (1955).

12. In his correspondence, John Brown used male pronouns to refer to Tubman, as if only masculine attributes could match her accomplishments. She Richard Warch and Jonathan Fanton, eds., *John Brown* (Englewood, N.J.: Prentice Hall, 1973), 39–40.

13. Lillie B. Chace Wyman, "Harriet Tubman," *New England Magazine* 14, no. 1 (March 1896), 117.

14. Tubman might have been bedridden with illness in Massachusetts at the time. See her interview with Elizabeth Carter, in Joseph Thomas and Marsha McCabe, eds., *Spinner: People and Culture in Southeastern Massachusetts* (New Bedford, Mass.: Spinner Publications, 1987), 4:66–67.

15. Megan McClard, *Harriet Tubman: Slavery and the Underground Railroad* (Englewood Cliffs, N.J.: Silver Burdett, 1991), 37.

16. The Reverend J. S. Lane, *Maryland Slavery and Maryland Chivalry* (Philadelphia: Collins Printer, 1858), 24.

17. Bradford, *Scenes in the Life of Harriet Tubman*, 36.

18. John Bell Robinson, *Pictures of Slavery and Anti-Slavery* (1863; reprint,

Miami, Fla.: Mnemosyne Publishing, 1969), 331.

19. Ibid., 323.

20. Ibid., 324, 327

21. William Andrews and H. L. Gates Jr., eds., *The Civitas Anthology of African American Slave Narratives* (Washington, D.C.: Civitas/Counterpoint, 1999), 4.

22. Ibid., 5.

23. Charles Davis and Henry Louis Gates Jr., eds., *The Slave's Narrative* (New York: Oxford University Press, 1985), xvii.

24. Ibid., 323–27.

25. Frank A. Wilmot, *Disclosures and Confessions, etc.* (Philadelphia: Barclay and Company, 1860), 26–30.

26. Ibid., 11.

27. Ibid., 20.

28. Ibid., 35, 37.

29. Ibid., 14, 36, 38.

30. See *(Boston) Commonwealth*, July 17, 1863.

31. Bradford, *Scenes in the Life of Harriet Tubman*, 34–35.

32. *Liberator*, July 8, 1859.

33. William Wells Brown, *The Rising Son* (Boston: A. G. Brown, 1874), 536.

34. *Commonwealth*, July 17, 1863.

35. For example, see the archives of H-Minerva and other electronic lists at h-net@msu.edu (keyword search Harriet Tubman) for discussions of Tubman and gun use.

36. For differing but equally colorful accounts see Frank C. Davis, "The Moses of Her People," *New York Herald Sunday Magazine*, September 22, 1907, and "A Slave in the Family," in Samuel H. Adams, *Grandfather Stories* (New York: Random House, 1953), 270.

37. "Harriet Tubman is Dead," *Auburn Citizen*, March 11, 1913.

38. Such institutions range from the Harriet Tubman Museum in Macon, Georgia, to the Harriet Tubman Resource Center on the African Diaspora, York University (Toronto, Canada), to the Harriet Tubman Crisis Service Support in Minneapolis.

10. FLIGHT AND FIGHT

1. Edward McPherson, *The Political History of the United States during the Great Rebellion,* 2d ed. (Washington, D.C.: Philp and Solomons, 1865), 237.

Frederick Douglass, *Life and Times of Frederick Douglass: His Early Life as a Slave, His Escape from Bondage, and His Complete History* (1892; reprint, London: Collier Books, 1969), 266. A far larger number of slaves attempted unsuccessfully to escape the South, while others fled temporarily into the Southern countryside before returning on their own or being recaptured. See John Hope Franklin and Loren Schweninger, *Runaway Slaves: Rebels on the Plantation* (New York: Oxford University Press, 1999), 279–82.

2. The best discussion of these Southern initiatives is in William W. Freehling, *The Road to Disunion: Secessionists at Bay, 1776–1854* (New York: Oxford University Press, 1990).

3. Kenneth Stampp, ed., *The Causes of the Civil War*, 3d rev. ed. (New York: Simon and Schuster, 1991), 62; Charles B. Dew, *Apostles of Disunion: Southern Secession Commissioners and the Causes of the Civil War* (Charlottesville: University Press of Virginia, 2002), 10–12, 30, 33, 53, 63–65.

4. Roy P. Basler, et al., eds., *The Collected Works of Abraham Lincoln* (New Brunswick: Rutgers University Press, 1953), 4:160, 263. Hereafter referred to as Basler, *CW*.

5. Ibid., 4:48–49.

6. E. McPherson, *Political History*, 286.

7. James M. McPherson, *The Negro's Civil War: How American Negroes Felt and Acted during the War for the Union* (1965; reprint, Urbana: University of Illinois Press, 1982), 11, 18.

8. Philip S. Foner, ed., *The Life and Writings of Frederick Douglass* (New York: International, 1975), 3:99.

9. Stephens was a free black Northerner who worked as a cook and personal servant for an officer in the Union's Army of the Potomac early in the war. While performing those duties, he sent reports about what he saw and heard to the New York *Weekly Anglo-African*. Donald Yacavone, ed., *A Voice of Thunder: The Civil War Letters of George E. Stephens* (Chicago: University of Illinois Press, 1997), 15, 138, 151.

10. Ibid., 146–47, 138; J. McPherson, *Negro's Civil War*, 57–58; Leon F. Litwack, *Been in the Storm So Long: The*

Aftermath of Slavery (New York: Knopf, 1979), 61, 127.

11. William H. Lee to L. P. Walker, May 4, 1861, Record Group 109, Confederate War Department, Letters Received, entry 5, no. 957, National Archives; Litwack, *Been in the Storm So Long*, 127–30.

12. US War Department, *The War of the Rebellion: A Compilation of the Official Records of the Union and Confederate Armies* (Washington, D.C.: Government Printing Office, 1880–1901), series 2, vol. 1, 750, hereafter referred to as *O.R.*; Litwack, *Been in the Storm So Long*, 54.

13. Benjamin F. Butler, *Butler's Book: Autobiography and Personal Reminiscences* (Boston: A. M. Thayer, 1892), 1:256–58.

14. J. McPherson, *Negro's Civil War*, 28.

15. Ibid., 237–38, 195, 286–87, 44.

16. E. McPherson, *Political History*, 245–51.

17. Ibid., 211–12, 254, 239, 196.

18. Bell Irvin Wiley, *Southern Negroes: 1861–1865* (Baton Rouge: Louisiana State University Press, 1965), 10–11.

19. Basler, *CW*, 5:423, 144, 318.

20. Ibid., 5:434.

21. Ibid., 6:29–30, 5:537.

22. J. McPherson, *Negro's Civil War*, 65; Litwack, *Been in the Storm So Long*, 21.

23. Ibid., 55.

24. William T. Sherman, *Memoirs* (New York: Appleton, 1875), 2:180–81.

25. Leslie A. Schwalm, *A Hard Fight for We: Women's Transition from Slavery to Freedom in South Carolina* (Urbana: University of Illinois Press, 1997), 99; Clarence L. Mohr, *On the Threshold of Freedom: Masters and Slaves in Civil War Georgia* (Athens: University of Georgia Press, 1986), 78; Litwack, *Been in the Storm So Long*, 53; Robert Manson Myers, ed., *The Children of Pride: A True Story of Georgia in the Civil War* (New Haven: Yale University Press, 1972), 930.

26. Wiley, *Southern Negroes*. 18; James L. Roark, *Masters Without Slaves: Southern Planters in the Civil War and Reconstruction* (New York: Norton, 1977), 82, 89.

27. *Lynchburg Virginian*, March 16, 1865; *Macon Telegraph and Confederate*, October 29, 1864; *(Raleigh) North Carolina Standard*, November 16, 1864; *Richmond Sentinel*, November 24, 1864, and February 16, 1865.

28. Litwack, *Been in the Storm So Long*, 59, 189, 147–50; Myers, *Children of Pride*, 1247.

29. James M. McPherson, *What They Fought For, 1861–1865* (New York: Doubleday, 1995), 59, 67; Yacavone, *A Voice of Thunder*, 161, 170; Bell Irvin Wiley, *The Life of Billy Yank: The Common Soldier of the Union* (Baton Rouge: Louisiana State University, 1981), 44; Reid Mitchell, *Civil War Soldiers* (New York: Penguin, 1988), 104.

30. *O.R.*, series 3, 1:133; J. McPherson, *Negro's Civil War*, 22.

31. E. McPherson, *Political History*, 249.

32. Ibid., 197, 274; Litwack, *Been in the Storm So Long*, 73; Basler, *CW*, 6:30.

33. Dudley Taylor Cornish, *The Sable Arm: Black Troops in the Union Army, 1861–1865* (Lawrence: University of Kansas Press, 1990), 265, 288; Basler, *CW*, 8:1–2; Joseph T. Glatthaar, *Forged in Battle: The Civil War Alliance of Black Soldiers and White Officers* (New York: Penguin, 1990), 167.

34. J. McPherson, *Negro's Civil War*, 168; Glatthaar, *Forged in Battle*, 122, 79.

35. Ibid., 122, 135; Litwack, *Been in the Storm So Long*, 75, 111; Edward Pollard to Jefferson Davis, January 13, 1865, Record Group 109, Confederate War Department, Letters Received, entry 5, 16-P-1865, National Archives, Washington, D.C.; *Macon Telegraph and Confederate*, October 12, 1864.

36. Litwack, *Been in the Storm So Long*, 200.

37. Thomas Wentworth Higginson, *Army Life in a Black Regiment* (1869; reprint, Boston: Beacon, 1970), 47; W. E. B. Du Bois, *Black Reconstruction in America, 1860–1880* (1935; reprint, Cleveland: World, 1968), 30.

38. Litwack, *Been in the Storm So Long*, 249.

11. WHY THE UNDERGROUND RAILROAD, AND WHY NOW?

1. The 2003 "National Underground Railroad Family Reunion Festival: Reuniting the Spirit of Freedom" met in Philadelphia on June 27–29. The event included exhibits, a book fair, reenactments, oral history interviews, tours, and presentation of a model for a William Still statue. See the festival's Web site for more details [www.undergroundrr.com].

2. Charles L. Blockson, *The Underground Railroad: First-Person Narratives of Escapes to Freedom in the North* (New York: Prentice Hall, 1987), ix.

3. William H. Siebert, *The Underground Railroad from Slavery to Freedom* (New York: Macmillan, 1898), 2, 43, 91.

4. Ibid., 30. On Torrey see Stanley Harrold, *Subversives: Antislavery Community in Washington, D.C., 1828–1865* (Baton Rouge: Louisiana State University Press, 2003), 64–93.

5. Siebert, *Underground Railroad*, 351. The address of the NPS Web site is [www.cr.nps.gov/ugrr].

6. Ibid., 11–12.

7. James Baynes to Siebert, March 14, 1896, Hodge, Iowa; H. D. Platt to Siebert, March 20, 1826, Franklin, Nebraska; and no author, four-page sketch, "Underground Railroad," from Clinton County, Iowa. See Wilbur Siebert Papers, Houghton Library, Harvard University, especially Illinois, vol. 5, and Iowa, vol. 1.

8. H. B. Leeper to Siebert, undated likely 1896, Princeton, Illinois; and H. D. Platt to Siebert, March 20, 1896, Franklin, Nebraska, Siebert Papers, Illinois, vol. 5.

9. C. D. Booth, "Ashtabula as a Station on the UGRR," report for US History 13 for Professor A. B. Hart, Harvard University, Siebert Papers, Ohio vol. 2; "True Story of the Underground Railway," *(Marysville, Ohio) Tribune*, September 29, 1897, Siebert Papers, Ohio, vol. 1.

10. H. D. Platt to Siebert, March 20, 1896, Franklin, Nebraska, Siebert Papers, Illinois, vol. 5; Henry M. Higgins to Siebert, October 30, 1895, Hillsboro, Ohio, Siebert Papers, Ohio, vol. 1.

11. Nathan Irvin Huggins, *Harlem Resaissance* (New York: Oxford University Press, 1971), 255–56.

12. Willis Boughton to Siebert, January 5, 1894, Athens, Ohio; Mrs. Levi P. Monse Gould to Siebert, March 7, 1896, Siebert Papers, Ohio, vol. 10.

13. Larry Gara, *The Liberty Line: The Legend of the Underground Railroad* (Lexington: University of Kentucky Press, 1961), 2–3, 36, 153.

14. John Hope Franklin and Loren Schweninger, *Runaway Slaves: Rebels on the Plantation* (New York: Oxford University Press, 1999), 282.

15. Ibid., 210–19, 228–33.

16. Ibid., 209, 221.

17. William Still, *The Underground Railroad* (1872; reprint, New York: Arno Press, 1968), 305–309.

18. Ibid., 27.

19. Carol Lasser, "The Underground Railroad in Oberlin: History and Memory," paper presented at the symposium "Threads of Freedom: The Underground Railroad Story in Quilts," Oberlin, Ohio, June 23, 2001.

20. "Abolitionist's Hiding Place for Slaves Found," *Baltimore Afro-American Ledger*, April 15, 1902. A special thanks to Shawn Alexander for sharing this article with me. Peter P. Hinks, "A Review of Stations on the Connecticut Underground Railroad," 2000. Copy provided by the author.

12. TELLING IT LIKE IT WAS AT ROKEBY

1. Wilbur H. Siebert, *The Underground Railroad from Slavery to Freedom* (New York: Macmillan, 1898).

2. The coincidence of this timing is actually rather fortuitous. George Robinson expressed some real hostility to the people of color his parents welcomed into their home and clearly shared the "malicious attitudes of other white Vermonters" rather than the egalitarian views of his parents. He may not have taken the time to answer Siebert's questionnaire as carefully and thoughtfully as his brother did. For George Robinson's attitudes, see George Gilpin Robinson to Rowland Evans Robinson, January 1, 1859, February 21, 1859, and March 27, 1859, Robinson Family Papers, Rokeby Museum, and Rowland Evans Robinson to George Gilpin Robinson, March 9, 1859, and April 2, 1859, Rowland Evans Robinson Papers, Rokeby Museum. For racial attitudes of antebellum Vermonters see Randolph A. Roth, *The Democratic Dilemma: Religion, Reform, and the Social Order in the Connecticut River Valley of Vermont, 1791–1850* (New York: Cambridge University Press, 1987), 273.

3. Robinson's determination to record his parents' work did not stop with his reply to Siebert. He went so far as

to annotate the family's copy of Siebert's book. Blind himself at the time, he had his wife underline Joseph Poland's name and write "a fraud—he was an anti-slavery man when it became fashionable to be one and not before. R. E. R." in the margin of page 107. Poland, Siebert's chief informant on Vermont, is mentioned again on page 130, where he is identified as the editor and publisher of an antislavery newspaper. "Editor" is crossed out and "printer" is written in the margin. Joseph Poland was an active organizer of the Liberty Party in Vermont and editor of its newspaper and therefore in the opposite camp of the Garrisonian Robinsons. There might have been a more specific dispute, but his parents' opinion clearly made a lasting impression on Robinson.

4. Rowland Evans Robinson to Wilbur H. Siebert, August 19, 1896. Siebert Papers, Houghton Library, Harvard University.

5. Wilbur H. Siebert, *Vermont's Anti-Slavery and Underground Railroad Record* (1937; reprint, New York: Negro University Press, 1969).

6. Rowland Evans Robinson, *Out of Bondage* (Boston: Houghton, Mifflin and Company, 1905). Page references given here are to the centennial edition, part of a comprehensive reprinting of Robinson's books to commemorate his birth in 1833. Rowland E. Robinson, *Out of Bondage and Other Stories* (Rutland, Vt.: Charles E. Tuttle, 1936).

7. Robinson created Danvis, a quintessential Vermont "hill town," and filled it with residents whose lives he chronicled from the early days of Vermont statehood to the Civil War. He took the writing of dialect seriously and recorded the western Vermont twang that has all but disappeared, along with Quaker plain and French Canadian speech and the odd Southern or Irish accent. His six books about Danvis are *Uncle Lisha's Shop*, 1887; *Sam Lovel's Camps*, 1890; *Danvis Folks*, 1894; *Uncle Lisha's Outing*, 1896; *A Danvis Pioneer*, 1900; and *Sam Lovel's Boy*, 1901.

8. Siebert, *Vermont's Anti-Slavery Record*, 75. Siebert may have picked this up from the biographical sketch of Robinson his daughter, Mary, wrote in 1921 and published in the centennial edition reprint of *Out of Bondage*. In it, she says, "Most of the anecdotes in his written works he had actually heard," but she was speaking of his Danvis books and not of the Underground Railroad stories.

9. The stories were collected in book form in 1905, but "Out of Bondage" first appeared in the *Atlantic Monthly* in 1897. It seems possible, if not likely, that Siebert's questionnaire gave Robinson the idea to write *Out of Bondage*.

10. See "Out of Bondage," 21–48, and "The Mole's Path," 49–60.

11. See, for example, Terence Martin, "Rowland Evans Robinson: Realist of the Outdoors," *Vermont History* 23 (January 1955): 3–15. The poet Hayden Carruth made an interesting comment on this aspect of Robinson's work: "The point is not that certain ingredients of Robinson's Danvis are actual while others are fictional, but that the amalgam he made of them, forged in affection, is neither fact, in the statistical sense, nor fiction, in the novelistic sense; it is simpler, but purer. Doubtless at a modest level, it is truth enlarged, the kind of superreal generalization at which all imaginative writing aims." See Hayden Carruth, "Introduction: Vermont's Genius of the Folk," in *Danvis Tales: Selected Stories by Rowland E. Robinson* (Hanover, Vt.: University Press of New England, 1995).

12. Robinson, *Out of Bondage*, 37, 45. Rowland Evans Robinson saved his bitterest prejudice for French Canadians, "the white nigger of the North." See David Budbill, "Editor's Preface," in *Danvis Tales*, p. xiii, and Rowland E. Robinson, *Vermont: A Study of Independence* (Boston: Houghton Mifflin, 1892; reprint, Rutland, Vt.: Charles E. Tuttle, 1975), 328–32, where he says, for example, "They were an abominable crew of vagabonds, robust, lazy men and boys, slatternly women with litters of filthy brats, and all as detestable as they were uninteresting."

13. Mary Robinson Perkins, *Out of Bondage*, 11.

14. Letter from Rowland Thomas Robinson to Wilbur H. Siebert, October 28, 1935, mss. 116, Siebert Papers, Ohio Historical Society, Columbus.

15. In his introduction to *Danvis Tales* (p. lvii), Hayden Carruth says, "Much that has been written about the 'slave room' at Rokeby seems nonsense. Unless the older part of the house was altered at some later date—and this is not evident—the room can never have been 'secret,' nor can the back stairway leading to it. For that matter, Ferrisburg [sic] is no more than fifty miles from Canada. . . . A slave who had safely reached Ferrisburg [sic] could be reasonably sure that no southern agent would have come so far north in his pursuit, and although precautions were still taken against the treachery of local southern sympathizers, the extreme subterfuge practiced at stations farther south was no longer needed. Granted, Robinson does introduce southern agents into one or two of his stories about runaway slaves in Ferrisburg [sic]; but of all the characters in his dramatis personae these strike me as least credible, closest to the stereotypes of Victorian melodrama."

16. See Jane Williamson, "Rowland T. Robinson, Rokeby, and the Underground Railroad in Vermont," *Vermont History* 69 (Winter 2001): 19–3l. Some parts of the current essay are based on this earlier one.

17. Oliver Johnson to Rowland Thomas Robinson, January 27, 1837, Rowland Thomas and Rachel Gilpin Robinson Papers, Rokeby Museum.

18. Charles Marriott to Rowland Thomas Robinson, March 14,1842, Rowland Thomas and Rachel Gilpin Robinson Papers, Rokeby Museum.

19. William M. Wiecek, "Slavery and Abolition Before the United States Supreme Court, 1820–1860," *Journal of American History* 65 (1978): 34–59.

20. Ephram Elliott to Rowland Thomas Robinson, April 9, 1837; Rowland Thomas Robinson to Ephram Elliott, May 3, 1837; and Ephram Elliott to Rowland Thomas Robinson, June 7, 1837, Rowland Thomas and Rachel Gilpin Robinson Papers, Rokeby Museum.

21. David M. Ludlum, *Social Ferment in Vermont, 1791–1850* (New York: Columbia University Press, 1939), chaps. 5 and 6; John Myers, "The

Beginning of Antislavery Agencies in Vermont, 1832–1836," *Vermont History* 36 (summer 1968): 126–41; John Myers, "The Major Efforts of Anti-Slavery Agents in Vermont, 1836–1838," *Vermont History* 36 (fall 1968): 214–29; Reinhard O. Johnson, "The Liberty Party in Vermont, 1840–1848: The Forgotten Abolitionists," *Vermont History* 47 (fall 1979): 258–75; Thomas D. Morris, *Free Men All: The Personal Liberty Laws of the North, 1780–1861* (Baltimore: Johns Hopkins University Press, 1974), 219.

22. John Hope Franklin and Loren Schweninger, *Runaway Slaves: Rebels on the Plantation* (New York: Oxford University Press, 1999), 160, 286–89.

23. This report was found by Raymond Paul Zirblis, *Friends of Freedom: The Vermont Underground Railroad Survey* (Montpelier: Vermont Division for Historic Preservation, 1996); see "Hold the Miscreant Up that Freemen May See Him!" *Green Mountain Freeman*, August 23, 1844, and "The Georgia Slaveholder and His Catchpole," *Green Mountain Freeman*, December 20, 1844.

24. Oliver Johnson to Rowland Thomas Robinson, January 27, 1837, Rowland Thomas and Rachel Gilpin Robinson Papers, Rokeby Museum.

25. Joseph H. Beale to Rowland Thomas Robinson, July 12, 1844, Rowland Thomas and Rachel Gilpin Robinson Papers, Rokeby Museum.

26. Rachel Gilpin Robinson to Ann King, January 9, 1844, Ann King Papers, Rokeby Museum.

13. READING FREEDOM'S MEMORY BOOK

1. Irene C. Tallman, "Auburn's Shrine to Faithful Slave Now Silent, Dark," *(Auburn) Citizen-Advertiser*, December 24, 1971.

2. Irene C. Tallman, "Future of Harriet Tubman Home Discussed by Clergy," *(Auburn) Citizen-Advertiser*, April 10, 1972.

3. Auburn officials ordered the ruins of Tubman's Home for the Aged to be demolished in 1944. Bishop William J. Walls was then in charge of the Western New York Conference of the African Methodist Episcopal Zion Church. See W. J. Walls, *Harriet Tubman Home: Its Present and Its Future* (Auburn: AME Zion Church, circa 1954), a commemorative pamphlet.

4. Kathy Kiely and Richard Benedetto, "Clinton Visits a Treasure in Need," *USA Today*, September 2, 1999.

5. This included a $450,000 "bricks and mortar" grant obtained in 2000 from the federal "Save America's Treasures" program as well as a $40,000 "planning and funding" grant awarded in 1999. When Hillary Clinton visited the Tubman site in July 1998, she announced a $10,000 gift from philanthropist Bitsy Folger of Washington, D.C. A number of New York State grants have been given, the largest of which was an award announced in March 2001 of $284,000 to restore the Harriet Tubman Home and develop the accompanying historic site. See "$284,000 Grant Pledged for Harriet Tubman Home," *(Albany) Times Union*, March 10, 2001. Also see Caroline Chen, "Rebuilding History: Architects Work on Restoration of Tubman Historic Sites," *(Syracuse) Post-Standard*, February 14, 2002.

6. Blockson chaired the National Underground Railroad Committee for the National Park Service. His article on the Underground Railroad that appeared in a 1984 issue of *National Geographic* magazine served as a harbinger of the current revival. See Charles L. Blockson, "Escape from Slavery: The Underground Railroad," *National Geographic* 166, no. 1 (July 1984): 3–39.

7. Gene Palmer, "Group Revives to Honor Tubman," *Syracuse Herald-Journal*, March 27, 1991. The Harriet Tubman Boosters, formed in 1956, had not met for twenty years.

8. Arch Merrill, *The Underground: Freedom's Road and Other Upstate Tales* (New York: American Book-Stradford Press, 1963).

9. Helene C. Phelan, *"And Why Not Every Man?": An Account of Slavery, the Underground Railroad, and the Road to Freedom in New York State's Southern Tier* (Interlaken, N.Y.: Heart of the Lakes Publishing, 1987).

10. Wilbur H. Siebert, *The Underground Railroad from Slavery to Freedom* (New York: Macmillan, 1898). See the three microfilm reels in the W. H. Siebert Collection, New York Underground Railroad Materials, Ohio Historical Society, Columbus.

11. Articles about the history of the Underground Railroad in specific locales in New York State appeared prior to this revival of interest, but they were written before a statewide effort was made to pull the various strands of the story together. See, for example, William S. Bailey, "Underground Railroad in Southern Chautauqua County," *New York History* 33 (January 1935): 53–63. For a more thorough discussion of the existing historiography pertaining to the Underground Railroad in New York State see Milton C. Sernett, "'On Freedom's Trail': Researching the Underground Railroad in New York State," *Afro-Americans in New York Life and History* 25 (January 2001): 7–32. Emerson Klees, formerly an executive with Eastman Kodak in Rochester, published a popular, though not always accurate, compendium of Underground Railroad stories in 1997. See Emerson Klees, *Underground Railroad Tales with Routes Through the Finger Lakes Region* (Rochester: Friends of the Finger Lakes Publishing, 1997).

12. Larry Gara, *The Liberty Line: The Legend of the Underground Railroad* (Lexington: University of Kentucky Press, 1961).

13. Based in Bainbridge, New York, George Sands serves as the regional coordinator of the Central Leatherstocking Region of the Forging the Freedom Trail Project. His Web site is [www.freedomtrail.org/home.htm].

14. *New York Freedom Trail Program Study: Report to the Commission* (New York: Schomburg Center for Research in Black Culture, October 1999).

15. On March 21, 2002, Gretchen Sorin, chair, and Sandy Stuart, coordinator to commission members, sent letters to commission members, informing them that the New York State Freedom Trail Commission had run out of funding "as a result of budgetary constraints."

16. Heritage New York Program description announcement, August 21, 2001.

17. Samuel Gruber, "Where is Our Freedom Trail?" *Syracuse Herald-American*, April 1, 2001.

18. See Judith Wellman and Milton C. Sernett, *Uncovering the Freedom Trail in Syracuse and Onondaga County* (Syracuse: Preservation Association of Central New York, 2002). The Preservation League of New York State provided funding for the report. Also see "Creating the Madison County Freedom Trail Commission," Resolution 247, September 11, 2001.

19. The Southern Tier Underground Railroad Commission organized to serve Broome, Chenango, Chemung, Cortland, Delaware, Otsego, Schoharie, Schuyler, Steuben, Tompkins, and Tioga counties. See George Basler, "Fugitive Slaves Found Help Here: Exhibition Highlights Tier's Role in Rescue Effort," *(Binghamton) Press and Sun Bulletin*, January 29, 2002.

20. Janet Gramza, "House with Dual History: Valley Home's Builder Owned a Slave; a Son was Abolitionist," *(Syracuse) Post-Standard*, February 16, 2002. William H. Sabine, a slave owner, built the house at 9 Academy Green in the Valley neighborhood of Syracuse. One of his sons became an abolitionist and another, Joseph F. Sabine, participated in the rescue of William Henry, or Jerry, in 1851.

21. Debates in Albany and elsewhere in New York about revisions to the school curricula echoed the controversy over National History Standards. See Gary B. Nash, Charlotte Crabtree, and Ross E. Dunn, *History on Trial: Culture Wars and the Teaching of the Past* (New York: Vintage Books, 2000).

22. *New York State Freedom Trail Program Study*, Appendix F. Legislation authorizing the New York State Freedom Trail involved the amendment of an education law passed in 1996. The relevant section reads (with the 1997 addition in italics): "In order to promote a spirit of patriotic and civic service and obligation and to foster in children of the state moral and intellectual qualities which are essential in preparing to meet the obligations of citizenship in peace or in war, the regents of The University of the State of New York shall prescribe courses of instruction in patriotism, citizenship, and human rights issues, with particular attention to the study of the inhumanity of genocide, slavery (*including the freedom trail and underground railroad*), the Holocaust, and the mass starvation in Ireland from 1845 to 1850, to be maintained and followed in all the schools of the state." Cited from "An Act to amend the education law and the parks, recreation and historic preservation law, in relation to creating the New York State Freedom Trail program," State of New York Assembly, 8458BB, June 26, 1997.

23. Nancy Shute, "New Routes to Old Roots," *Smithsonian* 32 (March 2002): 78. "Why 'Roots' Hit Home," *Time* (February 14, 1977): 69–71.

24. In 1996 Robert Shear designed one of the earliest Web sites with useful information about the Underground Railroad and its historical context in New York State; see [www.nyhistory.com]. The Web site of the New York State Freedom Trail [www.nysfreedom.nysed.gov] has not been updated for some time or been made interactive. The Freedom Trail Commission attempted to start a listserv, though it was not widely used.

25. Personal communication with Christopher Densmore, March 13, 2002.

26. Personal communication with Hadley Cruczek-Aaron, June 20, 2002.

27. Milton C. Sernett, *North Star Country: Upstate New York and the Crusade for African American Freedom* (Syracuse: Syracuse University Press, 2002). *(Syracuse) North Star*, December 8, 1848. On Gerrit Smith and the question of race see John Stauffer, *The Black Hearts of Men: Radical Abolitionists and the Transformation of Race* (Cambridge: Harvard University Press, 2002).

28. Tendai Mutunhu, "John W. Jones: Underground Railroad Station-Master," *Negro History Bulletin* 41 (March–April 1978): 814–18. Austin Steward, *Twenty-Two Years a Slave and Forty Years a Freeman* (1857; reprint, with an introduction by Graham Russell Hodges, Syracuse: Syracuse University Press, 2002). Stephen Myers, editor of the *Northern Star and Freedman's Advocate*, whom Frederick Douglass called one of "the forwarders from Albany" (Douglass, *Life and Times*, 266–67), deserves additional biographical treatment. Thomas James, *Wonderful Eventful Life of Rev. Thomas James, By Himself* (Rochester: Post-Express Printing Company, 1887). Sernett, *North Star Country*, 8–9, 262–64. Jermain W. Loguen, *The Rev. J. W. Loguen, as a Slave and as a Freeman: A Narrative of Real Life* (Syracuse: J. G. R. Truair and Company, 1859); Carol M. Hunter, *To Set the Captives Free: Reverend Jermain Wesley Loguen and the Struggle for Freedom in Central New York, 1835–1872* (New York: Garland Publishing, 1993). Dorothy Porter, "David Ruggles: An Apostle of Human Rights," *Journal of Negro History* 28 (January 1943): 23–50. On Tudor Grant see Judith Wellman, "Larry Gara's Liberty Line in Oswego County, New York, 1838–1854: A New Look at the Legend," *Afro-Americans in New York Life and History* 25 (January 2002): 33–56. On Catharine Harris's Underground Railroad activities in Jamestown, New York, see the local history articles written for the *(Jamestown) Evening* in 1902 by C. R. Lockwood, as edited and posted on the Internet by Christopher Densmore on March 21, 2000 [ublib.buffalo.edu/libraries/units/archives/urr/jamestown.html]. Tom Calarco, "Reverend Abel Brown, Forgotten Abolitionist," paper presented at the Conference on New York State History, Hartwick College, Oneonta, New York, on June 12, 1999. Calarco discovered a copy of C. S. Brown's *Memoir of Rev. Abel Brown* (Worcester, 1849), written by Brown's widow after his untimely death at the age of thirty-four. See also Tom Calarco, *The Outpost to Freedom: The Underground Railroad in Northern New York* (Jefferson, N.C.: McFarland and Company, 2003).

29. While historian for Monroe County, Shirley Cox Husted conducted pioneering research on the Underground Railroad in Rochester and its environs. See Shirley Cox Husted, "'Black and White Together!': Paths Towards Freedom on the Underground Railroad," *Sweet Gift of Freedom* (Rochester: County of

Monroe, 1986), 1:2–24. Hugh C. Humphreys, "'Agitate! Agitate! Agitate!': The Great Fugitive Slave Convention and Its Rare Daguerreotype," *Madison County Heritage* 19 (1994): 3–64. Sernett, *North Star Country*, 136–45. Monique Patenaude Roach, "The Rescue of William 'Jerry' Henry: Antislavery and Racism in the Burned-Over District," *New York History* 82 (spring 2001): 135–54.

30. Rebecca Schwarz-Kopf, *The Underground Railroad in the North Country, and Early Accounts of African-American Life, Abolitionists and Newspapers in Northern New York and Vermont* (Plattsburgh, N.Y.: Studley Printing and Publishing, 2001).

31. Wellman reports on many of these contributions in her essay "The Underground Railroad and the National Register of Historic Places: Historical Importance vs. Architectural Integrity," *Public Historian* 24 (winter 2002): 11–30. The Web site she developed for Oswego County is found at [www.oswego.edu/Acad_Dept/a_and_s/history/ugrr].

32. Janet Gramza, "All-White, All-Black Churches Find Links in History," *Syracuse Herald American*, February 25, 2001.

33. Personal communication with Paul and Mary Stewart, June 10, 2002. The site visit to Albany and the Underground Railroad tour were on June 14, 2001. The address of the Stewarts' Web site is [www.ugr-workshop.com].

34. Jones is credited with aiding more than eight hundred fugitives. After the Elmira Civil War prison camp opened in July 1864, Jones became responsible for the internment of Confederate soldiers at Elmira's Woodlawn Cemetery. "Slavery to Freedom; the Life of John W. Jones, Once a Slave, Now a Rich Citizen," *(Elmira) Telegram*, January 3, 1885. William S. Ramsdell, "Woodlawn's Sexton: John W. Jones (1817–1900)," *Chemung Historical Journal* (September 1997): 4668–71. The site visit and interview with Barbara S. Ramsdell occurred on July 13, 2001.

35. Mary Perham, "Lucy Brown Fights to Keep Elmira's Black History Alive," *(Corning) Leader*, February 18, 2001.

Personal communication with Lucy Brown, June 14, 2002. For an insightful discussion of Cord's influence on Twain see Shelly Fisher Fishkin, *Lighting Out for the Territory: Reflections on Mark Twain and American Culture* (New York: Oxford University Press, 1998), 84–91.

36. Carol Kammen, "The UGRR and Local History," *Cultural Resources Management* 21 (1998): 11, published by the National Park Service, U.S. Department of the Interior.

37. Barbara Franco, "The Cardiff Giant: A Hundred Year Old Hoax," *New York History* 50 (October 1969): 421–40. The Cardiff Giant, unearthed on a central New York farm in 1869, turned out to be a 2,990-pound piece of gypsum made to look like an ancient figure and not a petrified "giant" from biblical times.

38. In answer to the question, "Do we know who carved these faces?" a brochure produced by the Onondaga Historical Association to accompany a traveling exhibition that featured them states: "No, we can never be sure. But they were discovered in a basement passageway that archaeologists date to the mid-nineteenth century. The former church building once housed a congregation of active abolitionists and a minister who was involved with the Underground Railroad. That these faces may have been carved by fugitive slaves makes them worthy of preservation and interpretion [*sic*] as symbols of that era." See *Symbols of a Journey*, Onondaga Historical Association, Syracuse, New York.

39. The church's cornerstone was laid in 1845, and the structure was completed in 1849. Of the building as an Underground Railroad stop, historian Monroe Fordham says, "Although providing assistance to fugitive slaves was a violation of federal law, it was widely held that the Michigan Street Baptist Church was a station on the 'underground railroad.' By the late nineteenth century, such stories had attained legendary status." See Monroe Fordham, "Origins of the Michigan Street Baptist Church, Buffalo, New York," *Afro Americans in New York Life and History* 21 (January 1997), 13. See also Donn Esmonde, "New Effort Made to Restore

Abolitionist-Linked Church," *Buffalo News*, September 10, 2001. Cottrell's preservation efforts and interest in promoting the tourism potential of the Underground Railroad renaissance have drawn national attention. See, for example, Maria Mallory, "Bound for the Promised Land: Retracing the Footsteps of a Runaway," *U.S. News and World Report*, April 14, 1997.

40. Quoted in Randal C. Archibold, "Decaying Depots on the Tracks to Freedom: New Interest in the Underground Railroad Inspires an Effort to Preserve its Landmarks," *New York Times*, July 10, 2001.

41. Brian Meyer, "Underground to Forefront: Michigan Ave. Named Urban Renewal Area," *Buffalo News*, June 19, 2002. See the Michigan Street Urban Design Plan, Buffalo, New York, prepared for the Michigan Street Preservation Corporation by Hamilton Houston Lownie, Architects LLC, 2002. Interview and site visit by Milton Sernett to the Michigan Street Baptist Church and Nash Home, June 21, 2002.

42. Judith Wellman, "James Watkins Seward: Common Criminal or Hero of the Freedom Trail?," paper delivered at the annual meeting of the Organization of American Historians/National Council on Public History, Washington, D.C., April 12. 2002.

14. THE PLACES AND COMMUNITIES OF THE UNDERGROUND RAILROAD

1. Charles L. Blockson, "Escape from Slavery: The Underground Railroad," *National Geographic* 166, no. 1 (July 1984): 3.

2. House Committee on Resources, *Hearings Before the Subcommittee on National Parks and Public Lands*, 105th Cong., July 22, 1997, 27.

3. The advisory committee included nine members with expertise in African American history, historic preservation, museum work, and public programs. The members were Vivian Abdur-Rahim, Thomas Battle, Ancella Bickley, Charles Blockson (chair), John Fleming, Barbara Hudson, Rose Powhatan, Glennette Turner, and Robin Winks.

4. US Department of the Interior, "Underground Railroad: Special Resource Study, Management Concepts, Environmental Alternatives," 1995, v.

5. The Web site address of the National Underground Railroad Network to Freedom is [www.cr.nps.gov/ugrr].

6. Ser Seshshab Heter and C. M. Boxley, "Forks of the Road Enslavement Market Terminus," Network to Freedom Application, 2001.

15. A SACRED DRAMA

1. *Colored American*, October 20, 1838. This essay is indebted to my year-long conversations with colleagues in the Black Studies department at Amherst College. I am especially grateful to Professor Jeffrey Ferguson. My thinking about melodrama and race began in our extraordinary conversations.

2. Quoted in David Blight, *Race and Reunion: The Civil War in American Memory* (Cambridge: Belknap Press of Harvard University, 2001), 23.

3. Quoted in Theophus Smith, *Conjuring Culture: Biblical Formations of Black America* (New York: Oxford University Press, 1994), 68.

4. Jeffrey Mason, *Melodrama and the Myth of America* (Bloomington: Indiana University Press, 1993), 21.

5. Robert Heilman, *Tragedy and Melodrama: Versions of Experience* (Seattle: University of Washington Press, 1968), 79.

6. William Still, ed., "Peter Petty," in *The Underground Railroad* (1872; reprint, Chicago: Johnson Publishing, 1970), 168. Still recorded this account on March 22, 1858.

7. Ibid., 167.

8. "Charles Thompson," in ibid., 142–43.

9. Ibid., 143.

10. "Letter from George Rhoads," in ibid., 139.

11. Albert Raboteau, "The Blood of the Martyrs Is the Seed of Faith": Suffering in the Christianity of American Slaves," in *The Courage to Hope: From Black Suffering to Human Redemption*, eds. Quinton Hosford Dixie and Cornel West (Boston: Beacon Press, 1999), 33.

12. Sarah Bradford, *Harriet Tubman, the Moses of Her People* (New York: Corinth Books, 1961), 61. Italics added for emphasis.

13. Jean Humez, "In Search of Harriet Tubman's Spiritual Autobiography," *National Women's Study Association Journal* 5, no. 2 (summer 1993): 163.

14. "George Solomon, Daniel Neall, Benjamin R. Fletcher and Maria Dorsey," in Still, *Underground Railroad*, 65.

15. "A Slave Girl's Narrative (1859)," in ibid., 107.

16. "Five Years and One Month Secreted (1853)," in ibid., 190.

17. The African American jeremiad consists of "the constant warnings issued by blacks to whites, concerning the judgment that was to come for the sin of slavery." Millions of people view America as a chosen nation with a covenantal duty to deal justly with the blacks. See Wilson Moses, *Black Messiahs and Uncle Toms: Social and Literary Manipulations of a Religious Myth* (University Park: Pennsylvania State University Press, 1982), 29–30.

18. "Arrival of Jackson, Isaac and Edmundson Turner from Petersburg," in Still, *Underground Railroad*, 111.

19. Werner Sollors, *Beyond Ethnicity: Consent and Descent in American Culture* (New York: Oxford University Press, 1986), 41. Also see Eddie Glaude Jr., *Exodus! Religion, Race, and Nation in Early Nineteenth Century Black America* (Chicago: University of Chicago Press, 2000), 44.

20. Quoted in Albert Raboteau's essay "African-American, Exodus, and the American Israel," in Albert Raboteau, *A Fire in the Bones* (Boston: Beacon Press, 1995), 39. The sermon is reprinted in Conrad Cherry, ed., *God's New Israel: Religious Interpretations of American Destiny* (Englewood Cliffs, N.J.: Prentice-Hall, 1971), 43.

21. Sacvan Bercovitch, *The Rites of Assent: Transformation in the Symbolic Construction of America* (New York: Routledge, 1993), 33.

22. Ibid., 33-34.

23. Ibid., 39.

24. According to Bercovitch, in the mid-nineteenth century the symbols of errand were reworked as America's Manifest Destiny. America, the Redeemer Nation, was now "popularly conceived as spreading the blessings of democracy, free enterprise, and Protestantism across the continent." The story of Exodus and the idea of being God's chosen people justified, to some degree, the conquest and subordination of other people. The backdrop of this change was the revision of the Puritan errand: Exodus was now the property of all Anglo-American settlers and heralded "one city on a hill." The foundation was then laid for America's civil religion. See Glaude, *Exodus! Religion, Race, and Nation*, specifically chap. 3.

25. Vincent Harding, "The Uses of the Afro-American Past," in *The Religious Situation*, 1969, ed. Donald R. Cutter (Boston: Beacon Press, 1969), 829–40.

26. David Walker's *Appeal to the Coloured Citizens of the World, but in Particular, and Very Expressly, to Those of the United States of America* (New York: Hill and Wang, 1965).

27. Ibid., xiv.

28. Ibid., 66.

29. Peter Hinks, *To Awaken My Afflicted Brethren: David Walker and the Problem of Antebellum Slave Resistance* (University Park: University of Pennsylvania Press, 1997), 55.

30. "Arrival of Jackson, Isaac and Edmondson Turner from Petersburg" in Still, *Underground Railroad*, 110.

31. Here I am adapting Kenneth Burke's definition of ideology. Burke writes that ideology is an "aggregate of beliefs sufficiently at odds with one another to justify opposite kinds of conduct." This understanding of ideology places a premium on the kind of interpretative activity that, I believe, is taking place with the various ways the Exodus story is being used. See Kenneth Burke, *Counter Statement* (Berkeley: University of California, 1968), 163.

32. Blight, *Race and Reunion*, 237.

ILLUSTRATION CREDITS

b bottom
l left
m middle
r right
t top

National Underground Railroad Freedom Center: v; Archives and Special Collections, Amherst College: ixt, 7, 14, 15, 16, 22, 27, 29, 31, 34, 38, 39, 40, 41, 42, 44, 47, 54, 56, 59, 60, 63, 64, 71, 73, 82, 85, 96, 139, 141, 143, 146, 150, 152, 153, 154, 166, 167, 173, 176, 178, 179, 180, 181, 184, 186, 189, 191, 204, 212, 213, 222, 224, 230b, 240, 242, 253, 257, 258, 264, 262, 281, 282, 292, 293, 294, 297, 300; Indiana Historical Society: ixb; Louise Minks: xi, 103, 192, 289; Library of Congress: 2, 21, 37, 49, 51, 52, 53, 69, 77, 80, 81t, 84, 87, 88, 99, 119, 120, 130, 134, 136, 144, 168, 170, 171, 183, 187, 196, 200, 202, 203, 205, 208, 221, 223, 225, 227, 230t, 243, 299, 303; Tuskegee Institute Archives: 3; Ed Dwight: 4; Morris Library, Southern Illinois University: 8, 9; Abby Aldrich Rockefeller Folk Art Center, Colonial Williamsburg, Virginia: 17; Gibbes Museum of Art, Charleston, South Carolina: 19; Library of Virginia, Richmond: 20, 25; Davidson College Archives: 23; Library Company of Philadelphia: 24, 75, 78, 228; private collection: 26; Massachusetts Historical Society: 28t, 87; New York Historical Society: 28b, 35, 126b, 155, 163, 218, 292; Jack Naylor Collection: 30; Miriam and Ira D. Wallach Division of Art, Prints, and Photographs, New York Public Library: 36, 129; J. P. Altmayer Collection: 43; National Archives of Canada: 45; Colonial Williamsburg Foundation: 48; Historic New Orleans Collection: 57; Schomburg Center for Research in Black Culture: 68, 102, 118, 160, 206, 207, 217; Trustees of the Boston Public Library: 70, 81b, 159; Newton Historical Society, Newton, Massachusetts: 76; Picture Research Consultants, Topsfield, Massachusetts: 79, 86, 172, 229, 237, 302; Slavery Library Archives, Talladega College, Talladega, Alabama: 90; Ohio Historical Society: 91, 111, 239; Documenting the American South Collection, University of North Carolina, Chapel Hill: 97; John Vlach: 98, 100, 101, 105, 106, 107, 109b, 110, 123, 259, 262r; National Park Service: 109tm, 283, 286; Washington County Historical Society: 112t; Uncle Tom's Cabin Historic Site: 112b; Florida Museum of Natural History: 125; Manigault Papers, Southern Historical Collection, University of North Carolina, Chapel Hill: 126t; Chester County Historical Society, West Chester, Pennsylvania: 138; Boston African American National Historic Site: 140; Onondaga Historical Association: 145, 275, 289; Chicago Historical Society: 157; Missouri Historical Society: 164; Bostonian Society, Old State House, Boston, Massachusetts: 165; State Historical Society of Wisconsin: 169; University of Virginia Library: 190, 301; Brooklyn Museum of Art: 193; Abby Aldrich Rockefeller Art Center, Williamsburg, Virginia: 197; Paul Collins: 199; Smithsonian American Art Museum: 209; J. Paul Getty Museum: 215; Amistad Research Center, Tulane University, New Orleans, Louisiana: 220; Wild Swan Theater, Ann Arbor, Michigan: 123; © 2002 John Steventon: 235; Cincinnati Art Museum—photo by Tony Walsh: 236; Rokeby Museum, Ferrisburgh, Vermont: 250, 251, 252, 254, 255, 256; Milton Sernett and Ruth Potter: 262l; Rochester Public Library: 261, 270; Madison County Historical Society: 263, 268, 269, 270; Milton Sernett and State Historical Society of Wisconsin: 271, 272, 277; Chemung County Historical Society: 273; Eric Wensel, *The Leader*, Corning, New York: 274; Buffalo and Erie County Historical Society: 276; Oberlin College Archives, Oberlin, Ohio: 280; Ser Seshishab Heter-C. M. Boxley and Diane Miller: 284; Valerie Chang and Jeff Greer: 285; *Black Voice News*: 287; Indiana Department of Natural Resources, Division of Historic Preservation and Archaeology: 188; Kansas State Historical Society, Topeka, Kansas: 293.

INDEX

Italics page numbers indicate illustrations